EXPANDED EDITION

Love and Betrayal

A Catullus Reader

Gilbert Lawall
The University of Massachusetts Amherst

Bruce Arnold
Mount Holyoke College

Andrew Aronson
The University of Southern Maine

Elizabeth Baer
Pittsfield (MA) Public Schools

Boston, Massachusetts
Chandler, Arizona
Glenview, Illinois
Upper Saddle River, New Jersey

Photo Credit

Cover: © Phoenix Art Group, Inc., Richard Franklin "To Go Beyond," Courtesy of Grand Image Ltd., Seattle, WA

Acknowledgments

Grateful acknowledgment is made for extracts of copyrighted material from the following: **Appleton-Century-Crofts** J. William Hebel and Hoyt H. Hudson, eds. *Poetry of the English Renaissance 1509–1660*. New York: Appleton-Century-Crofts, 1929. **Aris & Phillips Ltd.** John Godwin, ed. *Catullus: Poems 61–68*. Warminster: Aris & Phillips Ltd., 1995. John Godwin, ed. *Catullus: The Shorter Poems*. Warminster: Aris & Phillips Ltd., 1999. **Bibliothèque de la Pléiade** Gustave Cohen, ed. *Oeuvre complète de Ronsard*. Bibliothèque de la Pléiade. Paris: Librairie Gallimard, 1950. **George Braziller, Inc.** Gary Wills, ed. *Roman Culture: Weapons and the Man*. New York: George Braziller, Inc., 1966. **Clarendon Press** R.A.B. Mynors, ed. *C. Valerii Catulli Carmina*. Oxford: Clarendon Press, 1958, 1960. **The Classical Quarterly** A.S. Gratwick. "*Vale, Patrona Virgo*: The Text of Catullus 1.9." *The Classical Quarterly* 52 (2002) 305–20. J.G.F. Powell. "Two Notes on Catullus." *The Classical Quarterly* 40 (1990) 199–206. **The Estate of Horace Gregory** Excerpt from "The Poems of Catullus" by Horace Gregory (W.W. Norton, 1972). Copyright © 1956, 1972 by the Estate of Horace Gregory. Used by permission of The Estate of Horace Gregory. **Faber & Faber Ltd.** Ezra Pound. *The Translations of Ezra Pound*. London: Faber & Faber Ltd., 1954. **Groton School** G.P. Goold, ed. *C. Valerii Catulli Carmina*. Groton: Groton School, 1973. **Harcourt Brace & World, Inc.** T.S. Eliot. *The Complete Poems and Plays 1909–1950*. New York: Harcourt Brace & World, Inc., 1971 © by Esme Valerie Eliot. **Harvard University Press** Elmer Truesdell Merrill, ed. *Catullus*. Cambridge: Harvard University Press, 1893, rpt., 1951. **The Hudson Review, Inc.** *The Hudson Review*, Vol. V, No. 1 (Spring 1952). The Hudson Review, Inc. **Johns Hopkins University Press** Excerpts from "Catullus 11: Atque in perpetuum, Lesbia, ave atque vale" by Gloria S. Duclos from *Arethusa* 9. Excerpts from pp. 78–88. Copyright © 1976 *Arethusa*. Used by permission of the Johns Hopkins University Press. **Latomus** Charles Segal. "The Order of Catullus, Poems 2–11." *Latomus* 27 (1968) 305–21. **Macmillan Publishing Co.** Kenneth Quinn, ed. *Catullus: The Poems*. London: Macmillan Publishing Co., 1970. *Literature of The Western World* (Vol. 1), "Chaucer's Canterbury Tales," Theodore Morrison, tr. London: Macmillan Publishing Co., 1984. **Oxford University Press** C.J. Fordyce, ed. *Catullus: A Commentary*. Oxford: Oxford University Press, 1961, 1965, 1966. **Penguin Putnam, Inc.** Peter Whigham, tr. *The Poems of Catullus*. New York: Penguin Classics, 1966. **Phoenix** T. Goud, "Who Speaks the Final Lines? Catullus 62: Structure and Ritual." *Phoenix* 49 (1995) 23–32. **Smith College** Eleanor Shipley Duckett. *Catullus in English Poetry*. Smith College Classical Studies 6 (1925). **University of Oklahoma Press** Daniel H. Garrison, ed. *The Student's Catullus*. Norman: University of Oklahoma Press, 1989. **University of Toronto Press** D.F.S. Thomson, ed. *Catullus: Edited with a Textual and Interpretative Commentary*. Toronto: University of Toronto Press, 1997.

Note: Every effort has been made to locate the copyright owner of material reproduced in this component. Omissions brought to our attention will be corrected in subsequent editions.

PEARSON

ISBN-13: 978-0-13-320478-0
ISBN-10: 0-13-320478-2

11   17

CONTENTS

INTRODUCTION

Catullus has commonly proved to be a potent resource against boredom for those students who otherwise may think of Roman authors as old fuddy-duddies. The youthful hero who tells his elders exactly what he thinks of them and then begs his girlfriend to give him hundreds and thousands of kisses right now before it's too late grips the interest of most young people who are in their early years of studying Latin. Catullus has been Western civilization's poster child for youthful alienation, and thus his life elicits ready sympathy on the part of the casual reader. What students should know, therefore, about the poet's life and poetry may not always seem entirely useful when first coming to grips with this author, but it may serve to help them, on further reflection, to understand the many portions of the Catullan corpus that do not immediately bubble up on the page with gushing romantic sentiment.

It might strike the modern student of Catullus as odd that the Latin love poets, who in subsequent generations looked back to him as a model for their own work, described him as **doctus Catullus**. His designation as "learned" derives primarily from the fact that he belonged to the first generation of Latin poets to be significantly instructed in and shaped by the aesthetic sensibilities and literary practices of Greek poets of the third century B.C., several hundred years before his own day and age (Catullus' dates are usually given as 84–54 B.C.). Alexander the Great had founded Alexandria in 331 B.C. as the administrative center of Greek rule in Egypt, and his successors, the Ptolemies, built and cultivated a great library there, which became the most important center of Greek literature and learning during the Hellenistic era (323–31 B.C.). The most notable of the third century Alexandrian or Hellenistic Greek poets was Callimachus, who espoused a critical awareness of literary form, scrupulous attention to refinement in composition, and elegant erudition. He made fun of long, continuous narrative poems that were still being written in imitation of Homer, comparing them to the muddy Euphrates River. He himself experimented with short poems, such as epigrams, hymns, and personal invective, books of discontinuous, episodic narratives, and a miniature epic or "epyllion"; in his treatment of myth he gave some attention, as did other Alexandrians poets, to exploring the feelings of lovers. He attached more importance to themes of personal and scholarly interest than to the communal and moralistic values common to the traditional epic and dramatic poetry of archaic and classical Greece. Many of the features of Callimachus' innovative poetic program were deliberately taken up in the poetry of Catullus and presumably in the poetry, no longer extant, of other Latin poets of that period who were associated loosely with Catullus. These are the very ones whom Catullus' older contemporary

Cicero called **poētae novī** and *neoteroi* (a Greek word meaning "newer" or "rather new"), terms that expressed his disdain for what he regarded as their "modern" tendencies. As we have seen, these tendencies had been around for several hundred years in the Greek world, but they seemed revolutionary to many in the Roman world who still preferred the traditional epic and dramatic poetry of the early Latin writers Naevius (late third century B.C.) and Ennius (239–169 B.C.), with their patriotic and nationalistic themes.

Some of the Latin poets who shaped the neoteric revolution in Italy, such as C. Helvius Cinna and Licinius Calvus, were close friends of Catullus and are warmly acknowledged in his poetry; many of them came from Cisalpine Gaul, as did Catullus himself, who was a native of Verona. Prominent among them was Valerius Cato, who settled at Rome as a grammarian and teacher of poetry in the Alexandrian tradition. We also hear of a Greek poet, Parthenius of Nicaea, who was brought to Rome from Bithynia by Cinna and whose presence in Rome stimulated interest in Alexandrian literature and especially in the poetry of Callimachus. There can be little doubt that such friendships and associations with poets who were engaged in experimenting with new styles of thinking, writing, and living during the mid seventies and the sixties B.C. had a profound influence on the youthful Catullus' own destiny as a poet.

According to Jerome (ca. A.D. 347–420), who relied on Suetonius (ca. A.D. 70–130), our poet lived only thirty years. Thus, if we assume that the last datable allusions in his poetry fall in the final year of his life, we may speculate that he lived from approximately 84 to 54 B.C. (Jerome himself gives the dates as 87–57 B.C., which cannot be right.) At some time in his life, Catullus took up residence in Rome, where he came into contact with many of the men prominent in politics and literature who are known to us through historical sources. He is antagonistic toward a great many of the influential politicians of the time, such as Caesar, Pompey, Memmius, Clodius, Calpurnius Piso, and Vatinius, as well as lesser satellites such as Gellius and Mamurra, Caesar's chief engineer in his Gallic campaigns. In addition, poets like Volusius and Suffenus, who were apparently working in the tradition of Latin epic going back to the *Annals* of Ennius over a century before, come in for harsh criticism. The great city of Rome certainly opened unparalleled opportunities for enjoying the urbane intellectual, social, and poetic life that engaged Catullus so deeply, yet on the other hand he was outraged by much of what passed for culture, literature, and politics in the capital. He was always an outsider to some extent, and this allowed him to view the Roman élite from the perspective of his own discomfort, perhaps something like that of a Midwesterner living in New York City, unclouded by the prevailing political ideologies and social practices of the day—mostly corrupt from his perspective.

The most notable topic that extends its influence throughout Catullus' brief poetic career is a love affair with a woman he calls Lesbia, a name that alludes to Sappho, the famous Greek love poet of the island of Lesbos (seventh to sixth centuries B.C.). The Lesbia of Catullus' poetry is thus at least in part a literary creation who is meant to recall the emotion and the artistry of Sappho. Two of Catullus' most important poems, which describe critical moments in his turbulent affair with the woman he calls Lesbia, are written in a meter reminiscent of Sappho, and both contain allusions to her poetry as the poet describes his own feelings. In part, then, a literary creation, Catullus' affair with Lesbia is usually regarded also as reflecting an affair that he had in real life with a beautiful, captivating, and talented woman named Clodia, who was most likely the wife of Q. Caecilius Metellus Celer, governor of Cisalpine Gaul in 62–61 B.C. and consul in 60 (died 59 B.C.). Nothing that Catullus' poetry says about his relationship with Lesbia/Clodia can be corroborated by other sources, and much that he relates seems more appropriate to a literary fiction than a literary autobiography. Some readers prefer to think of "Catullus" and "Lesbia" as they appear in the poems as fictional or semi-fictional literary characters or **persōnae**, *dramatic masks, dramatic characters*, that may have little or no relationship to Catullus or Lesbia/Clodia as real people. However that may be, Catullus' poems offer the first example we have from ancient literature of the poetic record of an affair (imaginary, real, or a combination of the two) extending over time with a beginning, middle, and end. Catullus is also the first poet of whom we have any record who wrote in a subjective manner about his own (or what purports to be his own) love affair as it developed over the course of time.

In the first eleven poems there is an interesting array of pieces that treat Catullus' love affair with a **puella**, who is sometimes explicitly named as Lesbia. These poems appear to offer the outlines of an affair: first the poet's attraction to the **puella** (poems 2 and 3), then his courting of her love (poems 5 and 7), then a realization that she is no longer interested (poem 8), and finally the dissolution of the affair in bitter acrimony as the poet finds himself betrayed by a mistress whom he has discovered to be wildly promiscuous (poem 11).

The theme of betrayal recurs throughout Catullus' poems—sometimes betrayal by his **puella** and sometimes betrayal by his male friends and associates: hence the title of this book. As you read the poems relating to the "affair" with "Lesbia," you will want to think about the extent to which these poems may have been prompted by actual events in the poet's affair with a real woman and the extent to which they are fictional, literary creations. Whether you regard them as more biographical or more fictional, you will likely find yourself wanting to locate and rearrange all

of the "Lesbia" poems into a cycle that makes emotional and psychological sense of the ups and downs of the love affair. Two things that you
will certainly find are that the poems often allude to Greek models
(Sappho, Callimachus, and other Hellenistic poets) and that they are
works of supreme poetic artistry that repay very careful attention to their
poetic craftsmanship, something on which the neoteric poets all prided
themselves. While possibly inspired by actual moments in a real-life affair with Clodia the wife of Metellus (known as **Clōdia Metellī**),
Catullus' poems are also creations that he prayed would "endure through
the years for more than one century" (1.10) because of what they have to
say to readers of all generations, our own no less than any other.

One other significant event in the biography of the poet is clearly
marked for the reader as a major contributor to his embitterment: his
year-long tenure of service on the provincial staff of Gaius Memmius in
Bithynia, which can be dated with all probability to 57–56 B.C. Memmius
was considered an expert in literary matters and was a patron of the Roman poet Lucretius. This powerful man's involvement in the literary
scene at Rome may have been a factor in Catullus' acquaintance with him
and his being appointed to his personal staff. Things did not work out,
however, as Catullus planned, and he levels some nasty vituperation at
Memmius in poems 10 and 28.

In Rome Catullus depended upon the sympathy of a few close
friends such as Veranius and Fabullus and of fellow neoterics such as
Licinius Calvus and Cinna. Among these close friends Catullus cultivated a life style based on **ōtium**, *leisure*, and devoted to friendship, love,
and poetry. The key term describing the ideal relationships among the
people in this circle of friends is **urbanitās** (its opposite is **rūsticitās**),
and readers of Catullus soon discover a range of other words that the
poet repeatedly uses when writing about the sophisticated urbane values
and interactions among the members of his social and literary coterie.

By Catullus' own testimony there were few in the élite circles with
whom he was on good terms. This was the age of the so-called First Triumvirate, an agreement made in 60 B.C. between Julius Caesar, Pompey
the Great, and Marcus Crassus with the design of controlling political affairs at Rome and reserving the choicest political offices for themselves
and their followers. The pact was symptomatic of the destructive ambi-
tions and illegal maneuvering that undermined political life during the
fifties and led ultimately to its cataclysmic collapse in civil war at the end
of the decade. Many of Catullus' poems raise what is almost a "voice in
the wilderness," protesting against the unrestricted greed and social
crassness that were so prevalent at the time. In particular, Catullus sin-
gles out Caesar and Pompey and their underlings for scathing criticism.

Another disheartening event in Catullus' life was the death of his

brother, whose grave in the vicinity of Troy Catullus visited and com-
memorated with the justly famous and moving poem 101. There seems
to have been deep affection between the brothers, and Catullus' tragic
sense of loss over his brother's death appears also in poems 65 and 68.

Catullus seems to have admired the traditional value set upon the
Roman family, as the hymn to Diana (34) and the two wedding poems (61
and 62) indicate. Suetonius reports (*Life of Julius Caesar* 73) that Catullus'
father enjoyed Caesar's friendship and that the son on one occasion apol-
ogized to Caesar for the libelous verses he had written against him. While
it is difficult to imagine Catullus abandoning his deep-seated hatred toward the budding dictator and his minions, there is no difficulty in sup-
posing that the poet undertook such a reconciliation in deference to his father's ties of hospitality, which may have been important for the family's
influence and business contacts.

The problems of understanding Catullus' poetry extend beyond the
mysteries of his personal life. The text itself of the poems has spawned
many questions and insoluble conundrums. Our modern editions of the
text descend from three manuscripts copied in the fourteenth century, all
of which are derived from a single version, now lost, that managed to
make it through the Middle Ages. That single copy had many errors, for
which much scholarly work has produced some plausible corrections, and
some fragmentary parts that have never been adequately explained or in-
tegrated with their surrounding poems. You will encounter some of
these textual problems in the poems contained in this book, and there will
be some discussion of them in the notes. Examination and comparison of
variant readings will give you opportunities to read passages closely and
to evaluate the implications of variant readings for the tone and meanings
of the poems.

There is another thorny problem presented by the text that has
prompted much scholarly debate. Did Catullus arrange part or all of the
poems in his corpus in the order in which we now have them, or is the
collection a miscellany gathered together by a posthumous editor? The
first poem in the corpus as we have it is a piece dedicating a **novus libellus**, *a new little papyrus roll*, to a certain Cornelius. The problem is that the
word **libellus** seems to imply a single, short papyrus roll, but the 2,289
lines of poetry in the present corpus exceed what would have comfortably fit on the literary papyrus rolls of which we have knowledge. Many
scholars, therefore, assume a threefold division of Catullus' poetry, which
would have originally been transmitted on three separate rolls: poems 1–
60 (848 lines), poems 61–64 (795 lines), and poems 65–116 (646 lines). These
divisions are not arbitrary but coincide with major breaks in the grouping
of poems by genre or meter. The first 60 poems are short, personal com-
positions, often addressed to a specific recipient, written in a variety of

meters (and thus called "polymetric"), the most common of which is the hendecasyllabic meter. The second group of four long poems may all be said to treat marriage in one form or another, including the two epithalamia, which recall one of the favorite genres of poetry that Sappho worked in. This group also includes a highly polished short epic or epyllion on the wedding of Peleus and Thetis. The poems of the final group are all written in the elegiac meter, a common meter for writing love poetry. Most of these poems are short epigrams, a literary type recalling one of the favorite genres of Hellenistic poets such as Callimachus, who loved the brief compass and compressed expression of this poetic form. Other scholars have produced other divisions of the poems, and some hold that the **novus libellus** dedicated to Cornelius may have included only poems 2–11 or 2–14. However this may be, Catullus' poetry from one end of the corpus to the other features recurrent themes, such as love, friendship, betrayal, social commentary, and discussions of literary practice, and the range of different genres in which he writes is truly impressive. He appears to have given examples in Latin of the most important kinds of short poetry that were written by the Greeks before him, including both the Hellenistic poets and earlier lyric poets such as Sappho.

In closing, it may be noted that there are arguments in favor of regarding Catullus as a performer of some of his poems. At first he would have written his poems on wax tablets; later they were gathered into collections and transferred to rolls of papyrus. In the meantime, he may have recited poems of his to groups of friends at gatherings called "recitations" or at banquets of élite citizens. Some poems such as 8 and 10 are reminiscent of scenes in the Roman comedies of Catullus' predecessors, Plautus and Terence. You should keep this in mind as you study Catullus' poems, and you should not confine your attention to the poems as presented on the written page. Read them aloud by yourself and in front of a live audience of classmates. Pay close attention to tone and modulation of voice, sounds of words, rhythms, rhetorical devices, and nuances of expression as if you were an actor on a stage trying to communicate your understanding of the poem as vividly as possible to your audience. Ham it up and make your audience appreciate the poetry to its fullest.

*   *   *

This second edition of *Love and Betrayal* has been expanded with the addition of the following poems: 14a, 30, 40, 60, 64.50–253, 65, 68.1–40, and 69.

TIME LINE

84 A plausible date for the birth of Catullus (see Introduction).
81 Sulla dictator after returning from campaign in Asia against
   Mithradates and civil war against Marians in Italy.
78 Death of Sulla.
75 Beginning of Cicero's career as quaestor in Sicily.
70 First consulship of Pompey and Crassus.
   Birth of Vergil.
66 Cicero as praetor delivers speech *De imperio Pompei*.
65 Birth of Horace.
63 Consulship of Cicero and suppression of the Catilinarian conspiracy.
62 After campaigning in the East, Pompey settles affairs there and
   returns to Rome, disbanding his army.
62–60 Approximate period of Catullus' move to Rome.
61 Governorship of Metellus Celer in Cisalpine Gaul.
60 Caesar returns from a provincial command in Spain and forms the so-
   called First Triumvirate, an illegal agreement for sharing power
   with Pompey and Crassus.
59 Caesar's consulship, during which he receives Cisalpine Gaul and
   Illyricum under the *lex Vatinia*.
58 P. Clodius is tribune and brings about the exile of Cicero.
57 Rioting in Rome between Clodius and Milo.
   Cicero returns from exile.
   Catullus spends the year on the staff of C. Memmius in Bithynia.
56 Cicero delivers the *Pro Caelio*.
   Renewal of the so-called First Triumvirate at Luca.
   Catullus returns to Italy.
55 Second consulship of Pompey and Crassus.
   Caesar bridges the Rhine and later invades Britain.
54 Pompey governs Spain while remaining near Rome.
   Caesar makes a second invasion of Britain.
   Crassus prepares in Syria for a campaign against the Parthians.
   Last datable allusions in the poetry of Catullus (to the campaigns in
   Britain and Parthia), probably indicating that he died about this
   time or in the next couple of years.
53 Crassus defeated and killed in the military disaster at Carrhae.
52 Caesar finally subdues powerful rebellion in Gaul.
50 Caesar crosses the Rubicon into Italy, beginning civil war with
   Pompey and the Senate.
48 Caesar defeats Pompey at Pharsalus.
44 Caesar becomes dictator for life and is assassinated on the Ides of
   March.

USING THIS BOOK

The running vocabularies facing the Latin passages contain most of the words that are not in *ECCE ROMANI*, Books I and II, published by Prentice Hall. Words the meaning of which can be easily deduced are not given in the running vocabularies. A word that is in *ECCE ROMANI*, Books I and II, is included in the facing vocabulary if it is being used in a sense different from the sense in which it is used in that series. Words not given on the facing pages will be found in the vocabulary at the end of the book, thus allowing this book to be used after completion of any standard Latin program. When words that appear in the facing vocabularies reappear in later poems, they are glossed again on the facing page. This facilitates reading of the poems in any order; the vocabulary aids will always be there no matter in what order the poems are read. Note that a word that is glossed on the facing page and then reappears later in the same poem is not normally glossed at this later reappearance and may not appear in the end vocabulary. Look for the word in the earlier glosses for the poem.

The format of vocabulary entries is similar to that in the *ECCE ROMANI* series, with two major modifications. First, information about the Latin words themselves—in particular, information about the individual parts of compound verbs and of some nouns and adjectives—is given in brackets. Second, cross references to uses of the same or similar words in other poems are given in parentheses after the Latin word in question. Tracking down these cross references helps the reader build up an awareness of some of the distinctive features of Catullus' diction and expression.

Several definitions are usually given for the Latin words, with the most basic meaning of the word coming first and an appropriate meaning for the context coming last. Definitions and translations are given in italics. Words or phrases that help round out a definition but are not part of the definition itself are enclosed in parentheses. Words or phrases that fill out a suggested translation to make it more complete or to make it better English are placed in square brackets.

When reading a poem of Catullus from this book for the first time, one should not look at the facing vocabulary and notes at all but should read through the Latin of the poem, making as much sense of it as possible. When reading it a second or third time, one usually goes from the right-hand page to the vocabulary on the left-hand page, noting the italicized meanings, especially the last one given, for any unfamiliar words, and back again to the right-hand page. Only after one has grasped the sense of the poem should one look more closely at the vocabulary entries, the grammatical notes, and the other information on the left-hand page.

The Latin texts of the poems of Catullus as printed in this book are for the most part those that appear in the Oxford Classical Text edition of the poems of Catullus, edited by R. A. B. Mynors and published in 1958. Much scholarly attention has been directed to the text of the poems of Catullus since Mynors' edition; the most recent comprehensive edition of the poems produced in the English-speaking world is that of D. S. F. Thomson, *Catullus: Edited with a Textual and Interpretative Commentary*, University of Toronto Press, 1997. At a number of points Thomson and other modern editors have supplied readings that seem to be preferable to those of Mynors. In the present book we have often made note of these in special sections labeled **Text** appearing beneath the notes on the left-hand page or beneath lines of the poem on the right-hand page. Rarely we have incorporated readings different from those of Mynors in the poems as printed on the right-hand pages, and we have then given the Oxford Classical Text version in a section labeled **Text** on the left-hand page.

The Latin texts of the poems on the right-hand pages of this book are followed by study questions. Usually these are of two sorts, labeled **Initial Explorations** and **Discussion**. Beginning with poem 62, we provide only one set of questions, labeled **Explorations**. Detailed comparison with other poems is frequently invited in sections labeled **Comparison**. Passages from Greek and Latin literature for comparison with specific lines of poem 64 are gathered at the back of the book after poem 109.

The poems as presented in this book are often divided into segments printed on successive pages so that the facing vocabularies and notes and the questions will always be on the same page-spread as the related segments of the poems. It is very important, however, to see the poem in its entirety and to be able to mark it in various ways as one studies its structure, its poetic devices, and so forth. We accordingly provide for the teacher large-print versions of the poems at the end of the *Teacher's Guide*. Teachers may use these as masters for making overhead transparencies, and they may photocopy them and distribute them to students for their use.

In preparing the vocabularies and notes on the left-hand pages and the questions accompanying the poems, the following reference books were heavily used, and the authors wish to acknowledge their profound debt to them:

Grammar
> Greenough, J. B., and G. L. Kittredge, A. A. Howard, and Benjamin L. D'Ooge, eds. *Allen and Greenough's New Latin Grammar for Schools and Colleges*. Boston: Ginn and Company, 1931.

Dictionaries (listed in chronological order)
> Sir William Smith and Sir John Lockwood, eds. *Chambers Murray*

Latin-English Dictionary. Cambridge: Cambridge University Press, 1933.

P. G. W. Glare, ed. *Oxford Latin Dictionary.* Oxford: Clarendon Press, 1982.

Simon Hornblower and Antony Spawforth, eds. *Oxford Classical Dictionary.* 3rd ed. Oxford: Oxford University Press, 1996.

Editions and Commentaries (listed in chronological order)

Elmer Truesdell Merrill, ed. *Catullus.* Cambridge: Harvard University Press, 1893, rpt., 1951.

R. A. B. Mynors, ed. *C. Valerii Catulli Carmina.* Oxford: Clarendon Press, 1958, 1960.

C. J. Fordyce, ed. *Catullus: A Commentary.* Oxford: Oxford University Press, 1961, 1965, 1966.

G. P. Goold, ed., *C. Valerii Catulli Carmina.* Groton, Mass.: Groton School, 1973.

Kenneth Quinn, ed. *Catullus: The Poems.* New York: Macmillan, 1970, 1973.

Daniel H. Garrison, ed. *The Student's Catullus.* Norman: University of Oklahoma Press, 1989.

John Godwin, ed. *Catullus: Poems 61–68.* Warminster: Aris & Phillips Ltd., 1995.

D. F. S. Thomson, ed. *Catullus: Edited with a Textual and Interpretative Commentary.* Toronto: University of Toronto Press, 1997.

John Godwin, ed. *Catullus: The Shorter Poems.* Warminster: Aris & Phillips Ltd., 1999.

Brief excerpts from these commentaries are quoted where appropriate in this student's book and in the *Teacher's Guide*.

POETIC AND RHETORICAL DEVICES
AND FIGURES OF SPEECH

The following poetic and rhetorical devices and figures of speech occur in the selections from Catullus' poetry included in this book. Definitions are followed by representative examples (some of the definitions in this section and the section on metrical terms are formulated to be consistent with those in *Love and Transformation: An Ovid Reader*, edited by Richard A. Lafleur and published by Scott Foresman-Addison Wesley, 2nd ed., 1999).

Allegory: Gr., "speaking differently," a prolonged metaphor, i.e., a type of imagery involving the extended use of a person or object to represent some concept outside the literal narrative of a text, e.g., the extended simile of the flower in the garden to represent the desirability of virginity in 62.39–44.

Alliteration: deliberate repetition of sounds, usually of initial consonants but also of initial stressed vowels, in successive words, for emphasis and for musical and occasionally onomatopoetic effect, e.g.: **Cui dōnō lepidum novum libellum** (1.1, with consonance and assonance as well as alliteration); cf. assonance and consonance.

Anaphora: Gr., "carrying back," repetition of words or phrases at the beginning of successive clauses, often with asyndeton, for emphasis and emotional effect, e.g., **Ō factum male! Ō miselle passer!** (3.16)

Anastrophe: Gr., "turning back," the reversal of normal word order, as with a preposition following its object, often with the effect of emphasizing the word(s) placed earlier, e.g., **ōrāclum Iovis inter aestuōsī** (7.5).

Antithesis: Gr., "set against, in opposition," sharp contrast of juxtaposed ideas, e.g., **amant amantur** (45.20).

Apostrophe: Gr., "turning away," a break in a narrative to address some person or personified thing present or absent, sometimes for emotional effect, sometimes to evoke a witness to a statement being made, e.g., **Amastri Pontica et Cytōre buxifer** (4.13).

Ascending Tricolon: see Tricolon Crescens.

Assonance: repetition of internal or final vowel or syllable sounds in successive words, for musical and sometimes onomatopoetic effect, e.g.: **cui dōnō lepidum novum libellum / āridā modo pūmice expolītum?** (1.1–2); cf. homoioteleuton.

Asyndeton: Gr., "without connectives," omission of conjunctions where one or more would ordinarily be expected in a series of words, phrases, or clauses, underscoring the words in the series, e.g., **perfer, obdūrā** (8.11); cf. polysyndeton.

Chiasmus: Gr., "crossing," arrangement of words, phrases, or clauses in an oppositional, ABBA order, often to emphasize some opposition or to draw the elements of the chiasmus closer together, e.g., **frātrēs** (noun - A) : **ūnanimōs** (adjective - B) :: **anum** (adjective - B) : **mātrem** (noun - A) (9.4).

Conduplicatio: "repetition," for emphasis and emotional effect, e.g., **passer mortuus est meae puellae, / passer, dēliciae meae puellae** (3.3–4).

Consonance: repetition of consonants at the beginning, middle, or end of words (thus overlapping with the term *alliteration*), e.g., **quae tū volēbās nec puella nōlēbat** (8.7); cf. alliteration.

Ellipsis: Gr., "a falling short," omission of one or more words necessary to the sense of a clause but easily understood from the context; often a form of the verb **sum**, e.g., **salapūtium [est] disertum** (53.5); **Chommoda dīcēbat, sī quandō commoda vellet / dīcere, et īnsidiās Arrius hīnsidiās** (84.1–2; see note on passage).

Enjambement or **Enjambment**: "a straddling," delay of the final word or phrase of a sentence (or clause) to the beginning of the following verse, to create suspense or emphasize an idea or image, e.g., **sed identidem omnium / īlia rumpēns** (11.19–20).

Hendiadys: Gr., "one through two," use of two nouns connected by a conjunction to express a single complex idea, instead of having one noun modified by an adjective; the usual effect is to give equal prominence to an image that would ordinarily be subordinated, especially some quality of a person or thing, e.g., **pestem perniciemque** (76.20), literally *plague and ruin = ruinous plague.*

Homoioteleuton: Gr., "like ending," a recurrence of similar endings in successive words, e.g., **Cui dōnō lepid<u>um</u> nov<u>um</u> libell<u>um</u> / āridā modo pūmice expolī<u>tum</u>** (1.1–2); cf. assonance and polyptoton.

Hyperbaton: Gr., "a stepping across, transposition," a violation of usual word order for special effect, e.g., <u>**nōn inmerentī quam mihī meus venter,**</u> **/ dum sūmptuōsās appetō,** <u>dedit</u>**, cēnās** (44.8–9), where **dedit**, the verb of the relative clause in line 8, is delayed and interrupts the **dum** clause in line 9. Also here the relative pronoun **quam** does not stand at the beginning of its clause as is usual but comes as the third word in its clause (delayed relative).

Hyperbole: Gr., "a throwing beyond, exaggeration," self-conscious exaggeration for rhetorical effect, e.g., **Vērānī, omnibus ē meīs amīcīs/ antistāns mihi <u>mīlibus trecentīs</u>** (9.1–2).

Hysteron Proteron: Gr., "the latter put as the former," a reversal of the natural, logical, or chronological order of terms or ideas, e.g., **ut tēcum loquerer simulque ut essem** (50.13), where the idea of conversing is placed before the idea of being together, which would be prerequisite to any conversation; the more important idea is put first for emphasis, out of chronological order.

Interlocking Order or **Synchysis**: Gr., "a pouring together," an interlocking arrangement of related pairs of words in an ABAB pattern, often emphasizing the close connection between two thoughts or images, e.g., **Vatīniāna / meus crīmina Calvus** (53.2–3).

Irony: Gr., "pretended ignorance," the use of language with a meaning opposite its literal meaning, e.g., Catullus' reference to himself as **pessimus omnium poēta** in 49.6 is often interpreted as ironic.

Litotes: Gr., "plainness," a form of deliberate understatement in which a quality is described by denying its opposite, usually intensifying the statement, e.g., **nōn sānē illepidum neque invenustum** (10.4).

Metaphor: Gr., "carrying across, transference," an implied comparison, using one word for another that it suggests, usually with a visual effect, e.g., **palmulīs** (4.5), *little palms* (of hands) = *blades* (of oars); cf. simile.

Metonymy: Gr., "change of name," a type of imagery in which one word, generally a noun, is employed to suggest another with which it is closely related, e.g., **neque ūllius natantis impetum trabis** (4.3), where **trabis**, *timber*, is used in place of **nāvis**, *ship*; this figure is a hallmark of high poetic or epic style and allows the poet to avoid prosaic, commonplace words (such as **nāvis**); this example of metonymy is also an example of synecdoche (see below).

Onomatopoeia: Gr., "the making of words" (adjective, *onomatopoetic* or *onomatopoeic*), use of words the sounds of which suggest their meaning or the general meaning of their immediate context, e.g., **pīpiābat** (3.10), *used to chirp*.

Oxymoron: Gr., "pointedly foolish," the juxtaposition of incongruous or contradictory terms, e.g., **tacitum cubīle clāmat** (6.7).

Personification: "person making," a type of imagery by which human traits are attributed to plants, animals, inanimate objects, or abstract ideas, which are then addressed and which may speak as if they were human, e.g., **Phasēlus ille, quem vidētis, hospitēs, / ait fuisse nāvium celerrimus** (4.1–2).

Pleonasm: Gr., "excess," use of more words than necessary, repetition of the same idea in different words, e.g., **quam tē libenter quamque laetus invīsō** (31.4).

Polyptoton: Gr., "many case endings," repetition of the same word or of words from the same root but with different endings, e.g., **quīcum lūdere, quem in sinū tenēre, / cui prīmum digitum dare appetentī** (2.2–3); cf. homoioteleuton.

Polysyndeton: Gr., "using many connectives," use of a greater number of conjunctions than usual or necessary, often to emphasize the elements in a series, e.g., **ōtiōque et urtīcā** (44.15).

Prolepsis: Gr., "taking beforehand, anticipation," attribution of some characteristic to a person or thing before it is logically appropriate, especially application of a quality to a noun before the action of the verb has created that quality, e.g., **miserō quod omnīs/ ēripit sēnsūs mihi** (51.5–6), not *from miserable me* but *from me [and makes me] miserable*.

Simile: "like," an explicit comparison (often introduced by ut, **velut**, **quālis**, or **similis***)* between one person or thing and another, the latter generally something more familiar to the reader (frequently a scene from nature) and thus more easily visualized, e.g., **amōrem, / quī illius culpā cecidit velut prātī/ ultimī flōs** (11.22–23), cf. metaphor.

Synchysis: see Interlocking Order above.

Synecdoche: Gr., "understanding one thing with another," a type of metonymy in which a part is named in place of an entire object, or a material for a thing made of that material, or an individual in place of a class, e.g., **vēnimus larem ad nostrum** (31.9), where **larem ... nos-**

trum is named in place of **domum nostram** to focus attention on a key element of the concept of home and to avoid the commonplace word **domum**; cf. metonymy.

Tmesis: "cutting," separation of a compound word into its constituent parts, generally for metrical convenience, e.g., **mala . . . dīcit** (83.1) = **maledīcit.**

Transferred Epithet: application of an adjective to one noun when it properly applies to another, often involving personification and focusing special attention on the modified noun, e.g., **Nam tē nōn <u>viduās</u> iacēre noctēs** (6.6), where **viduās** logically describes the person referred to with the pronoun **tē** but modifies **noctēs** grammatically.

Tricolon Crescens or **Ascending Tricolon:** Gr., "having three members," a climactic series of three (or more) examples, illustrations, phrases, or clauses, each (or at least the last) more fully developed or more intense than the preceding, e.g., <u>**quīcum lūdere, quem in sinū tenēre,**</u> / <u>**cui prīmum digitum dare appetentī**</u> / <u>**et ācrīs solet incitāre morsūs**</u> (2.2–4).

Word-Picture: a type of imagery in which the words of a phrase are arranged in an order that suggests the visual image being described, e.g., **manūsque collō / ambās iniciēns** (35.9–10), where the words **manūs . . . ambās** surround the word **collō** just as the girl embraces the man's neck.

THE METERS OF CATULLUS' VERSE

Hendecasyllabic or Phalaecean (first found in Catullus 1):

Traditionally this meter is divided into feet as follows:

$$\underset{\smile}{\smile} \; \underset{\smile}{\smile} \; | \; - \smile \smile \; | \; - \smile \; | \; - \smile \; | \; - \underset{\smile}{\smile}$$

It is now regarded as preferable not to divide the line into feet as above but to give the scheme as follows:

$$\underset{\smile}{\smile} \; \underset{\smile}{\smile} \; - \smile \smile \; - \smile \; - \smile \; - \underset{\smile}{\smile}$$

This allows the third, fourth, fifth, and sixth syllables to be regarded as a choriamb ($- \smile \smile -$), which was one of the basic metrical patterns in lyric meters.

Pure Iambic Trimeter (found in Catullus 4 and used by Catullus elsewhere only in poem 29, which is not in this book):

$$\smile - \smile - \mid \smile \parallel - \smile - \mid \smile - \smile \underset{\smile}{-}$$

The meter consists of three pairs of iambic feet, divided here by the two single vertical lines. The double vertical lines mark the caesura. The pattern is invariable, except that the final syllable may be either long or short.

Choliambic (first found in Catullus 8):

The choliambic meter is based on the iambic trimeter (three pairs of iambic feet):

$$\underset{\smile}{-} - \smile \overset{\smile\smile}{-} \mid \underset{\smile}{-} \parallel - \smile - \mid \smile - - \underset{\smile}{-}$$

In the choliambic (Gr., "limping iambic") meter, the next to the last syllable is long instead of short, thus producing the limping effect. Note where substitutions are possible.

Sapphic Strophe (used by Catullus only in poems 11 and 51):

Traditionally this meter is divided into feet as follows:
Three lines (Lesser Sapphic) $- \smile \mid - \underset{\smile}{-} \mid - \parallel \smile \smile \mid - \smile \mid - \underset{\smile}{-}$

One line (Adonic) $\qquad\qquad - \smile \smile \mid - \underset{\smile}{-}$

It is now regarded as preferable not to divide the line into feet as above but to give the scheme as follows:

Three lines (Lesser Sapphic) $- \smile - \underset{\smile}{-} - \parallel \smile \smile - \smile - \underset{\smile}{-}$

One line (Adonic) $\qquad\qquad - \smile \smile - \underset{\smile}{-}$

This allows one to recognize choriambs ($- \smile \smile -$) as basic constituents of this lyric meter.

Greater Asclepiadean (used by Catullus only in poem 30)

The Greater Asclepiadean contains three choriambs ($- \smile \smile -$), often with a diaeresis (see below) after the first and the second choriamb as follows:

$$- - \mid - \smile \smile - \parallel - \smile \smile - \parallel - \smile \smile - \mid \smile \underset{\smile}{-}$$

Catullus 34

Three lines (Glyconic)   ⏓ ⏓ – ‿ ‿ – ‿ ⏓
One line (Pherecratean)   ⏓ ⏓ – ‿ ‿ – ⏓

Dactylic Hexameter (Catullus 62 and 64):

– ⏗ | – ⏗ | – ‖ ⏗ | – ⏗ | – ⏗ | – ⏓

– ⏗ | – ⏗ | – ‿ ‖ ‿ | – ⏗ | – ⏗ | – ⏓

– ⏗ | – ‖ ⏗ | – ⏗ | – ‖ ⏗ | – ⏗ | – ⏓

– ⏗ | – ‖ ⏗ | – ⏓ | – ‿ ‖ ‿ | – ⏗ | – ⏓

Spondees may be substituted for dactyls in the first five feet, but the substitution of a spondee in the fifth foot is rare. Double vertical lines indicate where caesuras may occur.

Elegiac Couplet (first found in Catullus 65):

Hexameter: – ⏗ | – ⏗ | – ⏗ | – ⏗ | – ⏗ | – ⏓

Pentameter: – ⏗ | – ⏗ | – | / – ‿ ‿ | – ‿ ‿ | ⏓

For caesuras in the hexameter, see above under **Dactylic Hexameter**. In the pentameter, the second half of the third foot and the second half of the sixth foot of a hexameter have been truncated, thus giving two sets of two and a half feet (= five feet or a pentameter). A diaeresis (here frequently coinciding with a pause in the sense) normally occurs after the third foot of the pentameter (marked here with a forward slash).

METRICAL TERMS

The following metrical terms will be found to be useful.

Caesura: a pause between words occurring within a metrical foot; the effect is to emphasize the word immediately preceding or, less often, following; cf. diaeresis.
Consonantal i and u: the vowels *i* and *u* become consonants before vowels.
Choriamb: a metrical foot with the pattern – ‿ ‿ – .

Dactyl: a metrical foot with the pattern - ˇ ˇ .

Diaeresis: a pause between words coinciding with the end of a metrical foot, less common than caesura and sometimes employed to emphasize the word immediately preceding or, less often, following.

Diastole: lengthening of an ordinarily short vowel (and hence the syllable containing it), usually when it occurs under the ictus and before a caesura; sometimes reflecting an archaic pronunciation; for an example, see poem 62.4.

Elision: Lat., "bruising," the partial suppression of a vowel or diphthong at the end of a word when the following word begins with a vowel or with *h*. A final *m* does not block elision, and thus the letters *um* of **cum** are elided in poem 1.5: **iam tum, cum‿ausus es ūnus Ītalōrum**.

Golden Line: a line of dactylic hexameter verse with words arranged as follows: adjective a : adjective b :: verb :: noun a : noun b, e.g., **irrita ventōsae linquēns prōmissa procellae** (64.59).

Hexameter: a line of poetry consisting of six metrical feet.

Hiatus: Lat., "gaping," omission of elision; this is generally avoided, but when it does occur it emphasizes the word that is not elided or coincides with a pause in the sense, e.g., **Ō factum male! Ō miselle passer!** (3.16; **male!** and **Ō** do not elide).

Hypermetric Line: a line containing an extra syllable, which elides with the word at the beginning of the next line, e.g., **prātī / ultimī** (11.22–23). Elision of this sort is called *synapheia* (see below).

Iambic Shortening: words with a metrical pattern of a short syllable followed by a long syllable, e.g., **sciō**, could be pronounced as two short syllables in ordinary speech. In Catullus 2.6 this carries over into **nescio**. A number of examples will be found in Catullus, e.g., **volo** for **volō** (6.16).

Iambus (Iamb): a metrical foot with the pattern ˇ - .

Ictus: Lat., "stroke," the verse accent or beat, falling on the first long syllable in each foot.

Pentameter: the second line of an elegiac couplet.

Spondaic line: a line of dactylic hexameter verse with a spondee in the fifth foot, e.g., **ipsius ante pedēs flūctūs salis allūdēbant** (64.67).

Spondee: a metrical foot with the pattern - - .

Synaeresis: Gr., "taking together," occasional pronunciation of the vowel *i* as a consonant *y* before a vowel, e.g., **cōnūbium** (62.57), normally four syllables, pronounced as *cōnūbyum*, three syllables. So, perhaps also **omnium** (11.19).

Synapheia or **Synaphaea**: Gr., "binding," elision at the end of one line with a word at the beginning of the next, e.g., **prātī / ultimī** (11.22–23); **prātī** elides with **ultimī**.

Syncope or **syncopation**: Gr., "striking together, cutting short," omission of a letter or a syllable from the middle of a word, e.g., **saeclō** (1.10) = **saeculō; nōrat** (3.6) = **nōverat.**

Synizesis: Gr., "settling together, collapsing," the pronunciation of two vowels as one syllable without forming a diphthong, e.g., **deinde.**

Systole: shortening of a vowel that was ordinarily long, e.g., **illius** (3.8) for **illīus.**

Trochee: a metrical foot with the pattern - ‿ .

LEXICAL AND GRAMMATICAL TERMS

Archaism: deliberate use of old-fashioned words or forms no longer in common currency.

Asterisks: e.g., ***stanō** (8.11), indication of a hypothetical form not actually found in surviving written documents.

Diminutives: the suffixes **-ulus, -olus** (after a vowel), **-culus, -ellus,** and **-illus** form diminutive adjectives and nouns, often expressing endearment and affection, sometimes pity, e.g., **Cui dōnō lepidum novum libellum** (1.1), *[my] dear little papyrus roll.*

Hapax: Gr., "once only," a term applied to some of the words in the running vocabularies, indicating that the word to which it is applied occurs only here in extant Latin literature.

Inceptive Verbs: verbs with an **-sc-** infix such as **cognōscō** are called inceptive verbs and often denote the beginning (cf. Lat. **incipiō**, *to begin*) of an action. Thus, **cognōscō** means *to get to know, learn, become acquainted with.* The inceptive infix **-sc-** appears only in the present stem of inceptive verbs, and forms of these verbs derived from the perfect stem are not translated as inceptive. The perfect tense of **cognōscō**, for example, **cognōvī**, means *to have come to understand, to know* and may often best be translated in context as a present tense, *I know.* The pluperfect of inceptive verbs may often best be translated as an imperfect.

Impersonal Verbs: impersonal verbs such as **libet (lubet)** + dat., *(it) is pleasing* (to), do not appear in the first or second persons and do not have personal subjects. In dictionaries the subject is given as the impersonal *it*, and this word may be used in your translation. There will often, however, be an infinitive, a phrase, or a clause introduced by **ut** and with its verb in the subjunctive that serves as the actual grammatical subject of the impersonal verb. Thus, in Catullus 2.6, the words **lubet iocārī** may be translated *it pleases [her] to play*, with the infinitive filling out the meaning of the impersonal verb, or we may translate *to play pleases [her]*, with the infinitive serving as the subject of the impersonal verb. You may translate either way, but in the notes in this book the actual grammatical subjects of impersonal verbs will usually be pointed out and used as subjects in translations.

LOVE AND BETRAYAL
SELECTIONS FROM CATULLUS

Meter: hendecasyllabic

1   **lepidus, -a, -um** [colloquial word, common in Plautus and Terence, and
recalling the Greek word *leptos*, "slender, subtle, refined," associated with
the verse of the Hellenistic Greek poet Callimachus], *witty, amusing;
delightful, charming.*
libellus, -ī, m. [dim. of **liber, librī,** m., *papyrus roll* (the ancient form of what
we think of as a book)], *little papyrus roll.*

2   **āridus, -a, -um,** *dry.*
modo, adv., *only; recently, just now.*
pūmex, pūmicis, f. here, though usually m., *pumice-stone* (used like sandpa-
per to smooth the ends of a papyrus roll).
expoliō [**ex-,** *thoroughly* + **poliō, -īre, -īvī, -ītus,** *to polish*], **-īre, -īvī, -ītus,** *to
smooth, polish.*

3   **Cornēlius, -ī,** m., *Cornelius* (Cornelius Nepos, ca. 110–24 B.C., historian, biog-
rapher, and poet of light verse. Nepos, like Catullus, was a Transpadane;
he was considerably older than Catullus, and he had important
connections in Rome, being a friend of Atticus and Cicero. He regarded
Catullus and Lucretius as the most elegant poets of their age; see his *Life of
Atticus* 12.4).
namque, conj., *for.*

4   **esse aliquid:** colloquial, *[they] were [worth] something, were [really] something.*
nūgae, -ārum, f. pl., *nonsense; trifles.*

5   **iam tum, cum:** *already at that time, when.*
ausus es: from the semi-deponent verb **audēre.**
ūnus Ītalōrum: *the [only] one of the Italians, alone of Italians.*

6   **aevum, -ī,** n., *age, generation; time.*
omne aevum: *all recorded history.* The work of Cornelius Nepos referred to
here was entitled *Chronica* (= *Annals*) and was a universal history of the
Greco-Roman world in three papyrus rolls.
explicō [**ex-,** *out* + **plicō, -āre, -āvī, -ātus,** *to fold; to roll*], **-āre, -āvī, -ātus,** *to
make known, explain, give an account of; to unfold, unroll.*
carta, -ae, f., *sheet of papyrus;* by extension, *papyrus roll* (i.e., sheets of papyrus
glued together), *volume* (of written work).

7   **doctus, -a, -um,** *full of learning, learned.*
Iuppiter: *by Jupiter! = I swear it!*
labōriōsus, -a, -um, *involving much work; painstaking, laborious.*

Text

The reading of line 9 (see next page spread) has been debated for centuries. First
we give the version printed in the Oxford Classical Text (1958), and then we give
lines 8–10 with the more recent reading of line 9 proposed by A. S. Gratwick (2002).

CATULLUS 1

Dedication

Catullus dedicates his new papyrus roll of verse to Cornelius Nepos.

1 Cui dōnō lepidum novum libellum *To whom do I dedicate*
2 āridā modo pūmice expolītum? *this new small delightful*
3 Cornēlī, tibi: namque tū solēbās *To you Cornelius*
4 meās esse aliquid putāre nūgās
5 iam tum, cum ausus es ūnus Ītalōrum
6 omne aevum tribus explicāre cartīs
7 doctīs, Iuppiter, et labōriōsīs.

continued

Initial Explorations

1. How does Catullus describe his **libellus**? (1–2)
2. Examine each word that Catullus uses to describe his **libellus** in the first two lines. How could each word simultaneously describe both the physical appearance of the **libellus** and also the quality of the poetry within it?
3. Why does Catullus use the diminutive form **libellum**? (1)
4. Identify examples of alliteration, assonance, and homoioteleuton in the first two lines. What effects are produced by these poetic devices?
5. How is **modo** in line 2 related to **novum** in line 1? How is **expolītum** in line 2 related to **lepidum** in line 1? How do these words form a chiasmus?
6. Identify the rhetorical figure involved in the words **solēbās / meās . . . nūgās** (3–4). What is its effect?
7. Why has Catullus chosen Cornelius as the recipient of his **libellus**? (3–4)
8. How by word choice and word order has Catullus drawn an effective contrast between Cornelius' estimation of the poet's work and Catullus' own description of it? (4)
9. In line 5 Catullus commends Cornelius for being a bold writer. What did Cornelius dare to produce? (5–6)
10. a. How does Catullus further characterize Cornelius and his literary production? (5–7)
    b. What is the tone of Catullus' description of Cornelius' literary achievement and how is that tone produced?
    c. What are some of the implications of Catullus' use of the two adjectives **doctīs** and **labōriōsīs** (7)?
11. Compare line 6 with line 1, and line 7 with line 2. How do Catullus' and Cornelius' respective works of poetry and history differ?

8   **habē tibi**: a legal phrase used when transferring property from one person to another, *take possession of X for yourself!*

    quisquis, quisquis, quidquid, indefinite pronoun/adjective, *whoever, whatever*.

        quidquid hoc libellī: supply **est**, *whatever this [is] of a little papyrus roll.*

9   **quāliscumque, quāliscumque, quālecumque**, indefinite adjective, *of whatever sort*.

        quālecumque: idiomatically, *such as it is.*

    quod: connecting relative and subject of the jussive subjunctive **maneat** (10), *and may it. . . .*

    patrōna, -ae, f., *patroness.*

    OR with Gratwick's reading of line 9

    patrōcinium, -ī, n., *patronage; advocacy.*

        Patrōcinī: supply **tuī**, referring to Cornelius.

    ergō, prep. + gen., always following its noun, *in witness of.*

10   **perennis, -is, -e** [**per-**, *through* + **annus, -ī**, m., *year*], *lasting through the years.*

        perenne: predicate adjective, modifying **quod** (9).

    saeclum, -ī, n. [syncope for **saeculum**], *age; lifetime; generation; century.*

8   Quārē habē tibi quidquid hoc libellī
9   quālecumque; quod, ō patrōna virgō,
10   plūs ūnō maneat perenne saeclō.

or with Gratwick's reading of line 9:

8   Quārē habē tibi quidquid hoc libellī,
9   quālecumque aliquid. Patrōcinī ergō
10   plūs ūnō maneat perenne saeclō.

Initial Explorations

12. What does the legal phrase **habē tibi** (8) imply about what Catullus is doing in this poem?
13. What, if anything, does the indefinite **quidquid** (8) imply about the contents of the **libellus**?
14. What does the word **quālecumque** (9) imply about Catullus' evaluation of his **libellus**?
15. To whom do you suppose the word **virgō** (9) refers?
16. What prayer does Catullus make to the **virgō**? (9–10)
17. Explain the tension that exists between the wish in the final line and the poet's earlier assessment of his work.
18. How does Gratwick's reading of line 9 change things?

Discussion

1.   Which reading of line 9 makes more sense within the poem as a whole?
2.   Why does Catullus choose Cornelius as the recipient of his **libellus**?
3.   What does the poem say about Catullus' **libellus** and about what Catullus valued in his poetry and thought noteworthy about it?
4.   What does Catullus admire about Cornelius and his *Chronica*?

Meter: hendecasyllabic

1   **passer, passeris,** m., *small bird* (usually thought to be a *sparrow*, but taken by
some to be a *blue thrush*; the word and its diminutive, **passerculus,** were
used as terms of endearment).
     passer: vocative, picked up by **tēcum** in line 9.
   dēliciae, -ārum, f. pl. [usually pl. in form, sing. in meaning], *pleasure, delight;
pet; darling, sweetheart.*
   puella, -ae, f., *girl; girlfriend, sweetheart.*
     meae puellae: genitive.
2   **quīcum:** = **quōcum.**
     quīcum lūdere: all the infinitives in lines 2–4 are dependent on **solet** (4);
the subject (*she*) is the **puella** (1).
   sinus, -ūs, m., *fold of a toga; lap; bosom.*
3   **prīmum digitum:** *fingertip.*
   appetō [**ad-,** *toward, against* + **petō, petere, petīvī, petītus,** *to look for, seek; to
attack*], **appetere, appetīvī, appetītus,** *to try to reach; to seek instinctively; to
desire; to attack.*
     cui . . . appetentī: the participle, completing the line framing, may be
translated with **cui** as a substantive, *to whose eager attack.*
       quīcum (2) **. . . quem . . . / cui** (3): polyptoton and anaphora.
4   **ācer, ācris, ācre,** *keen, sharp.*
     ācrīs: = **ācrēs,** *i*-stem nouns and adjectives commonly retain their original
spelling in the accusative plural.
   incitō [**in-,** *in, into* + **citō, -āre, -āvī, -ātus,** *to set in motion, rouse*], **-āre, -āvī,
-ātus,** *to urge on, arouse, provoke.*
   morsus, -ūs, m., *nibble, bite, peck* (of a bird).

CATULLUS 2

A Pet Bird

*Catullus wishes that the pet bird of his **puella** could satisfy his needs as well as it appears to satisfy hers.*

1   Passer, dēliciae meae puellae,
2   quīcum lūdere, quem in sinū tenēre,
3   cui prīmum digitum dare appetentī
4   et ācrīs solet incitāre morsūs,

continued

Initial Explorations

1.   The words **passer, meae,** and **puellae** in line 1 inform us of a triangle of relationships that this poem will explore. Identify the members of the triangle.
2.   What does the word **dēliciae** with its range of meanings tell us about how the poet views the relationship between the **puella** and the **passer**?
3.   Describe each of the interactions between the **puella** and the **passer** in lines 2–4.
4.   Identify the clauses of an ascending tricolon in lines 2–4.
5.   In addition to its literal meaning, what suggestive meaning does the infinitive **lūdere** carry in this context? (2)
6.   Of the words **quem in sinū tenēre**, which one adds an erotic coloring to the scene? (2)
7.   What is the relationship between the actions of the **puella** in line 3 and in line 4? Can something more than innocent play be seen here?
8.   What meaning of the verb **appetere** is most appropriate in translating the participle **appetentī** (3)? How does this word contribute an amorous overtone to the scene?
9.   Why is the verb **solet** (4) important? What does it add to the description of the behavior of the **puella**?
10. Discuss the words **ācrīs . . . morsūs** (4). In what direction do these two words take the poet's description of the scene? Elsewhere Catullus uses similar language of lovers' kisses: e.g., Catullus 8.18, **Quem basiābis? Cui labella mordēbis?** *Whom will you kiss? Whose little lips will you bite?* and 68.126–28, *the dove is said always to snatch kisses with her biting beak* (**mordentī . . . rōstrō**) *more wantonly than even an especially passionate woman.* How does this affect your understanding of the scene here?

27

5　**cum**: *whenever*; **cum** may introduce a general temporal clause with its verb in the indicative describing repeated action.

　　dēsīderium, -ī, n., *desire, longing; something longed for, object of desire; sweetheart.*

　　niteō, nitēre, *to shine; to be beautiful, be radiant.*

　　　　dēsīderiō meō nitentī: usually interpreted as dative with **lubet** (6), *to the radiant object of my desire*, but some, including Godwin and Thomson, regard **dēsīderiō meō** as ablative and translate *to [her] radiant with desire for me.*

6　**nesciō quis, nesciō quid**, indefinite pronoun [only the **quis, quid** part changes form; lit., *I don't know who, I don't know what*], *someone or other, something or other.*

　　　　nescio: iambic shortening carries over here into the compound **ne-scio**.

　　lubet: archaic for **libet**, impersonal + dat., *(it) is pleasing* (to).

　　　　lubet: the subject is the infinitive **iocārī**.

　　iocor, -ārī, -ātus sum, *to jest, joke; to play a game.*

　　　　iocārī: governing **cārum nescio quid** as internal or cognate accusative, *to play some dear game or other.*

7　**sōlāciolum, -ī**, n. [dim., probably coined by Catullus] + gen., *slight relief (from), small comfort (for).*

　　　　et sōlāciolum: a second internal or cognate accusative with **iocārī**, *and to play at a small comfort (for her. . . .).* The Renaissance scholar Guarinus suggested reading **ut** instead of **et**. He is followed by Thomson. This **ut** would be translated *as.* Line 7 would then clarify the vague **cārum nescio quid** in line 6; the **puella** plays with the **passer** *as a small comfort for her heartache.*

　　dolor, dolōris, m., *pain, smart, heartache.*

8　**acquiēscō** [**ad-**, intensive prefix + **quiēscō, quiēscere, quiēvī, quiētūrus**, *to fall asleep; to rest*], inceptive, **acquiēscere, acquiēvī**, *to quiet down, find rest.*

　　　　ut . . . acquiēscat: either a result or more likely a purpose clause.

　　ārdor, ārdōris, m., *fire; heat; passionate desire.*

9　**sīcut**, adv., *just as.*

　　ipsa: literally, *[she] herself*; here perhaps, *your mistress*, in the sense that **ipse** and **ipsa** often refer to the master and mistress of the household and owner and overseer of household slaves and workers.

　　possem: *would that I could, if only I could*; the imperfect subjunctive here expresses an unrealized wish in present time.

　　　　tēcum . . . possem: note the strict correspondence between the meter and the individual words in the line.

10　**trīstīs**: for the ending, see the note on **ācrīs** in line 4.

　　levō, -āre, -āvī, -ātus, *to lighten, alleviate, relieve.*

　　cūra, -ae, f., *care; emotional distress; anguished emotion; feeling.*

5 cum dēsīderiō meō nitentī

6 cārum nescio quid lubet iocārī,

7 et sōlāciolum suī dolōris,

8 crēdō, ut tum gravis acquiēscat ārdor:

9 tēcum lūdere sīcut ipsa possem

10 et trīstīs animī levāre cūrās!

Initial Explorations

11. The words **dēsīderiō meō nitentī** (5) may be translated *to the radiant object of my desire* or *to [her] shining with longing for me*. Does one translation seem to be more appropriate than the other? Need one choose?

12. Why, according to the poet, is the **puella** playing with the **passer**? (5–8) Include in your answer reference to the three line-ending words, **iocārī**, **dolōris**, and **ārdor**. To what extent is the **passer** described as a surrogate lover?

13. How does the presence of the parenthetical word **crēdō** qualify the statements in lines 7 and 8? What level of knowledge of the true intentions of the **puella** does this word suggest on the part of the poet?

14. Is the **puella** or the **passer** the center of the poet's interest in lines 1–8?

15. What is the poet's wish in line 9? in line 10?

16. What is implied by the use of the imperfect subjunctive (**possem**, 9) for the poet's wish?

Discussion

1. What is the relationship between Catullus and the **puella**?

2. How satisfactory is this poem as an introduction to a cycle of poems devoted to the love affair between Catullus and the **puella**?

Meter: hendecasyllabic

1   **tam ... quam:** *as ... as.*
    grātus, -a, -um + dat., *welcome* (to), *pleasing* (to).
      Tam grātum est: *It is as pleasing.* The three lines printed here as Catullus
      2b are joined together with poem 2 in the manuscripts, but most editors
      separate them as a fragment of a poem, the remainder of which is now
      lost (similar things happen elsewhere in the Catullan corpus). If they
      were to be joined after line 10 of poem 2, that line would end with a
      comma and the lines of 2b would complete the sentence. The main rea-
      son editors usually print 2b as a fragment of a separate poem is the
      change in the mood of the verbs. Catullus says in 2.9 *if only I could play*
      with you, using the imperfect subjunctive **possem**. If fragment 2b is to be
      joined to that statement, it is odd that Catullus continues with the indica-
      tive **est**, *it is as pleasing as*, when we would naturally expect the subjunc-
      tive, *it would be as pleasing as*. Furthermore, the comparison to Atalanta
      (see below) does not appear to illuminate or fit easily with any of the
      themes of Catullus 2.
    ferunt: *they say.*
    puellae: Atalanta, the swift huntress, whose hand in marriage Hippomenes
      (or Milanion; the name of her successful suitor differs in the sources) won
      by throwing three golden apples given him by Venus aside off the race
      course at intervals during his race with Atalanta, the prize of which would
      be marriage with her. Atalanta stopped to pick up the apples and so lost
      the race. According to one version of the story she deliberately wasted
      time in retrieving the last apple because she had fallen in love with Hip-
      pomenes (or Milanion) and wanted to lose the race so that he would marry
      her (see Ovid, *Metamorphoses* 10.560–704).
2   **pernīx, pernīcis,** *swift.*
    aureolus, -a, -um [dim. of **aureus, -a, -um,** *golden*], *golden.*
    mālum: note the macron; do not confuse with **malus, -a, -um.**
3   **quod:** relative pronoun.
    zōna, -ae, f. [Greek loan word], *girdle* (worn by unmarried girls).
    soluit: pronounce as three syllables here (usually spelled **solvit**).

CATULLUS 2b

Atalanta

This fragment of a poem compares a personal pleasure to Atalanta's delight with the golden apple.

. . . .

1 tam grātum est mihi quam ferunt puellae
2 pernīcī aureolum fuisse mālum,
3 quod zōnam soluit diū ligātam.

Discussion

Could these lines make sense as an ending to Catullus 2?

Meter: hendecasyllabic

1   **lūgeō, lūgēre, lūxī, lūctus,** *to grieve, mourn.*
    Venus, Veneris, f., *Venus (goddess of love); charm.*
    Cupīdō, Cupīdinis, m., *Cupid (son of Venus and god of love); desire.*
      Venerēs Cupīdinēsque: Catullus is calling upon all the Venuses and Cu-
        pids in the world, i.e., all the manifestations of charm and desire.
2   **quantum, -ī,** n., pronoun, *whatever amount.*
    quantum est: the third vocative with **lūgēte:** *whatever amount [of] . . . there is*
      = *however many [of] . . . there are,* a colloquial expression.
    venustus, -a, -um, *endowed/involved with Venus; attractive, charming.*
    venustiōrum: the comparative adjective may be translated *rather/quite. . . .*
      hominum venustiōrum: perhaps, *of men who are quite caught up in the*
        bonds of Venus herself, i.e., *who are deeply in love.*
4   **passer . . . meae puellae:** cf. line 3; conduplicatio, as often in dirges.
    dēliciae: see note to line 1 of Catullus 2.
    passer, dēliciae meae puellae: = Catullus 2.1, vocative there, nominative
      here.
6   **mellītus, -a, -um** [**mel, mellis,** n., *honey*], *honey-sweet*
    erat: the subject is **passer.**
    nōscō, nōscere, nōvī, nōtus, inceptive, *to get to know, learn;* perfect, *to know*
      (a person or thing).
      nōrat: syncope for **nōverat;** the pluperfect translates into English as an
        imperfect with the meaning *used to know.*
7   **ipsam:** = **dominam,** *its/his mistress* (modified by **suam** in line 6), compare
    ipsa in Catullus 2.9.
    puella mātrem: supply **nōvit.**
8   **sēsē:** an alternate form of **sē.** The form **sēsē** may originally have conveyed
    greater emphasis, but often it is indistinguishable in sense from the simple
    sē.
    gremium, -ī, n., *bosom, lap.*
    illius: = **illīus,** with short *i* for the sake of the meter.
9   **circumsiliō** [**circum-,** *around* + **saliō, salīre, saluī, saltus,** *to jump, leap*], **cir-**
    cumsilīre, *to jump/leap/hop around.*
    modo . . . modo: *now . . . now.*
10   **domina, -ae,** f., *mistress (female head of a household); owner; female ruler; mis-*
    tress (a woman loved by a man but not married to him).
    usque, adv., *continuously.*
    pīpiō, -āre [onomatopoetic], *to chirp, peep.*

CATULLUS 3

Death of the Pet Bird

Catullus eulogizes the pet bird.

1   Lūgēte, ō Venerēs Cupīdinēsque,
2   et quantum est hominum venustiōrum:
3   passer mortuus est meae puellae,
4   passer, dēliciae meae puellae,
5   quem plūs illa oculīs suīs amābat.
6   Nam mellītus erat suamque nōrat
7   ipsam tam bene quam puella mātrem,
8   nec sēsē ā gremiō illius movēbat,
9   sed circumsiliēns modo hūc modo illūc
10   ad sōlam dominam usque pīpiābat;

continued

Initial Explorations

1. Whom does the poet call upon to grieve? Why does he invoke these gods and men? (1–2)
2. Locate and analyze two ascending tricola in lines 1–2 and 4–5.
3. Lines 4–10 recall Catullus 2. Compare the relationship of the **passer** and the **puella** in these lines with lines 1–4 of Catullus 2. What are the similarities and differences?
4. With what word earlier in the poem does **mellītus** (6) correspond? How does the word **mellītus** contribute to our understanding of the relationship between the **puella** and the **passer** as expressed in this poem?
5. The verb **nōrat** (6) may connote a knowing in carnal or sexual as well as mental terms. What limitation does line 7 place on the dual meaning of **nōrat** in this context? Why is that significant?
6. The word **gremiō** (8) reminds the reader of **sinū** in Catullus 2.2. How has the bird's behavior at the bosom or on the lap of the **puella** changed between poems?
7. Comment on the impression produced by the polysyllabic participle placed next to four choppy and elided adverbs in line 9.
8. What do the words **ad sōlam dominam usque pīpiābat** (10) say about the relationship of the bird to the **puella**? Which meaning of the word **domina** is most appropriate? In the context of the scene described in lines 4–10, is more than one meaning of the word applicable?

11   **tenebricōsus, -a, -um** [a colloquial formation from **tenebrae, -ārum**, f. pl., *darkness, gloom*], *dark, gloomy.*

12   **quisquam, quisquam, quicquam**, indefinite pronoun, *anyone, anything.*
        negant . . . quemquam: *they say that no one. . . .*

13   **male sit**: colloquial, + dat., *may it go badly* (for), *curses* (on).
        tenebrae, -ārum, f. pl., *darkness, gloom.*

14   **Orcus, -ī**, m., *Orcus* (god of the underworld); *death; the underworld.*
        quae . . . dēvorātis: *you who. . . .*
        bellus, -a, -um [colloquial, cf. the more formal **pulcher, pulchra, pulchrum**, *beautiful, handsome, lovely*], *handsome, pretty.*

15   **mihi**: *from me*, dative of separation with **abstulistis.**

16   **Ō factum male!**: *O misfortune!* (literally, *[thing] done badly*).
        misellus, -a, -um [dim. of **miser, misera, miserum**, *wretched*], *wretched little, poor little.*

17   **opera, -ae**, f., *effort; deed.*
        tuā . . . operā: idiomatic, *because of your doing.*
        meae puellae: genitive, with **ocellī** (18).

18   **flendō**: *from. . . .*, gerund, ablative of cause.
        turgidulus, -a, -um [dim. of **turgidus, -a, -um**, *swollen*], *slightly swollen/ puffed.*
        rubeō, rebēre, *to be red.*
        ocellus, -ī, m. [dim. of **oculus, -ī**, m., *eye*], *dear eye, little eye.*
        turgidulī . . . ocellī: colloquial diminutives expressing endearment or compassion.

Text

16   **male! Ō**: hiatus emphasizes the pathos of the exclamations. Goold, however, emends as follows, eliminating the hiatus:

> 16   Ō factum male, quod, miselle passer,
> 17   tuā nunc operā meae puellae
> 18   flendō turgidulī rubent ocellī!

17   Instead of **tuā**, Thomson prints **vestrā**, referring to the **malae tenebrae / Orcī** (13–14), whereas **tuā** would refer to the **passer** (16). Thomson gives lines 15–17 as follows (note the different punctuation):

> 15   tam bellum mihi passerem abstulistis
> 16   (ō factum male! ō miselle passer!);
> 17   vestrā nunc operā meae puellae

11 quī nunc it per iter tenebricōsum
12 illūc, unde negant redīre quemquam.
13 At vōbīs male sit, malae tenebrae
14 Orcī, quae omnia bella dēvorātis:
15 tam bellum mihi passerem abstulistis.
16 Ō factum male! Ō miselle passer!
17 Tuā nunc operā meae puellae
18 flendō turgidulī rubent ocellī.

Initial Explorations

9. What journey must the bird now make? (11–12) How is it portrayed? What is its mythological background? Do the word **tenebricōsum** and the sentiment expressed in line 12 reinforce or undercut the gravity of the loss? Is there an element of parody here?

10. Whom does the poet curse? (13–14) What specific reason does the poet give for uttering the curse?

11. In a surprising conclusion, what is the bird (or the shades of Orcus if Thomson's reading is accepted) blamed for? (17–18) Does the traditional text or Thomson's emendation make better sense?

12. What feelings does the poet express in the final line? How does he express them?

13. Where in the poem do you find shifts in sentiment and tone? Describe the sentiment and tone of each section of the poem.

14. Read the poem aloud and in meter. Describe the effects of the various sound and metrical patterns in the poem, such as (a) the repetition of double *l*'s and the resulting linkage among words, (b) the resonance of *m*'s in lines 6–7, (c) the multiple elisions and onomatopoeia in lines 9–10, (d) the contrast between mono- or disyllabic words in the first half of line 11 and the polysyllabic word at the end of the line, (e) the repetitions in lines 13–15 (**malae . . . male; bella . . . bellum**) and the anaphora and exclamations in line 16, and (f) the soft liquid sounds of line 18.

Discussion

1. How is the **passer** given human qualities in the image of a lover?

2. How does the portrayal of the **passer** with the **puella** in Catullus 3 complement that in Catullus 2?

3. How does the death of the **passer** open the way for future developments in Catullus' love for the **puella**?

Meter: iambic trimeter

1   **phasēlus, -ī,** m. [Greek loan word meaning *bean*], *small boat, yacht* (named **phasēlus** from its resemblance to a bean-pod).
     hospes, hospitis, m., *guest; stranger.*
2   **ait:** pronounce as two syllables.
     ait fuisse . . . celerrimus: *says that it/he was the swiftest.* . . . The **phasēlus** uses Greek grammar, for, unlike Latin, Greek uses the nominative case in indirect statement and does not express the subject of the indirect statement when that subject is the same as the subject of the verb of saying; normal Latin would be **ait sē fuisse . . . celerrimum.**
          ait . . . / neque (3) **. . . / nequīsse** (4): *and [it/he] says that it/he was not unable;* either litotes = *and [it/he] says that it/he was able* or a denial of a denial = *and [it/he] denies that it/he was not able* (as if someone had said or might say that it/he was not able).
3   **natō, -āre, -āvī, -ātūrus,** *to swim; to float; to sail.*
     impetus, -ūs, m. [a word associated with epic poetry], *strong forward movement, speed.*
     trabs, trabis, f., *tree trunk; wooden beam; timber;* by metonymy in poetry, *boat.*
4   **nequeō, nequīre, nequīvī/nequiī** (perfect infinitive, **nequīsse**), *to be unable.*
     praetereō [**praeter-**, *past, by* + **eō, īre, iī/īvī, itūrus,** *to go*], **praeterīre, praeterīvī/praeteriī, praeteritus,** *to go past; to surpass.*
     sīve . . . sīve, conj., *whether . . . or.*
     palmula, -ae, f. [dim. of **palma, -ae,** f., *palm* (of the hand)], *little palm* (of the hand); metaphorically, *blade of an oar; oar.*
5   **opus est,** impersonal idiom, *(it) is necessary.*
          opus foret (= **esset**): *was necessary;* the subject is **volāre.** Dependent clauses in indirect statement have their verbs in the subjunctive.
     volō, -āre, -āvī, -ātūrus, *to fly.*
     linteum, -ī, n., *linen; towel, napkin; sail.*
6   **Et hoc negat . . . negāre lītus** (7): *And it/he denies that the shore . . . denies this [claim],* i.e., that it/he was the swiftest ship. In addition to **lītus,** the infinitive **negāre** has four other subjects in the indirect statement: **īnsulās** (7), **Rhodum** (8), **Propontida** (9), and **sinum** (9).
     mināx, minācis, *menacing, threatening* (in word or action).
     Hadriāticum, -ī, n., *Adriatic Sea.*
7   **-ve,** enclitic conj., *or.*
     Cyclades, Cycladum, f. pl., *Cyclades* (a group of islands in the Aegean Sea).
          Cycladās: Greek accusative plural.
8   **Rhodus, -ī,** f., *Rhodes* (an island in the Aegean Sea, east of the Cyclades).
     nōbilis, -is, -e, *well-known, famous.*
     horridus, -a, -um, *bristling* (of hair); *rough, choppy* (of the sea).
     Thracius, -a, -um, *Thracian, on the Thracian side* (referring to Thrace, a territory in northeast Greece).
          Thrāciam: Thomson prints **Thrāciā,** ablative of **Thāciās, -ae,** f. [Greek loan word], *Thracias* (a wind blowing from a direction west of north); **Thrāciā** would be ablative of instrument or cause with **horridam.**

CATULLUS 4

A Ship Retired from Service

The poet commemorates the retirement of a well-traveled ship.

1   Phasēlus ille, quem vidētis, hospitēs,
2   ait fuisse nāvium celerrimus,
3   neque ūllius natantis impetum trabis
4   nequīsse praeterīre, sīve palmulīs
5   opus foret volāre sīve linteō.
6   Et hoc negat minācis Hadriāticī
7   negāre lītus īnsulāsve Cȳcladās
8   Rhodumque nōbilem horridamque Thrāciam

Initial Explorations

1. Who is the speaker? Whom does the speaker address? What is the speaker doing? (1)
2. What claim does the speaker report that the **phasēlus** makes for itself/himself? (2)
3. What denial does the speaker report that the **phasēlus** makes in lines 3–5? What is the tone of the denial? What is the flavor of the words attributed to the **phasēlus** here?
4. In continuing to insist on its/his swiftness, what tone does the **phasēlus** use in lines 6–9?
5. What words describe the dangers of the waters through which the **phasēlus** claims to have sailed so swiftly? (6–9)
6. Find four words that suggest that the **phasēlus** is being personified. Find one word that suggests it/he is like a bird. What two words suggest the personification of nature? (2–9)

9   **Propontis, Propontidis** or **Propontidos**, f. [**pro-**, *in front of*, + **Pontus, -ī**, m.,
     Pontus, the Black Sea], *Propontis* (the ancient name for the Sea of Marmora,
     situated between the Aegean to the west and the Black Sea to the east).
         Propontida: Greek accusative.
     trux, trucis, *harsh, savage, pitiless* (of persons); *cruel, savage* (of the sea).
     Ponticus, -a, -um, *Pontic* (referring to the Pontus, the Black Sea).
     sinus, -ūs, m., see Catullus 2.2; here, *bay, gulf, sea*.
         horridamque Thrāciam (8) / **Propontida**: the three-word phrase is bal-
         anced by **trucemve Ponticum sinum**.
10   **iste, ista, istud**, *that, that* (that you see).
11   **comātus, -a, -um**, *long-haired; having much foliage, leafy*.
     Cytōrius, -a, -um, *Cytorian, of Mt. Cytorus* (a mountain on the southern shore
         of the Black Sea, rising up behind the port cities of Amastris and Cytorus).
     iugum, -ī, n., *yoke; mountain ridge*.
12   **sībilus, -ī**, m., *whistling sound*.
     ēdō [**ex-, ē-**, *out* + **dō, dare, dedī, datus**, *to give*], **ēdere, ēdidī, ēditus**, *to put
         out; to produce, let out; to utter*.
     coma, -ae, f., *hair; foliage, leaves*.
13   **Amastris, Amastris**, f., *Amastris* (a port city on the southern coast of the Black
     Sea).
         Amastri: Greek vocative.
     Cytōrus, -ī, m., *Cytorus* (both the name of a port city on the southern coast of
         the Black Sea that was absorbed by Amastris and the name of the mountain
         behind it, famous as a source of box wood).
     buxifer, buxifera, buxiferum [**buxus, -ī**, f., *box tree* + **-fer, -fera, -ferum**, *car-
         rying, bearing*], *producing boxwood trees, boxwood-bearing*.
         buxifer: compounds of this sort are a common feature of older Latin po-
         etic style.
14   **tibi**: since Cytorus was absorbed by Amastris, the two locations are addressed
         with a singular pronoun.
     haec: either *these things* (just mentioned in lines 10–12) or *the following events*;
         haec is the subject of **fuisse** and **esse** in indirect statement.
     cognitus, -a, -um, *recognized, well known*.
15   **ultimus, -a, -um**, *farthest; earliest*.
     orīgō, orīginis, f., *beginning*.
         ultimā ex orīgine: i.e., from its/his earliest days.
16   **stetisse dīcit**: the **phasēlus** is the subject of **dīcit** and of the three infinitives
         stetisse, imbuisse (17), and **tulisse** (19). Normally Latin would use **sē** as
         subject of the infinitives in indirect statement, but the ship is again using a
         Greek construction for indirect statement in which no subject needs to be
         expressed if it is the same as the subject of the introductory verb, here **dīcit**.
     cacūmen, cacūminis, n., *peak, summit*.

9   Propontida trucemve Ponticum sinum,

10 ubi iste post phasēlus anteā fuit

11 comāta silva; nam Cytōriō in iugō

12 loquente saepe sībilum ēdidit comā.

13 Amastri Pontica et Cytōre buxifer,

14 tibi haec fuisse et esse cognitissima

15 ait phasēlus: ultimā ex orīgine

16 tuō stetisse dīcit in cacūmine,

continued

Initial Explorations

7. Describe a chiastic arrangement of words in lines 8–9.

8. The speaker, quoting the denials of the **phasēlus**, leads us back to its/his place of origin in lines 6–9. With what words does the poet endow the **phasēlus** with human attributes and abilities when it/he stood as a forest on Mt. Cytorus? (10–12)

9. Whom did the speaker address in line 1? What does the speaker now address in line 13? What is the technical term for the rhetorical figure involved here?

10. Once more the **phasēlus** is said to refer to an authority for its/his veracity. (13–15) To what does it/he refer now and to what did it/he refer for its/his veracity before?

11. The word **haec** (14) could refer to what comes before it or to what comes after it. Do you think it refers backward or forward? Present reasons for your answer.

17 **imbuō, imbuere, imbuī, imbūtus,** *to dip, wet* (for the first time, as if in a rite of initiation).

18 **impotēns, impotentis [in-,** *not* + **potēns, potentis,** *having power* (over), *able to control*], *powerless, impotent; powerless* (over oneself), *lacking self-control; wild, violent, raging.*

fretum, -ī, n., *strait, narrows; sea.*

19 **erus, -ī,** m., *master; owner.*

laevus, -a, -um, *left, on/from the left.*

   laeva sīve. . . . : the first **sīve** has been omitted here: *whether on/from the left or. . . .*

20 **vocāret . . . / . . . incidisset** (21): for the use of the subjunctive here, see the note to line 5. Note the change in tense from imperfect (*a breeze was calling/inviting*) to pluperfect (*had fallen*).

aura, -ae, f., *breeze.*

utrumque: modifying **pedem** (21).

Iuppiter, Iovis, m., *Jupiter;* (by metonymy) *sky; wind.*

21 **secundus, -a, -um** [from **sequor, sequī, secūtus sum,** *to follow*], *following* (in order), *second;* of wind, *following* (producing a tail wind), *favorable;* of deities, *favorable, kindly.*

pēs, pedis, m., *foot; sheet* (rope fastening the lower corners of a sail to the ship).

22 **vōtum, -ī,** n., *vow* (promise made to a god to do something in exchange for the god's granting of a request for help).

lītorālis, -is, -e, *of/belonging to the shore.*

   lītorālibus deīs: i.e., gods of the sea, who commonly had temples on the shore and to whom sailors in distress would pray that the gods bring them safely to shore.

23 **sibi:** *by itself/himself,* dative of agent with the perfect passive infinitive **esse facta,** which in the indirect statement replaces a pluperfect indicative, *had been made;* the **cum** clause is then in secondary seqence (imperfect subjunctive).

venīret: the subject is the **phasēlus.**

24 **novissimus, -a, -um** [superlative of **novus, -a, -um,** *new*], *most recent, latest, last to be reached.*

   ā marī (23) / **novissimō . . . ad . . . lacum:** i.e., *from the last sea* (to be crossed, usually identified as the Adriatic) *to the lake* (often identified as the Benacus, Lake Garda, where Catullus' ancestral home was located on the promontory of Sirmio).

ad usque + acc., *all the way to.*

limpidus, -a, -um, *unclouded, clear, limpid.*

lacus, -ūs, m., *lake.*

Text

24 **novissimō:** a Renaissance conjecture replacing the superlative adverb **novissimē.** The adverb would mean *lastly/after all else* and is probably to be preferred here (Thomson prints it in his text). The phrase **ā marī** (23) would then refer to the Pontus or Black Sea, where the voyage began.

17   tuō imbuisse palmulās in aequore,
18   et inde tot per impotentia freta
19   erum tulisse, laeva sīve dextera
20   vocāret aura, sīve utrumque Iuppiter
21   simul secundus incidisset in pedem;
22   neque ūlla vōta lītorālibus deīs
23   sibi esse facta, cum venīret ā marī
24   novissimō hunc ad usque limpidum lacum.

continued

Initial Explorations

12.   What rhetorical figure is involved in the repetition of **tuō** (16, 17)?
13.   Find words that continue the personification of the **phasēlus** and of nature. (14–24)
14.   What word again calls attention to the dangers of the waters through which the **phasēlus** sailed? (18)
15.   How had the **phasēlus** emphasized its/his versatility before? How does it/he do it now? (19–21)
16.   What is the final boast of the **phasēlus**? (22–24)

25   **haec**: *these events.*
        fuēre: = **fuērunt**.
        reconditus, -a, -um, [**re-**, *back* + **conditus, -a, -um**, *hidden, concealed*], *hidden,*
            secluded.
26   **seneō, senēre**, *to be old; to spend one's old age.*
        quiēs, quiētis, f., *relief from labor, rest.*
        tibi: a singular pronoun is here used to refer to the twins, Castor and Pollux,
            who, as Merrill (12) explains, "were often spoken of . . . under one name,—
            that of Castor being more frequently used."
27   **gemellus, -a, -um**, *twin-born, twin.*
        Castor, Castoris, m., *Castor* (Castor and his twin brother Pollux were the sons
            of Zeus and Leda; as the constellation Gemini they were traditionally
            considered protectors of sailors and ships).
        gemellus, -ī, m., *twin.*
        gemelle Castoris: i.e., Pollux.

Comparisons

Cicero in his *Tusculan Disputations* (1.101) gives this Latin translation of a famous
epigram written by the Greek poet Simonides commemorating the Greeks under
the command of Leonidas who fell at Thermopylae fighting against the Persian
invaders. Compare it with the opening of Catullus 4:

Dīc, hospes, Spartae nōs tē hīc vīdisse iacentēs,
    dum sānctīs patriae lēgibus obsequimur.

lēx, lēgis, f., *law.*
obsequor, obsequī, obsecūtus sum + dat., *to obey.*

Compare the following translation of a Greek epigram written by Macedonius the
Consul (first century A.D.; *Palatine Anthology* 6.69) with the conclusion of Catullus 4:

Crantas, after many voyages, dedicated his ship to Poseidon,
    anchoring it firmly in the floor of the temple;
now that it is aground it cares no longer for the breeze; on this ground
    Crantas stretching out sleeps without fear.

25   Sed haec prius fuēre: nunc recondita
26   senet quiēte sēque dēdicat tibi,
27   gemelle Castor et gemelle Castoris.

Initial Explorations

17.   At what point does the speaker again stop letting the **phasēlus** speak for it-
       self/himself?
18.   The words **prius** and **nunc** in line 25 complete the temporal circle of the
       poem, from the present (**quem vidētis**, 1) to the past (**ait fuisse**, 2) to the pre-
       sent (**nunc . . . / senet**, 25–26). What picture does the speaker present of the
       phasēlus in its/his retirement?
19.   To whom does the **phasēlus** dedicate itself/himself and why?
20.   What rhetorical device used earlier in the poem is used again in the last line?
21.   What is the effect of the meter used in this poem?

Discussion

1.   Examine the structure of the poem as a whole. Define an "introduction," a
      "conclusion," and a "center." Then locate lines that move toward the center
      and lines that move away from the center.
2.   In what ways does the **phasēlus** betray its/his origin as a Greek ship?
3.   In what ways is the **phasēlus** similar to the legendary Argo?
4.   The **phasēlus** is personified. What personality or traits of character does
      it/he project as the speaker reports its/his words?
5.   How do you think the speaker feels about the **phasēlus**? How do you feel
      about it/him?

Meter: hendecasyllabic

1   **vīvō, vīvere, vīxī, victūrus**, *to live; to live* (in the full sense of the word), *really live, enjoy life.*
   Vīvāmus ... amēmus / ... / ... aestimēmus (3): hortatory subjunctives.
   Lesbia, -ae, f., *Lesbia* (the name or pseudonym of the woman to whom the poem is addressed; see Introduction).
   atque, conj., *and also; and what is more, and in fact, and indeed.*
2   **rūmor, rūmōris,** m., *rumor; gossip.*
   sevērus, -a, -um, *severe in judgment, strict, stern.*
   sevēriōrum: for translation of the comparative, see note to Catullus 3.2.
3   **aestimō, -āre, -āvī, -ātus,** *to estimate the worth of, value.*
   as, assis, m., *copper Roman coin; penny, cent.*
   ūnius assis aestimāre, idiom, *to value X* (acc.) *as worth just one cent*, genitive of indefinite value. The *i* of **ūnius** is here short for the sake of the meter.
4   **sōlēs:** from **sōl, sōlis,** m., *sun.*
   occidō [**ob-,** *against* + **cadō, cadere, cecidī, cāsūrus,** *to fall*], **occidere, occidī, occāsūrus,** *to fall; to die; to sink, set* (of celestial bodies).
5   **nōbīs:** emphatic by position, serving as dative of reference, *for us,* with **occidit brevis lūx** and as dative of agent, *by us,* with **est ... dormienda** (6). Thomson places a comma after **nōbīs,** allowing **nōbīs** to be taken only with **est ... dormienda** (6).
   semel, adv., *once, once and for all.*
   cum semel occidit: either present or perfect indicative in a present-general temporal clause, *whenever ... once sets* or *whenever ... has once set.* Present-general temporal and conditional clauses take the present or perfect indicative in the subordinate clause and the present indicative in the main clause (here **est ... dormienda**). The pronoun **nōbīs** will then refer to humankind in general, not to Catullus and Lesbia as individuals.
6   **est ... dormienda:** gerundive of obligation or passive periphrastic, *must be slept,* with the dative of agent, **nōbīs** (5).
   perpetuus, -a, -um, *continuous, everlasting.*
7   **Dā mī:** note the reversed and lengthened repetition of vowel sounds from the previous word **dormienda.**
   bāsium, -ī, n., *kiss.*
   bāsia: the word is first attested in Catullus and is rare in later poets; the normal words for *kiss* are **ōsculum** and **suāvium/sāvium.**
8   **dein:** = **deinde.**
9   **usque,** adv., *continuously, without a break.*

CATULLUS 5

Give me a thousand kisses!

The poet invites Lesbia to a life of love.

1   Vīvāmus, mea Lesbia, atque amēmus,
2   rūmōrēsque senum sevēriōrum
3   omnēs ūnius aestimēmus assis!
4   Sōlēs occidere et redīre possunt:
5   nōbīs cum semel occidit brevis lūx,
6   nox est perpetua ūna dormienda.
7   Dā mī bāsia mīlle, deinde centum,
8   dein mīlle altera, dein secunda centum,
9   deinde usque altera mīlle, deinde centum.

continued

Initial Explorations

1. To whom is this poem addressed? Who is Lesbia? What does the name signify? Of what significance is its position in the line here?
2. With what two exhortations does the poet frame the first line? How does the second exhortation explain the first? How do these exhortations jar with traditional Roman values?
3. How would a well-brought-up young Roman woman react to Catullus' exhortations in line 1?
4. How does Catullus in lines 2–3 anticipate reservations that Lesbia might have?
5. How does Catullus encourage Lesbia to evaluate the **rūmōrēs** of the stern old men? (2–3)
6. What do assonance, alliteration, and word placement contribute to the effect of line 3?
7. What is meant by the phrase **carpe diem**? How do lines 4–6 introduce this theme?
8. Identify, analyze, and comment on the meaning of the imagery and the antitheses in lines 4–6.
9. How does the demand for kisses (7–9) result logically from what the poet has said so far in the poem?
10. How would you characterize Catullus' demand for kisses, and what would the stern old men think of it?

10   **multa mīlia**: supply **basiōrum** as partitive genitive.

      fēcerīmus: future perfect indicative, with long *i* here. In addition to mean-
            ing simply *will have made*, the verb may be understood here in a special
            commercial sense of *making up* or *reaching* a specific sum of money.

11   **conturbō** [con-, *thoroughly* + **turbō, -āre, -āvī, -ātus**, *to stir up, throw into con-
            fusion*], **-āre, -āvī, -ātus**, *to mix up, confound*.

      nē sciāmus: negative purpose clause. The danger for them is that "to count
            one's blessings is to invite Nemesis and the evil eye" (Fordyce, 108).

12   **quis, qua/quae, quid**, indefinite pronoun after **nē**, *anyone, anybody, somebody,
            anything, something*.

      nē quis malus: *so that no evil person* (lit., *so that somebody evil . . . not . . .*).

      invideō [in-, *in, on* + **video, vidēre, vīdī, vīsus**, *to see*], **invidēre, invīdī, in-
            vīsus** + dat., *to cast an evil eye* (on), *cast spells* (upon); *to envy*.

      invidēre: use one of the first two translations of the verb given above;
            supply **nōbīs**.

13   **cum**: *when*.

      tantum, -ī, n., *such a quantity, so much; so great a number*.

      tantum: with **bāsiōrum**. According to widely held beliefs of magic, some-
            one knowing the exact number of a person's possessions or actions could
            cast a destructive spell upon them or upon the person.

      sciat: subjunctive by attraction to the subjunctive in the purpose clause.

Text

11   **conturbābimus illa, nē sciāmus**: as a technical commercial term, the verb
      conturbāre may mean *to throw one's accounts* (**ratiōnēs**) *into confusion* (in
      order to give a deceptive appearance of bankruptcy), *to go bankrupt*. The
      technical commercial meaning may be appropriate after lines 7–10; when
      used in this sense, the verb is intransitive and never has an expressed di-
      rect object; one would then place the comma after **conturbābimus** instead
      of after **illa**, and **illa** (*those things* = *the sum, the total*) would be taken with **nē
      sciāmus**:

      11   conturbābimus, illa nē sciāmus
            we will throw our accounts into confusion (i.e., fraudulently claim
            bankruptcy), *so that we may not know them* (i.e., the kisses, how
            many they were)

      Fordyce remarks, "they will cheat the evil eye [see line 12], as the
      bankrupt cheats his creditors, by faking their books" (108).

10   Dein, cum mīlia multa fēcerīmus,
11   conturbābimus illa, nē sciāmus,
12   aut nē quis malus invidēre possit,
13   cum tantum sciat esse bāsiōrum.

Initial Explorations

11.   Analyze the rhetorical effects produced by sound, rhythm, and movement in lines 7–11.
12.   How does line 11 set up a contrast between passion and rationality?
13.   What two threats to the love between himself and Lesbia does Catullus want to protect against? (11–13)

Discussion

1.   How would you divide the poem into sections?
2.   The **malus**, *evil person*, of line 12 is usually thought to represent the stern old men of line 2. To what extent is the following conclusion justified: "The association, or identification, of the *malus* and his envy with the *senes severi* shows them up as hypocrites, and their moral censure stands discredited"? (Fredricksmeyer, 443)
3.   In opposition to the **senēs sevērī** and the **malus**, Catullus stakes out a moral defense of the life of love in this poem. How, in lines 4–6, has he also staked out a rational defense of the life of love?
4.   Assume that the woman addressed as **mea Lesbia** in this poem is the same as the person referred to as **mea puella** in Catullus 2 and 3. To what extent is Catullus 5 an appropriate next step in Catullus' courtship of the **puella**?

Comparisons

Catullus 5 was widely imitated in the Renaissance and later. Compare the following versions, one French and the rest British.

Pierre de Ronsard
(1524–85)

La Lune est coustumiere
De naistre tous les mois,
Mais quand nostre lumiere
Est esteinte une fois,
Longuement sans veiller
Il nous faut sommeiller.

Tandis que vivons ores,
Un baiser donnez-moy,
Donnez-m'en mille encores.
Amour n'a point de loy,
A sa Divinité,
Convient l'infinité.

Thomas Campion
(1567?–1619)

My sweetest Lesbia let us live and love,
And though the sager sort our deedes reprove,
Let us not way them: heav'ns great lampes doe dive
Into their west, and strait againe revive,
But soone as once set is our little light,
Then must we sleepe one ever-during night.

Ben Jonson
(1571/72–1637)

Come, my Celia, let us prove,
While we can, the sports of love;
Time will not be ours for ever,
He at length our good will sever.
Spend not then his gifts in vain:
Suns that set, may rise again;
But if once we lose this light,
'Tis with us perpetual night.
Why should we defer our joys?
Fame and rumour are but toys.
Cannot we delude the eyes
Of a few poor household spies?
Or his easier ears beguile,
So removed by our wile?
'Tis no sin love's fruit to steal,
But the sweet thefts to reveal,
To be taken, to be seen,
These have crimes accounted been.

Robert Herrick
(1591–1674)

Come, let us goe, while we are in our prime;
And take the harmlesse follie of the time.
   We shall grow old apace, and die
   Before we know our liberty.
   Our life is short; and our dayes run
   As fast away as do's the Sunne:
And as a vapour, or a drop of raine
Once lost, can ne'r be found againe:
   So when or you or I are made
   A fable, song, or fleeting shade;
   All love, all liking, all delight
   Lies drown'd with us in endlesse night.
Then while time serves, and we are but decaying;
Come, my *Corinna*, come, let's goe a Maying.

Richard Crashaw
(1613?–49)

Come and let us live my deare,
Let us love and never feare,
What the sowrest fathers say:
Brightest Sol that dyes to day
Lives againe as blith to morrow;
But if we darke sons of sorrow
Set: O then how long a Night
Shuts the eyes of our short light!
Then let amorous kisses dwell
On our lips, begin and tell
A thousand, and a hundred score,
An hundred and a thousand more,
Till another thousand smother
That, and that wipe off another.
Thus at last when we have numbred
Many a thousand, many a hundred,
Wee'l confound the reckoning quite
And lose our selves in wild delight:
While our joyes so multiply
As shall mocke the envious eye.

Andrew Marvell
(1621–78)

Had we but world enough, and time,
This coyness, lady, were no crime.
We would sit down and think which way
To walk, and pass our long love's day;
Thou by the Indian Ganges' side
Shouldst rubies find; I by the tide
Of Humber would complain. I would
Love you ten years before the Flood;
And you should, if you please, refuse
Till the conversion of the Jews.
My vegetable love should grow
Vaster than empires, and more slow.
An hundred years should go to praise
Thine eyes, and on thy forehead gaze;
Two hundred to adore each breast,
But thirty thousand to the rest;
An age at least to every part,
And the last age should show your heart.
For, lady, you deserve this state,
Nor would I love at lower rate.

But at my back I always hear
Time's winged chariot hurrying near;
And yonder all before us lie
Deserts of vast eternity.
Thy beauty shall no more be found,
Nor in thy marble vault shall sound
My echoing song; then worms shall try
That long preserved virginity,
And your quaint honor turn to dust,
And into ashes all my lust.
The grave's a fine and private place,
But none, I think, do there embrace.

Now, therefore, while the youthful hue
Sits on thy skin like morning glew,
And while thy willing soul transpires
At every pore with instant fires,
Now let us sport us while we may;
And now, like am'rous birds of prey,
Rather at once our time devour,

Than languish in his slow-chapped power.
Let us roll all our strength, and all
Our sweetness, up into one ball;
And tear our pleasures with rough strife
Through the iron gates of life.
Thus, though we cannot make our sun
Stand still, yet we will make him run.

Meter: hendecasyllabic

1   **Flāvius, -ī**, m., *Flavius* (unknown except for mention in this poem).
        dēliciās: see Catullus 2.1; here, *darling, sweetheart.*
2   **nī**: = **nisi**, conj., *if . . . not, unless.*
        nī sint: *if she weren't. . . . , unless she were. . . .* ; the present instead of the im-
           perfect subjunctive in the protasis of a contrary-to-fact condition is an ar-
           chaic usage; **vellēs** (3) and **possēs** (3) are the verbs of the apodosis.
        illepidus, -a, -um [**in-**, *not* + **lepidus, -a, -um**, see Catullus 1.1], *without*
           grace/refinement; without charm.
        inēlegāns, inēlegantis, *lacking in taste, without refinement.*
3   **dīcere**: + dat. and acc., *to tell* (someone, **Catullō**, 1) *about* (something, **dēliciās**
        tuās, 1).
        taceō, -ēre, -uī, -itus, intransitive, *to be silent, to keep quiet;* transitive, *to be*
           silent about (something, **dēliciās tuās**, 1).
4   **vērum**, conj., *but.*
        nescio quid: see vocabulary note on Catullus 2.6, **nesciō quis**.
        nescio quid: + partitive genitive, *something of a . . . = some . . .*
        febrīculōsus, -a, -um [adjective formed from the noun **febris, febris**, f.,
           fever], *fever-ridden, feverish.*
5   **scortum, -ī**, n., *whore.*
        hoc: object of **fatērī**.
        pudet, -ēre, -uit, impersonal, *(it) makes* (someone) *ashamed.*
        pudet: **fatērī** is the subject; supply **tē** as object.
        fateor, fatērī, fassus sum, *to admit.*
6   **viduus, -a, -um**, *without a husband/wife/mate.*
        viduās . . . noctēs: accusative of duration of time; note the transferred epi-
           thet.
        iacēre: *to lie* (in bed).
        tē nōn viduās iacēre noctēs: indirect statement dependent on **clāmat**;
           nōn may be taken with either **viduās** or **iacēre**.
7   **nēquīquam**, adv., *in vain.*
        nēquīquam: with **tacitum**.
        cubīle, cubīlis, n., *bed.*
        clāmat: four nouns in lines 7–11 serve as subjects of this verb.
8   **serta, -ōrum**, n. pl., *wreathes.*
        Syriō . . . olīvō: *Syrian perfume* (olive oil from Syria was used as a base for
           perfumes).
        fragrō, -āre, -āvī, -ātūrus + abl., *to smell strongly* (of).
        fragrāns: neuter nominative singular, modifying **cubīle** (7).
9   **pulvīnus, -ī**, m., *pillow.*
        peraequē, adv. [strengthened form of **aequē**], *equally.*
        hic: scanned as a long or heavy syllable (originally written **hicc**).

CATULLUS 6

Who is your mistress, Flavius?

The poet asks a friend to tell him about his mistress.

1 · Flāvī, dēliciās tuās Catullō,
2 nī sint illepidae atque inēlegantēs,
3 vellēs dīcere nec tacēre possēs.
4 Vērum nescio quid febrīculōsī
5 scortī dīligis: hoc pudet fatērī.
6 Nam tē nōn viduās iacēre noctēs
7 nēquīquam tacitum cubīle clāmat
8 sertīs ac Syriō fragrāns olīvō,
9 pulvīnusque peraequē et hic et ille

continued

Initial Explorations

1. Study the diction of lines 1–5. What important words recall words used in earlier poems? What words import a new tone? What is the effect of the combination of different kinds of diction?
2. What effect is achieved by the use of **Catullō** instead of **mihi** in line 1? Note the line framing.
3. What does Catullus know about Flavius' activities? What does he not know? (1–5)
4. Based on his friend's silence about the identity of the woman he is in love with, what does Catullus assume about her? (2–5)
5. What does Catullus suggest that Flavius is ashamed to admit? (4–5) What incongruity does the juxtaposition of **scortī** and **dīligis** suggest?
6. How is the bed personified? (7)
7. What does the bed shout? (6–7).
8. Why is the bed described as **nēquīquam tacitum** (7)?

10   **attrītus, -a, -um** [**ad-**, *to, toward; thoroughly* + **trītus, -a, -um,** *worn*], *worn down,*
        battered, crumpled.
      tremulus, -a, -um, *trembling.*
      quassus, -a, -um, *shaken.*
        quassa: transferred epithet, in sense describing the bed.
11   **argūtātiō, argūtātiōnis,** f. [a Catullan coinage; **argūtor, -ārī, -ātus sum,** *to*
        chatter, prattle, babble, from **arguō, arguere, arguī, argūtus,** *to accuse; to*
        prove guilty, convict], *loquacious speaking; creaking.*
      inambulātiō, inambulātiōnis, f., *a walking up and down, a pacing back and forth*
        (like an orator at a trial); hence, *a restless motion.*
12   **nīl**: = **nihil**; subject of **valet.**
      stuprum, -ī, n., *dishonor, disgrace, debauchery.*
      valet: + infinitive, *is strong enough* (to), *is able* (to).
      nihil: the subject is repeated for emphasis.
      tacēre: cf. **tacēre** (3); here, *to keep X secret.*
13   **tam**: modifying **ecfutūta.**
      latus, lateris, n., *side, flanks* (of a person).
        latera: a euphemism (one reference of the word is to the seat of male
          strength and vigor), translate, *body.*
      ecfutūtus, -a, -um [**ex-**, *completely* + perfect passive participle of **futuō,**
        futuere, futuī, futūtus, *to have sexual relations with* (a woman)], *worn out*
        with sex.
      pandō, pandere, *to spread out.*
        pandās, / . . . **faciās** (14): present subjunctives in a present contrary-to-fact
          condition. In archaic Latin the present as well as the imperfect subjunc-
          tive was used in present contrary-to-fact conditions, and the present
          subjunctive sometimes continued to be used in poetry.
14   **quis, qua/quae, quid,** indefinite pronoun after **nī,** *anyone, anybody, somebody,*
        anything, something.
      ineptiae, -ārum, f. pl., *instances of foolishness/absurdity/frivolity.*
        quid . . . **ineptiārum**: partitive genitive, *something foolish.*
15   **quisquis, quisquis, quidquid,** indefinite pronoun/adjective, *whoever, what-*
        ever.
          quidquid . . . **bonī malīque**: *whatever of good and bad* = *whatever good or*
            bad thing.
16   **volo**: = **volō** with iambic shortening.
      amor, amōris, m., *love;* pl., concrete, *the object of one's love, loved one.*
17   **lepidō**: see Catullus 1.1.
      vocāre: *to summon.*

10   attrītus, tremulīque quassa lectī
11   argūtātiō inambulātiōque.
12   Nam nīl stupra valet, nihil, tacēre.
13   Cūr? Nōn tam latera ecfutūta pandās,
14   nī tū quid faciās ineptiārum.
15   Quārē, quidquid habēs bonī malīque,
16   dīc nōbīs. Volo tē ac tuōs amōrēs
17   ad caelum lepidō vocāre versū.

Text

12   **Nam ... tacēre**: what is printed here is an emendation proposed by Haupt
      for the unintelligible manuscript reading, †**Nam inista prevalet**† **nihil**
      tacēre, which is printed in the Oxford Classical Text with the †'s surround-
      ing words thought to be corrupt. Thomson prints Haupt's emendation in
      his text, and we print it here. Godwin has Lachmann's **Nam nīl ista valet,**
      nihil, tacēre.

Initial Explorations

 9.   How does the bed (7–11) reveal the truth of the statement made in line 6?
10.   Comment on word placement and sound effects in the description of the bed?
      (7–11)
11.   How does Catullus refer to Flavius' activity in line 12?
12.   What imaginary objection from Flavius is the interrogative **Cūr?** (13) meant
      to address?
13.   How does Catullus in line 14 evaluate Flavius' activity?
14.   **Quārē** (15) implies that there is a logical connection between the request
      made in lines 15–16 and the previous part of the poem. Explain the connec-
      tion.
15.   In the last line and a half what does Catullus propose to do?

Discussion

 1.   Consider the poem as a parody of legal proceedings against Flavius. How
      does the mock trial develop? What language is borrowed from the court-
      room? What charges are brought? Who are the witnesses? How does Fla-
      vius defend himself? What is the verdict?
 2.   How do the last line and a half fit with the rest of the poem?
 3.   What does the poem celebrate?
 4.   If Catullus arranged his poems or at least the ones toward the beginning of
      the corpus in the order in which we now have them, why would he have put
      poem 6 here?

Meter: hendecasyllabic

1   **bāsiātiō, bāsiātiōnis,** f., *act of kissing, kiss.*
      bāsiātiōnēs: this abstract, polysyllabic noun, formed from **bāsium**, was coined and used only here by Catullus. With **tuae**, in the light of Catullus 5, = *your kissings [of me]*, but editors often understand *[my] kissings of you.*

2   **satis superque**: idiom, *enough and over, enough and more than enough.*

3   <u>Quam magnus</u> **numerus** . . . **iacet** (4) . . . **aut** <u>quam</u> **sīdera** <u>multa</u> (7) . . . **vident** (8) . . . ; <u>tam</u> **tē bāsia** <u>multa</u> **bāsiāre** (9) . . . **est** (10): *As great as the number . . . [that] lies . . . or <u>as many as</u> the stars . . . [that] see . . . ; for you to kiss <u>so many</u> kisses/to kiss you <u>so many</u> kisses is.* . . . The correlative **quam** in lines 3 and 7 is answered by **tam** in line 9; through two images of infinite numbers Catullus answers Lesbia's question from lines 1–2.
   Libyssa, -ae, f., adjective, *of Libya, Libyan.*
   harēna, -ae, f., *sand;* in collective sense, *sands.*

4   **lāsarpīcifer, -a, -um,** *producing* **lāsarpīcium/lāserpīcium** (a plant thought to have extraordinary curative powers for a wide variety of ailments; see Pliny, *Natural History* 22.100–6).
      lāsarpīciferīs: for the use of a compound adjective, see Catullus 4.13, **buxifer.**
   Cyrēnae, -ārum, f. pl., *Cyrene* (an ancient town in northwest Libya, but here the word is used of a vast region surrounding the town; the town Cyrene was founded in the 7th century B.C. by the legendary Battus, whose tomb is mentioned in line 6 of this poem. It was also the birthplace of the Greek poet Callimachus, whose style and theories of poetry influenced Catullus; Callimachus actually adopted *Battiades*, "Descendant of Battus," as his pen name).
      Cyrēnīs: locative.

5   **ōrāclum, -ī,** n. [syncope for **ōrāculum**], *oracle.*
   Iuppiter, Iovis, m., *Jupiter.*
      ōrāclum Iovis: the famous North African temple and oracle of Ammon, situated in the oasis of Siwa in the Libyan desert; Ammon was an Egyptian god who was identified by the Romans with Jupiter.
   inter: governing **ōrāclum** (note the anastrophe) and **sepulcrum** (8).
   aestuōsus, -a, -um [**aestus, -ūs,** m., *heat; the fire of love, passion*], *very hot, sweltering;* perhaps, *passionate.*
      aestuōsī: both meanings are possible, the former as a transferred epithet describing the location of the **ōrāclum**, the latter as an apt description of Jupiter.

6   **Battus, -ī,** m., *Battus* (see note to line 4 above).
   sacer, sacra, sacrum, *sacred.*

7   **sīdus, sīderis,** n., *star.*
   nox: an echo of Catullus 5.6.

8   **fūrtīvus, -a, -um,** *stolen; secret.*
   amor, amōris, m., *love;* pl. here, *love affairs; loves.*

CATULLUS 7

"How many kisses?"

Catullus draws upon two images of infinity to answer Lesbia's question.

1 Quaeris, quot mihi bāsiātiōnēs
2 tuae, Lesbia, sint satis superque.
3 Quam magnus numerus Libyssae harēnae
4 lāsarpīciferīs iacet Cyrēnīs
5 ōrāclum Iovis inter aestuōsī
6 et Battī veteris sacrum sepulcrum;
7 aut quam sīdera multa, cum tacet nox,
8 fūrtīvōs hominum vident amōrēs:

continued

Initial Explorations

1. What has Lesbia apparently asked Catullus? Why would she have asked such a question? (1–2)
2. The phrase **bāsiātiōnēs / tuae** (1–2) can be translated two different ways (see note on facing page). Can you argue for translating the phrase one way or the other, or is there deliberate ambiguity here?
3. Catullus inverts his answer by placing two images of infinite number first (3–8) and then giving his statement of how many kisses would suffice (9–10). What is the first image he evokes? (3–6)
4. Generally and specifically where are the sands located? (3–6)
5. The image of infinite sands (3–6) is elaborately developed. What do the connotations and associations of the following words and phrases add to the texture of the image? **lāsarpīciferīs** (4), **aestuōsī** (5), **Battī veteris** (6), and **sacrum sepulcrum** (6)
6. What is the second image? (7–8) How does it differ in tone and mood from the first? How is it similar? What personal reference does it contain?
7. Find three examples of chiasmus in lines 5–8.

9   bāsium, -ī, n., *kiss.*
     bāsiō, -āre, -āvī, -ātus, *to kiss.*
        tē bāsia multa bāsiāre: tē may be taken as the subject of the infinitive, *for*
           you to kiss so many kisses (compare Catullus 5, where Catullus asks Lesbia
           for hundreds and thousands of kisses), or the verb bāsiāre may govern
           the two accusatives, *to kiss you so many kisses.* Compare the two different
           ways of interpreting tuae in line 2 above.
10   vēsānus, -a, -um [vē-, *without, not* + sānus, -a, -um, *healthy, sane, sober* (in
        particular, free from the passion of love)], *insane, crazy, frenzied.*
     satis et super: see line 2.
11   quae: the antecedent is bāsia (9).
     pernumerō [per-, *thoroughly* + numerō, -āre, -āvī, -ātus, *to count*], -āre, -āvī,
        -ātus, *to make a full accounting of, count completely.*
     cūriōsus, -a, -um, *careful, attentive; inquiring, curious; meddlesome.*
12   possint: *could,* potential subjunctive.
     mala . . . lingua: second subject of possint.
     fascinō, -āre, -āvī, -ātus, *to charm, bewitch.*
        possint nec mala fascināre lingua: compare Catullus 5.12, aut nē quid
           malus invidēre possit, and with the cūriōsī here, compare the senēs
           sevēriōrēs of Catullus 5.2.

9 tam tē bāsia multa bāsiāre

10 vēsānō satis et super Catullō est,

11 quae nec pernumerāre cūriōsī

12 possint nec mala fascināre lingua.

Initial Explorations

8. In line 1, Catullus refers to himself with the first person pronoun, **mihi**; in line 10 the reference shifts to **Catullō**. What is the significance of this shift from first to third person?

9. What view of himself does the speaker take in using the phrase **vēsānō . . . Catullō**?

10. From whom and from what does the speaker wish to protect the kisses? (11–12) What does this echo in Catullus 5?

Discussion

1. How are Catullus 5 and 7 similar and how do they differ in basic matters of form and content?

2. How does Catullus 7 differ from Catullus 5 in style and tone?

3. What is the poet saying through his antithetical images of sand and stars?

4. Why does the poet use the word **bāsiātiōnēs** instead of **bāsia**, which he used in poem 5?

5. How does the third-person reference in the phrase **vēsānō . . . Catullō** (10) suggest that the poet is taking a new, objective perspective on himself and his passion?

6. What role do the **cūriōsī** play in this poem?

7. How would you, if you were Lesbia, respond to Catullus 7?

8. Why might Catullus have placed poem 6 in between poems 5 and 7?

Comparisons

The following poem by Ben Jonson combines themes from Catullus 5 and 7; the lyric of John Oldham is based on Catullus 7 alone.

Ben Jonson
(1571/72–1637)

Kiss me, sweet: the wary lover
Can your fauours keepe, and cover,
When the common courting jay
All your bounties will betray.
Kiss again! no creature comes;
Kiss, and score up wealthy sums
On my lips, thus hardly sundered,
While you breathe. First give a hundred,
Then a thousand, then another
Hundred, then unto the other
Add a thousand, and so more:
Till you equal with the store,
All the grass that Rumney yields,
Or the sands in Chelsea fields,
Or the drops in silver Thames,
Or the stars, that guild his streams,
In the silent Summer-nights,
When youths ply their stolen delights;
That the curious may not know
How to tell 'em as they flow,
And the envious, when they find
What their number is, be pined.

John Oldham
(1653–83)

Nay, *Lesbia*, never ask me this,
How many kisses will suffice?
Faith, 'tis a question hard to tell,
Exceeding hard; for you as well
May ask what sums of Gold suffice
The greedy Miser's boundless Wish:
Think what drops the Ocean store,
With all the Sands, that make its Shore:
Think what Spangles deck the Skies,
When Heaven looks with all its Eyes:
Or think how many Atoms came
To compose this mighty Frame:
Let all these the Counters be,
To tell how oft I'm kiss'd by thee:
Till no malicious Spy can guess
To what vast height the Scores arise;
Till weak Arithmetick grow scant,
And numbers for the reck'ning want:
All these will hardly be enough
For me stark staring mad with Love.

Meter: choliambic

1   **miser, misera, miserum**, *unhappy, miserable, wretched*; as a technical term describing lovers, *obsessed with erotic passion, lovesick.*

    dēsinās . . . / . . . dūcās (2): the second person jussive subjunctive is not commonly used with a definite person in mind, as here; it is a milder form of command than an imperative.

    ineptiō [ineptus, -a, -um, *foolish, silly*], **ineptīre**, *to be lacking in good judgment; to be a fool.*

2   **pereō [per-**, here of upset or perversity + **eō, īre, iī/īvī, itūrus**, *to go*], **perīre, periī, peritūrus**, *to die, perish.*

    perdō [per-, here of upset or perversity + **dō, dare, dedī, datus**, *to give*], **perdere, perdidī, perditus**, *to destroy; to lose.*

        quod . . . dūcās: a pithy, proverbial injunction; supply **id**, *that thing*, as the understood antecedent of **quod**: *consider* (an idiomatic usage of **dūcere**) *that thing* (amplified by **quod vidēs perīsse**) *to have been lost* (supplying **esse** with **perditum**). Compare Plautus, *Trinummus* 1026, **Quīn tū quod periit periisse dūcis?** *Why don't you consider what is gone as gone?*

        perīsse perditum: alliteration and verbal jingle.

3   **fulgeō, fulgēre, fulsī**, *to shine.*

    Fulsēre: = **Fulsērunt**.

    quondam, adv., *formerly, once.*

    candidus, -a, -um, *white; favorable; happy; bright.*

    sōlēs: from **sōl, sōlis**, m., *sun*; Thomson suggests that **sōlēs** here = **diēs**.

4   **ventitō [veniō, venīre, vēnī, ventūrus**, *to come* + **-itō**, iterative suffix denoting repeated action], **-āre, -āvī, -ātūrus**, *to come again and again.*

5   **nōbīs**: dative of agent; plural for singular.

    quantum, adv., *as much as.*

    nūlla: supply **puella**.

6   **cum**: *when*, delayed conjunction coming in the middle of its clause.

    iocōsus, -a, -um, *full of jest; funny, playful.*

    iocōsa: substantive, *playful things/experiences* (with a suggestion of lovers' play).

7   **nec . . . nōlēbat**: perhaps litotes = **volēbat**, but the double negative may suggest something less than enthusiastic reciprocity.

8   **fulsēre . . . sōlēs**: compare with line 3.

When you want...

CATULLUS 8

Catullus to Himself

The poet tells himself to harden his heart against his **puella**.

1 Miser Catulle, dēsinās ineptīre,
2 et quod vidēs perīsse perditum dūcās.
3 Fulsēre quondam candidī tibī sōlēs,
4 cum ventitābās quō puella dūcēbat
5 amāta nōbīs quantum amābitur nūlla.
6 Ibi illa multa cum iocōsa fīēbant,
7 quae tū volēbās nec puella nōlēbat,
8 fulsēre vērē candidī tibī sōlēs.

continued

Initial Explorations

1. What does the speaker's use of the vocative **Miser Catulle** (1) imply about the dramatic situation of this poem? Who is addressing whom? Why?
2. What do the words **miser** (1) and **ineptīre** (1) reveal about Catullus' view of his situation and its cause?
3. Explain the point of the command expressed in line 2.
4. Lines 3 and 8 serve as a frame for a nostalgic memory. What do the words **fulsēre . . . candidī tibī sōlēs** mean?
5. What picture do we get of the relationship between Catullus and the **puella** as presented in lines 4–7?
6. What does each of the following contribute to the meaning and the tone of lines 4–7: the iterative verb, hyperbole, repetition of sounds, and litotes (**nec . . . nōlēbat**)?

9   **Nunc iam**: *Now at last* (in contrast to what was true in the past).
     illa: i.e., the **puella**.
     volt: archaic form of **vult**.
     inpotēns, inpotentis [**in-**, *not* + **potēns, potentis**, *having power* (over), *able to control*] (see Catullus 4.18, where editors print the alternate spelling, **im-**), *powerless, impotent; powerless* (over oneself), *lacking self-control, weak in will; wild, violent, raging.*
         inpotēns: vocative and perhaps concessive, *although weak in will.*
             inpotē<ns nōlī>: the letters in brackets are missing from the manuscripts and have been supplied by editors.
10   **quae fugit**: supply **eam** as the antecedent of **quae** and object of **sectāre**.
     sector [**sequor, sequī, secūtus sum**, *to follow* + **-tō**, iterative suffix], **-ārī, -ātus sum**, *to run after/chase after constantly.*
         sectāre: singular imperative of the deponent verb.
     vīve: colloquial usage of the verb **vīvere**, equivalent in meaning to **es** (imperative), *be!*
         nec miser vīve: for **miser**, see note to line 1: *don't be lovesick.*
11   **obstinātus, -a, -um** [**ob-**, *in the way of, against* + ***stanō**, a hypothetical form, cf. **stō, stāre**, *to stand*], *set firmly against, stubborn, determined, resolute.*
     perferō [**per-**, *through, completely* + **ferō, ferre, tulī, lātus**, *to carry, bear*], **perferre, pertulī, perlātus**, *to carry through to the end; to endure.*
     obdūrō [**ob-**, *in the way of, against* + **dūrō, dūrāre**, *to become hard*], **-āre, -āvī, -ātūrus** *to steel oneself, be resolute, tough it out.*
         perfer, obdūrā: asyndeton.
13   **requīrō** [**re-**, *again* + **quaerō, quaerere, quaesīvī, quaesītus**, *to seek, look for*], **requīrere, requīsīvī, requīsītus**, *to ask, inquire; to seek out, look for.*
     rogābit: the verb **rogāre** here carries the ideas of invitation, *to request a person be present, to invite*, and of seeking erotic favors, *to court, woo.*
     invītam: modifying **tē**.
14   **nūlla**: colloquial use of the adjective with emphatic adverbial force, *not at all, not ever again.* Compare line 5 where the adjective is used as a substantive.
15   **scelestus, -a, -um**, *accursed; wicked; unlucky, unfortunate.*
     vae, exclamation + dat. or (more rarely) + acc., *woe* (to), *alas* (for).
     Quae: interrogative adjective, modifying **vīta**.
     manet: here + dat., *is in store* (for), *awaits.*
16   **bellus, -a, -um**, *pretty.*
17   **dīcēris**: future passive (note the long *e*). Lesbia will suffer when Catullus no longer calls her his own **puella**, or so he insists.
18   **bāsiō, -āre, -āvī, -ātus**, *to kiss.*
     Cui: dative of reference expressing personal interest; translate *Whose. . . ?*
     labellum, -ī, n. [**labrum, -ī**, n., *lip* + **-lum**, dim. suffix], *little/dear lip.*
     mordeō, mordēre, momordī, morsus, *to nibble, bite.*
19   **dēstinātus, -a, -um** [**dē-**, *down, thoroughly, completely* + ***stanō**, a hypothetical form, cf. **stō, stāre**, *to stand*], *fixed* (in one's mind), *determined, stubborn, firmly set.*
         dēstinātus: cf. **obstinātā mente** (11); note the force of the different prefixes.

9   Nunc iam illa nōn volt; tū quoque, inpotē<ns, nōlī>,
10   nec quae fugit sectāre, nec miser vīve,
11   sed obstinātā mente perfer, obdūrā.
12   Valē, puella. Iam Catullus obdūrat,
13   nec tē requīret nec rogābit invītam.
14   At tū dolēbis, cum rogāberis nūlla.
15   Scelesta, vae tē, quae tibī manet vīta?
16   Quis nunc tē adībit? Cui vidēberis bella?
17   Quem nunc amābis? Cuius esse dīcēris?
18   Quem bāsiābis? Cui labella mordēbis?
19   At tū, Catulle, dēstinātus obdūrā.

Initial Explorations

7.   With what temporal adverb earlier in the poem does the phrase **Nunc iam** (9) correlate?

8.   How does Catullus describe the situation as being different now? (9)   How does he characterize himself, and what does he order himself to do? (9)

9.   How does the pairing of **inpotēns** and **nōlī** (9) intimate Catullus' dilemma in the poem?

10. How do the words **nec quae fugit sectāre** (10) reverse the memory of the relationship with the **puella** in line 4?

11. How do the iterative verbs **ventitābās** (4) and **sectāre** (10) link and characterize Catullus' behavior before and now?

12. Line 11 concludes Catullus' address to himself, which began in line 1. Comment on his choice of words, use of prefixes, and use of asyndeton in line 11.

13. Beginning with line 12, who is now addressing whom? In what frame of mind is the speaker of this line? With what does he greet his **puella**? What will he not do? (13)

14. What is the purpose of the statement in line 14, the exclamation in line 15, and the rhetorical questions in lines 15–18? For what is the **puella** to be pitied?

15. In warning the **puella** of the consequences of her change of heart toward him by listing the causes of grief that await her (13–18), Catullus is in fact reliving memories of his love affair with her. Do his memories have a beginning, middle, and end? Do they move toward a climax? What echoes of earlier poems do you find in these memories? What is happening to Catullus' professed resolve?

16. In the last line we again hear the voice of the Catullus of the first eleven lines of the poem. Why does Catullus need to repeat at the end of the poem (19) the command that he had already delivered in line 11? Compare **dēstinātus**

(19) with **obstinātā mente** (11). What different meaning does the different prefix create in line 19?
17. What effects are produced by the meter of the poem? What tone is produced by absence of enjambement?

Discussion

1. Reread the poem and note words, phrases, and sounds that are repeated. What is significant about the repeated words, phrases, and sounds? What do the repetitions add to the meaning of the poem?
2. How does Catullus 8 fit into the story of Catullus' love affair with the **puella**/Lesbia as recorded in Catullus 2, 3, 5, and 7? Does it come as a surprise? Does it seem to fit?

Comparison

Compare the following version of Catullus 8:

Thomas Campion
(1567?–1619)

Harden now thy tyred hart, with more then flinty rage;
Ne'er let her false teares henceforth thy constant griefe asswage.
Once true happy dayes thou saw'st when shee stood firme and kinde,
Both as one then liv'd and held one eare, one tongue, one minde:
But now those bright houres be fled, and never may returne;
What then remaines but her untruths to mourne?

Silly Traytresse, who shall now thy carelesse tresses place?
Who thy pretty talke supply, whose eare thy musicke grace?
Who shall thy bright eyes admire? what lips triumph with thine?
Day by day who'll visit thee and say "th'art onely mine?"
Such a time there was, God wot, but such shall never be:
Too oft, I feare, thou wilt remember me.

Meter: hendecasyllabic

1   **Vērānius, -ī,** m., *Veranius* (a member of Catullus' inner circle of friends, who
      has just returned home from provincial service in Spain; he is also men-
      tioned in poems 12, 28, and 47).
      omnibus: take with **meīs amīcīs.**

2   **antistō (antestō) [ante-,** *before* + **stō, stāre, stetī, statūrus,** *to stand*], **antistāre,**
      antistitī + dat., *to surpass, be superior* (to), *be worth more* (than).
      mihi: ethical dative, *in my eyes.*
      trecentī, -ae, -a, *three hundred* (often of an indefinitely large number).
      mīlibus trecentīs: supply **amīcīs,** dative with **antistāns.**

3   **penātēs, penātium,** m. pl. [**penus, -ūs,** f., *food, provisions* (of the household)],
      penates (traditional gods of the household, protectors of the food supply).

4   **ūnanimus, -a, -um,** *of one mind; harmonious; loving.*
      anus, -ūs, f., *old woman;* as an adjective, *old, aged.*

5   **beātus, -a, -um,** *happy; fortunate; supremely happy, blessed, blissful.*
      Ō mihi nūntiī beātī: remember that **nūntius** can mean *messenger* or *mes-*
      sage; exclamatory nominative here (instead of the usual exclamatory ac-
      cusative); either *O messengers (with) fortunate news for me* (implying that
      Catullus heard the news of Veranius' return from more than one source)
      or more probably plural for singular, *O blissful message for me.*

6   **vīsō, vīsere, vīsī,** *to go and look at/view* (something); *to see.*
      Hibērēs, Hibērum, m. pl., *Iberians, Spaniards.*

7   **nārrantem:** supply **tē** (6).
      loca: this word, masculine in the singular, has both masculine and neuter
      forms in the plural.
      factum, -ī, n., *exploit; deed.*
      nātiō, nātiōnis, f., *people, race, tribe.*

8   **applicō [ad-,** *to, toward* + **plicō, -āre, -āvī, -ātus,** *to fold, bend*], **-āre, -āvī, -ātus**
      to bring into contact; to draw (something) *close.*
      collum, -ī, n., *neck.*
      collum: supply **tuum.**

9   **suāvior (sāvior) [suāvis, -is, -e,** *pleasant*], **-ārī, -ātus sum,** *to kiss.*
      suāviābor: Thomson prints **sāviābor.**

10 **Ō quantum est hominum beātiōrum:** *O whatever amount there is of. . . .* = *O*
      however many . . . there are, cf. Catullus 3.1–2, **ō Venerēs Cupīdinēsque, /** et
      quantum est hominum venustiōrum. In the present poem, however, the
      quantum clause is not vocative as it is in Catullus 3 but is an exclamatory
      accusative. It is then to be taken in a partitive sense with **quid** (best trans-
      lated as if it were **quis**) in the next line: *O of all the rather blissful men there*
      are, who is . . . ?

11 **quid:** neuter, picking up the neuter **quantum** (10), but best translated *who*
      (see note above).
      laetius . . . beātius: modifying **quid.**
      -ve, enclitic conj., *or.*

CATULLUS 9

Joyous news!

Catullus welcomes his close friend Veranius back from Spain.

1   Vērānī, omnibus ē meīs amīcīs
2   antistāns mihi mīlibus trecentīs,
3   vēnistīne domum ad tuōs penātēs
4   frātrēsque ūnanimōs anumque mātrem?
5   Vēnistī. Ō mihi nūntiī beātī!
6   Vīsam tē incolumem audiamque Hibērum
7   nārrantem loca, facta, nātiōnēs,
8   ut mōs est tuus, applicānsque collum
9   iūcundum ōs oculōsque suāviābor.
10 Ō quantum est hominum beātiōrum,
11 quid mē laetius est beātiusve?

Initial Explorations

1.   By means again of large numbers (compare Catullus 5 and 7), what point about Veranius does the hyperbole make? (1–2)
2.   Behind the simplicity and colloquialism of the Latin in this poem are strong sentiments that celebrate the return of Catullus' close friend. How does Catullus imagine that Veranius' reunion with his home and family unfolded? (3–4)
3.   Identify a tricolon in lines 3–4 and a chiasmus in line 4.
4.   News of Veranius' arrival home precedes the anticipated reunion of the speaker with his friend. What sequence does the speaker anticipate when the two friends are reunited? How is the intimacy of their friendship revealed through the sequence? (6–9)
5.   Lines 6–9 contain three verbs; identify the members of an ascending tricolon in this sentence.
6.   As Veranius is singled out by a hyperbole at the start of the poem, who is singled out at the end by an equally strong hyperbole? (10–11)
7.   Note that line 10 is almost identical with line 2 of Catullus 3. Does this repetition serve any purpose?
8.   Reread the poem and note recurring sound patterns, especially of the letters *m* and *n*. What important words in the poem echo Veranius' name by beginning with the letter *v*? Where is asyndeton used effectively? What do the three elisions in line 6 highlight? Locate strongly placed front and end words in particular lines throughout the poem.

Discussion

1. At what points would you divide the poem into three parts?
2. Printed below are lines from a poem by the third century B.C. Greek poet Theocritus. Catullus may have known this poem, and he may have taken his cue for his repetition of **vēnistī** (3, 5) from the Greek words of Theocritus' poem that are translated "You have come. . . /you have come. . . . " What similarities and what differences between the two poems do you notice? What purpose might Catullus have had in mind in echoing the words from Theocritus?
3. How do the close friendship and bonding between Catullus and Veranius contrast with the relationship between the poet and his **puella** in the preceding poem?

Comparison

The opening lines of Theocritus' *Idyll* 12 are addressed to the poet's boyfriend:

You have come, dear boy; after two nights and days
you have come. But lovers grow old in a day.
As much as spring is sweeter than winter, the apple than the sloe,
as much as the ewe is fleecier than the lamb,
as much as a maiden is more desirable than a thrice-wed woman,
as much as the fawn is swifter than the calf, as much as the
clear voiced nightingale surpasses all other birds in its singing,
so have you cheered me with your appearance, and I run to you
as a traveler runs to a shady oak from the roasting sun.

Meter: hendecasyllabic

1 **Vārus, -ī**, m., *Varus* (a Varus is also addressed in Catullus 22; he may have been Alfenus Varus, a jurist and official in Cisalpine Gaul possibly addressed in Catullus 30.1, or Quintilius Varus, friend of Vergil and Horace).

meus: *my friend*, a colloquialism. The speaker of the poem is Catullus (25).

amōrēs: *girlfriend, love*, cf. Catullus 6.16.

2 **vīsō, vīsere, vīsī** (see Catullus 9.6), *to go and look at/view* (something); + **ad** + acc., *to go and visit* (a person, often a sick person).

   vīsum: this may be a rare supine of **vīsere**, *to go and visit his* (sick?) *girl-friend/love*, or it may be the supine of **vidēre**, *to have a look at* (Quinn), or it may be the perfect passive participle of **vidēre**, modifying **mē** (1), and be taken with **ōtiōsum [esse]**, *me seen to be at leisure*.

forum, -ī, n., *forum, public square, piazza*.

ōtiōsus, -a, -um [**ōtium, -ī**, n., *spare time; time free from serious occupations; leisure; idleness*], *not occupied by business or politics, having nothing to do, at leisure*.

3 **scortillum, -ī**, n. [hapax; dim. of **scortum, -ī**, n., *prostitute, whore*, see Catullus 6.5], *dear little/young prostitute/whore*.

   scortillum: in apposition to **amōrēs** (1); Varus had perhaps romantically called her his **amōrēs**, but Catullus with some disparagement refers to her with this word, which he apparently coined.

repente, adv., *suddenly; at first glance*.

4 **sānē**, adv., *certainly, truly;* concessive, *admittedly, to be sure*.

illepidus, -a, -um [**in-** *not* + **lepidus, -a, -um**, *elegant, charming; smart, witty*] (cf. Catullus 6.2), *without charm/wit*.

invenustus, -a, -um [**in-**, *not* + **venustus, -a, -um**, see Catullus 3.2], *without beauty, without charm*.

   nōn . . . illepidum . . . invenustum: litotes.

5 **Hūc**: *To this place, Here*, probably to where the woman lived.

ut: *when*.

incidō [**in-**, *in, on* + **cadō, cadere, cecidī, cāsūrus**, *to fall*], **incidere, incidī, incāsūrus** + dat., *to fall into/onto; to fall to one's lot; to occur, arise*.

   incidēre: = **incidērunt**; topics of conversation came up at random.

6 **quid . . . / . . . quō modō** (7) **. . . / . . . quōnam . . . aere** (8): three indirect questions stating topics of conversation; the questions, addressed to Catullus, pass quickly from an inquiry about the province of Bithynia (where Catullus served for a year) to the profitability of his year abroad.

7 **sē habēret**: *it held itself, it was faring*.

8 **quīnam, quaenam, quodnam** [**quī, quae, quod**, *what, which?* + **nam**, particle, *now*], interrogative adjective, *what kind of?*

prōsum [**prō-**, expressing advantage + **sum, esse, fuī, futūrus**, *to be*], **prōdesse, prōfuī**, *to be of use;* + dat., *to benefit, profit* (someone).

   prōfuisset: the subject is still Bithynia.

aes, aeris, n., *copper, bronze; money*.

   quōnam . . . aere: ablative of source, *from what kind of money*.

CATULLUS 10

Visiting Varus' New Girlfriend

The poet, caught in a shameless lie, defends himself by vilifying the woman.

1   Vārus mē meus ad suōs amōrēs
2   vīsum dūxerat ē forō ōtiōsum,
3   scortillum, ut mihi tum repente vīsum est,
4   nōn sānē illepidum neque invenustum.
5   Hūc ut vēnimus, incidēre nōbīs
6   sermōnēs variī, in quibus, quid esset
7   iam Bīthȳnia, quō modō sē habēret,
8   et quōnam mihi prōfuisset aere.

continued

Text

et quōnam (8): Thomson prints **ecquōnam**, *whether. . . from any.*

Initial Explorations

1. Unlike the earlier poems, Catullus 10 does not set up the situation of a dramatic dialogue in which Catullus addresses someone. There is no addressee. What form does this poem take? (1–4)
2. What are Catullus' first impressions of the woman that Varus takes him to visit? (3–4)
3. What direction does their conversation take? (5–8)
4. Locate the members of a tricolon in lines 6–8.

9 **id quod erat**: *that which was*, i.e., *the truth*.
   nihil: with **esse** (10), *there was nothing* = *there was no profit*.
   ipsīs: usually interpreted as meaning *for the natives*; some editors take it as
   modifying **praetōribus** (10) and regard **neque . . . / nec** (10) as a
   colloquial pleonasm, thus **neque ipsīs / nec praetōribus** (possibly plural
   for singular; see next note) . . . **nec cohortī** = *neither for the governor himself
   nor for his staff*.

10 **praetor, praetōris**, m., *magistrate; governor*.
   praetōribus: possibly plural for singular; the praetor, or, more properly,
   the propraetor was appointed by the Senate to govern a province for a
   year. Catullus served under Gaius Memmius in 57 B.C., when the latter
   served as the governor of Bithynia.
   cohors, cohortis, f., *cohort; bodyguard; retinue, staff*.
   cohortī: the **cohors praetōria** had evolved by Catullus' time into a fash-
   ionable assembly of young men, called **comitēs**, *companions*, who accompanied a provincial governor on his tour of duty. In some cases, as
   probably with Memmius, poets and artists were enlisted to provide cultural relief amid provincial backwaters.

11 **cūr**: *[as to] why*.
   quisquam, quisquam, quicquam, indefinite pronoun, *anyone, anything*.
   ūnctus, -a, -um, *oiled, anointed*; metaphorical, *enriched*.
   caput ūnctius: *a more oiled head*, = *a more richly combed head of hair*; the use of
   expensive hair lotions at banquets and celebrations was a mark of class
   and prosperity in Rome.
      caput ūnctius referret: = *should return enriched*. Catullus is implying
      that with Memmius as governor, no one in his entourage was able to
      make any profit.

12 **praesertim**, adv., *especially*.
   quibus esset: dative of the possessor, *[those] who had*. . . .
   irrumātor, irrumātōris, m., *a man who forces others to engage in unnatural sex
   with him; a pervert*; generally, *an s.o.b.*

13 **praetor**: C. Memmius, governor of Bithynia in 57/56 B.C.; he was a man of
   reputed literary taste, favoring, as did Catullus, Greek Alexandrian
   poetry; a patron of the Latin poet Lucretius, he took both Catullus and the
   poet C. Helvius Cinna with him to Bithynia.
      irrumātor / praetor: the governor may literally have abused his staff
      sexually, but the words may be taken figuratively to suggest the
      disdain with which the governor treated his staff. Catullus excoriates
      Memmius for sexual abuse of his staff in poem 28.
   nec faceret: *and he was not considering*.
   esset (12) . . . / . . . **faceret** (13): relative clauses in indirect statement
      require the subjunctive.
   pilus, -ī, m., *a hair*.
      pilī: genitive of value, *worth a hair*.

9   Respondī id quod erat, nihil neque ipsīs
10 nec praetōribus esse nec cohortī,
11 cūr quisquam caput ūnctius referret,
12 praesertim quibus esset irrumātor
13 praetor, nec faceret pilī cohortem.

continued

TEXT

nec (10): Goold prints **nunc**.

Initial Explorations

5. How does Catullus characterize his reply to these questions? (9)
6. Locate three words or phrases with the colloquial flavor of everyday or street language in lines 11–13.
7. How does Catullus characterize his service on the governor's staff in Bithynia? What complaints does he make?   (9–13)

14   **quod illīc / nātum dīcitur esse** (15): *[that] which is said to have been born there*
      = *[that] which is said to be native to that place;* the **lectīca octōphoros** (note the
      Greek adjectival ending), *litter carried by eight men,* was proverbially
      associated with the kings of Bithynia.
15   **comparāstī:** syncope for **comparāvistī.**
16   **ad lectīcam:** *for [the purpose of carrying] a litter, to carry a litter.*
      puellae: *in the eyes of the girl,* ethical dative (cf. Catullus 9.2, **mihi**).
17   **mē facerem:** *I might make myself [out as]. . . .*
      beātus, -a, -um, *happy; wealthy; fortunate.*
        beātiōrem: not *more. . . .* but *rather. . . .*
          ūnum . . . beātiōrem: *the one [fellow] in particular [who was] rather
          fortunate;* note the sense of **ūnum** here, *one in particular, one above all
          others.*
18   **malignē,** adv., *stingily, scantily, insufficiently.*
        nōn . . . mihi tam fuit malignē: *I didn't make out so badly.*
19   **quod:** *just because.*
      incidisset: supply **mihi.**
20   **parō, -āre, -āvī, -ātus,** *to prepare;* here and in lines 30 and 32, *to purchase, buy.*
      rēctus, -a, -um, *right, proper; tall; straight.*
21   **mī:** dative of the possessor.
      illīc: i.e., in Bithynia.
22   **grabātus, -ī,** m. [Greek loan word], *(a simple, poor man's) bed, cot.*
23   **collum, -ī,** n., *neck.*
      collocō [con-, *together* + **locō, -āre, -āvī, -ātus,** *to place*], **-āre, -āvī, -ātus,** *to place.*
24   **Hīc:** *At this point.*
      illa: i.e., Varus' girlfriend.
      decet, decēre, decuit, impersonal + acc., *(it) is fitting for, befits.*
      cinaedus, -a, -um [adjective made from the Greek loan word **cinaedus, -ī,**
      m., *catamite* (a male whore, usually regarded as exceedingly mercenary
      and opportunistic)], *resembling/typical of a cinaedus.*
        cinaediōrem: perhaps translate *the rather shamelessly opportunistic [girl].*
25   **quaesō, quaesere,** *to seek; to ask, beg.*
        Quaesō: *I beg, Please.*
      inquit, "mihi, mī: Thomson gives this line as **"Quaesō," inquit mihi, "mī
      Catulle, paulum.**
        mī: vocative of **meus.**
26   **iste, ista, istud,** *that* (of yours).
        istōs: *those [litter-bearers] of yours.*
      commodō [**commodus, -a, -um,** *convenient, beneficial* + **-ō,** verbal suffix],
      -āre, -āvī, -ātus, *to lend.*
        commoda: imperative with short *a* for the sake of the meter or possibly
          in imitation of colloquial speech.
      ad Serāpim: *to the temple of Serapis.* Serapis was an Egyptian goddess, who
      was popular in Rome, especially among women who went to her temple
      in the city for treatment of various illnesses.
27   **Mane:** iambic shortening = **Manē,** *Wait!*
      inquiī: perfect of **inquam;** the form is found only here in classical Latin.

14 "At certē tamen," inquiunt, "quod illīc
15 nātum dīcitur esse, comparāstī
16 ad lectīcam hominēs." Ego, ut puellae
17 ūnum mē facerem beātiōrem,
18 "Nōn," inquam, "mihi tam fuit malignē,
19 ut, prōvincia quod mala incidisset,
20 nōn possem octō hominēs parāre rēctōs."
21 At mī nūllus erat nec hīc neque illīc,
22 frāctum quī veteris pedem grabātī
23 in collō sibi collocāre posset.
24 Hīc illa, ut decuit cinaediōrem,
25 "Quaesō," inquit, "mihi, mī Catulle, paulum
26 istōs commoda: nam volō ad Serāpim
27 dēferrī." "Mane," inquiī puellae,

continued

Initial Explorations

8. What do Varus and the **scortillum** suppose that Catullus must have acquired in Bithynia and why? (14–16)
9. Why do you suppose that Varus and the **scortillum** remark that Catullus surely acquired these? (14–16)
10. What motivates Catullus' reply? To whom does he explain his motivation? (16–17)
11. What does Catullus say he was able to purchase? (20)
12. Is he telling the truth? How do we know? (21–23)
13. What does the **puella** request? (25–27) How does Catullus characterize her for making this request? (24) What reason does the **puella** give for her request? (26–27) Might she have some other reason for making it? If so, what is it?

28   **istud**: object of **parāvit** (30).

      modo, adv., *only; just now.*

29   **ratiō, ratiōnis**, f., *reason; ability to think; one's wits.*

      fūgit mē ratiō: a colloquial expression for one's wits going astray, causing
      one to make a mistake.

      sodālis, sodālis, m., *companion, buddy.*

30   **Cinna ... Gāïus**: Gaius Helvius Cinna, poet and friend of Catullus and au-
      thor of a poem titled *Zmyrna*, much admired by Catullus (see poem 95).

      Gāïus: scan as three syllables.

31   **vērum**, conj., *but.*

      utrum ... an ...: *whether [the litter-bearers are] ... or. ...*

      illius ... meī: *his ... mine*, possessive genitives; **illius** = **illīus**; **meī** is proba-
      bly the genitive of **ego**, although the genitive of **ego** is not usually used to
      show possession, the adjective **meus, -a, -um** being used instead (the form
      would be the same here, **meī**).

      quid ad mē: supply **attinet**, *is [that] of concern.*

32   **tam bene quam ... parārim** (= **parāverim**): supply **sī**, *just as well as if I have/
      had. . . .* , perfect subjunctive in a conditional clause of comparison.

33   **īnsulsus, -a, -um** [**in-**, *not* + **salsus, -a, -um**, *salted; salty; witty*; cf. **sāl, salis**,
      m., *salt*], *unsalted; without wit; without taste.*

      male: *especially, very, quite*, a colloquial use.

      vīvis: colloquial for **es** (see Catullus 8.10).

34   **esse neglegentem**: supply **quemquam**, *anyone*, or **mē**, *me*; the phrase
      [**quemquam/mē**] **esse neglegentem** is the subject of **nōn licet**, *[for any-
      one/for me] to be careless is not permitted.*

28   "istud quod modo dīxeram mē habēre,

29   fūgit mē ratiō: meus sodālis—

30   Cinna est Gāïus,—is sibī parāvit.

31   Vērum, utrum illius an meī, quid ad mē?

32   Ūtor tam bene quam mihī parārim.

33   Sed tū īnsulsa male et molesta vīvis,

34   per quam nōn licet esse neglegentem."

Initial Explorations

14.   What does the faltering speech of lines 27–30 imply about the speaker?

15.   What is unusual about the order of words in the first half of line 30? Why do you suppose the speaker does what he does here?

16.   Is Catullus' explanation in lines 29–30 credible?

17.   How does Catullus' assessment of the woman differ at the end of the poem (33–34) from what it was at the beginning (4)?

18.   What does Catullus imply about social manners in referring to himself as **neglegentem** (34)?

19.   Was Catullus **neglegēns**?

Discussion

1.   This poem does not have an addressee, but Catullus tells a story about himself. What are the consequences of this difference in form? How does this poem differ in tone from those preceding it?

2.   What device does the poet use to guide the reader's response to his portrayal of himself in this poem?

Meter: Sapphic Strophe

1   **Fūrī . . . Aurēlī**: vocative. Furius and Aurelius are two friends of Catullus, who are dealt with abusively in other poems but are seemingly presented as loyal comrades here.

       comitēs: vocative, in apposition to **Fūrī et Aurēlī**.

2   **sīve . . . sīve** (5), conjs., *whether . . . or. . . .*

       penetrābit and **gradiētur** (9): Catullus is the subject of these verbs in an extended travelogue that runs from line 2 through line 12. The correlative **sīve** in lines 2, 5, 6 (where the alternate form **seu** appears), 7, and 9 separates mention of the various places in the world that Furius and Aurelius are invited to visit with Catullus.

       extrēmus, -a, -um, *last; lying at the end; far distant;* (situated) *at the end of the world.*

          in extrēmōs . . . Indōs: *among the. . . .*

       penetrō, -āre, -āvī, -ātus, *to penetrate;* + **in** + acc., *to enter among.*

       Indī, -ōrum, m. pl., *inhabitants of India, Indians* (India marked the furthest extent of the conquests of Alexander the Great).

3   **lītus**: the shore of the ocean that was thought to surround the circle of the world's lands.

       ut, relative adv., *where.*

          ut: delayed relative adverb, coming as the second rather than the first word in its clause.

       longē, adv., *far.*

          lītus . . . longē: alliteration.

       resonō [**re-**, *back* + **sonō, sonāre, sonuī, sonitus**, *to sound*], **-āre, -āvī**, *to resound.*

       Eōus, -a, -um, *Eastern.*

4   **tundō, tundere, tutudī, tūsus**, *to strike, beat.*

          tunditur: the subject is **lītus**.

             tunditur undā: note the play on sounds.

CATULLUS 11

A Parting of the Ways

*Catullus sends a final message to his **puella**.*

1   Fūrī et Aurēlī, comitēs Catullī,
2   sīve in extrēmōs penetrābit Indōs,
3   lītus ut longē resonante Eōā
4   tunditur undā,

continued

Initial Explorations

1. Analyze the grammar of lines 2–12.
    a. What two verbs are introduced by the repeated conjunction **sīve**?
    b. What two verbs are parts of subordinate clauses within clauses introduced by **sīve**?
    c. What two prepositional phrases are parallel to one another?
    d. Where has the preposition **in** been omitted where it could have been expressed?
    e. What relative adverb has been delayed?
    f. What antecedent has been placed within the relative clause dependent on it?

5   **Hyrcānī, -ōrum,** m. pl., *the Hyrcanians* (a people who lived on the south
     shore of the Caspian Sea and were associated in the popular mind with the
     conquests of Alexander the Great).
     Arabēs, Arabum, m. pl., *the Arabians.*
        Arabas: Greek accusative plural.
     -ve, enclitic conj., *or.*
     mollis, -is, -e, *soft; luxurious.*
        in Hyrcānōs Arabasve mollēs: supply **penetrābit** from line 2.
6   **seu:** = **sīve.**
     Sagae, -ārum, m. pl., *the Sacae* (a nomadic Scythian people who lived east of
     the Caspian Sea and were dangerous enemies of Rome).
     sagittiferus, -a, -um [**sagitta, -ae,** f., *arrow* + **-fer, -fera, -ferum,** *carrying,*
     bearing], *arrow-bearing.*
     Parthī, -ōrum, m. pl., *the Parthians* (an eastern people whose kingdom
     reached from the Euphrates to the Indus and who were hostile to Rome;
     they were notorious for the skilled tactics of their mounted archers; in
     November, 55 B.C., Marcus Licinius Crassus set out with a Roman army to
     defeat the Parthians but was trapped and killed near Carrhae).
        Sagās sagittiferōsve Parthōs: supply **in,** *among.*
7   **quae . . . Nīlus** (8): the antecedent of **quae** is **aequora** (8), placed inside the
     relative clause.
     septemgeminus, -a, -um [**septem,** *seven* + **geminus, -a, -um,** *twin*], *seven-*
     fold (referring to the delta of the Nile).
     colōrō, -āre, -āvī, -ātus, *to color.*
8   **aequor, aequoris,** n., *a smooth, level surface; a level stretch of ground, plain; of-*
     ten, in sing. or pl., *the sea.*
        aequora: supply **in,** *into, onto;* **aequora** is the final item in the list of
        imagined localities dependent on **penetrābit** (2).
           colōrat / aequora Nīlus: probably referring to silt carried into the
           Mediterranean (**aequora** = *the sea*), but possibly referring to the
           Nile staining the *plains* (another possible meaning of **aequora**)
           with alluvial deposits during its annual flooding.

5 sīve in Hyrcānōs Arabasve mollēs,

6 seu Sagās sagittiferōsve Parthōs,

7 sīve quae septemgeminus colōrat

8   aequora Nīlus,

continued

Initial Explorations

2. The words **sagittiferōsve Parthōs** (6) allude to Crassus' expedition to
    Parthia, to which he set out in 55 B.C. and where he was defeated near Car-
    rhae in 53 B.C.; lines 9–12 refer to Caesar's bridging of the Rhine in 55 B.C.
    and his crossing into Britain in 55 and 54 B.C. Why do you suppose Catullus
    included this allusion in line 6 and these references in lines 9–12?

9 **gradior, gradī, gressus sum,** *to walk, go.*

10 **Caesar, Caesaris,** m., *Julius Caesar* (whose campaigns in Gaul, 58–51 B.C., are alluded to here; early in 54 B.C., Catullus, who had viciously lampooned Caesar and his henchmen in a number of poems, was reconciled with him).

 vīsō, vīsere, vīsī, *to go and look at/view* (something); *to visit.*

 monimentum/monumentum, -ī, n. [**moneō, -ēre, -uī, -itus,** *to remind; to warn* + **-mentum,** noun suffix], *reminder; memorial.*

 magnī: with **Caesaris:** line framing.

11 **Gallicus, -a, -um,** *of Gaul, Gallic.*

 Rhēnus, -ī, m., *the Rhine River* (the Rhine formed the natural boundary between Gaul and Germany; Caesar crossed the Rhine with his army in the summer of 55 B.C.).

 horribilis, -is, -e, *inspiring fear/horror; rough.*

  horribile aequor: i.e., the British Channel, which Caesar first crossed in August of 55 B.C. and again in the late summer of 54.

   Gallicum Rhēnum horribile aequor: asyndeton.

 ultimus, -a, -um, *far, distant.*

12 **Britannī, -ōrum,** m. pl., *inhabitants of Britain.*

13 **omnia haec:** i.e., the places and peoples in the previous list.

 quīcumque, quaecumque, quodcumque, indefinite relative pronoun, *whoever, whatever.*

  quaecumque: neuter accusative plural, *whatever.*

 voluntās, voluntātis, f., *will.*

14 **caeles, caelitis** [archaic and poetic], *dwelling in heaven;* as substantive, usually plural, **caelitēs, caelitum,** m. pl., *gods.*

 simul, adv., *in company, together; at the same time.*

 parātī: modifying the vocatives in line 1.

15 **pauca:** modifying **dicta** (16), the two words framing the two lines.

 nūntiō, -āre, -āvī, -ātus, *to announce.*

16 **nōn bona:** litotes; the "words" or message are the final two stanzas.

Text

11 **horribile aequor ulti- / mōsque Britannōs:** the manuscripts have **horribilēsque ulti- / mōsque Britannōs,** with both adjectives modifying **Britannōs:**

  11 Gallicum Rhēnum horribilēsque ulti-
  12 mōsque Britannōs,

With this reading, however, the meter is preserved only if elision does not occur between **horribilēsque** and **ulti-.** In order to avoid this hiatus, editors usually print the emendation **horribile aequor,** as in this text. Another reading, **horribilem gelū** [**gelū, -ūs,** n., *cold, frost, ice*], has also been proposed, with the adjective modifying **Rhēnum:**

  11 Gallicum Rhēnum horribilem gelū ulti-
  12 mōsque Britannōs,

9   sīve trāns altās gradiētur Alpēs,

10 Caesaris vīsēns monimenta magnī,

11 Gallicum Rhēnum horribile aequor ulti-

12   mōsque Britannōs,

13 omnia haec, quaecumque feret voluntās

14 caelitum, temptāre simul parātī,

15 pauca nūntiāte meae puellae

16   nōn bona dicta.

continued

Initial Explorations

3. Examine the elements of elevated style in lines 2–12.
    a. Identify examples of anaphora and of asyndeton.
    b. Comment on the effectiveness of word placement in line 2. Consider in particular the placement of the verb **penetrābit**.
    c. Identify the sound effects of the words in lines 3–4.
    d. Identify a chiastic noun-adjective, adjective-noun arrangement in lines 5–6.
    e. Describe the effect of the use of polysyllabic adjectives.
    f. Describe the effect of adverbial and adjectival words that convey ideas of distance, size, or stature.
4. Trace on a map the succession of places mentioned from line 2 to the end of line 12.
    a. What is the overall pattern?
    b. What word at the end rounds out the passage by echoing a word at the beginning?
    c. What do these words emphasize?
5. How is the elevated style of lines 1–12 continued in lines 13–14? Note hyperbole and poetic vocabulary.
6. a. What appears to be the purpose of the imagined or projected travels?
    b. Who will decide what travels will be undertaken?
    c. What is the relationship of Furius and Aurelius to Catullus?
7. Lines 1–16 constitute a single sentence. What is its main verb?
8. How do lines 15–16 depart from the elevated style of lines 1–4?
9. What word in lines 15–16 echoes what word in lines 13–14?

17   **Cum**: *With.*

       valeō, valēre, valuī, *to grow stronger; to thrive, prosper, fare well.*

         cum suīs vīvat valeatque: jussive subjunctives (the subject is **puella**) in a
           formula for leave-taking = *good-by to her with her. . . .* , but expressing
           more literal meanings as well: *may she live and may she fare well with
           her. . . .*

       moechus, -ī, m., *adulterer.*

18   **quōs**: with **trecentōs**, *300 of whom.*

       complector [con-, *together* + **plectō, plectere, plexī, plexus**, *to plait, twine*],
         complectī, complexus sum, *to embrace.*

         complexa: the perfect participle of a deponent verb is often best
           translated with a present participle in English.

       trecentī, -ae, -a, *three hundred* (often of an indefinitely large number).

         trecentōs: hyperbole; cf. Catullus 9.2, **mīlibus trecentīs**.

19   **omnium**: pronounce as two syllables by synaeresis or elide with the next line
       (synapheia; see lines 22–23).

20   **īlia, īlium**, n. pl., *groin, male organs.*

21   **respectō** [re-, *back* + **speciō, specere, spexī, specus**, *to see; to watch* + **-tō**,
       intensive or iterative suffix], **-āre**, *to look for.*

         respectet: jussive subjunctive again; the subject is **puella**.

22   **quī**: the antecedent is **amōrem**.

       illius: = **illīus**, referring to the **puella**.

       culpa, -ae, f., *fault, blame; wrongdoing;* (of sexual misconduct) *infidelity.*

         culpā: ablative of cause.

       prātum, -ī, n., *meadow.*

         prātī: the line is hypermetric, and the final syllable is elided (synapheia).

           prātī / ultimī: *of/at the furthest [part of a] meadow.*

23   **flōs**: supply **cadit**.

       praetereunte . . . / . . . arātrō (24): ablative absolute, not instrumental
       ablative, which would have required **praetereuntī**.

       postquam: delayed conjunction.

24   **arātrum, -ī**, n., *plow.*

17   Cum suīs vīvat valeatque moechīs,

18   quōs simul complexa tenet trecentōs,

19   nūllum amāns vērē, sed identidem omnium

20   īlia rumpēns;

21   nec meum respectet, ut ante, amōrem,

22   quī illius culpā cecidit velut prātī

23   ultimī flōs, praetereunte postquam

24   tāctus arātrō est.

Initial Explorations

10.   Does the message in lines 17–20 come as a shock after the buildup of lines 1–16? What is shocking about it?

11.   How are the style, tone, and perspective of lines 17–20 different from those of lines 1–16? Is hyperbole present in lines 17–20?

12.   In what ways is the scene described in lines 17–20 the opposite of the travels described in lines 1–12?

13.   Notice that two words are repeated in lines 17–20 from the previous stanza: **simul** (18) = **simul** (14) and **omnium** (19) = **omnia** (13). What contrast do these repetitions invite between the two groups of people and their activities, i.e., between Catullus and his male companions (**comitēs**) on the one hand and the **puella** embracing three hundred adulterers at a time on the other?

14.   What words in lines 17–20 express leave-taking? What words in lines 21–24 reiterate this message?

15.   Examine the simile of the flower and the plow.
    a.   What does the flower represent?
    b.   What does the plow represent?
    c.   What is the significance of the fact that the flower is at the edge of the meadow?
    d.   Is there any suggestion as to whether the plowman cuts the flower accidentally or on purpose?

16.   Look at the last line in each stanza. How does each last line bring its stanza to an effective closure?

Discussion

1.   Consider this poem as part of the cycle of poems dealing with Catullus' love affair with his **puella**/Lesbia. What position does this poem occupy in the cycle? What is different from the situation in Catullus 8?

2.   Gloria S. Duclos has compared the fifth stanza of Catullus 11 with Catullus 5 as follows. To what extent do you agree with her observations?

C.11 . . . is in some ways a response to . . . earlier enthusiasm. Just as Catullus now truly sees Lesbia for what she is, . . . so he also weaves into this last poem themes and verbal reminiscences from other poems to and about Lesbia. The most rapturous poem of the Catullus-Lesbia affair is c.5, which opens with the startling equation of living and loving: *vivamus atque amemus* (1). The two lovers are exhorted to live a life of loving and kissing, excluding all others. The isolation and uniqueness of Catullus and Lesbia in their love for each other are stressed in c.5. In the fifth stanza of c.11, there are ironic and bitter echoes of c.5. *Vivamus atque amemus* becomes *vivat valeatque* of 11.17. The union of the two lovers, expressed in the verbs, has been broken irrevocably and one partner now fornicates indiscriminately, to the disgust of the other. The percussive *centum, centum, centum* of 5.7,8,9 is ironically reflected in the *trecentos* of 11.18; Catullus now counts Lesbia's other lovers, not her kisses given to him. 5.1 and 11.17 show in the very word order how far apart the lovers have grown: *vivamus* and *amemus* encircle, as it were, the beloved *mea Lesbia*; living and loving should be the alpha and omega of the lovers' existence. In c.11, however, Lesbia is encircled, in the line as well as in life, by her adulterers, *cum suis . . . moechis*; she lives her life with them and thrives on her sexual excesses. The *amemus* of 5.1 is answered by the flat statement of 11.19: *nullum amans vere*, and the ecstatic exhortation of 5.1 degenerates into a true assessment of what Lesbia's "love" really is: *ilia rumpens* (11.20). It is not only Lesbia who has withdrawn from the *amemus*; Catullus' love, too, has gone, destroyed by Lesbia herself (11.21–22). Catullus had declared in c.5 that living and loving were the same thing and thus in c.11 he pictures his love dying as a flower dies; when love is gone, so is life extinguished.

      (Gloria S. Duclos, "Catullus 11: Atque in perpetuum, Lesbia, ave atque vale," *Arethusa* 9, 1976, 79–80)

3. The comparison of Catullus' love to a flower cut down as a plow passes by (22–24) is indebted to an image of a hyacinth in lines preserved from a wedding hymn written by the Greek poet Sappho (seventh to sixth centuries B.C.). It is fragment 105c:

    like the hyacinth that shepherds trample under foot in the mountains, and the purple flower <lies crushed> on the ground. . . .

Gloria S. Duclos has written as follows on this fragment of Sappho and the image of the flower in the last stanza of Catullus' poem. Again, to what extent do you agree with her observations?

The image which dominates this stanza, the lonely flower at the meadow's edge cut down by the plough, has its origin in a fragment attributed to Sappho. Catullus had used a variant of it in another, presumably earlier, poem (62.39–47), but what is interesting about its use in c.11 is the inversion to which Catullus has subjected it. In the Sapphic fragment, the hyacinth trampled by the shepherds is presumably likened to a maiden's virginity. The passage in c.62 explicitly compares the plucked flower to a girl's maidenhood. The image, then, is traditionally used to express the finality of a girl's loss of her virginity. In c.11, the finality is still there *(cecidit, 22)* but the subject of the image has been changed, the flower has become Catullus' love for Lesbia. As he inverted the first part of the Sapphic image from feminine to masculine, so also he transforms the second element from masculine to feminine, for the passing plough of the simile must correspond to Lesbia. Not only is ploughing ordinarily a masculine activity, but the metaphoric use of ploughing to denote male sexual activity is commonplace in ancient literature.

    Catullus has clearly reversed the usual terms of the image: the girl's virginity becomes Catullus' love, and the shepherds' trampling feet become

Lesbia's plough. In this final renunciation of his love, the poet's tendency to think of himself in feminine rather than masculine terms is . . . apparent.
(Duclos, 86–87)

4. Divide the poem into three parts according to the tenses of the indicative verbs. In what temporal direction do the poet's thoughts move? On what note does the poem end?

CATULLUS 1–11

Review Catullus 1–11

1. Outline the course taken by Catullus' love affair with Lesbia in poems 2, 3, 5, 7, 8, and 11, as they are arranged here (which need not be the order in which they were composed).

2. Note the theme of travel in poems 4, 9, 10, and 11.

3. Observe the theme of the whore in poems 6, 10, and 11.

4. Show how Catullus 11 recapitulates the main themes of the collection as a whole and provides an appropriate conclusion.

Make a diagram showing the pattern of relationships among the poems in the collection, noting how the themes of Lesbia, travel, and the whore are interwoven.

Charles Segal has argued that poems 1–11 "form a unified block held together by some coherent pattern of arrangement" (306), noting that "six of these poems concern Lesbia" and "are so arranged that they form a progression: from light to serious and from optimistic to bitter" (309). He sees a progression in "the terms of address . . . to Lesbia" (312), noting that in the final poem Catullus "refuses to address Lesbia at all or even to mention her name" (313). Throughout the Lesbia poems, Segal notes "a complex of related themes and images, namely love, death, light, and darkness" (314). He also calls attention to the placement of the poems dealing with travel and the whore, noting that Catullus 4 and 9 "are both happy poems" (318) and that in Catullus 11 "Lesbia is herself little better than a *scortum*" (318). (Charles Segal, "The Order of Catullus, Poems 2–11," *Latomus* 27, 1968, 305–21)

What other interrelations can you find among these poems? Consider the placement of Catullus 6 at the center of poems 1–11. Does Catullus 10 foreshadow the poem that follows it in any important ways? Do you think Catullus gathered these poems into a collection and arranged them in this order? If so, what does the collection as a whole say that the poems read individually do not? How is the collection greater than the sum of its parts?

Meter: hendecasyllabic

1   **Marrūcīnus, -a, -um,** *of/belonging to the Marrucini* (a people living on the Adriatic coast of central Italy).

         Marrūcīne Asinī: Asinius Marrucinus, an acquaintance of Catullus. The order of the **nōmen (Asinius)** and **cognōmen (Marrūcīnus)** is reversed. The family of the Asinii came from Teate, the chief town of the Marrucini.

     manū sinistrā: the left hand was proverbially associated with thievery.

2   **bellē**: for the adjective **bellus, -a, -um**, see on Catullus 3.14; the adverb has a colloquial tone, *nicely*.

     in iocō atque vīnō: i.e., at dinner parties full of joking and drinking.

3   **linteum, -ī**, n., *linen; towel, napkin.*

         lintea: see Catullus 4.5 for use of the word **linteum** in a different sense. The Romans brought their own napkins to dinner parties, and napkins were important because the Romans ate with their fingers.

     neglegentiōrum: substantive use of the adjective. Cf. Catullus 10.34.

4   **salsus, -a, -um** (cf. Catullus 10.33, **īnsulsa**), *salty; humorous, witty.*

     Fugit tē: *[It] escapes you. That's where you're wrong.* Cf. Catullus 10.29, **fūgit mē ratiō.**

     ineptus, -a, -um [in-, *not* + **aptus, -a, -um,** *tied, bound; appropriate, fitting*], *unaware of what is appropriate; silly, foolish.*

         inepte: cf. Catullus 6.14, **ineptiārum**, and 8.1, **ineptīre.**

5   **quamvīs [quam,** *as much as* + **vīs,** *you want/wish*], adv., *as much as you please; extremely, ever so.*

     sordidus, -a, -um, *filthy; sordid; disgraceful.*

     invenustus, -a, -um [in-, *not* + **venustus, -a, -um,** see Catullus 3.2 and 10.4], *without beauty, without charm.*

6   **Polliō, Polliōnis**, m., *Pollio* (brother of Asinius and most likely the Roman orator, historian, and poet, Gaius Asinius Pollio, 76 B.C.–A.D. 4., who was later a friend of Horace and Vergil and who founded the first public library in Rome).

7   **fūrtum, -ī**, n., *theft.*

     frātrī . . . fūrta: note the play on the sounds of these words.

     vel, particle, *even.*

     talentum, -ī, n. [Greek loan word], *talent* (a Greek unit of weight and an expression for a very large sum of money equaling the weight of a talent of gold or silver).

         vel talentō: *by [paying] even a talent*, ablative of means or instrument.

8   **mūtō, -āre, -āvī, -ātus,** *to change; to exchange; to undo.*

     velit: present subjunctive in a relative clause of characteristic.

         quī (7) . . . / . . . velit (8): i.e., he would give a talent for his brother's thefts to be undone.

     lepos, lepōris, m., *charm, grace; wit, humor*; pl., *pleasantry.*

CATULLUS 12

A Thief at Large

What has Asinius Marrucinus stolen? How does Catullus threaten to get it back? Why is it valuable?

1   Marrūcīne Asinī, manū sinistrā
2   nōn bellē ūteris: in iocō atque vīnō
3   tollis lintea neglegentiōrum.
4   Hoc salsum esse putās? Fugit tē, inepte:
5   quamvīs sordida rēs et invenusta est.
6   Nōn crēdis mihi? Crēde Polliōnī
7   frātrī, quī tua fūrta vel talentō
8   mūtārī velit: est enim lepōrum

continued

Initial Explorations

1. What words characterize Asinius and his crime in lines 1–5?
2. Why does Catullus mention Pollio, Asinius' brother? (6–9)

9   **differtus, -a, -um** [**dis-**, intensive + **farciō, farcīre, farsī, farsus**, *to fill, stuff*]
     + gen., *stuffed* (with), *chock-full* (of).
     facētiae, -ārum, f. pl., *cleverness; facetiousness, wit.*
10   **hendecasyllabī, -ōrum**, m. pl. [Greek loan word], *hendecasyllables* (eleven-
     syllable verses, the meter of this poem and a meter often used by Catullus
     for satire and abuse as well as for love poems).
     trecentī, -ae, -a, *three hundred* (often of an indefinitely large number).
     trecentōs: hyperbole; cf. Catullus 9.2 and 11.18.
12   **quod**: relative pronoun and subject of **movet**.
     aestimātiō, aestimātiōnis, f., *valuation; monetary worth, value.*
13   **vērum**, conj., *but.*
     mnēmosynum, -ī, n. [Greek loan word; only here in Latin], *souvenir,*
     memento, keepsake.
     sodālis, sodālis, m. (see Catullus 10.29), *companion, buddy.*
14   **sūdārium, -ī**, n., *sweat cloth, handkerchief, napkin.*
     Saetabus, -a, -um, *Saetaban, from Saetabis* (a town in Spain known for its linen
     goods).
     Hibērī, Hibērōrum, m. pl., *Iberians, Spaniards.*
     ex Hibērīs: *from the [land of the] Iberians*, i.e., from Spain.
     sūdāria Saetaba ex Hibērīs: alliteration.
15   **mihi mūnerī**: double dative, *to me for [the purpose of] a gift, to me as a gift.*
     mīsērunt mihi mūnerī: alliteration.
     Fabullus: he and **Vērānius** (16) were friends of Catullus, on provincial ser-
     vice in Spain; for Veranius, see Catullus 9.1.
16   **haec**: i.e., the **sudāria** (14).
     haec amem: supply **ut**, *that* (which is often left out from clauses used with
     impersonal verbs and the impersonal phrase **necesse est**); the clause
     [ut] haec amem is the subject of **necesse est**.
17   **ut**: *just as*, supply **amō**.
     Vērāniolus, -ī, m. [dim. of **Vērānius**], *dear Veranius.*

Text

9   **differtus**: the manuscripts have **dissertus** or **disertus**, *skilled in speaking,*
     which does not produce good sense; Thomson notes that the conjecture
     printed in our text, **differtus**, should take an ablative and not a genitive as
     here; Thomson proposes reading **disertē pater**, *clearly the father*, with the
     genitives in lines 8 and 9 depending on **pater** = *he is clearly the father [= the*
     very essence] of. . . . Thus:

     8   est enim lepōrum
     9   disertē pater ac facētiārum.

9   differtus puer ac facētiārum.

10   Quārē aut hendecasyllabōs trecentōs

11   exspectā, aut mihi linteum remitte,

12   quod mē nōn movet aestimātiōne,

13   vērum est mnēmosynum meī sodālis.

14   Nam sūdāria Saetaba ex Hibērīs

15   mīsērunt mihi mūnerī Fabullus

16   et Vērānius: haec amem necesse est

17   ut Vērāniolum meum et Fabullum.

Initial Explorations

3. What reading in line 9 makes more sense?
4. What threat does Catullus make in lines 10–11? What rhetorical device does he use to highlight the threat?
5. The poem ends on a sentimental note. Why does Catullus really want the napkin back?
6. In line 1, look closely at the two pairs of words. How do they echo each other?
7. Locate other pairs of words or phrases in the poem.

Discussion

1. What key words are used in the comparison of the two brothers in lines 4–9? How do they define a conception of **urbānitās**, i.e., the sophistication and manners appropriate to a refined city-dweller?
2. The literary genre of satire is often aimed at people who act in self-interested, thoughtless, greedy, and ultimately self-destructive ways. To what extent is this poem satirical, and what strategies does the poet use in lines 1–11 to bring Asinius to his senses and to correct his ways?
3. How does the poet's valuation of the napkin as expressed in the last section of the poem differ from that of Asinius?
4. Divide the poem into three sections. How do the themes of the poem develop from beginning to end?

Meter: hendecasyllabic

1   **mī:** vocative singular of **meus**, often used of close friends (compare Catullus 10.25).

       Fabullus, -ī, m., *Fabullus* (a dear friend of Catullus; see Catullus 12.17).

2   **paucīs . . . diēbus:** note how Catullus has framed the line with these two words.

       sī . . . favent: equivalent to our expression, *God willing;* the use of the present tense in the if-clause (protasis) of the future-more-vivid condition is colloquial.

       dī: = **deī,** nom. pl.

3   **attuleris:** the future perfect, used in the protasis of a future-more-vivid conditional sentence. Where is the second half or conclusion (apodosis)? What is the tense of the verb in the apodosis?

4   **nōn sine:** litotes, equivalent to **cum.**

       candidus, -a, -um (see Catullus 8.3, 8), *white, fair-skinned, pretty.*

5   **sāl, salis,** m. (see Catullus 10.33, **īnsulsa,** and 12.4, **salsum**), *salt;* by metonymy, *wit.*

       cachinnus, -ī, m. [onomatopoetic], *hearty laughter.*

6   **venustus, -a, -um** (see Catullus 3.2, 10.4, 12.5), *endowed/involved with Venus; attractive, charming.*

       noster: Catullus often uses the plural possessive adjective instead of the singular; translate, *my.*

7   **tuī Catullī:** genitive of possession with **sacculus** (8).

8   **sacculus, -ī,** m. [dim. of **saccus, -ī,** m., *sack, bag*], *little money bag.*

       arānea, -ae, f., *spider's web, cobweb.*

9   **contrā,** adv., *in return.*

       merus, -a, -um, *undiluted, pure.*

       amor, amōris, m., *love;* pl., *love affairs* (cf. Catullus 7.8), or concrete, *the object of one's love, loved one, girlfriend* (cf. Catullus 6.16 and 10.1).

          amōrēs: not *girlfriend* here; the phrase **merōs amōrēs** points forward to **unguentum** (11), a perfume that is anticipated in the phrase **merōs amōrēs,** "pure, unadulterated love" (Fordyce), "something you'll absolutely fall in love with" (Quinn), or "love's pure essence" (Ker in translating Martial 14.206.1, where Martial borrows Catullus' phrase **merōs amōrēs**).

10   **seu:** = **sīve,** *or if.*

       quis, qua/quae, quid, indefinite pronoun after **seu,** *anyone, anybody, somebody, anything, something.*

          seu quid . . . est: i.e., you could describe the perfume with some word or phrase other than **merōs amōrēs** if there is anything more delightful or more elegant than that.

       -ve, enclitic conj., *or.*

CATULLUS 13

A Fantasy of an Unusual Dinner

What prediction does Catullus make in the first half of the following poem? What does he promise in the second half?

1   Cēnābis bene, mī Fabulle, apud mē
2   paucīs, sī tibi dī favent, diēbus,
3   sī tēcum attuleris bonam atque magnam
4   cēnam, nōn sine candidā puellā
5   et vīnō et sale et omnibus cachinnīs.
6   Haec sī, inquam, attuleris, venuste noster,
7   cēnābis bene; nam tuī Catullī
8   plēnus sacculus est arāneārum.
9   Sed contrā accipiēs merōs amōrēs
10 seu quid suāvius ēlegantiusve est:

continued

Initial Explorations

1. What will Fabullus do? Where? When? On what condition? (1–2)
2. What does Catullus imagine that Fabullus will bring? (3–5)
3. Why can't Catullus provide the usual essentials of a good dinner? (7–8)
4. What will Fabullus receive in return? (9–10)

11   **unguentum, -ī**, n., *perfume*.

dabo: iambic shortening.

unguentum dabo: Catullus as host of the dinner party will provide the perfume that was usual on such occasions, but the perfume he will give Fabullus is no ordinary perfume. There is an allusion here to a jar of perfume that Venus gave to Phaon, a ferryman on the island of Lesbos, as a reward for his ferrying the goddess disguised as an old woman free of charge. When Phaon anointed himself with the perfume, women found him irresistible. The story goes that he attracted the love of the poet Sappho, but when she was rejected by him she committed suicide by jumping off a cliff at Leucas, an island off the west coast of Greece.

meae puellae: the **puella** is usually identified with Lesbia.

dōnārunt: syncope for **dōnāvērunt**.

Venerēs Cupīdinēsque: *[all the] Venuses and Cupids*; cf. Catullus 3.1.

13   **olfaciō, olfacere, olfēcī, olfactus** *to catch the scent of, smell*.

tū cum olfaciēs: temporal **cum** clause.

14   **tōtum . . . nāsum**: line framing. Where else has Catullus used line framing in this poem?

tōtum: take with either **tē** or **nāsum** or both.

ut tē faciant: indirect command; note the delayed position of **ut**.

11   nam unguentum dabo, quod meae puellae

12   dōnārunt Venerēs Cupīdinēsque,

13   quod tū cum olfaciēs, deōs rogābis

14   tōtum ut tē faciant, Fabulle, nāsum.

Initial Explorations

5.   What specifically will Catullus give Fabullus? (11–12)
6.   What will this make Fabullus do? (13–14)
7.   Structure:
      a.   Analyze the chiastic arrangement of phrases and words in lines 1–7 by
            finding in lines 6 and 7 words and phrases that correspond in reverse
            order to the following phrases and words in lines 1–4: **Cēnābis bene** (1),
            mī Fabulle (1), **sī . . . attuleris** (3), **cēnam** (4).
      b.   What three words positioned at the beginning of three of lines 1–7 echo
            one another?
      c.   The arrangement of words that you have analyzed in lines 1–7 rein-
            forces the tight logic of the statement being made in these lines, namely,
            that Fabullus will dine well if he brings the dinner, etc., with him. What
            Catullus will contribute is described in lines 9–14. Discuss the signifi-
            cance of the following correspondences between phrases and words in
            these lines and in lines 1–7: **accipiēs merōs amōrēs** (9) = **Haec . . . at-
            tuleris** (6); **unguentum dabo** (11) = **attuleris . . . / cēnam** (3–4); **puellae**
            (11) = **puellā** (4); **deōs** (13) = **dī** (2); and **Fabulle** (14) = **Fabulle** (1).

Discussion

1.   This poem is often described as an invitation to dinner. Is it? What would a
      normal dinner invitation be like, and how does this poem invert and parody
      what one would expect in a dinner invitation? How does this inversion and
      parody produce a humorous and comical effect?
2.   How does the structure of the poem set up an opposition between the dinner
      that Fabullus will provide and the perfume that Catullus will offer? Note the
      verbal correspondences that you analyzed above.
3.   What are the implications of the allusion to the perfume that Venus gave to
      Phaon?
4.   Is the poem a serious description of a possible dinner with Fabullus, or does it
      have some quite different purpose? If so, what is it?

Meter: hendecasyllabic

1　　**nī:** = nisi.
　　plūs oculīs meīs: cf. Catullus 3.5, **quem plūs illa oculīs suīs amābat.**
2　　**Calvus, -ī, m.,** *C. Licinius Calvus Macer* (a close friend of Catullus, an orator,
　　　　and one of the **poētae novī;** see Catullus 50, 53, and 96).
　　　　　　iūcundissime Calve: cf. Catullus 50.16, **iūcunde** (also addressed to
　　　　　　　　Calvus).
　　iste, ista, istud, often contemptuous or derogatory, *that* (of yours).
　　mūnere istō: *because of that gift of yours,* ablative of cause.
3　　**ōdī, ōdisse, ōsus,** perfect in form, present in meaning, *to hate.*
　　　　ōdissem: because no present system exists for this verb, this form serves as
　　　　　　an imperfect subjunctive and should be translated as the apodosis of a
　　　　　　present contrary-to-fact condition.
　　odium, -ī, n., *hatred.*
　　Vatīniānus, -a, -um, *of Vatinius* (Publius Vatinius, whom Calvus prosecuted
　　　　in 58, 56, and 54 B.C.; Vatinius was a tribune of the plebs who sponsored
　　　　bills granting Caesar Cisapline Gaul and Illyricum, and he served with
　　　　Caesar in Gaul. See Catullus 53 for reference to one of the trials, probably
　　　　in 54 B.C. for Vatinius' illegal electioneering practices in his succesful bid
　　　　for the praetorship in 56 B.C.).
　　　　　　odiō Vatīniānō, *with the hatred of Vatinius;* many commentators take this
　　　　　　　　to mean *the hatred Vatinius has for you,* but it may also mean *the hatred
　　　　　　　　you have* [or perhaps *everyone has*] *for Vatinius.*
5　　**cūr:** *[as to] why,* translate here *because of which.*
　　tot: with **poētīs.**
　　male perderēs: male is an intensifier here, *utterly.*
　　poētīs: Calvus sent Catullus a little papyrus roll of poems written by various
　　　　poets.
　　mē . . . male perderēs poētīs: alliteration.
6　　**Istī:** with **clientī;** the identity of the client is not yet revealed; later Catullus
　　　　guesses at a certain Sulla (9).
　　dī: = **deī,** nom. pl.
　　dī mala multa dent: a formulaic imprecation.
　　clientī: "Catullus depicts himself as suspecting that the only reason why
　　　　Calvus should have sent him a book of atrociously bad verses was that a
　　　　client, defended successfully by Calvus, had given it to him in token of
　　　　gratitude, and Calvus in his turn—as a joke—sent this unwanted present
　　　　on to Catullus" (Thomson).
7　　**impius, -a, -um,** *impious, unholy; wicked.*
　　　　tantum . . . impiōrum: *so many scoundrels* (Merrill), for the partitive
　　　　　　genitive with **tantum,** see Catullus 5.13, **tantum . . . bāsiōrum.**

CATULLUS 14a

A Horrible Gift for the Saturnalia

Catullus will settle the score.

1 Nī tē plūs oculīs meīs amārem,
2 iūcundissime Calve, mūnere istō
3 ōdissem tē odiō Vatīniānō:
4 nam quid fēcī ego quidve sum locūtus,
5 cūr mē tot male perderēs poētīs?
6 Istī dī mala multa dent clientī,
7 quī tantum tibi mīsit impiōrum.

continued

Initial Explorations

1. The first three lines are carefully crafted. Locate:
   a. a chiasmus
   b. repetition of words
   c. effective repetition of vowel sounds
   d. a play on words
   e. effective juxtaposition of two words
   f. two examples of effective elision
2. Judging from line 5, what did Calvus' gift do to Catullus?
3. Mention of Vatinius (3), whom Calvus prosecuted in court, introduces a legal element into the poem.
   a. In line 4, what question does the poet ask of Calvus as if he has been accused of something?
   b. In line 5, what punishment does Catullus complain about?
4. **Istī** in line 6 echoes **istō** in line 3. To whom does Catullus trace the origin of the gift? What does the poet pray will happen to this person?
5. Compare lines 4–5 with lines 6–7. Point out a chiasmus that highlights the charges and punishments directed at Catullus and at the person who sent the "gift" to Calvus.

8 **Quod sī:** *But if.*
   suspicor, -ārī, -ātus sum, *to suspect.*
   reperiō [re-, *back, again* **+ pariō, parere, peperī, partus,** *to procure, get*],
      reperīre, repperī, repertus, *to find; to get.*
         novum ac repertum / mūnus (9): hendiadys, *newly discovered gift, novel*
            form of gift.
9 **dat:** historical present, as is also **dispereunt (11).**
   Sulla, -ae, m., *Sulla* (otherwise unknown).
   litterātor, litterātōris, m., *elementary school teacher.*
      litterātor: "for surely no one but a schoolmaster (*litterator*) would ever
         think of paying the *honorarium* of his legal counsel with books" (Merrill).
10 **mī: = mihi.**
      nōn est mī male: *I am not unhappy* (Fordyce).
   beātus, -a, -um, *happy.*
      bene ac beātē: alliteration; translate freely, *utterly happy.*
11 **dispereō [dis-,** intensive **+ pereō , perīre, periī, peritus,** *to perish*], **disperīre,**
      disperiī, *to perish; to be destroyed; to be wasted.*
12 **horribilis, -is, -e** (see Catullus 11.11), *horrible; terrifying; dreadful.*
   sacer, sacra, sacrum, *sacred; holy; accursed.*
   libellus, -ī, m. [dim. of **liber, librī,** m., *papyrus roll* (the ancient form of what
      we think of as a book)] (see Catullus 1.1 and 8), *little papyrus roll.*
         horribilem et sacrum libellum: accusative of exclamation.
13 **scīlicet,** adv., often ironical or sarcastic, *of course.*
14 **mīstī:** syncope for **mīsistī.**
   continuus, -a, -um, *uninterrupted, unbroken, whole; very next.*
      continuō: see **Text.**
15 **Sāturnālia, Sāturnālium,** n. pl., *the festival of Saturn, the Saturnalia* (an ancient
      Roman festival, originally celebrated on December 17, but often extended
      over the following days; presents were exchanged, slaves were treated as
      equal or superior to their masters, and an atmosphere of freedom and
      merrymaking was cultivated).
16 **Nōn nōn:** note the repetition.
      Nōn . . . abībit: *This* (act of yours or this **mūnus**) *will not go away for you,* =
         You'll not get away with this (i.e., with sending this awful poetry).
   falsus, -a, -um, *wrong, erroneous; treacherous, faithless, deceitful.*
      false: see **Text.**
   sīc: i.e., "as a trick entirely at Catullus' expense" (Garrison).

8   Quod sī, ut suspicor, hoc novum ac repertum
9   mūnus dat tibi Sulla litterātor,
10 nōn est mī male, sed bene ac beātē,
11 quod nōn dispereunt tuī labōrēs.
12 Dī magnī, horribilem et sacrum libellum!
13 Quem tū scīlicet ad tuum Catullum
14 mīstī, continuō ut diē perīret,
15 Sāturnālibus, optimō diērum!
16 Nōn nōn hoc tibi, false, sīc abībit.

continued

Text

Thomson prints lines 14–15 as follows:

14 mīstī continuō, ut diē perīret
15 Sāturnālibus optimō diērum!

> The word **continuō** is here an adverb meaning *immediately*, and **Satur-nālibus** is in apposition to **diē . . . / . . . optimō diērum**: *on the best day of days, on the Saturnalia* (note the hyperbaton of **diē . . . / . . . optimō**). With the punctuation printed in our text above, **continuō** will modify **diē**: *on the very next day.*

16 **false**

> Godwin keeps this reading of the Oxford Classical Text (= manuscripts O and R) and translates the line, *No, you will not get away with it, you scallywag*, as if Calvus were a "villain" for what he did. Most editors accept the reading of manuscript G, **salse**, *you witty fellow!* (Thomson).

Initial Explorations

6. Why would Catullus be utterly happy if it were Sulla who had given the papyrus roll of poetry to Calvus? (8–11)
7. How does the tone of line 12 contrast with that of lines 8–11?
8. Lines 4 and 7 allude to wrongful actions on the part of Catullus and on the part of the person who sent the papyrus roll of poems to Calvus. What culpable action does Catullus accuse Calvus of in lines 13–15?
9. How does line 16 continue the legal thread in the poem?

17   **sī lūxerit**: literally, *if it* (i.e., the sun) *will have shone*, = *when dawn comes.*
      librārius, -ī, m., *copyist, bookseller.*

18   **scrīnium, -ī**, n., *a cylindrical case* (for holding papyrus rolls).
      Caesius, -ī, m., *Caesius* (otherwise unknown).
      Aquīnus, -ī, m., *Aquinus* (perhaps the Aquinius mentioned by Cicero,
         Tusculan Disputations 5.63, where Cicero comments on his conceit).
         Caesiōs, Aquīnōs: generalizing plurals, *poets such as. . . .*

19   **Suffēnus, -ī**, m., *Suffenus* (Catullus attacks Suffenus in poem 22 for his
         overblown and unwarranted pride in himself as a poet; the singular,
         following the generalizing plurals, and the enjambement single out
         Suffenus as being especially bad).
      colligō [**con-**, *together* + **legō, legere, lēgī, lēctus**, *to gather*], **colligere,**
      collēgī, collēctus, *to gather together, collect.*
      venēnum, -ī, n., *poison.*

20   **supplicium, -ī**, n., *punishment.*
      hīs suppliciīs: *with these as punishments* (Thomson).
      remūneror [**re-**, *back* + **mūneror, -ārī, -ātus sum**, *to present; to give*], **-ārī, -ātus**
      sum, *to pay back.*
         remūnerābor: picking up **mūnus** (9) and **mūnere** (2).

21   **Vōs**: personification and apostrophe of the bad poems that Calvus sent.
      hinc, adv., *from here.*
      intereā: i.e., until Catullus gets a chance to buy the others (Quinn).
      valēte abīte: asyndeton.

22   **malum pedem attulistis**: *you brought your bad feet* (**malum pedem**: sing. for
         pl., continuing the apostrohe of the bad poems that Calvus sent), with a
         pun on **pedem** as a foot of poetry, with **malum** suggesting "incompetence
         in the art of versification" (Thomson).

23   **saeclī**: = **saeculī**.
      incommodum, -ī, n., *misfortune; trouble.*
         saeclī incommoda: comic overstatement, *the nuisances of our times*
         (Fordyce).

17 Nam, sī lūxerit, ad librāriōrum

18 curram scrīnia, Caesiōs, Aquīnōs,

19 Suffēnum, omnia colligam venēna,

20 ac tē hīs suppliciīs remūnerābor.

21 Vōs hinc intereā valēte abīte

22 illūc, unde malum pedem attulistis,

23 saeclī incommoda, pessimī poētae.

Initial Explorations

10. How does Catullus plan to take the punishment that Calvus deserves into his own hands? (17–20)
11. The phrase **sī lūxerit** (17) and the verb **curram** (18) hint at Catullus' need to be quick in punishing Calvus. What reasons can you give for his haste?
12. Why is the verb **remūnerābor** (20) an apt choice for the occasion?
13. To whom or what are the final three lines addressed? What demand does Catullus make? (21–23)
14. Although there is time between the penning of this poem and the next morning, as indicated by the word **intereā** (21), why is Catullus' command an urgent one, expressed in the back-to-back imperatives **valēte abīte**?
15. In the last three lines, point out examples of:
    a. asyndeton
    b. metaphor
    c. hyperbole
    d. alliteration

Discussion

1. What is the structure of the poem? What is the significance of the line that is in the middle, and how do the lines to either side of it make up segments that respond to one another?
2. How does this poem celebrate Catullus and Calvus' friendship and their shared poetic/aesthetic values?

Meter: choliambic

1   **Suffēnus, -ī**, m., *Suffenus* (the poet about whom Catullus is writing this
        poem; he is mentioned in Catullus 14a.19; nothing of his work has sur-
        vived).
     iste, ista, istud, often contemptuous or derogatory, *that, that of yours.*
     Vārus, -ī, m., *Varus* (see on Catullus 10.1).
     probē, adv., *correctly; thoroughly, well.*
     nōscō, nōscere, nōvī, nōtus, inceptive, *to become acquainted with;* pf., *to know.*
        nōstī: syncope for **nōvistī**.
2   **venustus**: see Catullus 3.2, 10.4, 12.5, and 13.6.
     dicāx, dicācis, *clever with his tongue.*
     urbānus, -a, -um, *of the city; sophisticated* (in speech and manners); *urbane.*
3   **īdem**: pronoun, *the same* (person as previously mentioned); often, as here, in-
        troducing an inconsistency, translate, *and yet at the same time/on the other
        hand.*
     longē, adv., *by far.*
4   **esse**: take with **perscrīpta** in line 5 to form a perfect passive infinitive.
     illī: dative of agent.
     mīlia: supply **versuum**.
     aut decem aut plūra: modifying **mīlia**, as a kind of afterthought, the main
        point being that Suffenus writes verses by the thousands.
5   **perscrībō** [**per-**, *fully* + **scrībō, scrībere, scrīpsī, scrīptus**, *to write*], **per-**
        scrībere, perscrīpsī, perscrīptus, *to write out fully; to write down.*
     ut fit: *as it happens, as is usual/common.*
     palimpsestum, -ī, n. [from a Greek word meaning *scraped again*], *used
        papyrus* (parchment or papyrus from which the old writing has been
        scraped off, mentioned here as an example of ordinary, everyday writing
        material).
6   **relāta**: supply **esse**, *[to have been] written down;* the subject of the infinitive is
        mīlia (versuum) (4).
     carta, -ae, f. (see Catullus 1.6), *sheet of papyrus.*
        cartae . . . / . . . membrānae (7): supply **sed** to introduce this list.
     rēgius, -a, -um, *royal, fit for kings; high-quality, expensive.*
     liber, librī, m., *papyrus roll* (the ancient form of what we think of as a book).
7   **novī . . .** (6) / **novī**: anaphora.
     umbilīcus, -ī, m., *navel; stick/cylinder* (on which papyrus was rolled); pl.,
        knobs (at either end of the stick or cylinder of a papyrus roll).
     lōrum, -ī, n., *strap, leather tie.*
     ruber, rubra, rubrum, *red.*
     membrāna, -ae, f., *skin of a sheep or goat prepared for use as writing material,
        parchment; wrapper made of parchment.*
        membrānae: genitive or dative, *of/for the wrapper made of parchment.*

CATULLUS 22

On a Local Poetaster

Suffenus is a charming person, but as a poet—. Still, there is a Suffenus in us all.

1   Suffēnus iste, Vāre, quem probē nōstī,
2   homō est venustus et dicāx et urbānus,
3   īdemque longē plūrimōs facit versūs.
4   Putō esse ego illī mīlia aut decem aut plūra
5   perscrīpta, nec sīc ut fit in palimpsestō
6   relāta: cartae rēgiae, novī librī,
7   novī umbilīcī, lōra rubra membrānae,

continued

Text

6   **cartae rēgiae, novī librī**: Thomson prints **cartae rēgiae novae librī**, making the whole phrase refer to the sheets of the papyrus roll.
7   **lōra rubra membrānae**: Thomson punctuates **lōra rubra, membrānae**, with **membrānae**, *wrappers made of parchment*, nominative plural, thus:

      6   relāta: cartae rēgiae novae librī,
      7   novī umbilīcī, lōra rubra, membrānae,

Initial Explorations

1.   In lines 1–2, how does Catullus characterize Suffenus as a person?
2.   What picture of Suffenus as a poet does Catullus build up in lines 3–8?
3.   Does Catullus seem to approve or disapprove of Suffenus as a poet?

8   dērigō [dē-, *thoroughly* + regō, regere, rēxī, rēctus, *to keep* (things) *in line,*
      direct, rule], dērigere, dērēxī, dērēctus, *to arrange along a fixed line; to line,*
      rule (a sheet of papyrus).
      plumbum, -ī, n., *lead* (used for making lines on papyrus).
      pūmex, pūmicis, m. (see Catullus 1.2), *pumice-stone* (used like sandpaper to
      smooth the ends of a papyrus roll).
      omnia: subject, modified by dērēcta and aequāta.
      aequō, -āre, -āvī, -ātus, *to make level/smooth.*
        dērēcta plumbō et pūmice . . . aequāta: this line "is itself aequāta by
          having the participles at either end with the *p*-alliterated words in the
          middle" (Godwin, 138).
9   bellus, -a, -um (see Catullus 3.14, 15; colloquial, cf. the more formal pulcher,
      pulchra, pulchrum, *beautiful, handsome, lovely*), *handsome, pretty; charming;*
      "smart."
10   ūnus, -a, -um, *one* (of a class), *an ordinary, any old.*
      caprimulgus, -ī, m. [caper, caprī, m., *billy goat* + mulgeō, mulgēre, mulsī,
      mulsus, *to milk* (an animal)], *goat-milker, goatherd.*
      fōssor, fōssōris, m., *ditch digger.*
11   rūrsus, adv., *again, once again; on the other hand, contrariwise.*
      vidētur: supply esse or fierī.
      abhorreō [ab-, *from* + horreō, -ēre, -uī, *to bristle, shudder, tremble*], abhorrēre,
      abhorruī, *to shrink back from; to be out of accordance, be at variance; to be*
      different.
        abhorret: i.e., is different from the appearance he gave earlier.
      mūtō, -āre, -āvī, -ātūrus, *to change.*
12   putēmus: deliberative subjunctive; the "we" are Varus and Catullus.
      Quī: the antecedent is īdem in line 14; for a smoother translation, bring the
        idea expressed in īdem to the front, *The same man who.* . . .
      modo, adv., *only; just now.*
      scurra, -ae, m., *an urbane and witty man, a wit.*
13   quis, qua/quae, quid, indefinite pronoun after sī, *anyone, anybody, somebody,*
      anything, something.
      scītus, -a, -um [scīscō, scīscere, scīvī, scītus, inceptive, *to get to know*],
      knowing, shrewd, sharp.
        hāc rē scītius: ablative of comparison, i.e., than a scurra.
14   īdem: see notes on lines 3 and 12.
      īnfacētus, -a, -um [in-, *not* + facētus, -a, -um, *clever*], *witless.*
        īnfacētō . . . īnfacētior: some editions have īnficētō . . . īnficētior.
15   simul: = simul ac, conj., *as soon as.*
      poēma, poēmatis, n. [Greek loan word], *poem.*
      attingō [ad-, *to, toward* + tango, tangere, tetigī, tāctus, *to touch*], attingere, at-
      tigī, attāctus, *to touch; to undertake, put one's hand to.*
16   aequē . . . ac . . . cum: *equally/as* . . . *as when.*
      beātus, -a, -um, *happy.*

8   dērēcta plumbō et pūmice omnia aequāta.

9   Haec cum legās tū, bellus ille et urbānus

10 Suffēnus ūnus caprimulgus aut fossor

11 rūrsus vidētur: tantum abhorret ac mūtat.

12 Hoc quid putēmus esse? Quī modo scurra

13 aut sī quid hāc rē scītius vidēbātur,

14 īdem īnfacētō est īnfacētior rūre,

15 simul poēmata attigit, neque īdem umquam

16 aequē est beātus ac poēma cum scrībit:

17 tam gaudet in sē tamque sē ipse mīrātur.

continued

Initial Explorations

4. According to lines 9–11, what contradiction is noticed when one reads Suffenus' poetry?
5. How does Catullus further describe the contradictions in Suffenus? (12–15)
6. How does Suffenus feel about his activity as a poet? Are his feelings justified? (15–17)

18   **nīmīrum** [**nī-**, negative + **mīrum**, *it would be a wonder if . . . not*], particle, *without doubt, clearly.*

       idem: with a short *i*, neuter, internal accusative with **fallimur**.

       fallō, fallere, fefellī, falsus, *to mislead, deceive;* passive, *to be deceived, be mistaken.*

          idem . . . fallimur: *we make the same mistake.*

       quisquam, quisquam, quicquam, indefinite pronoun, *anyone, anything.*

19   **in aliquā rē**: *in some respect.* The second foot of this line consists of three short syllables.

       Suffēnum: *[as] a Suffenus.*

20   **Suus . . . error**: *one's own mistake/delusion.*

       quisque, quaeque, quidque, pronoun, *each, every one, every thing.*

          cuique: what case and number?

       attribuō, attribuere, attribuī, attribūtus, *to assign, allot.*

       error, errōris, m., *wandering; mistake; mental aberration, delusion.*

21   **mantica, -ae**, f., *wallet, knapsack* ("with one pocket resting on the back, one on the chest," Thomson).

          manticae quod . . . est: *[the part] of the knapsack that is. . . .*

18   Nīmīrum idem omnēs fallimur, neque est quisquam
19   quem nōn in aliquā rē vidēre Suffēnum
20   possīs. Suus cuique attribūtus est error;
21   sed nōn vidēmus manticae quod in tergō est.

Initial Explorations

7.   What observation on human nature does Catullus make in lines 18–21?
8.   How many elisions can you find in line 4? What effect do they produce?
9.   Find an example of asyndeton and describe its effect on the reader.

Discussion

1.   Repetition is an effective device in poetry; the same word or phrase used two
     or three times can emphasize a point or feeling. How does the repetition of
     īdem (3, 14, 15) reinforce the theme of this poem?
2.   Why are the terms **caprimulgus** and **fossor** (10) appropriate descriptions of
     Suffenus when he publishes his poetry?
3.   What point of literary criticism does Catullus make in this poem?
4.   Compare the external appearance and the inner contents of Suffenus' **librī**
     with those of Catullus' **libellus** as he describes it in his first poem.
5.   What larger moral does Catullus draw from his observations on Suffenus?

Comparison

Compare the ending of Catullus' poem with this fable of Phaedrus (Latin poet of
the first half of the first century A.D.):

De vitiīs hominum

Pērās imposuit Iuppiter nōbīs duās:
propriīs replētam vitiīs post tergum dedit,
aliēnīs ante pectus suspendit gravem.
  Hāc rē vidēre nostra mala nōn possumus;
aliī simul dēlinquunt, cēnsōrēs sumus.

Jupiter has put upon us two bags:
the one that is filled with our own faults he put on our back,
the other sagging with the faults of others he hung on our chest.
  For this reason we cannot see our own faults;
but as soon as others do something wrong, we become fault-finders.

—Phaedrus, *Fables* 4.10

Meter: hendecasyllabic

1   **minister, ministrī,** m., *servant, attendant;* of wine, *dispenser* (of) + gen.
      Minister: vocative, in apposition to **puer** (here referring to a slave boy).
     vetulus, -a, -um [dim. of **vetus, veteris,** *old*], *fairly old; good old.*
     Falernus, -a, -um, *Falernian* (referring to a district in northern Campania,
      famous for its wine).
          Falernī: supply **vīnī.**
2   **ingerō, ingerere, ingessī, ingestus,** *to heap on; to pour on/in* (abundantly).
      inger: form found only here = **ingere,** imperative singular.
     calix, calicis, m. [cf. Greek *kylix,* "drinking-cup"], *drinking cup;* here by
      metonymy, *the contents of drinking cups, wine.*
     amārus, -a, -um, *bitter;* of wine, *dry, tart.*
          amāriōrēs: comparative adjective, *drier;* the following lines indicate that it
          is intended here to mean *mixed with less water.*
3   **lēx, lēgis,** f., *law, dictate, decree.*
     Postumia, -ae, f., *Postumia* (name of the Roman matron who is presiding
      over this drinking party as **magistra bibendī,** *mistress of drinking,* replac-
      ing the usual **magister bibendī,** the individual who decided on the wine
      and the proportion of water, **lympha,** cf. 5, to pure wine, **merum,** cf. 7, that
      was to be drunk. This may be the same Postumia who was the wife of
      Servius Sulpicius Rufus and mistress of Julius Caesar, but this is only a
      guess; there may instead be an allusion here to the Lex Postumia from the
      time of the reign of King Numa that regulated the use of wine in certain
      rituals, see Pliny, *Natural History* 14.88).
4   **ēbriōsus, -a, -um,** *addicted to drink.*
     acinus, -ī, m., *berry; grape.*
5   **vōs:** i.e., the **lymphae,** which Catullus here addresses.
     quō lubet: archaic for **libet,** *to wherever [to go] pleases [you], to wherever it pleases
      [you] [to go].*
     hinc, adv., *from here.*
     lympha, -ae, f. [from Greek *nymphē,* "bride, nymph, water,"], *water-nymph;
      water.*
6   **perniciēs, -ēī,** f., *destruction, ruin.*
      vīnī perniciēs: in apposition to **lymphae.**
     sevērus, -a, -um (see Catullus 5.2), *severe in judgment, stern, strict.*
7   **merus, -a, -um** (see Catullus 13.9), *undiluted, pure.*
     Thyōniānus, -ī, m. [noun coined by Catullus; cf. **Thyōnē, Thyōnēs,** f., *Thy-
      one* (another name for Semele, the mother of Bacchus); **Thyōneus, -ī,** m.,
      Thyoneus (a name of Bacchus); cf. formations such as **Caesariānus,** *a sup-
      porter of Caesar,* and **Pompeiānus,** *a supporter of Pompey*], *a follower/adherent
      of Bacchus.*
          Thyōniānus: Catullus and his fellow neoteric poets coined many new
          words.
               Hīc merus est Thyōniānus: perhaps, *Here is an undiluted Thyonian*
               = *Here is a follower of Bacchus who drinks his wine undiluted,* perhaps
               referring to Catullus himself.

CATULLUS 27

Stronger drink, please!

Catullus sets the serving boy straight at a drinking party.

1   Minister vetulī puer Falernī,
2   inger mī calicēs amāriōrēs,
3   ut lēx Postumiae iubet magistrae
4   ēbriōsō acinō ēbriōsiōris.
5   At vōs quō lubet hinc abīte, lymphae,
6   vīnī perniciēs, et ad sevērōs
7   migrāte. Hīc merus est Thyōniānus.

Initial Explorations

1.   How is the juxtaposition of the words **vetulī** and **puer** particularly effective?
2.   What is unusual about the person in charge of the drinking on this occasion?
3.   What is striking about the choice, sound, and arrangement of the words in line 4? What poetic devices are used?
4.   What rule for the drinking was laid down by Postumia? (2–4)
5.   How does the speaker go beyond Postumia's provisions for drinking? (5–7)

Discussion

1.   Where does the poem divide into segments, and how does line 4 fit in?
2.   Compare this poem with the lines of Anacreon and Diphilus quoted below. What are the similarities? How does Catullus' poem move to a climax?
3.   What role do the **sevērī** play in this poem? How does their role here compare with their role in Catullus 5?

Comparisons

Boy, come, bring me a bowl. . . . Pour in ten ladles of water and five of wine, so that I may again play the part of the god of wine decorously.

—Anacreon (Greek lyric poet, sixth century B.C., fragment 356a)

Now pour us something to drink. Give stronger stuff, by Zeus, boy! For everything watery is an evil for the soul!

—Diphilus (Greek comic poet, fourth century B.C., fragment 58K)

Meter: greater Asclepiadean

1   **Alfēnus, -ī**, m., *Alfenus* (perhaps Alfenus Varus, a shoemaker in Cremona,
    not far from Catullus' native Verona, who studied law in Rome and
    became consul in 39 B.C.; he may be the same Varus as in 10.1 and 22.1,
    though the identification is by no means certain).
    immemor, immemoris, *forgetful, not remembering one's obligations.*
    ūnanimus, -a, -um (see Catullus 9.4), *of one mind, harmonious; loving.*
    falsus, -a, -um, *wrong, erroneous; treacherous, faithless, deceitful.*
    sodālis, sodālis, m. (see Catullus 10.29 and 12.13), *companion, buddy.*
        ūnanimīs . . . sodālibus: dat. with **false** and "'generalized' plural
        (singular in reference)" (Thomson).
2   **nīl**: adverbial, *not at all, in no way.*
    misereō, -ēre, -uī, *to pity, to feel pity.*
        miseret: impersonal, *pity for X (gen.) afflicts Y (acc.); here, you feel no pity for*
        X (**tuī dulcis amīculī**).
    dūrus, -a, -um, *hard; rough; cruel.*
    dulcis, -is, -e, *sweet, pleasant, dear.*
    amīculus [dim. of **amīcus, -ī**, m., *friend*], **-ī**, m., *pal, buddy.*
        amīculī: the diminutive suggests an emotional tone.
            tē . . . dūre, tuī dulcis: note the alliteration and the play on the words **tē**
            and **tuī** and on **dūre** and **dulcis**.
3   **iam (2) . . . Iam . . . iam**: the anaphora implies urgency.
    prōdō [**prō-**, *forward* + **dō, dare, dedī, datus**, *to give*], **prōdere, prōdidī,**
    prōditus, *to betray.*
        mē prōdere: supply **nōn dubitās** from later in the line.
    dubitō, -āre, -āvī, -ātus, *to doubt; to waver; to hesitate.*
    fallō, fallere, fefellī, falsus, *to deceive.*
    perfidus, -a, -um, *breaking faith, treacherous, false, deceitful.*
4   **Nec** and **Quae** (5): see **Text**.
    impius, -a, -um, *undutiful, impious.*
    fallāx, fallācis, *treacherous, deceitful.*
        fallācum: = **fallācium**; the adjective here picks up **fallere** (3) and **false** (1).
    caelicola [**caelum, -ī**, n., *heaven* + **colō, colere, coluī, cultus**, *to inhabit,*
        dwell], **-ae**, m./f., *god/goddess.*
            caelicolīs: the word has an epic flavor, and the line is reminiscent of
                Homer, *Odyssey*, 14.83, "Surely the blessed gods do not love
                cruel/shocking/abominable/reckless deeds," referring to the deeds
                of the suitors of Penelope in Odysseus' palace in Ithaca.
5   **dēserō, dēserere, dēseruī, dēsertus**, *to abandon, desert.*
        mē miserum dēseris: **miserum** is proleptic, = *you desert me [and make me]*
        pitiable/miserable.
    in malīs: Quinn notes that "the details of Catullus' misfortune are not part of
        the poem's hypothesis."
6   **faciant . . . habeant**: deliberative subjunctives in rhetorical questions.
    cui: masculine or neuter, *in whom* or *in what.*

CATULLUS 30

To a False-hearted Friend

Catullus warns Alfenus that he will regret having forsaken him.

1 Alfēne immemor atque ūnanimīs false sodālibus,
2 iam tē nīl miseret, dūre, tuī dulcis amīculī?
3 Iam mē prōdere, iam nōn dubitās fallere, perfide?
4 Nec facta impia fallācum hominum caelicolīs placent.
5 Quae tū neglegis ac mē miserum dēseris in malīs.
6 Ēheu quid faciant, dīc, hominēs cuive habeant fidem?

continued

Text

Godwin prints lines 4–5 as follows:

4 Nunc facta impia fallācum hominum caelicolīs placent,
5 quōs tū neglegis ac mē miserum dēseris in malīs?

> In the Oxford Classical Text as printed above there is no *neither* to correspond to the *nor* of **Nec** (4), and there is no logical antecedent for the relative pronoun **Quae** (5). Godwin prints conjectures of Baehrens (**nunc** for **nec**) and Guarinus (**quōs** for **quae**). Thomson keeps the readings of the Oxford Classical Text, accepting **nec** as a mere negation (= **nōn**), and agreeing with Fordyce that the antecedent of **quae** is broader than the words **facta impia** (4); Thomson translates **quae tū neglegis** as "you care nothing for <the consequences of> your disloyal actions."

Initial Explorations

1. In using the two adjectives **immemor** and **falsus** to address Alfenus, what first impression of his friend does Catullus give us? (1)
2. Thomson describes the phrase **ūnanimīs . . . sodālibus** (1) as a "'generalized' plural (singular in reference)." What does this mean?
3. What complaints does Catullus bring against Alfenus in lines 2 and 3?
4. How does Catullus portray himself in line 2?
5. What effective repetitions and placement of words are there in lines 2 and 3?
6. In what context does Catullus develop his complaint against Alfenus? (4)
7. In what action has Alfenus shown his neglect of the gods' will, and what is its result? *(continued on page 115)*

7   **tūte**: emphatic form of **tū**.

     animam trādere: *to commit my life and soul* (Thomson); supply **tibi**, *to you*. "To some extent **animam trādere** picks up **ūnanimīs** (1)" (Quinn).

     inīquus, -a, -um [**in-**, *not* + **aequus, -a, -um**, *level, equal, equally matched*], *unequal; ill-matched; unfair.*

     mē: take this first as object of **iubēbās** and subject of **animam trādere** and then as object of **indūcēns** (8).

8   **indūcō** [**in-**, *in* + **dūcō, dūcere, dūxī, ductus**, *to lead*], **indūcere, indūxī, inductus**, *to lead in; to entice.*

     tūtus, -a, -um, *safe.*

     mī: = **mihi**.

     forent: = **essent**, from **fore**, the alternative future infinitive of **sum, esse, fuī, futūrus**, *to be.*

9   **Īdem**: emphasizing the contrast between Alfenus in the past (7–8) and in the present (9–10).

     retrahō [**re-**, *back* + **trahō, trahere, trāxī, tractus**, *to draw*], **retrahere, retrāxī, retractus**, *to draw back, withdraw.*

     ac: connecting **retrahis** and **sinis** (10).

     factum, -ī, n., *deed.*

10   **irritus, -a, -um**, *null and void; empty; unrealized; non-existent.*

     irrita: proleptic, translate predicatively, *[as] non-existent* or *[and make them] non-existent*. The image of winds carrying away words and making them as if they had never been spoken is a commonplace in Greek literature (see Homer, *Odyssey* 8.408–409), and will appear again in Catullus 64.59 and 142, 65.17, and 70.4.

     ac: connecting **ventōs** and **nebulās āereās**.

     nebula, -ae, f., *fog; cloud.*

     āereus [Greek, *aerios*], **-a, -um**, *of the air, airy.*

11   **oblīvīscor, oblīvīscī, oblītus sum**, *to forget.*

     oblītus es: picking up the idea of **immemor** (1) and contrasting with **meminērunt** (11) and **meminit** (11).

     Fidēs: picking up **fidem** (6).

12   **paenitet, -ēre, -uit**, impersonal, *regret for* X (gen.) *afflicts* Y (acc.); here, *you will regret your deed.*

     quae . . . tuī: the basic structure of the relative clause is **quae . . . faciet**, *who will make/bring it about*; the verb of effort governs a substantive clause of result, **tē ut paeniteat postmodo factī . . . tuī**, with a delayed conjunction (**tē ut** = **ut tē**).

        tē ut paeniteat postmodo factī faciet tuī: note framing **tē . . . tuī** and the play on the etymologically related words **factī . . . faciet**.

     postmodo, adv., *later.*

     factī: picking up **facta** (4 and 9).

7   Certē tūte iubēbās animam trādere, inīque, mē

8   indūcēns in amōrem, quasi tūta omnia mī forent.

9   Īdem nunc retrahis tē ac tua dicta omnia factaque

10   ventōs irrita ferre ac nebulās āereās sinis.

11   Sī tū oblītus es, at dī meminērunt, meminit Fidēs,

12   quae tē ut paeniteat postmodo factī faciet tuī.

Initial Explorations

8.   How does line 6 continue to develop the religious aspect of Catullus' complaint?

9.   To whom is line 6 addressed?

10.   What two words are effectively placed in line 7?

11.   The vocatives **false** (1) and **perfide** (3) called attention to Alfenus' treachery and deceit. To what does the vocative **inīque** (7) call attention?

12.   In the light of the first half of the poem, what particular meaning might the word **tūta** have here? (8)

13.   The word **Īdem** (9) could be deleted. What does its presence add?

14.   The chiasmus of **mē : indūcēns** (7–8) :: **retrahis : tē** (9) gets to the heart of Catullus' grievance. What verb in line 5 foreshadows the grievance expressed here?

15.   What do the second half of line 9 and line 10 add to what is said in the first half of line 9?

16.   What words in line 11 echo words earlier in the poem?

17.   In lines 11–12, find examples of polyptoton, chiasmus, asyndeton, and alliteration.

Discussion

1.   How is the poem organized with regard to past, present, and future?

2.   How does the poem shift between the human and the divine?

Meter: choliambic

1   **paene īnsulārum**: = **paenīnsulārum**. The genitives in line 1 depend on the
     word **ocelle** (2).
     Sirmiō, Sirmiōnis, f., *Sirmio* (a small peninsula or promontory overlooking
     Lake Garda, Lago di Garda in Italian, the ancient **lacus Bēnācus**, where
     Catullus' family had a villa).

2   **ocellus, -ī**, m. [dim. of **oculus, -ī**, m., *eye*], *little eye, dear eye*; figurative, *jewel*.
     ocelle: vocative (affectionate diminutive), in apposition to **Sirmiō** (1). The
     word **ocelle** is used as a term of endearment for a person in Catullus 50.19.
     quīcumque, quaecumque, quodcumque, indefinite relative pronoun, *who-
     ever, whatever, whichever*.
     liquēns, liquentis, *clear*.
     stagnum, -ī, n., *pool; lake*.

3   **vastus, -a, -um**, *desolate*; of the sea, *dreary, endless, vast*.
     uterque Neptūnus: i.e., each of the two Neptunes, referring to the tradition
     that there was a Neptune of saltwater seas and one of fresh-water lakes.

4   **quam ... quamque**: *how ... and how. ...*
     invīsō, invīsere, invīsī, invīsus, *to come to see, to visit* (a person); *to look upon*.

5   **mī**: dative with **crēdēns**.
     Thūnia (Thȳnia), -ae, f., *Thynia* (the country on the south shore of the Black
     Sea inhabited by the Thyni).
     Bīthūnus (Bīthȳnus), -a, -um, *Bithynian, of/belonging to Bithynia* (the Roman
     province in Asia Minor inhabited by the Thyni and the Bithyni).
         Thūniam atque Bīthūnōs / ... campōs (6): objects of **līquisse** (6).

6   **līquisse**: = **relīquisse**.
     tūtus, -a, -um, *safe, secure*.
     in tūtō: *in one piece, in safety*.
     solūtīs ... cūrīs: ablative of comparison; instead of translating *than cares that
     have been relieved*, turn the idea expressed in the participle into a noun;
     compare **ab urbe conditā** = *from the foundation of the city*.
     beātius: for the word, see note on 9.5.

8   **repōnō** [**re-**, *back* + **pōnō, pōnere, posuī, positus**, *to put, place*], **repōnere,
     reposuī, repositus**, *to put aside*.
     peregrīnus, -a, -um, *foreign*.
     peregrīnō / labōre (9): the phrase refers to the hardships of travel and pub-
     lic service in foreign lands.

9   **fessī**: = **dēfessī**.
     lar, laris, m., *household god*; by synecdoche, *home*.

10   **acquiēscō** [**ad-**, intensive + **quiēscō, quiēscere, quiēvī, quiētūrus**, *to fall
     asleep; to rest*], **acquiēscere, acquiēvī**, inceptive, *to find rest*.
     lectō: = **in lectō**.

11   **ūnus, -a, -um**, here, *alone*.
     prō, prep. + abl., *for; in return for, in compensation for*.
     Hoc est quod ūnum est prō: *This is [that] which alone is in compensation
     for.... = This is what alone makes up for. ...*

CATULLUS 31

Coming Home after Work

Catullus arrives home to his villa at Sirmio in the spring of 56 B.C. for a welcome rest after spending a trying year in Bithynia on the staff of Gaius Memmius.

1 Paene īnsulārum, Sirmiō, īnsulārumque
2 ocelle, quāscumque in liquentibus stagnīs
3 marīque vastō fert uterque Neptūnus,
4 quam tē libenter quamque laetus invīsō,
5 vix mī ipse crēdēns Thūniam atque Bīthūnōs
6 līquisse campōs et vidēre tē in tūtō.
7 Ō quid solūtīs est beātius cūrīs,
8 cum mēns onus repōnit, ac peregrīnō
9 labōre fessī vēnimus larem ad nostrum,
10 dēsīderātōque acquiēscimus lectō?
11 Hoc est quod ūnum est prō labōribus tantīs.

continued

Initial Explorations

1. What is the tone of the poet's opening address to Sirmio? (1–3)
2. a. What words and phrases are paired in these lines?
   b. Which words are arranged in a chiasmus?
3. What does the poet reveal in lines 4–6 about what he is doing now and what he has done in the recent past?
4. a. Locate an example of anaphora in lines 4–6.
   b. Locate three pairs of words in these lines.
   c. What effect do such figures of speech and pairing of words have on the reader?
5. What further factual information does the poet reveal about himself in lines 7–10?
6. What emotions or feelings does the poet express in lines 7–10?
7. Locate the members of an ascending tricolon in lines 7–10. Which of the three clauses in the tricolon is the longest? Which is climactic?
8. What words or phrases in lines 7–10 are set in contrast or concordance with each other?
9. With what word in line 7 does **labōribus** (11) correspond?

12　　**venustus, -a, -um**: see Catullus 3.2, 10.4, 12.5, 13.6.

　　　erus, -ī, m., *master* (especially of a household); *owner* (of a piece of property);
　　　　lord (used of deities).　See Catulus 4.19.

　　　　　erō: "The poet . . . speaks of the place as a servant rejoicing in the return
　　　　　　of its master" (Godwin, 148).

　　　　　　　erō . . . / gaudente (13): ablative absolute.

　　　gaudē: personification.

13　　**gaudē** (12) **/ gaudente**: polyptoton.

　　　Lȳdius, -a, -um, *Lydian, Etruscan* (the area around Sirmio had once been
　　　　ruled by the Etruscans, who were thought to have come from Lydia in Asia
　　　　Minor).

　　　lacus, -ūs, m., *lake.*

14　　**rīdēte**: personification.

　　　quisquis, quisquis, quidquid, indefinite pronoun/adjective, *whoever, what-*
　　　　ever.

　　　domī: locative, idiomatically, *at your disposal, in your stock, in store,* but also *at*
　　　　home.

　　　cachinnus, -ī, m. [onomatopoetic] (see Catullus 13.5), *hearty laughter.*

　　　　quidquid . . . cachinnōrum: **quidquid** with its dependent partitive geni-
　　　　tive functions as internal or cognate accusative with the intransitive verb
　　　　rīdēte, *laugh whatever (of) hearty laughter;* we would say *with whatever*
　　　　hearty laughter.

Text

13　　**vōsque, ō Lȳdiae lacūs undae**: Thomson argues for reading **vōsque lūci-**
　　　dae lacūs undae:

　　　　　13　　gaudente, vōsque lūcidae lacūs undae

　　　[**lūdicus, -a, -um**, *clear, bright, translucent*] This eliminates the learned ref-
　　　erence to Lydia.　Goold prints **limpidae**, *clear, transparent,* in his text.

12 Salvē, ō venusta Sirmiō, atque erō gaudē
13 gaudente, vōsque, ō Lȳdiae lacūs undae,
14 rīdēte quidquid est domī cachinnōrum.

Initial Explorations

10. Locate the members of an ascending tricolon in lines 12–14. Which clause is longest? Is it also climactic?
11. Some editors eliminate the learned allusion in the description of the lake as Lydian and substitute descriptive adjectives instead (see **Text** on the opposite page). What arguments could you make for and against the substitution of descriptive adjectives?
12. How do lines 12–14 echo lines 1–3? How do these sets of lines provide an effective frame for the poem? How is the tone of lines 12–14 different from that of lines 1–3? Why is it different?

Discussion

1. This poem is an example of a literary genre that the ancients described with the Greek word *epibaterion*, which refers to a speech or poem recited by someone who steps onto the shore of his homeland upon returning from travels abroad. The Greek poem translated below is an example, representing the words of Odysseus upon his return home after the Trojan War and his subsequent wanderings. What similarities do you find with Catullus' poem? What differences?
2. What role does personification play in Catullus' poem? How is it important?
3. Compare Catullus 31 with Catullus 9 on Veranius' return home. What similarities and what differences do you find?

Comparison

Ithaca, hail! After my labors, after the bitter woes
of the sea, with joy I come to your soil, hoping to see
Laertes and my wife and my glorious only son.
Love of you enticed my heart; I have learnt for myself that
"Nothing is sweeter than a man's country and his parents."

—Anonymous, *Palatine Anthology* 9.458

Meter: The first three lines of each stanza are glyconics, the fourth line a pherecratean.

1   **Diāna, -ae**, f., *Diana* (Roman goddess identified with the Greek goddess
    Artemis).
    in fidē: *in the custody, under the protection* (as a patron would protect a client in
    Roman society).
2   **puellae et puerī**: subjects of **sumus** (1), both modified by **integrī**.
    integer, integra, integrum [**in-**, *not* + **tangō, tangere, tetigī, tāctus**, *to touch*],
    untouched; whole, complete; youthful; morally unblemished, chaste.
3   **<Diānam puerī integrī>**: this line, missing in the manuscripts, has been
    supplied by modern editors.
4   **canō, canere, cecinī, cantus**, *to sing of.*
5   **Lātōnia, -ae** [matronymic], f., *Latonia, daughter of Latona* (= Diana, daughter of
    Leto, who was called Latona by the Romans).
6   **prōgeniēs, -ēī**, f., *offspring.*
    Iuppiter, Iovis, m., *Jupiter, Jove* (king of the gods).
    maximī (5) / **magna prōgeniēs Iovis**: embedded phrasing and effective
    juxtaposition of **maximī** and **magna**.
7   **Dēlius, -a, -um**, *Delian, of/belonging to/on Delos* (island in the Aegean where
    Latona gave birth to Diana and Apollo under an olive tree).
8   **dēpōnō** [**dē-**, *down* + **pōnō, pōnere, posuī** (archaic **posīvī**), **positus**, *to put,
    place*], **dēpōnere, dēposuī** (archaic **dēposīvī**), **dēpositus**, *to put/lay down*
    (here used instead of a verb meaning *to give birth to*).
    olīvam: other accounts of the birth of Apollo and Artemis/Diana mention
    the tree as a palm or laurel.
9   **montium domina ut**: the subordinating conjunction introducing the pur-
    pose clause is delayed to third position.
        montium . . . / silvārumque (10) **. . . / saltuumque** (11) **. . . / amnium-
        que** (12): the genitives depend on **domina** (9) and list the places over
        which Diana presides as the goddess of wild beasts and of hunting.
    forēs: = **essēs**; the subject, *you*, refers to **Lātōnia** (5) = Diana.
10 **vireō, virēre, viruī**, *to be green.*
11 **saltus, -ūs**, m., *wooded pasture land.*
    reconditus, -a, -um, [**re-**, *back* + **conditus, -a, -um**, *hidden, concealed*], *hidden,
    secluded.*
        saltuumque reconditōrum / amniumque: line 11 is hypermetric and
        reconditōrum elides with the first word of the next line (synapheia).
12 **amnis, amnis**, m., *river.*
    sonō, sonāre, sonuī, sonitus, *to resound, echo.*
    sonantum: = **sonantium**.

CATULLUS 34

A Hymn to Diana

A chorus of unmarried boys and girls supplicates Diana as a goddess of nature and fertility in a traditionally styled hymn and makes a patriotic prayer.

1 Diānae sumus in fidē
2 puellae et puerī integrī:
3 <Diānam puerī integrī>
4   puellaeque canāmus.

5   Ō Lātōnia, maximī
6 magna prōgeniēs Iovis,
7 quam māter prope Dēliam
8   dēposīvit olīvam,

9 montium domina ut forēs
10 silvārumque virentium
11 saltuumque reconditōrum
12   amniumque sonantum:

continued

Initial Explorations

1. How does the first stanza introduce the hymn?
2. How do anaphora, conduplicatio, and chiasmus contribute to the tone of the first stanza?
3. How is Diana invoked in the second stanza? What is implied or stated about her parentage and her birth?
4. What deities do the adjectives **maximī** (5) and **magna** (6) describe? Why is it tactful for the adjective **maximī** to come before the adjective **magna**?
5. What function of Diana is celebrated in the third stanza?
6. What is the effect of the positioning of words in the third stanza?

13   tū ... dicta (14): with dicta, supply es (cf. es / dicta, 15–16).

    Lūcīna ... / Iūnō (14): Diana is here identified with Iūnō Lūcīna, Juno in her role as goddess of childbirth, a role Juno took over from the Greek goddess of childbirth Eileithyia, who was associated with Artemis.

14   dīcō, dīcere, dīxī, dictus, *to say; to tell; to name, call.*

    puerpera, -ae, f. [puer, puerī, m., *child* + pariō, parere, peperī, partus, *to give birth*], *woman in labor.*

      dolentibus (13) / ... puerperīs: dative of agent.

15   potēns, potentis [often describing sorcerers and witches], *powerful.*

    Trivia, -ae, f., *Trivia* (another name for Diana, as identified with the Greek goddess Hecate, goddess of the underworld and goddess of witchcraft and sorcery, worshiped at places where three roads meet: trivium, -ī, n., from trēs, tria, *three* + via, -ae, f., *road*).

    nothus, -a, -um, *bastard; not genuine, spurious; derivative;* here, *reflected.*

16   lūmen, lūminis, n., *light.*

    nothō (15) ... / ... lūmine: ablative of cause with es (15) / dicta.

    Lūna: once Diana was identified with the Greek goddesses Artemis and Hecate, she became a moon-goddess too. Artemis had already been identified with the Greek moon goddess, Selene. Note lūmine Lūna.

17   cursus, -ūs, m., *course* (here, of the moon).

    mēnstruus, -a, -um [mēnsis, mēnsis, m., *month*], *monthly.*

18   mētior, mētīrī, mēnsus sum, *to measure.*

    mēnstruō (17) / mētiēns: there is an etymological play on words here, since mēnstruus, mēnsis, and mētior are all derived from the same root; the Indo-European root also gave the English words *month* and *moon.*

    annuus, -a, -um, *annual, yearly, of/belonging to the year.*

19   rūsticus, -a, -um, *rustic, country.*

    agricolae: genitive with tēcta (20) or dative of reference (advantage).

20   tēctum, -ī, n., *roof; home; shed.*

    frūgēs, frūgum, f. pl., *grain; produce.*

    expleō, explēre, explēvī, explētus, *to fill.*

21   Sīs: with sāncta (22).

    quīcumque, quaecumque, quodcumque, indefinite adjective, *whatever.*

      quōcumque ... nōmine (22): ablative with sāncta (22), *sanctified with whatever name.* In hymns and prayers, it was common to appeal to the divinity with as many names as possible to be sure to incorporate the right one for the occasion and to include an open-ended appeal as here.

22   Rōmulus, -ī, m., *Romulus* (legendary first king of Rome).

    Rōmulī: with gentem (24).

    sāncta nōmine, Rōmulīque: hypermetric line with synapheia again.

23   antīquē, adv., *in olden times, long ago, of old.*

    antīquē: translate with solita es.

    solita es: from the semi-deponent verb solēre.

24   sōspitō [archaic, religious word from sōspes, sōspitis, *safe and sound*], -āre, *to preserve.*

    ops, opis, f., *help, aid.*

    gentem: take with Rōmulī (22).

13   tū Lūcīna dolentibus
14   Iūnō dicta puerperīs,
15   tū potēns Trivia et nothō es
16   dicta lūmine Lūna.

17   Tū cursū, dea, mēnstruō
18   mētiēns iter annuum,
19   rūstica agricolae bonīs
20   tēcta frūgibus explēs.

21   Sīs quōcumque tibi placet
22   sāncta nōmine, Rōmulīque,
23   antīquē ut solita es, bonā
24   sōspitēs ope gentem.

Initial Explorations

7. Locate the members of an ascending tricolon articulated by anaphora in lines 13–20.
8. Now look at the fourth stanza (13–16), and locate the members of a tricolon in this stanza. Is it an ascending tricolon?
9. What three aspects or manifestations of Diana are celebrated in the fourth stanza (13–16)? To what three Greek goddesses is she equivalent? What three realms are involved here?
10. Which manifestation of Diana mentioned in the fourth stanza (13–16) is elaborated in the fifth (17–20)? How does Diana in this manifestation benefit mankind?
11. What two prayers are expressed in the sixth stanza (21–24)? What is the relationship between them?
12. How is the last word, **gentem** (24), a fitting conclusion for the hymn?

Discussion

1. What conception of the goddess Diana is presented in the three stanzas (9–20) that celebrate her powers, and how does the poet organize his presentation of that conception of the deity?
2. To what extent does Catullus present, celebrate, and appeal to Diana as a particularly Roman goddess?

Meter: hendecasyllabic

1 **Poētae tenerō, meō sodālī, / . . . Caeciliō (2)**: datives with **dīcās** (2).
   tener, tenera, tenerum, *soft, delicate; sensitive; tender.*
   sodālis, sodālis, m. (see Catullus 10.29, 12.13, and 30.1), *companion, buddy.*
2 **velim . . . dīcās**: *I would like you to. . . .* , potential subjunctive (**velim**) introducing an indirect command; supply **ut** to introduce **dīcās**.
   Caecilius, -ī, m., *Caecilius* (known only from this poem).
   papȳrus, -ī, m., *papyrus* (paper made from papyrus reeds).
     papȳre: by metonymy the sheet of papyrus refers to the poem that Catul-
     lus is writing.
3 **Vērōna, -ae**, f., *Verona* (city in northern Italy, birthplace and family home of
   Catullus).
   veniat: supply **ut** to introduce a second indirect command.
   Novī . . . / Cōmī (4): *Novum Comum* (Comum, a town north of Milan and
   about 95 miles west of Verona; the name **Novum Cōmum** dates from 59
   B.C., when Julius Caesar repopulated the town with 5000 colonists);
   genitive with **moenia** (4).
   relinquēns: the subject is Caecilius.
4 **Lārius, -a, -um**, *Larian, of/belonging to Lake Larius* (now the Lago di Como,
   Lake Como, on the southern shore of which was situated **Novum Cōmum**,
   the modern Como).
5 **volo**: iambic shortening.
   cōgitātiō, cōgitātiōnis, f., *thought; opinion.*
6 **accipiat**: supply **ut** to introduce the indirect command.
7 **sapiō, sapere, sapīvī**, *to be wise.*
   vorō, -āre, -āvī, -ātus, *to devour.*
     viam vorābit: an unusual metaphor; note the alliteration.
8 **quamvīs**, relative adv. + subjunctive, *even if, although.*
   candidus, -a, -um (see Catullus 8.3, 8 and 13.4), *white, fair-skinned, pretty.*
   mīliēs, adv. = **mīliēns**, *a thousand times.*
     mīliēs: although this adverb should be translated with **revocet** (9), its
     placement suggests that the **puella** is a thousand times dazzling too.
9 **euntem**: present participle from **eō, īre**; supply **eum**.
   manūs: by synecdoche the word here may refer to arms.
   collum, -ī, n. (see Catullus 9.8), *neck.*
10 **iniciēns**: scanned with a long first syllable.
   roget morārī: poetic equivalent of **roget ut [Caecilius] morētur**.

CATULLUS 35

Go, papyrus, bring my friend!

The poet wants to convey some thoughts to his friend, but he understands his delay.

1	Poētae tenerō, meō sodālī,
2	velim Caeciliō, papȳre, dīcās
3	Vērōnam veniat, Novī relinquēns
4	Cōmī moenia Lāriumque lītus.
5	Nam quāsdam volo cōgitātiōnēs
6	amīcī accipiat suī meīque.
7	Quārē, sī sapiet, viam vorābit,
8	quamvīs candida mīliēs puella
9	euntem revocet, manūsque collō
10	ambās iniciēns roget morārī.

continued

Initial Explorations

1. How is Caecilius described in the first line? Identify the elements of a chiasmus.
2. Note that Catullus addresses the papyrus (2) on which he is writing and not Caecilius. How is this unusual? Why do you suppose he does this?
3. What does Catullus want the papyrus to tell Caecilius? (3–4)
4. Why does Catullus want Caecilius to come to Verona? (5–6)
5. Is there any suggestion as to what the **cōgitātiōnēs** (5) might be and who the mutual **amīcus** (6) might be?
6. What will Caecilius do if he is wise? (7)
7. How is the person of the verb **veniat** (3) dependent on Catullus' addressing the sheet of papyrus instead of addressing Caecilius directly? How does the person of this and the following verbs affect the tone of what is said here?
8. Who may hold Caecilius back in Novum Comum? (8–10) Why do you suppose she would do this?
9. What physical means of gaining her end does the **puella** employ? (9–10) How does the arrangement of words reflect her action?

11   **Quae**: the antecedent is **puella** (8); a relative pronoun at the beginning of a sentence is common in Latin as a link to the previous sentence; translate *And she. . . .*

       vēra: nom. pl., *true [things/reports].*

       nūntiō, -āre, -āvī, -ātus, *to announce.*

12   **dēpereō [dē-**, *thoroughly* + **pereō, perīre, periī, peritūrus**, *to perish]*, **dēperīre, dēperiī**, *to perish;* + acc., *to be madly in love with.*

       impotēns, impotentis [in-, *not* + **potēns, potentis**, *having power* (over), *able to control]* (see Catullus 4.18 and 8.9), *powerless, impotent; powerless* (over oneself), *lacking self-control; wild, violent, raging; uncontrollable.*

13   **quō tempore . . . / ex eō** (14): = **ex eō tempore quō**, *from that time at which;* then do not translate **ex eō** in line 14.

       lēgit: the **puella** is the subject.

       incohō, -āre, -āvī, -ātus, *to begin; to make a sketch/first draft of* (a literary work). **incohātus, -a, -um**, *just sketched out, unfinished, in progress, only begun.*

14   **Dindymon, -ī**, n., *Dindymon* (a mountain in Phrygia in northern Asia Minor, sacred to Cybele, the **Magna Māter**, Great Mother).

       Dindymī dominam: a phrase used to refer to Caecilius' poem, which was about Cybele. Note the alliteration.

       misellus, -a, -um [dim. of **miser, misera, miserum**, *wretched]* (see Catullus 3.16 and for **miser**, see Catullus 8.1), *poor little, wretched; lovesick.*

         misellae: supply **puellae**, genitive dependent on **medullam** (15).

15   **ignēs**: i.e., of passionate love.

       interior, interior, interius, gen., **interiōris**, *inner.*

       edunt: note the present tense; but translate, *(they) have been eating.*

       medulla, -ae, f., *marrow of bones; one's innermost parts, vitals, heart* (as the seat of emotions).

16   **ignōscō, ignōscere, ignōvī, ignōtus** + dat., *to forgive.*

       Sapphicus, -a, -um, *Sapphic, of Sappho* (Greek poet of Lesbos, seventh to sixth centuries B.C.).

       puella: vocative.

17   **mūsa, -ae**, f., *Muse.*

       Sapphicā (16) . . . / **mūsā**: *Sappho's Muse*, = a periphrasis for *Sappho the poet.*

       doctus, -a, -um (see Catullus 1.7), *full of learning, learned; well versed* (in poetry), *discriminating, tasteful.*

       venustus, -a, -um (see Catullus 3.2, 10.4, 12.5, 13.6, 31.12), *endowed/involved with Venus; attractive, charming.*

         venustē: *charmingly*, with **est . . . incohāta** (18); the context also suggests a secondary meaning for **venustē**—*in a manner that inspires erotic passion.*

18   **Magna . . . Māter**: perhaps the title of Caecilius' poem; note the line framing.

       Caeciliō: dative of agent.

11   Quae nunc, sī mihi vēra nūntiantur,
12   illum dēperit impotente amōre.
13   Nam quō tempore lēgit incohātam
14   Dindymī dominam, ex eō misellae
15   ignēs interiōrem edunt medullam.
16   Ignōscō tibi, Sapphicā puella
17   mūsā doctior; est enim venustē
18   Magna Caeciliō incohāta Māter.

Initial Explorations

10.   Is your answer to the second part of question 8 confirmed by lines 11–12?
11.   Why is it tactful for Catullus to include the words **sī mihi vēra nūntiantur** (11)?
12.   How does the description of the love of the **puella** for Caecilius harmonize with her imagined actions described in lines 8–10?
13.   When did the **puella** fall in love with Caecilius? (13–15)
14.   How does Catullus describe the intensity of the love felt by the **puella**? (14–15) Was the **puella** wretched (**misellae**, 14) before or after she fell in love? Why is the word **misellae** placed so early in its clause?
15.   For what does Catullus pardon the **puella**? (16)
16.   Up to this point the **puella** and her actions have been described in the third person. What reasons can you think of as to why Catullus now refers to the **puella** in the second person (**tibi**, 16) and addresses her directly in the vocative (**puella** / . . . **doctior**, 16–17)?
17.   Why does Catullus pardon the **puella**? (16–18)
18.   What word is repeated in the last line from the first section of the poem? What is the effect of this repetition?

Discussion

1.   Outline the poem's structure.
2.   What message is conveyed in the last six lines of the poem?

Meter: hendecasyllabic

1   **annālis, annālis**, m. [**annus, -ī**, m., *year*], *a book of chronicles or annals*; pl.,
        chronicles, annals (in several volumes).
            Annālēs: vocative: *Annals* of Volusius, referring to a verse chronicle writ-
               ten by the poet Volusius, who is lambasted here and in Catullus 95 for
               being a verbose writer.
    cacō, -āre, -āvī, -ātus, *to defecate; to expel as excrement; to defile with excrement.*
    carta, -ae, f. (see Catullus 1.6), *papyrus paper.*
2   **vōtum, -ī**, n., *vow* (a promise to dedicate or sacrifice something to a deity if
        the deity should grant a favor or answer a prayer); *offering or sacrifice made*
        in repayment of a vow, votive offering.
    solvō, solvere, solvī, solūtus, *to loosen, untie; to relax, relieve;* here, *to pay off,*
        discharge, fulfill.
            vōtum solvite: translate **vōtum** in the first of the two senses given in the
               vocabulary entry above.
    prō, prep. + abl., *for, on behalf of.*
4   **voveō, vovēre, vōvī, vōtus**, *to promise* (something to a god in return for a
        favor), *vow.*
            vōvit: echoing **vōtum** (2).
    sī . . . restitūtus essem / dēsīssemque (5) . . . / . . . / . . . **(sē) datūram**
        (esse) (7): *if I would be . . . and would . . . (she) would. . . .* , an example of a con-
        ditional sentence in an indirect statement, here, introduced by **vōvit**. The
        verb in the if-clause (protasis) is in the subjunctive since subordinate
        clauses in indirect statements use subjunctives; the verb in the conclusion
        (apodosis) is an infinitive in indirect statement. The type of the conditional
        sentence will determine the tense of the subjunctive and infinitive. In this
        case, Lesbia's vow was in the form of a future-more-vivid condition: **sī**
        Catullus mihi restitūtus erit dēsieritque trucēs vibrāre iambōs,
        dabō. . . . In indirect statement the future perfect indicatives become
        pluperfect subjunctives, and the future indicative becomes a future
        infinitive.
    sibi: i.e., the **puella**, presumably Lesbia.
    restituō [re-, *back, again* + **statuō, statuere, statuī, statūtus**, *to set; to stand up;*
        to place], **restituere, restituī, restitūtus**, *to set up again; to restore; to bring back;*
        + dat., *to reinstate in favor* (with).
5   **dēsīssem**: syncope for **dēsiissem**.
            essem (4) / **dēsīssem**que: note the play on sounds and the alliteration of
               s's in lines 4–5.
    trux, trucis, *fierce, vicious.*
    vibrō, -āre, -āvī, -ātus, *to fling, hurl* (as a spear or a bolt of lightning).
    iambus, -ī, m., *iamb; poem written in iambic meter* (including the choliambic or
        "limping iambic" meter); pl., *invective verses* (written in iambic meter).
            trucēs . . . iambōs: possibly referring to Catullus 37, a scabrous indict-
               ment of Lesbia's promiscuity, which is written in choliambics.

CATULLUS 36

Good riddance to the *Annals* of Volusius!

*Catullus at a time of estrangement from his **puella** eagerly sacrifices the Annals of Volusius to Vulcan, the fire-god, in fulfillment of a playful vow that his **puella** had made.*

1   Annālēs Volusī, cacāta carta,
2   vōtum solvite prō meā puellā.
3   Nam sānctae Venerī Cupīdinīque
4   vōvit, sī sibi restitūtus essem
5   dēsīssemque trucēs vibrāre iambōs,

continued

Initial Explorations

1. What is Catullus addressing in the opening lines and what command does he give? (1–2) On whose behalf is his command to be carried out? Who is the **puella**?
2. Analyze the first line as a chiasmus. What role do alliteration and assonance play in the effectiveness of the line?
3. What can we infer about recent events in the relationship of Catullus and his **puella** from lines 4 and 5?

6   ēlēctus, -a, -um [ēligō, ēligere, ēlēgī, ēlēctus, *to pick out, choose*], *select, choice.*
     ēlēctissima: with pessimī poētae, the word ēlēctissima creates an
        oxymoron and will mean *the very worst* (Thomson).
7   scrīptum, -ī, n., *writing, written work.*
     tardipēs, tardipedis [tardus, -a, -um, *slow* + pēs, pedis, m., *foot*], *slow-footed.*
        tardipedī deō: the slow-footed god is the limping Vulcan, the god of fire.
     datūram: = sē datūram esse.
8   īnfēlīx, īnfēlīcis [in-, *not* + fēlīx, fēlīcis, *fruitful, productive; auspicious; lucky*],
        unproductive, sterile; inauspicious; unlucky; cursed.
     ūstulō [ūrō, ūrere, ūssī, ūstus, *to burn*], -āre, -āvī, -ātus, *to char, scorch, burn.*
        ūstulanda: modifying scrīpta (7).
     lignum, -ī, n., *wood, firewood.*
        īnfēlīcibus . . . lignīs: firewood from trees thought to be īnfēlīx because
           they never grow from seed or bear fruit; such trees were consecrated to
           the gods of the underworld, condemned criminals were hung from them
           in primitive times, and their wood was used to burn deformed creatures
           thought of as prodigies or monsters (see Fordyce, 180).
9   hoc: supply vōtum.
     vīdit: i.e., *she knew* (that she was. . . .).
10   iocōsē, adv., *in jest, humorously, playfully.*
     lepidē, adv., *charmingly, pleasantly, wittily.*
        iocōsē lepidē: asyndeton.
     dīvus, -ī, m., *god.*
11   ō . . . creāta: O [goddess] created/born. . . . , i.e., Venus.
     caeruleus, -a, -um, *blue.*
     pontus, -ī, m., *sea.*
        caeruleō . . . pontō: ablative of origin; Aphrodite, Venus' Greek counter-
           part, was thought to have been born from the foam (Greek, *aphros*) of the
           sea.
12   quae: supply colis (14): *you who. . . .* ; the first of several relative clauses with
        anaphora naming the various locations at which Venus was worshiped
        throughout the Mediterranean world. In a hymn or appeal to a god or
        goddess, it was common practice to list the names and places of worship
        associated with the particular divinity. The verb colis (14) is understood in
        each clause.
     Īdalium, -ī, n., *Idalium* (a cult site of Aphrodite on the island of Cyprus).
     Ūriī, -ōrum, m. pl., *Urii* (possibly an alternate spelling for Urion [Greek] or
        Urium [Latin], a town in Apulia on the east coast of Italy). Nothing is
        known about worship of Venus there.
     apertus -a, -um, *open; exposed* (i.e., to the elements).
        apertōs: this describes Urii as an "open roadstead, in the nautical sense, in
           contrast to a safe, well-sheltered harbour" (Thomson, 298).

6 ēlēctissima pessimī poētae

7 scrīpta tardipedī deō datūram

8 īnfēlīcibus ūstulanda lignīs.

9 Et hoc pessima sē puella vīdit

10 iocōsē lepidē vovēre dīvīs.

11 Nunc, ō caeruleō creāta pontō,

12 quae sānctum Īdalium Ūriōsque apertōs

continued

Initial Explorations

4. What exactly did the **puella** promise, and on what conditions? (3–8)
5. What might the **puella** have had in mind when she spoke of **ēlēctissima pessimī poētae / scrīpta**? (6–7)
6. Locate elements of humor and wit in the vow as it is quoted in lines 3–8.
7. How does a phrase in line 9 answer a phrase in the vow of the **puella**?
8. What do lines 9–10 tell us about the attitude of the **puella** toward the vow she made?
9. What is bizarre about the vow made by the **puella**? How can it be said truly to have been made **iocōsē lepidē**?
10. What does the word **Nunc** (11) signal with regard to the structure of the poem?

13   **Ancōn, Ancōnis**, Greek acc. **Ancōna**, f., *Ancon* or *Ancona* (a seaport on the central east coast of Italy; a temple of Venus was located there, and representations of Venus appeared on its coins).

Cnidus, -ī, f., *Cnidus* (a city on the southwest coast of Asia Minor; Praxiteles' famous statue of Aphrodite stood in a temple in this city).

harundinōsus, -a, -um [**harundō, harundinis**, f., *reed*], *full of reeds* (reeds were exported from Cnidus and used for the production of paper).

14   **colō, colere, coluī, cultus**, *to cultivate; to live in.*

colis: deities were thought to dwell in the places where they were worshiped.

Amathus, Amathuntis, Greek acc. **Amathunta**, f., *Amathus* (a seaport town in Cyprus and cult site of Aphrodite).

Golgī, -ōrum, m. pl., *Golgi* (a town in Cyprus, famous for its very ancient cult of Aphrodite).

15   **Durrachium (Dyrrachium), -ī**, n., *Dyrrachium* (a seaport in southern Illyria, across the Adriatic from Brundisium and a prosperous trading center).

Hadria, -ae, f., *the Adriatic Sea.*

taberna, -ae, f., *shop; inn.*

Hadriae tabernam: in apposition to **Durrachium**. The town of Dyrrachium is described metaphorically as the *inn of the Adriatic* because sailors would frequently put in there. The town had a bad reputation, and the word **taberna** can be used of a house of ill repute. In Plautus, *Menaechmi* 258–62, the inhabitants of Dyrrachium are described as "the greatest pleasure-lovers and drinkers . . . lots of swindlers, cajolers . . . prostitutes nowhere in the world more blandishing." The word **taberna** has disreputable connotations in Catullus 37, the only other poem in which Catullus uses this word and possibly the poem referred to in the phrase **trucēs . . . iambōs** (above, line 5).

16   **face**: archaic for **fac**.

reddō [**re-**, *back* + **dō, dare, dedī, datus**, *to give*], **reddere, reddidī, redditus**, *to give back; to pay* (a debt); *to render* (ritual offerings); *to discharge, fulfill* (a vow).

acceptum face redditumque vōtum: the words **acceptum face . . . vōtum**, literally, *make the votive offering received* = **accipe vōtum**, *receive the votive offering* (note that **vōtum** is used here in the second of the two senses given in the vocabulary entry for line 2). The words **face redditum . . . vōtum** mean *regard the vow as discharged/fulfilled* (**vōtum** is used here in the first of the two senses given in the vocabulary entry for line 2).

17   **nōn illepidum neque invenustum**: see Catullus 10.4.

18   **vōs**: addressed again to the *Annals* of Volusius.

intereā: here not in its temporal sense, *meanwhile*, but in its adversative sense, *regardless, however that may be.*

19   **īnfacētiae, -ārum** [**in-**, *not* + **facētiae, -ārum**, f. pl., *skillfulness, cleverness, facetiousness*] (compare Catullus 22.14), *unrefinement, coarseness.*

īnfacētiārum: some editors print **īnficētiārum**.

rūris et īnfacētiārum: hendiadys.

13   quaeque Ancōna Cnidumque harundinōsam
14   colis quaeque Amathunta quaeque Golgōs
15   quaeque Durrachium Hadriae tabernam,
16   acceptum face redditumque vōtum,
17   sī nōn illepidum neque invenustum est.
18   At vōs intereā venīte in ignem,
19   plēnī rūris et īnfacētiārum
20   annālēs Volusī, cacāta carta.

Initial Explorations

11.   a.   What is the tone of the poet's invocation of Venus? (11–15)
      b.   How does it display the poet's learning?
      c.   Is it entirely serious, or does it contain some humor?
      d.   Is it a respectful eulogy of Venus' power?
12.   What does the poet request of Venus (16) after invoking her?
13.   What does Catullus mean in line 17?
14.   What does the use of the qualifying word **intereā** (18) imply?
15.   How does line 18 echo line 2?
16.   How does line 20 echo line 1?
17.   What is accomplished by Catullus' violating the symmetry of the opening and closing lines of the poem by adding line 19?

Discussion

1.   What does the poem imply about the present and future relationship between Catullus and the **puella**?
2.   Compare Catullus 36 with Catullus 35. What are some of the similarities and differences?

Meter: hendecasyllabic

1   **quīnam, quaenam, quodnam**, interrogative adjective, *what, just what.*
   mēns, mentis, f., *mind.*
      mala mēns: *mental derangement, sickness of mind* (Thomson).
      misellus [dim. of **miser, misera, miserum**, *poor, miserable, wretched*], **-a, -um**,
      poor little.
         miselle: see Catullus 3.16, **Ō miselle passer!**; here in Catullus 40.1 the
         diminutive suggests feigned pity or contempt.
      Rāvidus [**rāvus, -a, -um**, *gray; gray-eyed*], **-ī**, m., *Ravidus* (otherwise
      unknown).
         Rāvide: line 1 is one syllable too long; proposed solutions are either to
         consider the last syllable hypermetric, elliding with **agit** (a
         phenomnemon otherwise unheard of in hendecasyllables) or to
         presume a syncopated pronounciation of **Ravide** as disyllabic **Raude**.
2   **praeceps** [**prae-**, *in front, ahead* + **-ceps**, from **caput, capitis**, n., *head*],
   praecipitis, *headlong.*
   iambus, -ī, m. (see Catullus 36.2), *iamb, iambic verse of poetry;* pl., *lampoons.*
      in meōs iambōs: i.e., the very verses the poet is writing; the meter of this
      poem is not iambic, but the term **iambī** refers to poetry written as
      personal invective in the manner of the Greek poet Archilochus (7th
      century B.C.).
         Quaenam . . . (1) / . . . **iambōs** (2): note the repetition of *m*'s.
3   **Quis**: interrogative adjective here.
   tibi: take as both dative of agent with **advocātus** and as dative of reference
   with **excitāre** (4).
   advocō [**ad-**, *to, towards* + **vocō, -āre, -āvī, -ātus**, *to call*], **-āre, -āvī, -ātus**, *to*
   summon; to invoke.
      nōn bene advocātus: referring to the belief that an improperly
      performed ritual or an improper invocation of a deity might bring
      divine displeasure.
4   **vēcors, vēcordis** [**vē-**, *without, not* + **cor, cordis**, n., *heart; mind*], *mad, frenzied;*
   mentally deranged; senseless.
      vēcordem: picking up **mala mēns** (1).
5   **An**: supply **hoc facis**.
   vulgus, -ī, n., *masses; public; crowd.*
6   **quālubet**, adv., *no matter how, somehow or other, by any means, at any cost.*
   nōtus, -a, -um, *known, notorious.*
7   **Eris**: supply **nōtus**.
   quandoquidem, conj., *since.*
   meōs amōrēs: the pl. **amōrēs** is used in a concrete sense of a beloved person
      (cf. 6.16, **tuōs amōrēs**, and 10.1, **suōs amōrēs**); the phrase **meōs amōrēs**
      here probably refers to Catullus' beloved Juventius (cf. Catullus 15.1 and
      21.4, neither included in this book); Catullus never uses the term of Lesbia.
8   **cum**: preposition; translate freely, *at the risk of, though it involved* (Quinn).
   longā: of length of time; with **poenā**, = a punishment "that will not be
   quickly forgotten" (Quinn).

CATULLUS 40

You have gone after my beloved!

Ravidus will be notorious as a subject of Catullus' lampoons.

1   Quaenam tē mala mēns, miselle Rāvide,
2   agit praecipitem in meōs iambōs?
3   Quis deus tibi nōn bene advocātus
4   vēcordem parat excitāre rixam?
5   An ut perveniās in ōra vulgī?
6   Quid vīs? Quālubet esse nōtus optās?
7   Eris, quandoquidem meōs amōrēs
8   cum longā voluistī amāre poenā.

Initial Explorations

1. What three reasons does Catullus offer as to why Ravidus is behaving the way he is?
2. What has Ravidus done to offend Catullus?
3. What does Catullus threaten as punishment?

Discussion

1. How does the third reason that Catullus offers as to why Ravidus is behaving the way he is differ from the first two?
2. What suggests a more excited tone in lines 5–6?
3. What is ironic about the last two lines?

135

Meter: hendecasyllabic

1   **minimō . . . nāsō:** ablative of description, as are the other ablative phrases in
     lines 2–4.
2   **bellus, -a, -um** [colloquial, cf. the more formal **pulcher, pulchra, pulchrum,**
     beautiful, handsome, lovely], *handsome, pretty*.
     ocellus, -ī, m. [dim. of **oculus, -ī,** m., *eye*], *little/small eye*.
3   **siccus, -a, -um,** *dry*.
4   **sānē,** adv. (see Catullus 10.4), *certainly, truly, really*.
     nimis, adv., *too much, especially, very*.
     ēlegante: = **ēlegantī.**
        ēlegante linguā: here of elegant speech or wit rather than of physical ap-
        pearance.
5   **dēcoctor, dēcoctōris,** m. [**dēcoquō, dēcoquere, dēcoxī, dēcoctus,** *to boil
     down; to melt down; to squander money; to go bankrupt*], *insolvent debtor;
     bankrupt*.
     amīca: *paid mistress,* = the **puella** of line 1.
     Fōrmiānus, -a, -um, *from Formiae* (a resort town south of Rome).
        dēcoctōris . . . Fōrmiānī: usually identified as the bankrupt Mamurra,
        one of Caesar's generals, who had served in Gaul and whom Catullus at-
        tacks along with Caesar in poem 47 (not in this book); the girl would then
        be Ameana, his mistress, lampooned by Catullus in poem 41 (not in this
        book).
6   **tēn:** = **tē** + **-ne.**
     prōvincia: the Roman province of Cisalpine Gaul, where the woman re-
     ferred to in lines 1–5 lived.
7   **comparō** [**compar, comparis,** *similar, alike*], **-āre, -āvī, -ātus,** *to place together;
     to treat as equal; to compare*.
        comparātur: distinguish this verb from its homonym, **comparō** [**con-** *to-
        gether* + **parō, -āre, -āvī, -ātus,** *to prepare, get ready*], *to buy, obtain; to get
        ready*.
8   **saeclum, -ī,** n. [syncope for **saeculum**] (see Catullus 1.10), *era, age*.
     īnsapiēns, īnsapientis [**in-,** *not* + **sapiēns, sapientis,** *wise*], *unwise, foolish*.
     īnsapiēns: some editors print **īnsipiēns.**
     īnfacētus, -a, -um [**in-,** *not* + **facētus, -a, -um,** *clever, humorous*] (cf. Catullus
     12.9 **facētiārum,** 22.14 **īnfacētō est īnfacētior rūre,** and 36.19
     īnfacētiārum), *boorish, humorless, insensitive, tasteless*.
        īnfacētum: some editors print **īnficētum.**

CATULLUS 43

Hello, girl, with neither. . . .

Catullus describes a girl whom many consider attractive and even compare to Lesbia.

1   Salvē, nec minimō puella nāsō
2   nec bellō pede nec nigrīs ocellīs
3   nec longīs digitīs nec ōre siccō
4   nec sānē nimis ēlegante linguā,
5   dēcoctōris amīca Fōrmiānī.
6   Tēn prōvincia nārrat esse bellam?
7   Tēcum Lesbia nostra comparātur?
8   Ō saeclum īnsapiēns et īnfacētum!

Initial Explorations

1. Specifically, what does Catullus find distasteful about the girl? (1–4)
2. Identify examples of litotes in lines 1–4, and explain why the device is effective.
3. a. What other rhetorical device heightens the impact of lines 1–4?
    b. How is line 3 related to line 2 in positioning of words and sound of endings?
    c. What word in line 4 corresponds to **minimō** in line 1?
    d. Are the bodily features arranged in any particular order?
4. What does line 5 add to the disparaging attack on the girl?
5. What is the tone of the last three lines? What two rhetorical devices and what word emphasize the tone?
6. To what conclusion does Catullus come in the last line? What has led him to this conclusion?
7. How might this poem give us a glimpse of what the poet found most attractive about Lesbia?

Discussion

1. Summarize how Catullus in such a brief span draws a devastating portrait of the **puella** and her lover.
2. Why does the poet mention Lesbia in such an unpleasant context?

Comparisons

With **īnfacētum** (43.8), compare Catullus' use of other words to describe and evaluate the qualities of people and life around him in poems earlier in the collection:

facētus 12.9	**īnfacētus** 22.14; **īnfacētiae** 36.19
salsus 12.4	**īnsulsus** 10.33
venustus 3.2; 13.6; 22.2; 31.12; 35.17	**invenustus** 10.4; 12.5; 36.17
ēlegāns 13.10	**inēlegāns** 6.2
urbānus 22.2	**rūsticus** 34.19

*   *   *

For Catullus' adaptation of the following poem of Sappho, see page 153.

Sappho 31

1 Φαίνεταί μοι κῆνος ἴσος θέοισιν
2 ἔμμεν' ὤνηρ, ὄττις ἐνάντιός τοι
3 ἰσδάνει καὶ πλάσιον ἆδυ φωνεί-
4 σας ὐπακούει

5 καὶ γελαίσας ἰμέροεν, τό μ' ἦ μὰν
6 καρδίαν ἐν στήθεσιν ἐπτόαισεν·
7 ὡς γὰρ ἔς σ' ἴδω βρόχε', ὥς με φώναι-
8 σ' οὐδ' ἒν ἔτ' εἴκει,

9 ἀλλὰ κὰμ μὲν γλῶσσά ⟨μ'⟩ ἔαγε, λέπτον
10 δ' αὔτικα χρῷ πῦρ ὑπαδεδρόμηκεν,
11 ὀππάτεσσι δ' οὐδ' ἒν ὄρημμ', ἐπιρρόμ-
12 βεισι δ' ἄκουαι,

13 κὰδ δέ μ' ἴδρως κακχέεται, τρόμος δὲ
14 παῖσαν ἄγρει, χλωροτέρα δὲ ποίας
15 ἔμμι, τεθνάκην δ' ὀλίγω 'πιδεύης
16 φαίνομ' ἔμ' αὔτᾳ.

17 ἀλλὰ πὰν τόλματον, ἐπεὶ †καὶ πένητα†

Ezra Pound (1885-1972), a modern poet who also found himself at odds with the tastes and values of his time, translated Catullus 43 as follows. How well does the translation convey the tone of the original? Where has Pound taken liberties?

To Formianus' Young Lady Friend
After Valerius Catullus

All Hail; young lady with a nose by no means too small,
With a foot unbeautiful, and with eyes that are not black,
With fingers that are not long, and with a mouth undry,
And with a tongue by no means too elegant,
You are the friend of Formianus, the vendor of cosmetics,
And they call you beautiful in the province,
And you are even compared to Lesbia.

O most unfortunate age!

                    *   *   *

The following is a translation of the Greek poem on the opposite page.

Sappho 31

1   That man appears to me to be equal
2   to the gods, who sits opposite
3   you and listens to your sweet voice
4   close at hand

5   and your lovely laughter, which truly sets
6   the heart in my breast aflutter,
7   for when I look at you for a moment, I can
8   no longer speak,

9   but my tongue is tied, a thin
10 flame has at once run beneath my skin,
11 I cannot see even one thing with my eyes,
12   my ears are buzzing,

13 sweat pours down me, a trembling
14 takes hold of all of me, I am paler
15 than grass, and I seem to myself little
16   short of being dead.

17 But all must be endured/dared/ventured. . . .

Meter: choliambic

1   **fundus, -ī,** m., *farm, country estate.*
    noster: i.e., *my.*
        Ō funde noster: personification, as in Catullus' address to Sirmio in poem
        31.
    seu . . . seu, conj., *whether . . . or.*
    Sabīnus, -a, -um, *Sabine* (i.e., in the territory of the Sabines, a rustic, agricul-
        tural people living to the northeast of Rome, just beyond Tibur).
    Tīburs, Tīburtis, *of/belonging to Tibur* (the modern Tivoli, a fashionable re-
        sort town on the Anio River, eighteen miles northeast of Rome), *Tiburtine.*
        seu Sabīne seu Tīburs: vocative along with **funde noster.** Tibur was
        an expensive resort area; the Sabine hills and farming lands north of
        Tibur were less prosperous and pretentious. The argument in lines 1–
        5 is one of prestige: is the estate in the high- or low-rent district?
2   **autumō, -āre, -āvī, -ātus** [archaic], *to assert, insist.*
        autumant: the subject is the understood antecedent of **quibus;** translate:
        [they], for whom . . . , insist that you (**tē**). . . .
    quibus nōn est / cordī (3): idiom with double dative, *for whom . . . is not to/for
        the heart, is not dear/pleasing.* The subject is the infinitive **laedere** with its
        direct object **Catullum.**
3   **laedō, laedere, laesī, laesus,** *to hurt.*
    cordī est: supply **Catullum laedere** as subject.
4   **quīvīs, quaevīs, quodvīs** [**quī, quae, quod** + **vīs,** *you wish*], *any that you
        wish.*
    Sabīnum . . . esse: supply **tē;** parallel to **tē esse Tīburtem** (2); note the chias-
        tic arrangement of the infinitives and adjectives.
    pignus, pignoris, n., *stake, wager* (offered in a bet).
    contendō [**con-,** intensive + **tendō, tendere, tetendī, tentus,** *to stretch*], **con-
        tendere, contendī, contentus,** *to stretch; to hasten; to assert, maintain; to con-
        tend.*
5   **Sabīne . . . Tīburs:** vocative, as in line 1.
    sīve: = **seu.**
6   **fuī libenter:** *I was glad to be.*
    suburbānus, -a, -um, *located close to a city.*
7   **pectore:** ablative of separation.
    tussis, tussis, acc. **tussim,** f., *cough.*
8   **inmerēns, inmerentis** [**in-,** *not* + **merēns, merentis,** *deserving*], *undeserving.*
    quam: delayed relative pronoun; in normal word order it would occur at the
        beginning of this line. The verb for this relative clause is **dedit** in line 9,
        which oddly interrupts the **dum** clause in that line (an example of hyper-
        baton).
    mihī: the second *i* is sometimes long in poetry.
    venter, ventrī, m., *stomach.*

CATULLUS 44

Ō funde noster. . . .

As if praying to a deity, Catullus addresses his country estate in a poem of thanks that ends with a prayer.

1   Ō funde noster seu Sabīne seu Tīburs
2   (nam tē esse Tīburtem autumant, quibus nōn est
3   cordī Catullum laedere; at quibus cordī est,
4   quōvīs Sabīnum pignore esse contendunt),
5   sed seu Sabīne sīve vērius Tīburs,
6   fuī libenter in tuā suburbānā
7   vīllā, malamque pectore expulī tussim,
8   nōn inmerentī quam mihī meus venter,

continued

Initial Explorations

1. In what two ways do people refer to Catullus' country estate? (1–5)
2. Why do some people refer to it in one way and some the other way? (2–4)
3. What word in line 5 indicates how Catullus would like people to refer to his country estate?
4. How does line 5 echo line 1?
5. Why was Catullus glad to be at his country estate? (6–7)
6. How does Catullus describe himself in line 8? What figure of speech does he use?

9   **dum . . . appetō**: translate the present tense in a **dum** clause as an imperfect when the verb of the main clause is in the perfect tense.

sūmptuōsus, -a, -um, *expensive, costly; sumptuous.*

appetō [ad-, *to, toward* + **petō, petere, petīvī, petītus**, *to look for, seek*], **appetere, appetīvī, appetītus** (see Catullus 2.3), *to seek; to hunger after.*

dedit: hyperbaton, the verb is separated from the rest of its clause in line 8 and interrupts the subordinate clause in line 9, juxtaposing the two verbs. While Catullus desires sumptuous banquets (**appetō**), he is given (**dedit**) only a cold (see Godwin, 163).

10   **Sestiānus, -a, -um**, *of/belonging to Sestius* (Publius Sestius was a senator known for supporting conservative causes and for a dull, frigid speaking and writing style; he was quaestor in 63 B.C. and a friend of Cicero's).

      Sestiānus: take with **convīva**, *a Sestian guest*, an inflated way of saying *a guest of Sestius.*

dum: delayed conjunction, again meaning *while*, but with a hint of cause = *since.*

11   **ōrātiōnem**: a speech written by Sestius.

in: *against.*

Antius, -ī, m., *Antius* (possibly the C. Antius who was responsible for legislation against electoral fraud).

petītor, petītōris, m. [**petō, petere, petīvī, petītus**, *to look for, seek*], *one who seeks political office, a candidate.*

12   **venēnum, -ī**, n., *poison.*

pestilentia, -ae, f., *plague, pestilence.*

13   **hīc**, adv., *here; thereupon.*

gravēdō, gravēdinis, f. [**gravis, -is, -e**, *heavy*], *a head-cold.*

frequēns, frequentis, *repeated, frequent; constant.*

    gravēdō frīgida et frequēns tussis: chiasmus and alliteration.

14   **quassō, -āre, -āvī, -ātus**, *to shake.*

    quassāvit: the two subjects here take a singular verb.

usque, adv., *continuously.*

dum: *until.*

sinus, -ūs, m. (see Catullus 2.2), *fold of a toga; bosom.*

    tuum sinum: i.e., of the **fundus** (1) or its **vīlla** (7); personification again.

15   **recūrō [re-**, *back, again* + **cūrō, -āre, -āvī, -ātus**, *to look after, take care of*], **-āre, -āvī, -ātus**, *to restore* (by medical treatment), *cure.*

ōtium, -ī, n., *leisure; rest.*

urtīca, -ae, f., *stinging nettle* (a plant with small green flowers and stinging hairs, recommended for treating the cough).

      ōtiōque et urtīcā: the use of **-que et** is archaic and an example of polysyndeton.

16   **grātēs, grātium**, f. pl. [archaic, used especially in religious contexts and eventually replaced by **grātiae**], *thanks.*

9   dum sūmptuōsās appetō, dedit, cēnās.

10   Nam, Sestiānus dum volō esse convīva,

11   ōrātiōnem in Antium petītōrem

12   plēnam venēnī et pestilentiae lēgī.

13   Hīc mē gravēdō frīgida et frequēns tussis

14   quassāvit usque, dum in tuum sinum fūgī,

15   et mē recūrāvī ōtiōque et urtīcā.

16   Quārē refectus maximās tibi grātēs

continued

Initial Explorations

7.   Judging from line 9, why does Catullus describe himself as **nōn inmerentī** in line 8?

8.   What does the phrase **Sestiānus . . . convīva** (10) imply about the status of being invited to dinner by Sestius?

9.   When did Catullus read Sestius' oration against Antius? Why do you suppose he would have read it? (10–12)

10. How does Catullus describe the oration? (12)

11. What happened to Catullus when he read the oration? (13–14)

12. How does the description of the oration in line 12 prepare for or explain what happened to Catullus as described in lines 13–14?

13. How did Catullus treat his illness? (14–15)

17   **ulcīscor, ulcīscī, ultus sum,** *to take vengeance on; to punish.*
       es ulta: the subject is the **vīlla** (7).
     peccātum, -ī, n., *error, fault.*
18   **dēprecor** [**dē-,** indicating a reversal + **precor, -ārī, -ātus sum,** *to pray*], **-ārī,**
       -ātus sum, *to try to avert by prayer.*
         Nec dēprecor . . . / . . . quīn (19) **. . . / . . . ferat frīgus** (20): *And I make*
           no prayer . . . to prevent . . . from bringing. . . .
     nefārius, -a, -um, *awful, abominable.*
     scrīpta, -ōrum, n. pl., *writings.*
19   **recepsō:** an archaic future formation from the verb **recipere,** here used as the
       equivalent of **recēperō,** the future perfect; the meaning of the verb here, *to*
       take up again, is different from its usual meaning, *to receive, take back.*
20   **mihi:** note the two short syllables here instead of the single long syllable
       usual in this place. Thomson prints **mī.**
     frīgus, frīgoris, n., *cold, chill; frigidity* (a term for the chilling flatness of style
       typified by the orations of Sestius).
21   **tunc . . . , cum. . . . :** *[only] then . . . , when.*
     liber, librī, m., *papyrus roll* (book in the form of a papyrus roll).
       malum librum: i.e., one of Sestius' abominable speeches written out on a
       papyrus roll.

17   agō, meum quod nōn es ulta peccātum.

18   Nec dēprecor iam, sī nefāria scrīpta

19   Sestī recepsō, quīn gravēdinem et tussim

20   nōn mihi, sed ipsī Sestiō ferat frīgus,

21   quī tunc vocat mē, cum malum librum lēgī.

Initial Explorations

14.   For what two things is Catullus grateful? (16–17)
15.   What was Catullus' **peccātum** (17)? What phrase earlier in the poem is recalled by Catullus' blaming himself for a **peccātum** here?
16.   The prayer as stated in lines 18–20 begins with a double negative, literally, *And I now make no prayer . . . to prevent.* . . . Rephrase and translate it as a positive prayer, introduced by *I pray that.* . . .
17.   Explain how the poet puns on the two different meanings of the word **frīgus** (20).
18.   What words earlier in the poem are recalled by the following words: **nefāria** (18), **gravēdinem et tussim** (19), **frīgus** (20).
19.   Why does Catullus think that Sestius deserves to catch a cold? (21)

Discussion

1.   Consider the poem as a kind of address to a deity. Locate the following:
      a.   Invocation
      b.   Narrative of service rendered by the deity
      c.   Expression of thanks by the speaker
      d.   Prayer
2.   In calling upon their deities, the Romans tried to be as inclusive as possible in listing the deity's names, epithets, or places of worship (see, for example, Catullus 34.9–22 and 36.12–15). How does Catullus work this inclusiveness of epithet into his invocation of his country estate? (1–5)
3.   The Romans tended to preserve archaic words, expressions, and forms in their religious language. Locate examples in this poem.
4.   What phrase and words in lines 17–18 might add to the religious tone of the poem?
5.   In one common form of ancient prayer, the suppliant prays that a god may turn some evil back upon its perpetrator, e.g., "If someone wrongs me, turn the wrong back upon him." How does Catullus' prayer in lines 18–21 fit this pattern?
6.   How is Sestius described and evaluated as a social figure in this poem?
7.   How comfortably does Catullus fit into the social world evoked by this poem?

Meter: hendecasyllabic

1   **Acmē, Acmēs,** Greek acc. **Acmēn,** f., *Acme* (name of a young woman, probably to be thought of as a Greek freedwoman; her Greek name means *summit, prime, flowering*).

       Septimius, -ī, m., *Septimius* (name of a young Roman man; it is not known whether Acme and Septimius were real people or not).

       suōs amōrēs: see Catullus 6.16 and 10.1; the phrase is in apposition to **Acmēn.**

2   **gremium, -ī,** n. (see Catullus 3.8), *lap.*

3   **nī:** = **nisi.**

       perditē, adv., *recklessly; desperately.*

       amāre: dependent on **parātus** (4).

       porrō, adv., *onward, hereafter, into the future, on and on.*

4   **assiduē,** adv., *continually, unceasingly.*

5   **quantum quī:** *as much as [he] who.*

       potis or **pote,** indeclinable adjective + infinitive, *having the power* (to), *able* (to).

           pote: supply **est** = **potest.**

       pereō [**per-,** here of upset or perversity + **eō, īre, iī/īvī, itūrus,** *to go*], **perīre, periī, peritūrus,** *to die, perish; to come to an end; to perish* (with love), *be madly in love.*

           perīre: = **perditē amāre.**

6   **Libya, -ae,** f., *Libya* (name used generally for all of North Africa).

       India, -ae, f., *India* (name used for much of Asia, including modern day India and China).

       tostus, -a, -um, *burned, sun-baked, scorched.*

7   **caesius, -a, -um,** *having gray-green eyes.*

       veniam obvius: + dative; optative subjunctive expressing a wish or prayer, *may I come face-to-face* (with).

8   **dīxit:** Septimius is the subject.

       Amor, Amōris, m., *Love, Cupid.*

       sinistrā . . . / dextrā (9): ablative of place where without a preposition.

           sinistrā ut ante / dextrā (9): the meaning of this refrain, repeated in lines 17–18, has prompted much discussion; most agree, however, that the god is giving his approval of the lovers' vows by sneezing twice. The words **ut ante,** *as before,* may be taken alternately with both **sinistrā** and **dextrā.**

9   **sternō, sternere, sternuī,** *to sneeze.*

       approbātiō, approbātiōnis, f., *approval.*

CATULLUS 45

A Love Duet

"The most charming picture in any language of a light and happy love" —*Munro*

1 Acmēn Septimius suōs amōrēs
2 tenēns in gremiō, "Mea," inquit, "Acmē,
3 nī tē perditē amō atque amāre porrō
4 omnēs sum assiduē parātus annōs,
5 quantum quī pote plūrimum perīre,
6 sōlus in Libyā Indiāque tostā
7 caesiō veniam obvius leōnī."
8 Hoc ut dīxit, Amor sinistrā ut ante
9 dextrā sternuit approbātiōnem.

continued

Initial Explorations

1. Describe the scene as presented in lines 1–2.
2. How do the first two words and the people to whom they refer contrast with one another?
3. How does the arrangement of subject and object in the first line visually undercut the sense of the line?
4. What letter do the words **Acmēn Septimius ... amōrēs** have in common?
5. Septimius describes his love for Acme in a conditional sentence with its protasis introduced by **nī**, *unless* (3). What does Septimius say about himself in the protasis? (3–5)
6. What does Septimius wish or pray for in the apodosis (6–7) of his conditional sentence?
7. How do Septimius' words characterize his declaration of his love? (2–7)
8. Study the alliteration of *p*'s, *s*'s, and *q*'s in lines 3–5. How does sound reinforce sense?
9. For the Greeks, "right" was regarded as lucky and "left" as unlucky; the reverse was true in early times for the Romans, but later they tended to adopt the Greek way of thinking. Remember that Acme is Greek and Septimius Roman and that Acme is sitting on Septimius' lap and facing him. How would you interpret Amor's intentions in lines 8–9?

10   **leviter**, adv., *lightly, gently*.
      caput: i.e., her own.
      reflectō [re-, *back* **+ flectō, flectere, flexī, flexus,** *to bend*], **reflectere, reflexī,
      reflexus,** *to bend back*.
11   **dulcis, -is, -e,** *sweet*.
      ocellus, -ī, m. [dim. of **oculus, -ī,** m., *eye*] (see Catullus 3.18), *dear eye, little eye*.
12   **purpureus, -a, -um,** *purple, crimson; radiant, glowing*.
      suāvior (sāvior) [suāvis, -is, -e, *pleasant*], **-ārī, -ātus sum,** *to kiss*.
         suāviāta: Thomson prints **sāviāta**. Translate the perfect participle of the
         deponent verb with a present tense.
13   **Sīc**: take with **serviāmus** (14), optative subjunctive expressing a wish or
      prayer.
      Septimillus, -ī, m. [dim.], *dear little Septimius*.
14   **dominō**: i.e., Amor.
      usque, adv., *continuously*.
15   **ut**: *as surely as*. Acme's main thought, namely that her love is greater than
      Septimius', is expressed in the subordinate clause introduced by **ut** (15–16),
      and she offers proof of this in her wish or prayer expressed in lines 13–14.
      There is no direct equivalent in English of the fairly common sentence
      structure of **sīc** + optative subjunctive in the main clause and **ut** +
      indicative in the subordinate clause in Latin. To make better sense of the
      construction, Fordyce (207) offers the following paraphrase: "As I hope we
      may serve to the end the one master (i.e. Amor) whom we now own (*huic*),
      the passion that burns in me is far fiercer than yours."
      ācer, ācris, ācre, *keen; sharp; strong; violent; intense*.
16   **medulla, -ae,** f. (see Catullus 35.15), *marrow of bones; one's innermost part, vi-
      tals, heart* (as the seat of emotions).
         ignis . . . medullīs: cf. **ignēs . . . medullam,** Catullus 35.15.

10   At Acmē leviter caput reflectēns

11   et dulcis puerī ēbriōs ocellōs

12   illō purpureō ōre suāviāta,

13   "Sīc," inquit, "mea vīta Septimille,

14   huic ūnī dominō usque serviāmus,

15   ut multō mihi maior ācriorque

16   ignis mollibus ārdet in medullīs."

17   Hoc ut dīxit, Amor sinistrā ut ante

18   dextrā sternuit approbātiōnem.

continued

Initial Explorations

10. What is Acme's physical response to Septimius' declaration of his love? (10–12)

11. How does Acme's declaration of her love for Septimius (13–16) differ from his for her (2–7)? Include in your answer a description of how Acme's wish or prayer expressed with the optative subjunctive differs from that of Septimius.

12. Study the alliteration of *m*'s, *l*'s, and *s*'s in lines 13–16.
     a.   How does sound reinforce sense?
     b.   How many *p*'s did Septimius use in his speech?
     c.   How many *m*'s does Acme use?
     d.   How are these letters related to the names Septimius and Acme?

13. What words in Acme's speech repeat or recall words in Septimius'?

19   **auspicium, -ī**, n., *sign, omen.*
      profectī: modifying the subjects, Acme and Septimius.
20   **animus, -ī**, m., *mind* (as the seat of consciousness and thought); *soul, heart* (as
          the seat of feelings and emotions).
      amant amantur: asyndeton and antithesis.
21   **misellus, -a, -um** [dim. of **miser, misera, miserum**, *wretched; lovesick* (see
          Catullus 8.1)] (see Catullus 3.16), *poor little, wretched little, lovesick little.*
22   **māvult quam**: *prefers* X *to.*
      Syriās Britanniāsque: *[all] the Syrias and Britains [in the world]*; Septimius
          may be thinking of the wealth of plunder available from military service
          on the borders of the Roman empire. Mention of Syria and Britain may
          help provide a date for the poem; in 55 B.C. Crassus set out for Syria and
          Parthia, and Caesar led his first invasion of Britain (see Catullus 11.6 and
          12 for references to Parthia and Britain).
24   **dēliciae, -ārum**, f. pl. [usually pl. in form, sing. in meaning] (see Catullus 2.1),
          pleasure, delight; pet; darling, sweetheart.
          dēliciās facere, idiom, *to find pleasure.*
      libīdō, libīdinis, f., *sexual appetite/desire*; pl., *lovemaking.*
          dēliciās libīdinēsque: translate as hendiadys.
25   **beātus, -a, -um** (see Catullus 9.8), *happy; fortunate; supremely happy, blessed,
          blissful.*
26   **Venus, Veneris**, f., *Venus* (the goddess of love); *lovemaking.*
      auspicātus, -a, -um, *auspicious.*

19   Nunc ab auspiciō bonō profectī
20   mūtuīs animīs amant amantur.
21   Ūnam Septimius misellus Acmēn
22   māvult quam Syriās Britanniāsque:
23   ūnō in Septimiō fidēlis Acmē
24   facit dēliciās libīdinēsque.
25   Quis ūllōs hominēs beātiōrēs
26   vīdit, quis Venerem auspicātiōrem?

Initial Explorations

14.   In what ways does the language of line 19 suggest an army marching out to battle?
15.   In what two ways does line 20 emphasize the reciprocity of Acme and Septimius' love?
16.   Compare the arrangement of words in line 21 with that in line 1.
17.   What is said about Septimius in lines 21–22?
18.   What is said about Acme in lines 23–24?
19.   Identify the corresponding words in lines 21 and 23 and in lines 22 and 24.
20.   Identify the corresponding words in lines 25 and 26.
21.   What is the expected answer to the rhetorical questions in lines 25 and 26?

Discussion

1.   Divide the poem into its three major sections, and divide the third section into subsections.
2.   Septimius and Acme have been described as "spokesmen, as it were, of their sexes." Discuss the way they are portrayed in the poem and evaluate the applicability of this statement.
3.   Some readers have thought that the picture of an ideal love affair presented in the poem is too good to be true and have seen ironic double meanings undercutting its idyllic surface. What elements of irony, if any, do you detect in the poem?
4.   What lines show Septimius' adherence to the saying "Make love, not war"? To what extent did Catullus share this preference?

Meter: hendecasyllabic

1   vēr, vēris, n., *spring.*
     ēgelidus, -a, -um [ex-, *thoroughly; without* + gelū, -ūs, n., *frost; cold*], *extremely*
         cold; having the chill removed, no longer chill.
     tepor, tepōris, m., *warmth*; pl., *warm weather.*
2   furor, furōris, m., *rage, fury.*
     furor: "usually used of human madness and passion" (Godwin, 166).
     aequinoctiālis, -is, -e [aequus, -a, -um, *equal* + nox, noctis, f., *night*],
         equinoctial (i.e., at the spring equinox in the stormy month of March).
             aequinoctiālis: take with caelī.
3   Zephyrus, -ī, m., *Zephyr* (the personified west wind of springtime).
     silēscō, silēscere, inceptive, *to become silent.*
     aura, -ae f., *wind, breeze.*
         aureīs: an archaic spelling of the ablative (of instrument or cause with
             silēscit), scanned as two syllables. Thomson prints aurīs.
4   Linquantur: = Relinquantur.
         Linquantur: Catullus left Bithynia, where he had served on the governor's
             staff, in spring of 56 B.C. (see Catullus 10).
     Phrygius, -a, -um, *Phrygian* (referring to an area in central and north west-
         ern Asia Minor, including the western part of Bithynia).
5   Nicaea, -ae, f., *Nicaea* (one of the two major cities in Bithynia, its rival being
         Nicomedia, the seat of Roman provincial government).
     ūber, ūberis, *rich, fertile.*
     aestuōsus, -a, -um (see Catullus 7.5), *very hot, sweltering.*
         Nicaeae . . . ager ūber aestuōsae: note the embedded phrase **ager ūber**
             with identical endings, the arrangement of noun : noun : adjective :
             adjective, and the repeated *ae* sounds.
6   clārus, -a, -um, *bright; brilliant; famous.*
     Asia, -ae f., *Asia* (a Roman province on the western coast of what is now
         Turkey, famous for its Greek cities such as Pergamum and Ephesus).
     volō, -āre, -āvī, -ātūrus, *to fly.*
7   praetrepidāns, praetrepidantis [prae-, *ahead; very* + trepidō, -āre, -āvī,
         -ātūrus, *to tremble*], *trembling with anticipation.*
     aveō, avēre, *to wish, want, long* (to do something).
     vagor, -ārī, -ātus sum, *to wander.*
8   vigēscō, vigēscere, inceptive, *to grow strong, come alive.*
9   dulcis, -is, -e, *sweet.*
     coetus, -ūs, m., *group, band.*
         coetūs: vocative plural; comitum . . . coetūs: the members of the gover-
             nor's staff, his **cohors**, cf. Catullus 10.10.
10   longē: take with ā domō profectōs.
     quōs: delayed relative pronoun.
     profectōs: referring to the entire journey and not just to its beginning.
11   variē, adv., *variously; by different routes.*
         dīversae variē: pleonasm.

CATULLUS 46

Spring has arrived.

The poet is eager to journey home.

1   Iam vēr ēgelidōs refert tepōrēs,
2   iam caelī furor aequinoctiālis
3   iūcundīs Zephyrī silēscit aureīs.
4   Linquantur Phrygiī, Catulle, campī
5   Nicaeaeque ager ūber aestuōsae:
6   ad clārās Asiae volēmus urbēs.
7   Iam mēns praetrepidāns avet vagārī,
8   iam laetī studiō pedēs vigēscunt.
9   Ō dulcēs comitum, valēte, coetūs,
10   longē quōs simul ā domō profectōs
11   dīversae variē viae reportant.

Initial Explorations

1. What do the first three lines of the poem celebrate and what feelings do they evoke? What does Catullus urge in lines 4–6? What does he state in lines 7–8? Whom does he address and with what feelings in the last three lines?
2. Repetition of words, letters, and sounds is significant in this poem. Why is the word **iam** repeated four times?
3. Words that have the letter *v* in them are central to the poem. Locate these words and describe the pattern that you see in their use. What sounds link words within lines 4, 5, and 9? What prefix links lines 1 and 11?
4. Compare and contrast line 1 with line 7 and lines 2 and 3 with line 8. How does the arrival of spring influence and mirror the poet's state of mind?
5. Find examples of chiasmus in lines 5–6 and 7–8. Why are they effective?
6. Does the tone of the last three lines differ from that of the rest of the poem? If so, how?

Discussion

1. Divide the poem into groups of lines as follows:
    a. 1–3
    b. 4–6
    c. 7–8
    d. 9–11
   How do lines 7–8 relate to lines 1–3?

continued

How do lines 9–11 relate to lines 4–6?

2. Study the poet's use of the following words in the poem: **ēgelidōs** (1), **volē-mus** (6), **praetrepidāns** (7), and **vigēscunt** (8). How is each word especially appropriate and expressive in its context?

Comparisons

The arrival of spring has served as a metaphor for many poets. Read the following excerpts from Chaucer's *The Canterbury Tales* and T. S. Eliot's *The Waste Land*. What aspects of spring and springtime activity do these two passages share with Catullus 46? How are the attitudes of the three poets toward spring similar and how are they different?

As soon as April pierces to the root154
The drought of March, and bathes each bud and shoot
Through every vein of sap with gentle showers
From whose engendering liquor spring the flowers;
When zephyrs have breathed softly all about
Inspiring every wood and field to sprout. . . .
Then off as pilgrims people long to go,
And palmers to set out for distant strands
And foreign shrines renowned in many lands.
                              —Geoffrey Chaucer, ca. 1340–1400

April is the cruellest month, breeding
Lilacs out of the dead land, mixing
Memory and desire, stirring
Dull roots with spring rain.
                                        —T. S. Eliot, 1888–1965

Meter: hendecasyllabic

1 **disertus, -a, -um,** *articulate, eloquent.*
   Rōmulus, -ī, m., *Romulus* (first king of Rome).
   nepōs, nepōtis, m., *grandson; descendant.*
2 **quot,** indeclinable adjective, *as many as.*
   fuēre: = **fuērunt.**
   Mārcus Tullius, -ī, m., *Marcus Tullius Cicero* (106–43 B.C., Rome's greatest
      orator and a contemporary of Catullus; here addressed formally with
      praenōmen and **nōmen,** as if in the Senate).
5 **pessimus . . . poēta:** cf. Catullus 36.6, **pessimī poētae,** possibly referring to
      Catullus.
6 **tantō . . . quantō** (7), *as much . . . as.*
7 **patrōnus, ī,** m., *patron, defender, advocate* (in a court of law).
   patrōnus: supply **es.**

Comparison

Christopher Smart (1722–71)

(Imitated after Dining with Mr. Murray)

O Thou, of British orators the chief
That were, or are in being, or belief;
All eminence and goodness as thou art,
Accept the gratitude of Poet Smart,—
The meanest of the tuneful train as far,
As thou transcend'st the brightest at the bar.

CATULLUS 49

A Thank You Note to Cicero

For what is the poet thanking Cicero? Is he sincere or ironic?

1   Dīsertissime Rōmulī nepōtum,
2   quot sunt quotque fuēre, Mārce Tullī,
3   quotque post aliīs erunt in annīs,
4   grātiās tibi maximās Catullus
5   agit pessimus omnium poēta,
6   tantō pessimus omnium poēta,
7   quantō tū optimus omnium patrōnus.

Initial Explorations

1. What is the effect of anaphora and the ascending tricolon in lines 2–3?
2. What is the effect of the particular way Cicero is addressed in line 2?
3. Locate five superlative adjectives in the poem.
4. Locate examples of parallel word order.
5. Locate examples of letters repeated at the beginning of words.
6. Locate examples of homoioteleuton.
7. What is the structure of the poem?

Discussion

1. What indication, if any, does Catullus give for why he is thanking Cicero with this poem?
2. On the surface, this is a very flattering poem of thanks to Cicero. Some readers have felt that it is ironic. What is there in the poem that could lead one to suspect irony on the part of Catullus?

Meter: hendecasyllabic

1   **hesternus, -a, -um,** *of/belonging to yesterday.*
        Hesternō . . . diē: *Yesterday.*
        Licinius, -ī, m., *C. Licinius Calvus Macer* (a close friend of Catullus, an orator
        and one of the **poētae novī**; see Catullus 14a, 53, and 96).
        ōtiōsus, -a, -um [**ōtium, -ī,** n., *spare time; time free from serious occupations;*
        leisure; idleness] (see Catullus 10.2), *not occupied by business or politics, hav-*
        ing nothing to do, at leisure.
            ōtiōsī: modifying the subject of **lūsimus** (2). Catullus describes himself
                and Calvus spending an afternoon together, when other people were
                engaged in business (**negōtium**).
2   **lūsimus:** *we played/had fun,* the verb is often used of writing poetry and in
        particular of composing playful light verse, as opposed to doing serious
        business in the real world.
        tabella, -ae, f., *board;* pl., *waxed tablets* (for writing).
3   **conveniō, convenīre, convēnī, conventūrus,** *to come together, meet, assem-*
        ble; to make an agreement; impersonal, *(it) is agreed.*
            convēnerat (nōs) esse dēlicātōs: the infinitive phrase is the subject of
                the impersonal verb.
        dēlicātus, -a, -um, *at ease, self-indulgent, frivolous.*
4   **versiculus, -ī,** m. [dim. of **versus, -ūs,** m., *verse*], *a brief line of verse;* pl., *light*
        verse; scraps of verse.
        nostrum: partitive genitive of **nōs.**
5   **numerus, -ī,** m., *number; meter.*
        numerō: = **in numerō.**
        modo . . . modo, adv., *now . . . now.*
        illōc: = **illō,** with retention of a demonstrative suffix, **-c(e),** seen in **hic, haec**
        hoc.
            modo hōc modo illōc: cf. Catullus 3.9, **modo hūc modo illūc.**
6   **reddēns mūtua:** *exchanging [verses] in turn,* perhaps capping one another's
        verses.
        per iocum atque vīnum: cf. Catullus 12.2, **in iocō atque vīnō.**
7   **Atque:** here introducing a following event, *And then.*
        illinc, adv., *from there.*
        lepos, lepōris, m. (see Catullus 12.8), *wit, humor; charm.*
8   **facētiae, -ārum,** f. pl. (see Catullus 12.9, 36.19, and 43.8), *cleverness; facetious-*
        ness, wit.
            lepōre (7) **/. . . facētiīsque:** cf. Catullus 12.8–9 **lepōrum / . . .**
                facētiārum.
9   **miserum:** an adjective suggesting lovesickness; compare the opening word
        of Catullus 8.
        iuvō, iuvāre, iūvī, iūtus, *to help, benefit, relieve.*
10   **ocellus, -ī,** m. [dim. of **oculus, -ī,** m., *eye*], (see Catullus 3.18 and 45.11) *dear*
        eye, little eye.

CATULLUS 50

Inflamed by Poetry

The poet details how moved he was by a literary evening at his friend's.

1   Hesternō, Licinī, diē ōtiōsī
2   multum lūsimus in meīs tabellīs,
3   ut convēnerat esse dēlicātōs:
4   scrībēns versiculōs uterque nostrum
5   lūdēbat numerō modo hōc modo illōc,
6   reddēns mūtua per iocum atque vīnum.
7   Atque illinc abiī tuō lepōre
8   incēnsus, Licinī, facētiīsque,
9   ut nec mē miserum cibus iuvāret
10 nec somnus tegeret quiēte ocellōs,

continued

Initial Explorations

1. a. When were Catullus and Calvus together?
    b. What were they doing?
    c. Where were they?
    d. Was anyone else there?
2. How are the two men and their activity characterized? (1–6)
3. In what state of mind did Catullus depart from Calvus? (7–8)

159

11   **tōtō**: with **lectō**.
      indomitus, -a, -um [**in-**, *not* + **domitus, -a, -um**, *subdued by taming, broken in,*
          tamed], *unable to be controlled, unbridled; wild.*
      furor, furōris, m., *rage, fury; madness, delirium.*

12   **versō** [**vertō, vertere, vertī, versus**, *to turn* + iterative suffix **-sō**], **-āre, -āvī,**
          -ātus, *to keep turning around, to turn over and over.*
          versārer: passive used in middle/reflexive sense, *I was turning myself, I*
              was tossing and turning.

13   **ut essem**: supply **tēcum** from the first half of the line.
          ut tēcum loquerer simulque ut essem: hysteron proteron.

14   **At ... postquam**: **At** introduces the main clause in line 16; **postquam** is in
          delayed position.
      labōre: *with suffering/pain.*
      membrum, -ī, n., *limb* (of the body).
          membra: subject of **iacēbant** (15).

15   **sēmimortuus, -a, -um** [perhaps a Catullan coinage], *half-dead.*
          sēmimortua: hyperbole.
      lectulus, -ī [dim. of **lectus, -ī**, m., *bed*], *little bed.*

16   **iūcunde**: supply **amīce**. In poem 14a.2, Catullus addresses Calvus as **iū-**
          cundissime Calve.
      poēma, poēmatis [Greek loan word], n., *poem.*

17   **ex quō**: introducing a relative clause of purpose.
      perspiciō [**per-**, *through; thoroughly* + **speciō, specere, spexī, spectus**, *to see,*
          observe], **perspicere, perspexī, perspectus**, *to see clearly, perceive.*
      dolor, dolōris, m. (see Catullus 2.7), *pain, agony.*

18   **audāx, audācis**, *bold; reckless, presumptuous.*
          audāx: Thomson translates *over-confident [of my affection].*
      cave: = **cavē** by iambic shortening; the imperative governs the indirect
          command **(nē) ... sīs**, *beware of being. . . .*
      prex, precis, f., *prayer.*
          precēs ... nostrās: = the wishes expressed in line 13.

19   **ōrāmus**: parenthetical.
      dēspuō [**dē-**, *down* + **spuō, spuere, spuī, spūtus**, *to spit*] **dēspuere**, *to spit*
          out; to reject, scorn, spurn.
      ocelle: here as a term of endearment, *dearest one;* cf. Catullus 31.2.

20   **Nemesis, Nemeseōs** [Greek loan word], f., *Nemesis* (goddess of retribution).
      reposcō [**re-**, *back* + **poscō, poscere, poposcī**, *to demand, ask for*], **reposcere**,
          to demand back; exact.

21   **vehemēns, vehementis**, *violent; strong-willed, powerful.*
          vehemēns: scanned as two syllables; sometimes printed as **vēmēns**.
      laedō, laedere, laesī, laesus, *to hurt, harm; to displease, offend.*
      cavētō: the formal future imperative, *make sure you do not, beware of* +
          infinitive.

11   sed tōtō indomitus furōre lectō

12   versārer, cupiēns vidēre lūcem,

13   ut tēcum loquerer simulque ut essem.

14   At dēfessa labōre membra postquam

15   sēmimortua lectulō iacēbant,

16   hoc, iūcunde, tibī poēma fēcī,

17   ex quō perspicerēs meum dolōrem.

18   Nunc audāx cave sīs, precēsque nostrās,

19   ōrāmus, cave dēspuās, ocelle,

20   nē poenās Nemesis reposcat ā tē.

21   Est vehemēns dea; laedere hanc cavētō.

Initial Explorations

4. What were the consequences for Catullus of being inflamed with Calvus' charm and wit? (9–13)
5. When and why did Catullus write the present poem? (14–17)
6. Of what does Catullus warn Calvus? What are Catullus' **precēs**? (18–19)
7. With what does Catullus threaten Calvus? (20–21)

Discussion

1. Catullus describes Calvus and himself with the words ōtiōsī (1) and dēlicātōs (3). How is their life-style characterized in this poem? What would more traditionally-minded Romans such as the senēs sevēriōrēs referred to in Catullus 5.2 think about Catullus and Calvus' life-style here?
2. How does the poetic encounter with Calvus affect Catullus? What kind of language or what metaphor does Catullus use to describe the effect? Compare poem 35.

Meter: Sapphic strophe

1 **Ille:** *That man* (unknown and perhaps fictional).
    mī: take with **vidētur.**
  pār, paris + dat., *equal* (to).

2 **fās,** indeclinable, n., *that which is right or permissible by divine or natural law.*
    sī fās est: *if it is in accordance with divine or natural law; if it is possible.*
  superō, -āre, -āvī, -ātus, *to overcome, defeat; to be superior to, surpass.*
    superāre: supply **vidētur.**
  dīvus, -ī, m., *god.*

3 **adversus, -a, -um,** *turned toward, facing, opposite.*
    adversus: this may be an adjective, an adverb, or a preposition governing
    tē.

5 **dulcis, -is, -e,** *sweet.*
    dulce: = **dulciter.**
  miserō: take in agreement with **mihi** (6), dative of separation (*from . . .*). For
    the word **miser** as a staple of erotic vocabulary, see Catullus 50.9 **miser** and
    8.1 **Miser.**
  quod: *[a thing] that/which [thing],* subject of **ēripit** in line 6.
  omnīs: = **omnēs;** in early Latin and in many of the poets, the accusative plu-
    ral of i-stem nouns and adjectives often ends in **-īs.**

6 **sēnsus, -ūs,** m., *sensation* (i.e., ability to perceive by the senses).
  simul: supply **ac,** *at the same time as, as soon as.*

7 **aspiciō [ad-,** *to, toward* + **speciō, specere, spexī, spectus,** *to see, observe],* **as-**
  picere, aspexī, aspectus, *to catch sight of.*
  est super: = **superest,** *remains, is left.*
    simul tē, (6) **/ . . . aspexī, nihil est super:** *as soon as I [ever] catch sight of*
    you, nothing is left. . . . , perfect tense in the temporal clause and present in
    the main clause = a present general temporal structure, in which we
    regularly translate the perfect tense with a present tense in English and
    to which we may add the word *ever* to emphasize the generality of the
    statement.

8 **<vōcis in ōre,>:** this line is missing from the manuscripts. Editors have
    made various suggestions, such as **vōcis in ōre** (supplied in the text here)
    and **Lesbia, vōcis,** with the genitive dependent on **nihil** in line 7.

CATULLUS 51

Lesbia's Devastating Effect on Catullus

This poem may have been the first in the cycle of love poems to Lesbia.

1	Ille mī pār esse deō vidētur,
2	ille, sī fās est, superāre dīvōs,
3	quī sedēns adversus identidem tē
4	spectat et audit
5	dulce rīdentem, miserō quod omnīs
6	ēripit sēnsūs mihi: nam simul tē,
7	Lesbia, aspexī, nihil est super mī
8	<vōcis in ōre,>

continued

Initial Explorations

1. Three people are involved in the first two stanzas of this poem. Who are they? What exactly are we told about the identity of each of them?
2. What rhetorical figure links the first two lines?
3. What does the poet accomplish by adding the second line?
4. Why does the poet add the parenthetical **sī fās est**?
5. What is the man referred to by the word **ille** doing? (3–5)
6. What is the woman doing? (5)
7. To what does **quod** (5) refer?
8. The pronoun **mihi** (6) is modified by **miserō** (5). Is it better to take **miserō** as an attributive adjective (*from miserable/lovesick me*) or to take it proleptically (*from me [and makes me] miserable/lovesick*)? Why is the adjective placed so early, even ahead of the relative pronoun that introduces the clause within which the adjective functions grammatically?
9. How does the word **miserō** (5) set the poet in opposition to the man referred to by the word **ille**?
10. What words in the first stanza are echoed by **simul tē / . . . aspexī** (6–7) in the second?
11. What contrast is being drawn between Catullus in the second stanza and the man referred to by the word **ille** in the first?

9   **torpeō, torpēre,** *to be numb, be paralyzed.*
       tenuis, -is, -e, *thin.*
       sub, prep. + acc., *under; down into.*
       artus, -ūs, m., *joint; limb.*

10   **dēmānō [dē-,** *down* + **mānō, -āre, -āvī, -ātūrus,** *to flow*] **-āre, -āvī, -ātūrus,** *to flow down.*
       suōpte: the suffix **-pte** intensifies the reflexive possessive adjective.

11   **tintinō, -āre,** *to make a ringing sound; to have a ringing sensation, to ring.*
       auris, auris, f., *ear.*

12   **lūmen, lūminis,** n., *light;* pl., *eyes.*

13   **ōtium, -ī,** *spare time; time free from serious occupations; leisure; idleness.*

14   **exsultō [ex-,** *thoroughly* + **saltō, -āre, -āvī, -ātus,** *to dance*], **-āre, -āvī,** *to leap about, dance; to run riot; to rejoice without restraint;* + abl., *to exult/revel* (in).
       nimium, adv., *too much.*
       gestiō [gestus, -ūs, m., *movement* (of the limbs in dancing)], **-īre, -īvī,** *to desire eagerly; to make expressive movements/gestures; to act without restraint, be elated, exult.*

15   **beātus, -a, -um,** *happy, fortunate; wealthy.*
       et rēgēs . . . et beātās / perdidit urbēs (16): Catullus may be thinking of the fabulously wealthy and prosperous King Croesus of Lydia, whose city, Sardis, was sacked by the Persian king, Cyrus. Croesus had foolishly lowered his defenses by disbanding his allied army and was intending to wait until the next spring and the arrival of additional allied forces before continuing his war against Cyrus. Cyrus attacked Croesus with his defenses down and captured and sacked his city. See Herodotus 1.77 and 79.

9   lingua sed torpet, tenuis sub artūs

10   flamma dēmānat, sonitū suōpte

11   tintinant aurēs, geminā teguntur

12   lūmina nocte.

13   Ōtium, Catulle, tibī molestum est:

14   ōtiō exsultās nimiumque gestīs:

15   ōtium et rēgēs prius et beātās

16   perdidit urbēs.

Initial Explorations

12.   What four debilitating effects does Catullus describe in lines 9–12?
13.   Examine the positions of the nouns and the verbs in the four clauses in lines 9–12. What parallel arrangements of nouns and verbs and what chiastic arrangement can you find?
14.   What letters in lines 9–12 create effective alliteration?
15.   Find a transferred epithet in lines 9–12.
16.   What two words are most effectively juxtaposed in lines 9–12?
17.   How does the final clause, **geminā . . . / . . . nocte** (11–12), provide a fitting climax for the list of debilitating effects? How is the placement of the word **nocte** significant?
18.   What rhetorical figure is most prominent in the final stanza? (13–16)
19.   Point out several ways in which the placement of words and arrangement of clauses in the final stanza parallel the placement of words and arrangement of clauses in the first stanza of the poem.
20.   In the second and third stanzas Catullus has listed ways in which he is physically debilitated and devastated whenever he looks at Lesbia. On what does he place blame for this happening to him? (13)
21.   How does Catullus rebuke himself for his employment of his *leisure/idleness* (**ōtium**)? (14)
22.   How is the effect of **ōtium** on kings and wealthy cities (15–16) a heightened parallel to the effect that looking at Lesbia has on Catullus?
23.   How does Catullus' excessive indulgence in **ōtium** (14) account for his inability to look at Lesbia and listen to her sweetly laughing the way that the man referred to by the word **ille** is able to do?

Comparison

Compare this poem with Catullus 50:

Catullus 50

Hesternō, Licinī, diē ōtiōsī
multum lūsimus in meīs tabellīs,
ut convēnerat esse dēlicātōs:
scrībēns versiculōs uterque nostrum
lūdēbat numerō modo hōc modo illōc,
reddēns mūtua per iocum atque vīnum.
Atque illinc abiī tuō lepōre
incēnsus, Licinī, facētiīsque,
ut nec mē miserum cibus iuvāret
nec somnus tegeret quiēte ocellōs,
sed tōtō indomitus furōre lectō
versārer, cupiēns vidēre lūcem,
ut tēcum loquerer simulque ut essem.
At dēfessa labōre membra postquam
sēmimortua lectulō iacēbant,
hoc, iūcunde, tibī poēma fēcī,
ex quō perspicerēs meum dolōrem.
Nunc audāx cave sīs, precēsque nostrās,
ōrāmus, cave dēspuās, ocelle,
nē poenās Nemesis reposcat ā tē.
Est vēmēns dea; laedere hanc cavētō.

Catullus 51

Ille mī pār esse deō vidētur,
ille, sī fās est, superāre dīvōs,
quī sedēns adversus identidem tē
     spectat et audit

dulce rīdentem, miserō quod omnīs
ēripit sēnsūs mihi: nam simul tē,
Lesbia, aspexī, nihil est super mī
     <vōcis in ōre,>

lingua sed torpet, tenuis sub artūs
flamma dēmānat, sonitū suōpte
tintinant aurēs, geminā teguntur
     lūmina nocte.

Ōtium, Catulle, tibī molestum est:
ōtiō exsultās nimiumque gestīs:
ōtium et rēgēs prius et beātās
     perdidit urbēs.

1. In what ways are Catullus' encounters with Calvus and with Lesbia similar? In what ways are they dissimilar?
2. Compare the effects suffered by Catullus from his poetic encounter with Calvus with the effects suffered by Catullus when he looks at Lesbia.
3. What role does **ōtium** play in the two poems?
4. What resolution of his plight does Catullus envision in poem 50? What resolution of his plight does the final stanza of poem 51 hint at?

Another Comparison

The first three stanzas of the poem at the left below by the Greek poetess Sappho of Lesbos (seventh to sixth centuries B.C.) provided a model for Catullus when he wrote the first three stanzas of poem 51. Compare this translation of Sappho's poem (number 31 in modern editions of her work) with Catullus' poem printed next to it. For the Greek text of Sappho's poem, see page 124.

Sappho 31	Catullus 51

That man appears to me to be equal
to the gods, who sits opposite
you and listens to your sweet voice
    close at hand
	Ille mī pār esse deō vidētur,
	ille, sī fās est, superāre dīvōs,
	quī sedēns adversus identidem tē
	    spectat et audit

and your lovely laughter, which truly sets the heart in my breast aflutter, for when I look at you for a moment, I can no longer speak,	dulce rīdentem, miserō quod omnīs ēripit sēnsūs mihi: nam simul tē, Lesbia, aspexī, nihil est super mī <vōcis in ōre,>

but my tongue is tied, a thin
flame has at once run beneath my skin,
I cannot see even one thing with my eyes,
    my ears are buzzing,
	lingua sed torpet, tenuis sub artūs
	flamma dēmānat, sonitū suōpte
	tintinant aurēs, gemmā teguntur
	    lūmina nocte.

sweat pours down me, a trembling
takes hold of all of me, I am paler
than grass, and I seem to myself little
    short of being dead.
	Ōtium, Catulle, tibī molestum est:
	ōtiō exsultās nimiumque gestīs:
	ōtium et rēgēs prius et beātās
	    perdidit urbēs.

But all must be endured/dared/ventured. . . .

[The rest of the poem is lost.]

1. What are the major changes that Catullus has made in adapting the first three stanzas of Sappho's poem? What reasons can you suggest for his having made each of these changes?
2. What is Catullus doing in writing a completely different fourth stanza?

More Comparisons

Compare Sappho 31 with the selections from other Greek and Latin poets cited below:

1 That man appears to me to be equal
2 to the gods, who sits opposite
3 you and listens to your sweet voice
4   close at hand

5 and your lovely laughter, which truly sets
6 the heart in my breast aflutter,
7 for when I look at you for a moment, I can
8   no longer speak,

9 but my tongue is tied, a thin
10 flame has at once run beneath my skin,
11 I cannot see even one thing with my eyes,
12   my ears are buzzing,

13 sweat pours down me, a trembling
14 takes hold of all of me, I am paler
15 than grass, and I seem to myself little
16   short of being dead.

17 But all must be dared/ventured/endured. . . .

Sappho's description of her physical symptoms served as a model for later poets when describing women falling in love at first sight. Compare the following description by Apollonius of Rhodes (third century B.C. Hellenistic Greek poet) of Medea falling in love with Jason at first sight when she was shot by the arrow of Eros (Cupid) in *Argonautica*, Book 3. Pay particular attention to the underlined words.

> [Eros] put the notched end of the arrow in the middle of his bowstring, and then immediately he drew apart both hands and shot at Medea; speechlessness seized her. He himself darted out of the high-roofed hall rejoicing; but the arrow burned deep in the young woman's heart, like a flame. She was constantly casting glances back at Jason, and whatever sensible thoughts she had fluttered from her mind in her lovesickness, nor did she have memory of anything else, but her heart overflowed with sweet pain. . . . Such was the baleful love that, rolled tightly under her heart, was blazing secretly; her soft cheeks turned pale, then red, due to the anguish of her mind.

Later, Medea, alone in her bedroom, is wracked by the pangs of her love for Jason:

> Her heart within her breast palpitated wildly. . . . And always a pain distressed her within, smoldering through her skin and around her tender nerves and all

the way under the lowest bone of her head, where the harshest pain makes its way in, when never-tiring Eros plants troubles in the breast. (3.755–65)

Her physical symptoms are again catalogued when she has a rendezvous with Jason to give him the magic that will save him from the fire-breathing bulls:

When he appeared, he stirred up the torments of love. And her heart then fell out of her breast, and her eyes of their own accord were covered with mist, and a warm blush seized her cheeks. She lacked the strength to lift her knees forward or backward, but her feet were fixed in place beneath her. (3.961–65)

Another third century B.C. Hellenistic Greek poet, Theocritus, wrote of the love at first sight experienced by a fictional woman named Simaetha for a young man named Delphis. Simaetha describes her love at first sight:

When I saw him, I lost my mind, and my heart was pierced with fire, poor me! and my beauty melted away. I had no further thought for that procession, nor do I know how I got home, but a parching sickness shook me, and I lay in bed ten days and ten nights. . . . And my skin often turned pale yellow, and all the hair was falling from my head, and only my bones and my skin remained. (2.82–90)

She then describes her second encounter with Delphis:

My whole being went colder than snow, and from my forehead sweat streamed forth like damp dew, and I was not able to speak. . . . And my beautiful skin all became stiff like that of a wax doll. (2.106–10)

The Latin poet Lucretius, a contemporary of Catullus, borrowed Sappho's imagery to describe the effects on the body of the overwhelming emotion of fear:

When the mind is moved by a more vehement fear, we see that the whole spirit through the limbs of the body shares in the sensation and that sweat and pallor come forth from the whole body, that speech is impaired and that the voice is lost, that the eyes are shrouded in mist, the ears ring, the limbs give way, and finally we often see men collapse from terror that afflicts the mind. (3.152–58)

Another Latin poet, Valerius Aedituus, writing a little before the time of Catullus, composed an epigram that seems to borrow imagery from Sappho's lyric:

Dīcere cum cōnor cūram tibi, Pamphila, cordis,
    quid mī abs tē quaeram, verba labrīs abeunt,
per pectus mānat subitō mihi sūdor:
    sīc tacitus, subidus, dum pudeō, pereō.

When I try to tell you, Pamphila, the pangs in my heart,
    what I seek from you, the words fail my lips,
sweat suddenly flows over my chest:
    thus in silence, aroused with lust, while ashamed, I perish.

1. What words or phrases in Sappho 31 are recalled as you read the underlined words and phrases in the passages above? In your opinion, do the descriptions of symptoms in the passages above seem to have been written so as to recall Sappho 31 in the reader's mind? If so, what purpose is served by such recall?

2. Sappho's is a female voice, and the descriptions of the catastrophic physical and emotional effects of love at first sight in Apollonius and Theocritus are descriptions of the effects suffered by women. Valerius Aedituus and Catullus adapted these descriptions that had by their time come to be traditionally associated with the physical and emotional suffering of women to describe their own suffering as men overcome by love. What is ironic or paradoxical about Catullus' appropriation to his own situation of Sappho and of her imagery that had become traditional in descriptions of the physical and emotional suffering of *women* falling in love at first sight?

3. How does an understanding of the tradition that lies behind Catullus' portrayal of himself in a female role as victimized by love contribute to an understanding of the unity of poem 51, including the last stanza?

A Final Comparison

Catullus 51

Ille mī pār esse deō vidētur,
ille, sī fās est, superāre dīvōs,
quī sedēns adversus identidem tē
    spectat et audit

dulce rīdentem, miserō quod omnīs
ēripit sēnsūs mihi: nam simul tē,
Lesbia, aspexī, nihil est super mī
    <vōcis in ōre,>

lingua sed torpet, tenuis sub artūs
flamma dēmānat, sonitū suōpte
tintinant aurēs, geminā teguntur
    lūmina nocte.

Ōtium, Catulle, tibī molestum est:
ōtiō exsultās nimiumque gestīs:
ōtium et rēgēs prius et beātās
    perdidit urbēs.

Catullus 11

Fūrī et Aurēlī, comitēs Catullī,
sīve in extrēmōs penetrābit Indōs,
lītus ut longē resonante Eōā
    tunditur undā,

sīve in Hyrcānōs Arabasve mollēs,
seu Sagās sagittiferōsve Parthōs,
sīve quae septemgeminus colōrat
    aequora Nīlus,

sīve trāns altās gradiētur Alpēs,
Caesaris vīsēns monimenta magnī,
Gallicum Rhēnum horribile aequor ulti-
    mōsque Brittannōs,

omnia haec, quaecumque feret voluntās
caelitum, temptāre simul parātī,
pauca nūntiāte meae puellae
    nōn bona dicta.

cum suīs vīvat valeatque moechīs,
quōs simul complexa tenet trecentōs,
nūllum amāns vērē, sed identidem omnium
    īlia rumpēns;

nec meum respectet, ut ante, amōrem,
quī illius culpā cecidit velut prātī
ultimī flōs, praetereunte postquam
    tāctus arātrō est.

Gloria S. Duclos compares the two poems as follows:

> There can be no question of the link between c.11 and what was probably the first poem [Catullus] wrote to Lesbia, c.51. There are formal connections: metrical (both are in the Sapphic stanza which Catullus never otherwise used); word usage (the prosaic adverb *identidem* appears only in these two poems, significantly in the same position in the line and verse but in startlingly different contexts); source (c.51 is a partial adaptation of a poem of Sappho and the final stanza of c.11 hinges on a Sapphic image). These seem to be consciously erected signposts for Lesbia that what was begun in *ille mi par esse deo videtur* is now ended in *cecidit velut prati ultimi flos*.

> There are more than formal parallels between these two poems. The images of c.51 have been deliberately reversed in the fifth stanza of c.11. The first stanza of c.51 creates a picture of quiet enchantment yet distance: a . . . figure

sits opposite Lesbia (*qui sedens adversus*, 3) and gazes at her constantly and listens to her sweet laughter; this in contrast to the poet himself who becomes witless when he looks at her, so powerful is her effect upon him. What has happened to this distant enchantment in c.11? Lesbia is now shown in the closest possible proximity (*quos simul complexa tenet*, 18), not to one . . . admirer, but to hundreds of adulterers (*moechis . . . trecentos*, 17–18), constantly (*identidem*, 19) performing upon them all (*omnium*, 19) sexual acts (*ilia rumpens*, 20). The Lesbia of c.51, who was the passive recipient of the gazes of her admirers, has been transformed into the voracious fornicator of c.11. The repetition of *identidem* underlines Catullus' purpose. In 51.3 it describes *te spectat et audit*—a man watches and listens to you constantly. In 11.19–20, Lesbia has become the subject, not the object, nor does she merely look and listen; she is *ilia rumpens*, and not of just one but of all her adulterers, and all at the same time and constantly (*identidem*). Grotesque pornography perhaps, but effective in expressing Catullus' contempt and hatred.

A comparable change has affected the poet too, between c.51 and c.11. The man who was struck dumb by the sight of Lesbia and was almost on the point of fainting (*lingua sed torpet . . . gemina teguntur lumina nocte*, 51.9, 11–12) has, in c.11, revived and found an all too bitter voice. Yet in c.11 he cannot bring himself to talk directly to Lesbia, as he had done in the earlier poem; he employs the device of intermediaries to convey his message of scorn. The intimate *te* of c.51 has become a contemptuous third person singular in the last two stanzas of c.11 and the simple indicatives have been transformed into the scathing commands of lines 17 and 21.

C.11, then, not only recalls c.51 but is in some ways a response to that earlier enthusiasm. . . . Catullus now truly sees Lesbia for what she is, as he had not when he first gazed on her in c.51. . . .

(Gloria S. Duclos, "Catullus 11: Atque in Perpetuum, Lesbia, Ave atque Vale," *Arethusa* 9, 1976, 78–79)

1. Study the chiastic arrangement of themes in the two poems when set side by side:

Poem 51		Poem 11	
A	B	B	A
Love at first sight:	**ōtium:**	**negōtium:**	Final parting
adaptation	destruction of	travel and	of the ways:
of Sappho	kings and cities	conquest	reminiscence
(lines 1–12)	(lines 13–16)	(lines 1–14)	of Sappho
			(lines 21–24)

2. How does the theme of travel developed in lines 1–14 of poem 11 answer the poet's self-rebuke for excessive indulgence in **ōtium** in poem 51.13–16?

3. How does the message of Catullus' final parting from Lesbia (11.21–24) echo and reverse his description of his original infatuation with her (51.1–12)?

Meter: hendecasyllabic

1   nesciō quis, nesciō quid, indefinite pronoun [only the quis, quid part
    changes form; lit., *I don't know who, I don't know what*], *someone or other, some-
    thing or other*.
        nescio: iambic shortening carries over here into the compound ne-scio.
    modo, adv., *just now*.
    corōna, -ae f., *garland; circle* (of people), *audience, crowd* (it was a common
        sight in Rome to see a circle of bystanders gathered in or around a basilica,
        a Roman law court, to watch a trial).

2   mīrificē [mīrus, -a, -um, *extraordinary, remarkable* + -ficus, adjectival suffix,
    making, causing + -ē, adverbial ending], adv., *in an amazing manner, in
    marvelous fashion*.
    Vatīniānus, -a, -um, *of Vatinius* (Publius Vatinius, whom Calvus prosecuted
        in 58, 56, and 54 B.C.; Vatinius was a tribune of the plebs who sponsored
        bills granting Caesar Cisalpine Gaul and Illyricum, and he served with
        Caesar in Gaul. The trial referred to in Catullus' poem was probably
        Calvus' prosecution of Vatinius in 54 B.C. for illegal electioneering prac-
        tices in his successful bid for the praetorship in 56 B.C. At Caesar's behest,
        Cicero defended Vatinius, and he was acquitted. In two other poems, 14a
        and 52, the latter not in this book, Catullus expresses hatred of Vatinius).

3   crīmen, crīminis, n., *crime, charge*.
    Vatīniāna (2) /... crīmina: *charges against Vatinius*.
    Calvus, -ī, m., *Gaius Licinius Calvus* (82–ca. 47 B.C., an orator, poet, and close
        friend of Catullus; see Catullus 14a, 50, and 96).
    explicō [ex-, *out* + plicō, -āre, -āvī, -ātus, *to fold; to roll*], -āre, -āvī, -ātus (see
        Catullus 1.6), *to make known, explain, give an account of; to unroll, unfold*.
        explicāsset: syncope for explicāvisset.

4   ait, *(he/she) says/said*.
    haec: *these things, the following*.

5   Dī magnī: cf. Catullus 14a.12, Dī magnī.
    salapūtium, -ī, n. [etymology and meaning unknown, sometimes thought to
        refer to a person of short stature; cf. putus, -ī, m., *boy*], *little runt*; [sometimes
        thought to be obscene, derived from salāx, salācis, *overly sexed, lascivious*],
        rake, lecher.
    disertus, -a, -um, *skilled in speaking, articulate*.
        salapūtium disertum: supply est, *the little runt/lecher is*. . . .
            disertum: not as strong a word as ēloquēns. Thomson translates, *the little
            runt can <actually> make a speech!*

7

CATULLUS 53

An Amusing Incident at the Law Court

What is the dramatic situation of this short poem? What did Catullus find humorous?

1 Rīsī nescio quem modo ē corōnā,
2 quī, cum mīrificē Vatīniāna
3 meus crīmina Calvus explicāsset,
4 admīrāns ait haec manūsque tollēns,
5 "Dī magnī, salapūtium disertum!"

Initial Explorations

1. How does the first word of the poem create suspense?
2. Find an example of interlocking order or synchysis in lines 2–3.
3. What word earlier in the poem does line 4 recall?
4. How long is the reader held in suspense before learning what it was that Catullus laughed at?

Discussion

1. Compare this poem with Catullus 50. How do both poems express Catullus' admiration of Calvus? Is the expression of Catullus' admiration diminished in any way by quoting the word **salapūtium**, which may contain a gross obscenity?
2. What does the word **meus** tell us about the relation between Catullus and Calvus? Would it seem that this poem was written before or after Catullus 50?
3. Apart from its meter, what makes Catullus 53 poetic?

Meter: choliambic

1 **leaena, -ae**, f., *lioness.*
  Libystīnus, -a, -um = Libycus, -a, -um, *of Libya.*
  montibus Libystīnīs: ablative of place where without a preposition.

2 **Scylla, -ae**, f., *Scylla* (Catullus has deliberately changed the description of
  Scylla from Homer's in *Odyssey* 12.85–92, where she is a monster that yelps
  like a newborn puppy and has twelve legs and six necks, each with a
  frightening head with three rows of deadly teeth; for other descriptions,
  see Lucretius 5.892–895, Vergil, *Aeneid* 3.424–428, and Ovid, *Metamorphoses*
  14.51–67).
  īnfimus [superlative of **īnferus, -a, -um**, *lower, below*], **-a, -um**, *lowest.*
  inguen, inguinis, n., *groin.*
  īnfimā inguinum parte: ablative with **lātrāns**, translate *from* or *with.*

3 **tam**: anticipating the result clause in lines 4–5.
  mēns, mentis, f., *mind.*
  dūrus, -a, -um, *hard; rough; cruel.*
  prōcreō [pro-, *forward* + **creō, -āre, -āvī, -ātus**, *to give birth to*], **-āre, -āvī,
  -ātus**, *to give birth to.*
  taeter, taetra, taetrum, *horrible, abominable, foul.*
    tam mente dūrā ... ac taetrā: ablative of description, predicate to **tē** (1):
      you, [a creature] with such a. . . .

4 **supplex, supplicis**, m., *suppliant.*
  novissimus, -a, -um, *newest, most recent, latest; last of a series; last before one's
  death; most extreme, utmost, greatest.*
  cāsus, -ūs, m., *fall; event; misfortune.*
    in novissimō cāsū: *in the newest* (i.e., most recent, latest) or *greatest
    misfortune.*

5 **contemnō** [con-, intensive + **temnō, temnere, tempsī, temptus**, *to scorn,
  despise*], **contemnere, contempsī, contemptus**, *to think little of, disregard,
  despise.*
    contemptam: predicative.
      contemptam habērēs, *you held X in contempt.*
  ā, interjection, *ah!*
  ferus, -a, -um, of animals, *not tame, wild;* of persons, *cruel, ruthless, inhuman.*
    ferō corde: ablative of description, dependent on an implied vocative, *[you
    creature] with . . .*

CATULLUS 60

You're not really a beast or a monster, are you?

Only one born from an unnatural mother could be so hardhearted.

1 Num tē leaena montibus Libystīnīs
2 aut Scylla lātrāns īnfimā inguinum parte
3 tam mente dūrā prōcreāvit ac taetrā,
4 ut supplicis vōcem in novissimō cāsū
5 contemptam habērēs, ā nimis ferō corde?

Comparisons

The literary topos that someone who is cruel must have had an unnatural parent, seen here in lines 1–3, has a long history.

In Homer's *Iliad* (16.33–35), Patroclus speaks the following words to Achilles, rebuking him for refusing to be moved by the embassy sent to supplicate him and attempting to persuade him to enter battle again and aid the hard-pressed Achaeans:

> Pitiless one, it seems then your father was not Peleus, the horseman,
> nor was Thetis your mother; but the gleaming sea gave birth to you
> and the towering rocks, because your mind is harsh.

In Euripides' *Medea* (1342–43), Jason addresses the following words to Medea after she has murdered their children:

> [You are a] lioness, not a woman, with a nature
> fiercer than Tyrrhenian Scylla.

Discussion

1. Catullus surely knew both passages cited above. What has he taken from each, and how has he blended the passages together?
2. What other connection is there between Catullus' poem and the passage from Homer and the context from which it comes?

A GLIMPSE OF A WEDDING: CATULLUS 62

"On the morning of the wedding day the auspices are taken and the bride, with her hair arranged in the special style of the *sex crines*,[1] wearing a *tunica recta*[2] bound with a woolen girdle, a flame-coloured veil, matching shoes, and a garland, is escorted by the *pronuba*[3] into the atrium of her parents' house. There the *pronuba* joins the right hands of the bride and groom, perhaps the most significant symbol of the wedding ceremony. Depending on the type of marriage, certain other rites are performed, usually including a sacrifice. The wedding banquet follows and extends until evening. At the sign of the evening star, preparation is made for the *domum deductio*.[4] The bride makes a show of resistance, fleeing to her mother's bosom. She is torn away from her mother and, with two young boys holding her arms and a third preceding them with a pine torch, the procession begins. At the threshold of the groom's house the door is anointed with oil or fat and decked with woolen garlands. The bride makes a final show of resistance and is carried across the threshold into the groom's house."

(T. Goud, "Who Speaks the Final Lines? Catullus 62: Structure and Ritual," *Phoenix* 49, 1995, 30–31.)

1 **sex crīnēs**:	crīnis, crīnis, m., *lock of hair, tress* (Roman brides had their hair parted into six plaits, and as married women they continued to arrange it this way).
2 **tunica rēcta**:	the name of the garment worn by the bride, perhaps so called from the fact that it was woven by a weaver standing upright (**rēctus, -a, -um**) in front of a warp-weighted loom.
3 **prōnuba**:	*bride's attendant*.
4 **domum dēductiō**:	the escorting of the bride from her parents' home to the home of the groom.

Catullus 62 presupposes that the bride has fled to her mother's bosom, and the poem begins with the rise of the evening star. Instead of immediate preparation for the **domum dēductiō**, Catullus has choruses of young men and girls compete in a singing contest, with the girls siding with the reluctant bride and the young men championing the cause of lawful wedlock. When the contest is over, the bride is apparently brought forth from her mother's embrace and is addressed directly along with the groom, apparently by the poet himself. When he has delivered his advice, the poem ends. The **domum dēductiō** would then begin, accompanied by a **hymenaeus** or wedding song.

Meter: dactylic hexameter

1   **Vesper, Vesperī**, m. [from the Greek *Hesperos*, "the evening star"], *the evening star* (Venus).
    cōnsurgō [con-, intensive prefix + **surgō, surgere, surrēxī, surrēctūrus**, *to rise*], **cōnsurgere, cōnsurrēxī, cōnsurrēctūrus**, *to rise up.*
    Olympus, -ī, m., *Mount Olympus* (a mountain range in Thessaly and Macedonia); *Olympus* (the home of the gods); *the sky, the heavens.*
        Olympō: ablative of place where without a preposition.
2   **exspectāta**: *eagerly awaited.*
    lūmen, lūminis, n., *light, radiance*; pl., *rays of light.*
3   **tempus**: supply **est.**
    pinguis, -is, -e, *fat; rich; bountiful.*
4   **dīcētur**: here, *will be sung*; **-tur** is scanned long by diastole.
    hymenaeus, -ī, m. [Greek loan word], *refrain* (in the song sung at a wedding); here, *wedding song.*
        iam veniet virgō, iam dīcētur hymenaeus: the maiden will be brought forth from her mother's embrace just after line 58, and the **hymenaeus**, the *wedding song*, will be sung in the procession to the groom's house that will begin at the conclusion of this poem.
5   **Hȳmēn** or **Hymēn**, m., *Hymen* (part of the refrain sung at a wedding; personified as the god of weddings).
    Hymenaeus, -ī, m., *Hymenaeus* (here personified as the god of weddings).
6   **cernō, cernere, crēvī, crētus**, *to discern, distinguish; to see.*
    innūpta, -ae, f., *unmarried woman, maiden.*
    contrā, adv., *in return; opposite, facing.*
7   **nīmīrum** [**nī-**, negative adverb + **mīrum**, *it would be a wonder if . . . not*], particle, *without doubt.*
    Oetaeus, -a, -um, *of/belonging to Mount Oeta* (a mountain in southern Thessaly), *Oetean.*
        Oetaeōs . . . ignēs: there was a cult of Hesperus, the evening star (= **Vesper**) on Mount Oeta.
    Noctifer, Noctiferī, m. [a Catullan coinage from **nox, noctis**, f., *night* + **-fer, -fera, -ferum**, adjectival suffix, *bringing*], *the Nightbringer, the evening star.*
8   **certēst**: = **certē est.**
    viden: = **vidēs** + **-ne**; note the iambic shortening; the singular is casually used although a group of people is being addressed.
    ut, adv., *how.*
    pernīciter, adv., *quickly, speedily, nimbly.*
    exsiliō [**ex-**, *out, up* + **saliō, salīre, saluī** or **saliī, salitus**, *to jump, leap*], **exsilīre, exsiluī**, *to jump/leap up.*
        exsiluēre: = **exsiluērunt**, indicative used colloquially instead of the subjunctive that would be expected in the indirect question.
9   **temere**, adv., *blindly, heedlessly; without reason, for nothing.*
    pār, paris, *equal; fair, reasonable; likely.*
        quod vincere pār est: [*that*] *which is likely to win.*

CATULLUS 62

A Glimpse of a Wedding

Choruses of young men and girls compete at a critical moment in a wedding cere-
mony. The wedding banquet is over, the bride has fled to her mother's bosom, the
evening star is rising, and a chorus of young men and a chorus of girls are about
to compete in responsive song. The chorus of young men notes the rising of the
evening star and directs its own members to rise. The chorus of girls sees the young
men rising and directs its own members to rise in opposition.

Chorus of Young Men:

1 Vesper adest, iuvenēs, cōnsurgite: Vesper Olympō
2 exspectāta diū vix tandem lūmina tollit.
3 Surgere iam tempus, iam pinguīs linquere mēnsās;
4 iam veniet virgō, iam dīcētur hymenaeus.

Refrain (sung by the guests at the banquet):

5 Hȳmēn ō Hymenaee, Hymēn ades ō Hymenaee!

Chorus of Girls:

6 Cernitis, innūptae, iuvenēs? Cōnsurgite contrā;
7 nīmīrum Oetaeōs ostendit Noctifer ignēs.
8 Sīc certēst; viden ut perniciter exsiluēre?
9 Nōn temere exsiluēre, canent quod vincere pār est.

Refrain (sung by the guests at the banquet):

10 Hȳmēn ō Hymenaee, Hymēn ades ō Hymenaee!

continued

Explorations

1. What similarities can you detect between the words of the two choruses? How does the chorus of girls model its words on those of the chorus of young men? (1–4 and 6–9)
2. What different attitudes do the two choruses take toward the evening star in their descriptions of it? (1–2 and 7)
3. How does the chorus of girls regard the young men's actions? (6–9)

11   **aequālis, aequālis,** m./f., *age-mate.*

       palma, -ae, f., *palm* (of the hand); *palm-tree; palm branch* (awarded for victory in a contest); *victory.*

       parātus, -a, -um, *ready, prepared; ready at hand.*

12   **aspiciō** [**ad-,** *to, toward* + **speciō, specere, spexī, spectus,** *to see, observe*], **aspicere, aspexī, aspectus,** *to look at; to look.*

       ut, adv., *how.*

         ut: delayed exclamatory adverb.

       meditor, -ārī, -ātus sum, *to think about, ponder; to plan, prepare; to rehearse.*

         meditāta: *the things they have rehearsed;* the perfect passive participle of this deponent verb is often passive in meaning.

       requīrō [**re-,** *again* + **quaerō, quaerere, quaesīvī, quaesītus,** *to seek, look for*], **requīrere, requīsīvī, requīsītus,** *to ask, inquire; to seek out, look/search for.*

         requīrunt: indicative (cf. **exsiluēre** in line 8); the **ut** clause here does not depend grammatically on **aspicite,** but the latter is simply a parenthetical interjection.

13   **memorābilis, -is, -e,** *worthy of being recorded, remarkable, memorable.*

         memorābile quod sit: relative clause of characteristic; note the delayed relative pronoun = [**id**] **quod memorābile sit.**

14   **nec mīrum:** *and no wonder;* cf. **nīmīrum** (7).

       penitus, adv., *deep within.*

       quae . . . labōrant: delayed relative pronoun; the relative clause here expresses cause, *since they. . . . ,* and would normally have its verb in the subjunctive.

15   **aliō . . . aliō:** *in one direction . . . in another direction; one way . . . another.*

       dīvidō, dīvidere, dīvīsī, dīvīsus, *to divide.*

       auris, auris, f., *ear.*

         aliō mentēs, aliō dīvīsimus aurēs: in contrast to the girls, who are inwardly concentrating all of their mental effort, the young men's attention is divided between their thoughts and what they hear.

16   **iūs, iūris,** n., *law.*

         iūre: ablative, *rightly, justly.*

       amat victōria cūram: a proverbial expression.

17   **saltem,** adv., *at least.*

       convertō [**con-,** intensive prefix + **vertō, vertere, vertī, versus,** *to turn*], *to turn* (upside down or around); *to direct, concentrate* (one's mind).

18   **dīcere:** *to sing.*

Chorus of Young Men:

11   Nōn facilis nōbīs, aequālēs, palma parāta est;
12   aspicite, innūptae sēcum ut meditāta requīrunt.
13   Nōn frūstrā meditantur: habent memorābile quod sit;
14   nec mīrum, penitus quae tōtā mente labōrant.
15   Nōs aliō mentēs, aliō dīvīsimus aurēs;
16   iūre igitur vincēmur: amat victōria cūram.
17   Quārē nunc animōs saltem convertite vestrōs;
18   dīcere iam incipient, iam respondēre decēbit.

Refrain (sung by the guests at the banquet):

19   Hȳmēn ō Hymenaee, Hymēn ades ō Hymenaee!

continued

Explorations

4.   How do the opening remarks of the chorus of young men (11–14) relate to what the chorus of girls has just said?
5.   How does the attitude of the girls toward the singing match, as the young men perceive it, differ from that of the young men themselves? (12–17)

20   **Hesperus, -ī,** m. [from the Greek *Hesperos*, "the evening star"; cf. **Vesper**, 1],
      Hesperus (the evening star).
      quis: interrogative adjective here instead of the usual **quī**; take with **ignis.**
      caelō: = **in caelō.**
      fertur: *is carried/borne.*

21   **Quī . . . possīs:** relative clause expressing cause, with the subjunctive, as
      normal; **possīs,** *have the heart to, can bear to* (Fordyce).
      nāta, -ae, f., *daughter.*
      complexū: ablative of separation.
      āvellō [ab-, *away* + **vellō, vellere, vellī** or **volsī** or **vulsī, volsus** or **vulsus,** *to*
      pull, pluck], **āvellere, āvellī** or **āvolsī** or **āvulsī, āvolsus** or **āvulsus,** *to*
      pull/pluck/tear away.

22   **retineō [re-,** *back* + **teneō, tenēre, tenuī, tentus,** *to hold, grasp*], *to hold back, hold*
      fast; to cling.

23   **ārdentī:** i.e., with passion or lust.

24   **captā . . . urbe:** ablative absolute expressing time, not comparative ablative
      with **crūdēlius.**

26   **caelō:** = **in caelō.**

27   **firmō, -āre, -āvī, -ātus,** *to make strong, reinforce, establish, confirm.*
      Quī . . . firmēs: see note to line 21.
      cōnūbium, -ī, n. [**con-,** *together* + **nūbō, nūbere, nūpsī, nūptūrus,** *to marry*],
      marriage.

28   **pangō, pangere, pepigī, pactus,** *to set, fix; to arrange* (a matter such as a
      wedding).
      pepigēre: = **pepigērunt.**

29   **prius quam:** *earlier than* = **priusquam,** conj., *before.*
      ārdor, ārdōris, m. (see Catullus 2.8), *heat; fire.*

30   **Quid:** with **optātius.**
      dīvus, -ī, m., *god.*
      fēlīx, fēlīcis, *fruitful; lucky; blissful; prosperous; happy.*
      fēlīcī: keep all the meanings of this word in mind here.
      optātus, -a, -um, *desired, welcome.*

The chorus of girls begins the singing match:

20   Hespere, quis caelō fertur crūdēlior ignis?
21   Quī nātam possīs complexū āvellere mātris,
22   complexū mātris retinentem āvellere nātam,
23   et iuvenī ārdentī castam dōnāre puellam.
24   Quid faciunt hostēs captā crūdēlius urbe?

Refrain (sung by the guests at the banquet):

25   Hȳmēn ō Hymenaee, Hymēn ades ō Hymenaee!

The chorus of young men replies:

26   Hespere, quis caelō lūcet iūcundior ignis?
27   Quī dēspōnsa tuā firmēs cōnūbia flammā,
28   quae pepigēre virī, pepigērunt ante parentēs,
29   nec iūnxēre prius quam sē tuus extulit ārdor.
30   Quid datur ā dīvīs fēlīcī optātius hōrā?

Refrain (sung by the guests at the banquet):

31   Hȳmēn ō Hymenaee, Hymēn ades ō Hymenaee!

continued

Explorations

6.   How do the girls' and the young men's conceptions of Hesperus differ, and
      how does this reflect their different attitudes toward the institution of
      marriage? (20–24 and 26–30)
7.   What words do the young men repeat from the girls' song in the same
      metrical positions? (20–24 and 26–30) What phrase of the girls do the young
      men reflect in their words **fēlīcī optātius hōrā** (30)?
8.   How do the changes that the young men make in lines 26 and 30 as they
      echo lines 20 and 24 of the girls reflect their different view of marriage from
      that of the girls?
9.   Analyze the relationship between word-placement and meaning in lines
      21–23.
10.   How does the chorus of young men in lines 27–29 respond to the
      apprehension and anxiety over marriage expressed by the girls in lines 21–
      24?

33   **namque**, conj., *for.*
     adventus, -ūs, m., *arrival.*
     custōdia, -ae, f., *protection, defense;* concrete, *a guard, watchman.*
34   **revertor** [re-, *back* + **vertō, vertere, vertī, versus**, *to turn*], **revertī, reversus
     sum**, *to turn around; to return.*
35   **mūtō, -āre, -āvī, -ātus**, *to change.*
     comprendō [con-, *together* or intensive + **prendō, prendere, prendī, prēn-
     sus**, *to take hold of*], *to take hold of; to catch.*
     Eōus, -ī, m. [**Ēōs**, f. (Greek loan word), *Dawn*], Eous, *the morning star* (Venus
     appears in the evening as the evening star and in the morning as the
     morning star, thus **īdem**, line 34, but it does this at different times of the
     year, not one evening and the next morning as is implied here).
          Eōus: in apposition to the subject of **comprendis**, *you catch [as] the
          morning star.*
36   **lubet**: archaic for **libet**, impersonal + dat., *(it) is pleasing* (to).
     fictus, -a, -um, *made up, pretended, feigned.*
     carpō, carpere, carpsī, carptus, *to pluck, pick; to criticize, carp at.*
     questus, -ūs, m., *complaint.*
37   **sī carpunt**: supply **tē**, the implied antecedent of **quem**.
     tacitus, -a, -um, *silent, quiet; secret.*

The chorus of girls compares Hesperus to a thief; only the first line of the stanza has survived:

32   Hesperus ē nōbīs, aequālēs, abstulit ūnam.

32b .   .   .   .

32c .   .   .   .

32d .   .   .   .

32e .   .   .   .

32f .   .   .   .

Refrain (sung by the guests at the banquet):

32g <Hȳmēn ō Hymenaee, Hymēn ades ō Hymenaee!>

The chorus of young men, in a stanza missing its first line, replies that when evening comes guards are wakeful and that the evening star, when appearing as the morning star, catches thieves:

32h .   .   .   .

33   namque tuō adventū vigilat custōdia semper.

34   Nocte latent fūrēs, quōs īdem saepe revertēns,

35   Hespere, mūtātō comprendis nōmine Eōus.

36   At lubet innūptīs fictō tē carpere questū.

37   Quid tum, sī carpunt, tacitā quem mente requīrunt?

Refrain (sung by the guests at the banquet):

38   Hȳmēn ō Hymenaee, Hymēn ades ō Hymenaee!

continued

Explorations

11.   How does the girls' comparison of Hesperus to a thief (32) relate to their earlier description of Hesperus' actions (20–24)?

12.   How does the part of the young men's reply preserved in lines 33–35 counter the girls' complaint that Hesperus is a thief?

13.   Of what do the young men accuse the girls in lines 36–37?

39   **saepiō, saepīre, saepsī, saeptus,** *to surround, enclose.*
       sēcrētus, -a, -um, *set apart; secret, hidden.*
       nāscor, nāscī, nātus sum, *to be born; to grow.*
       hortus, -ī, m., *garden;* pl., *pleasure-garden.*

40   **ignōtus, -a, -um,** *unknown.*
       convellō [con-, intensive prefix + **vellō, vellere, vellī** or **volsī** or **vulsī,**
         volsus or **vulsus,** *to pull, pluck*], **convellere, convellī, convolsus** or
         convulsus, *to pull/tear up, uproot.*
       arātrum, -ī, n., *plow.*

41   **mulceō, mulcēre, mulsī, mulsus,** *to touch lightly, caress.*
       aura, -ae, f., *breeze.*
       firmō, -āre, -āvī, -ātus, *to strengthen.*
       ēducō, -āre, -āvī, -ātus, *to bring up, nurture.*

41b   A line may have been lost from the manuscripts here or elsewhere in this
       section.

42   **optāvēre:** = **optāvērunt;** here and below, the gnomic perfect, a Greek usage,
       expressing a general truth; translate as present.

43   **tenuis, -is, -e,** *thin.*
       dēflōrēscō [dē-, *down* or expressing reversal + **flōreō, -ēre, -uī,** *to bloom* +
         -scō, inceptive suffix], **dēflōrēscere, dēflōruī,** inceptive, *to lose its blossom.*
       unguis, unguis, m., *fingernail.*

45   **dum . . . dum:** *as long as . . . so long.*
       intāctus, -a, -um, *untouched.*
       suīs: i.e., her friends, such as the young men and girls mentioned in line 47.

46   **castum . . . flōrem:** = **castitātis flōrem,** *the flower of her chastity.*
       āmittō [ab-, *away* + **mittō, mittere, mīsī, missus,** *to send, let go*], **āmittere,**
         āmīsī, āmissus, *to send away; to lose.*
       polluō, polluere, polluī, pollūtus, *to stain, violate, sully.*

The chorus of girls begins another theme:

39   Ut flōs in saeptīs sēcrētus nāscitur hortīs,

40   ignōtus pecorī, nūllō convolsus arātrō,

41   quem mulcent aurae, firmat sōl, ēducat imber;

41b   \<iam iam\>   .   .   .   .   .

42   multī illum puerī, multae optāvēre puellae:

43   īdem cum tenuī carptus dēflōruit unguī,

44   nūllī illum puerī, nūllae optāvēre puellae:

45   sīc virgō, dum intācta manet, dum cāra suīs est;

46   cum castum āmīsit pollūtō corpore flōrem,

47   nec puerīs iūcunda manet, nec cāra puellīs.

Refrain (sung by the guests at the banquet):

48   Hȳmēn ō Hymenaee, Hymēn ades ō Hymenaee!

continued

Explorations

14.   What is the final argument against marriage that the girls make? (39–47)

15.   The girls develop an elaborate simile comparing virginity or a virgin girl to a flower. How do details of the simile recall objections that the chorus of girls has already leveled against marriage? How do details of the simile counter what the young men have said in defense of the institution of marriage?

Comparison

The comparison of the maiden to a flower contained in the lines above may have been suggested to Catullus by the same Sapphic image that suggested the image of the flower cut down by the passing plow in Catullus 11.22–24. (See Catullus 11 above, Discussion question 3.) This image is contained in Sappho fragment 105c:

> like the hyacinth that shepherds trample under foot in the mountains, and the purple flower \<lies crushed\> on the ground. . . .

As Gloria S. Duclos explains: "In the Sapphic fragment, the hyacinth trampled by the shepherds is presumably likened to a maiden's virginity. The passage in c.62 explicitly compares the plucked flower to a girl's maidenhood. The image, then, is traditionally used to express the finality of a girl's loss of her virginity."

(Gloria S. Duclos, "Catullus 11: Atque in perpetuum, Lesbia, ave atque vale," *Arethusa* 9, 1976, 86)

49   **viduus, -a, -um,** *lacking a husband/wife;* of a grape vine, *not trained* (on a prop
     or a tree to support it), *not married* (to a prop or a tree to support it), *unwed.*
     nūdus, -a, -um, *naked;* of a field, *bare, open* (i.e., without trees on which
     grapevines could be trained).
     vītis, vītis, f., *grapevine.*
     arvum, -ī, n., *plowed field.*
50   **extollō [ex-,** *out* + **tollō, tollere, sustulī, sublātus,** *to lift, raise*], **extollere,** *to lift
     up.*
     mītis, -is, -e, *gentle;* of fruit, *sweet and juicy.*
51   **tener, tenera, tenerum,** *tender, delicate.*
     prōnus, -a, -um, *leaning forward, bending down, downward leaning.*
     dēflectō [dē-, *down* + **flectō, flectere, flexī, flexus,** *to bend*], **dēflectere,**
     dēflexī, dēflexus, *to bend down.*
     pondus, ponderis, n., *weight.*
     prōnō: transferred epithet.
52   **iam iam:** *now [it] all but.*
     contingō [con-, intensive + **tangō, tangere, tetigī, tāctus,** *to touch*], **contin-
     gere, contigī, contāctus,** *to touch.*
     rādīx, rādīcis, f., *root.*
     flagellum, -ī, n. [dim. of **flagrum, -ī,** n., *whip*], *whip; shoot* (of a grapevine).
53   **agricola, -ae,** m., *farmer.*
     coluēre: see note on **optāvēre** (42).
     iuvencus, -ī, m., *young bull/ox.*
54   **eadem:** supply **vītis** from line 49.
     ulmus, -ī, f., *elm tree.*
     marītō: noun, *[as its] husband,* in apposition to **ulmō** (feminine); the elm tree
     is thought of metaphorically as the husband and the grape-vine as its wife,
     clinging to it. Thomson prints **marītā,** adjective, *married,* modifying **ulmō**
     (feminine)
56   **innūpta:** the manuscripts have **intācta** here, parallel to its appearance in line
     45, but we may substitute **innūpta** from the fact that the ancient writer on
     education, Quintilian (9.3.16), gives line 45 as **dum innūpta manet, dum
     cāra suīs est,** probably quoting from memory and confusing lines 45 and
     56, putting **innūpta** in line 45 where it does not belong because he
     remembered the word from line 56 where it does belong.
     incultus, -a, -um, of land or plants, *not cultivated;* of people, *unadorned; un-
     courted; not cultivated/untended* (by relatives, friends, or acquaintances).
     senēscō senēscere, senuī, inceptive, *to grow old.*
57   **pār, paris** (cf. 9), *equal; similar; matching; well-matched.*
     cōnūbium, -ī, n., *marriage; a marriage partner.*
     cōnūbium: scan as three syllables with consonantal *i.*
     mātūrus, -a, -um, *ripe; fully-grown;* of time, *due, proper.*
     adipīscor, adipīscī, adeptus sum, *to get, obtain.*
58   **invīsus, -a, -um,** *hateful.*
     invīsa parentī: daughters were thought of as burdens on their fathers.

The chorus of young men replies:

49 Ut vidua in nūdō vītis quae nāscitur arvō,

50 numquam sē extollit, numquam mītem ēducat ūvam,

51 sed tenerum prōnō dēflectēns pondere corpus

52 iam iam contingit summum rādīce flagellum;

53 hanc nūllī agricolae, nūllī coluēre iuvencī:

54 at sī forte eadem est ulmō coniūncta marītō,

55 multī illam agricolae, multī coluēre iuvencī:

56 sīc virgō, dum innūpta manet, dum inculta senēscit;

57 cum pār cōnūbium mātūrō tempore adepta est,

58 cāra virō magis et minus est invīsa parentī.

Refrain (sung by the guests at the banquet):

58b <Hȳmēn ō Hymenaee, Hymēn ades ō Hymenaee!>

continued

Explorations

16. The young men reply by proposing a different simile. To what do they compare an unwed maiden?

17. The young men in their reply repeat many of the words of the girls, usually in the same metrical positions. Locate all such repetitions. In a number of cases the young men echo words, phrases, and lines from the song of the girls but vary them by substituting different words. Locate all such echoes.

18. How does the simile of the vine reverse the implications of the simile of the flower to present a positive rather than a negative conception of marriage?

59 **est tua**: these words complete the meaning of the previous line, which has been lost; the subject may have been **virginitās** (see line 62). There is disagreement among editors as to how to restore Catullus' Latin here. The manuscripts have **et tua nec** and **et tū nec**; the Oxford Classical Text has **Et tū nē**; others read **At tū nē**. We follow Goud's suggestion of **est tua, nec**.
nec pugnā: *and don't. . . .* ; a form of negative imperative.

60 **aequus, -a, -um**, *level; equal; fair, right.*
aequum est, idiom, *it is right.*
pater cui: delayed relative, lacking an antecedent; expand the line as follows: **Nōn aequum est pugnāre [cum eō] cui pater [tē] trādidit ipse.**
The verb **pugnāre** can take a prepositional phrase (**cum** + abl.), as in line 59 and as suggested here, or a dative as in line 64 below.

62 **virginitās, virginitātis**, f., *virginity.*
parentum: possessive genitive.

63 **patrīst**: = **patrī est**, dative of the possessor; Thomson prints **patris est**.

65 **gener, generī**, m., *son-in-law.*
iūs, iūris, n., *law; claims; rights.*
dōs, dōtis, f., *dowry* (wealth given by the father of a bride to her husband at marriage).

The bride is brought forth from the embrace of her mother, and the poet addresses her in the presence of the groom (the first line of this passage is missing):

58c   .   .   .   .

59   est tua, nec pugnā cum tālī coniuge, virgō.

60   Nōn aequum est pugnāre, pater cui trādidit ipse,

61   ipse pater cum mātre, quibus parēre necesse est.

62   Virginitās nōn tōta tua est, ex parte parentum est,

63   tertia pars patrīst, pars est data tertia mātrī,

64   tertia sōla tua est: nōlī pugnāre duōbus,

65   quī generō sua iūra simul cum dōte dedērunt.

Refrain (sung by the guests at the banquet, with the bride and groom joining in this time):

66   Hȳmēn ō Hymenaee, Hymēn ades ō Hymenaee!

The poem over, the wedding procession to the house of the groom would begin, accompanied by the **hymenaeus** *or wedding song.*

Explorations

19.   Which side of the singing match does the poet appear to favor here? Is there a winner and a loser? How does this stanza correspond to the stanza spoken by the chorus of young men in lines 11–18?

20.   What explanation does the poet give for why the bride should not fight against marriage but should obey her parents?

21.   What relationship does the explanation that the poet gives to the bride have to concerns expressed by the choruses in the singing match?

22.   How may the structure of the entire poem be diagrammed?

Ariadne's Lament: Catullus 64.50–253

These lines from Catullus 64 describe the coverlet that was spread on the bridal bed of Peleus and Thetis, the parents of the great Homeric hero, Achilles. Pictured is Ariadne, the daughter of King Minos of Crete. She is the young woman who fell in love with the Athenian hero Theseus when he came to Crete to confront the Minotaur, half-man and half-bull, in the labyrinth. Theseus, on his voyage back to Athens with Ariadne after successfully completing his mission with her help, has just abandoned her on the island of Dia. She laments his cruelty and faithlessness as she watches him sail away and calls down a curse upon him, which is fulfilled when Theseus approaches Athens, having forgotten to change the sails on his ship to let his father know that he was returning alive. His father, in despair, commits suicide.

*　　*　　*

In this selection from Catullus 64 there are a number of words that have a special prominence in the verbal and thematic texture of the poem, such as the word **immemor**, *forgetful*, which is applied to Theseus both when he abandons Ariadne and when he forgets the instructions of his father and consequently brings the curse of Ariadne down upon himself. We note each occurrence of such words and refer the reader to the immediately prior occurrence so that the reader can follow the patterns of these words back through the poem.

A number of words in the running vocabularies are marked with asterisks. These words are not glossed when they appear later in this poem, but they are included in the end vocabulary.

Meter: dactylic hexameter

50   ***vestis, vestis**, f., *clothing; cloth; coverlet.*
    prīscīs: transferred epithet, grammatically agreeing with **figūrīs** but going
       in sense with **hominum.**
    variō, -āre, -āvī, -ātus, *to adorn.*
    *figūra, -ae, f., *figure.*

51   **hērōs, hērōos** or **hērōis**, gen. pl., **hērōum**, m. [Greek loan word], *hero.*
    virtūs, virtūtis, f., *manliness; valor; worth; virtue;* here, *heroic deeds.*
    indicō, -āre, -āvī, -ātus, *to show.*

52   **fluentisonus, -a, -um** [hapax], *resounding with waves, wave-resounding.*
    fluentisonō . . . lītore: ablative of place from which without a preposition.
    *prōspectō [**prō-**, *forward* + **speciō, specere, spexī, spectus**, *to see; to watch* +
       -tō, intensive or iterative suffix], **-āre, -āvī, -ātus**, *to look out.*
       prōspectāns: describing the subject, **Ariadna** (54).
    *Dīa, -ae, f., *Dia* (an island five and a half miles from Heracleon, Crete;
       confused in the myth with Naxos).

53   ***Thēseus, Thēseī**, m., acc., **Thēsea**, voc., **Thēseu** (all except the accusative
       pronounced as two syllables), *Theseus* (Greek hero, son of Aegeus).
    *cēdō, cēdere, cessī, cessūrus, *to go; to go away; to depart; to recede.*
    *classis, classis, f., *fleet* (here of a single ship).
    tueor, tuērī, tuitus sum, *to look at, observe, see.*
    Thēsea cēdentem celerī cum classe tuētur: note the alliteration of *t*'s and
       c's.

54   **indomitus, -a, -um**, *untamed; wild; uncontrollable.*
    *Ariadna, -ae, f., *Ariadne* (daughter of Minos).
    *furor, furōris, m., *frenzy; fury; rage; anger; passionate desire.*
    indomitōs . . . furōrēs: the words for the uncontrollable emotions that
       Ariadne feels frame the line. Cf. Catullus 50.11, **indomitus furōre.**

55   **necdum**, conj., *and not yet.*
    etiam: here, *even,* modifying **quae vīsit.**
    sēsē: an emphatic **sē.**
    *vīsō [**videō, vidēre, vīdī, vīsus**, *to see* + **-ō**], **vīsere, vīsī**, *to see.*
    vīsit vīsere: polyptoton.

56   **utpote**, particle, *as one might expect, as is natural, no wonder.*
    utpote . . . quae: *no wonder, since she. . . . ,* introducing a relative clause of
       characteristic expressing cause with its verb in the subjunctive.
    *fallāx, fallācis, *deceitful; treacherous; deceptive; traitorous.*
    fallācī: sleep is traitorous because it allowed Theseus to escape unnoticed.
    excitō [**ex-**, *out* + **cieō, ciēre, cīvī, citus**, *to move, stir up* + **-tō**, iterative or
       intensive suffix], **-āre, -āvī, -ātus**, *to rouse, awaken.*

57   ***dēsertus, -a, -um**, *lonely, left alone.*
    *sōlus, -a, -um, *alone, lonely.*
    dēsertam . . . sōlā: pleonastic for emphasis.
    miseram: proleptic, *[and made] miserable.*
    cernō, cernere, crēvī, crētus, *to perceive, see.*

CATULLUS 64.50–253

Ariadne's Lament

Ariadne, deserted on the island of Dia, looks off over the sea as Theseus sails away.

50   Haec vestis prīscīs hominum variāta figūrīs
51   hērōum mīrā virtūtēs indicat arte.
52   Namque fluentisonō prōspectāns lītore Dīae,
53   Thēsea cēdentem celerī cum classe tuētur
54   indomitōs in corde gerēns Ariadna furōrēs,
55   necdum etiam sēsē quae vīsit vīsere crēdit,
56   utpote fallācī quae tum prīmum excita somnō
57   dēsertam in sōlā miseram sē cernat harēnā.

continued

Myth

52   **Dīa:** possibly an earlier name for Naxos. Homer in his version of the story may have been thinking of the island of Dia that lies off the north coast of Crete. In *Odyssey* 11.321–25, Ariadne is described as the beautiful daughter of evil-minded King Minos, and Theseus is said to have tried to take her to Athens. Before that could happen, she was slain on Dia by Artemis because of a mysterious testimony of Dionysus. Catullus follows a later version of the story, in which Theseus abandons Ariadne on Naxos, but he locates the story on Dia.

Text

56   **tum**
    Thomson reads **tunc**, as in manuscript O.

Initial Explorations

1. The description of an art object that interrupts a narrative is called in Greek an *ecphrasis*. How is the *ecphrasis* introduced in lines 50–51?
2. What does the artistic representation on the coverlet show? (50–51)
3. Who are the two characters represented in the first scene? What are they doing? From whose perspective does the poet describe the scene? (52–57)
4. What features of the language in lines 52–53 suggest the high style of epic poetry? What word recalls Homer's version of the story?
5. How is Ariadne's state described in the first line in which she is named? (54)

58   **immemor . . . iuvenis:** i.e., Theseus; for **immemor,** cf. Catullus 30.1, **Alfēne immemor.**

pellō, pellere, pepulī, pulsus, *to beat, strike.*

vadum, -ī, n., *shallow water;* pl., *the waters of the sea.*

***rēmus, -ī,** m., *oar.*

59   ***irritus, -a, -um,** *vain; empty.*

ventōsus, -a, -um, *windy.*

  ventōsae . . . procellae: dative.

prōmissum, -ī, n., *promise.*

procella, -ae, f., *strong wind, gale.*

  irrita . . . procellae: a golden line (adjective a : adjective b :: verb :: noun a : noun b).

60   **procul,** adv., *far away.*

alga, -ae, f., *seaweed.*

  ex algā: i.e., from the seaweed on the beach.

***maestus, -a, -um,** *sorrowful, gloomy; grieving; sad.*

***Mīnōis, Mīnōidis,** f., *daughter of Minos* (here, Ariadne).

ocellus, -ī, m. [dim. of **oculus, -ī,** m., *eye*], (see Catullus 3.18, 45.11, and 60.10) *dear eye, little eye.*

61   **saxeus, -a, -um,** *of rock, of stone, stony.*

  saxea ut: = ut saxea.

effigiēs, -ēī, f., *statue, image.*

bacchāns, bacchantis, f., *bacchante* (female worshiper of Bacchus/Dionysus).

prōspiciō [pro-, *forward* **+ speciō, specere, spexī, spectus,** *to see; to watch*], **prōspicere, prōspexī, prōspectus,** *to see before one; to watch.*

  prōspicit, ēheu, / prōspicit (62): repetition to emphasize the pathos of Ariadne's situation.

62   ***cūra, -ae,** f., *care; emotional distress; anguished emotion* (cf. Catullus 2.10, **cūrās**).

flūctuō, -āre, -āvī, -ātūrus, *to rise in waves; to be agitated; to seethe.*

58   Immemor at iuvenis fugiēns pellit vada rēmīs,
59   irrita ventōsae linquēns prōmissa procellae.
60   Quem procul ex algā maestīs Mīnōis ocellīs,
61   saxea ut effigiēs bacchantis, prōspicit, ēheu,
62   prōspicit et magnīs cūrārum flūctuat undīs,

continued

Comparisons

59   **irrita ventōsae linquēns prōmissa procellae.**

Compare:
Catullus 30.9–10:
    īdem nunc retrahis tē ac tua dicta omnia factaque
    ventōs irrita ferre ac nebulās āeriās sinis.

Catullus 70.3–4:
    Dīcit: sed mulier cupidō quod dīcit amantī
      in ventō et rapidā scrībere oportet aquā.

Initial Explorations

6.   How is the mental state of Theseus described in line 58? How does the poetic image of line 59 reinforce the point of line 58?

7.   How is the deep emotion of the sad *daughter of Minos* conveyed in lines 60–62 through a simile, editorial interjection, and a striking metaphor?

63   **flāvus, -a, -um,** *yellow; blond.*
>   **flāvō:** heroes and heroines are often described as having blond hair (e.g.,
>   Dido in Vergil, *Aeneid* 4.590).

subtīlis, -is, -e, *delicate.*

***vertex, verticis,** m., *whirlpool; top; top of the head, head.*

***mitra** [Greek loan word], **-ae,** f., *headdress* (a cloth or cap worn by Greek girls
at night).
>   **flāvō ... subtīlem vertice mitram:** interlocking word order or
>   synchysis.

64   **contegō** [con-, *thoroughly* + **tegō, tegere, tēxī, tēctus,** *to cover*], **contegere,**
>   **contēxī, contēctus,** *to cover up, protect, cover.*
>   **nōn contēcta ... pectus:** this is an archaism in which the perfect passive
>   participle is used in a reflexive sense denoting an action that one
>   performs upon oneself, *not having covered her breast, not covering her
>   breast.*

vēlō, -āre, -āvī, -ātus, *to clothe, veil.*
>   **vēlātum:** a pleonasm, repeating the idea expressed in **contēcta.**

pectus, pectoris, n., *chest; breast.*

***amictus, -ūs,** m., *clothing* (here a Greek chiton).
>   **levī ... amictū:** ablative of means with **vēlātum,** *veiled with light clothing.*

65   **teres, teretis,** *smooth.*

strophium, -ī, n. [Greek loan word], *twisted band* (supporting a woman's
breasts).

lactēns, lactentis, *milky; milk-white.*

vinciō, vincīre, vīnxī, vīnctus, *to bind.*

papilla, -ae, f., *nipple; breast.*
>   **nōn lactentīs vīncta papillās:** *not binding ... ;* the same construction as
>   **contēcta ... pectus** above.

66   **omnia quae:** delayed relative pronoun, accusative plural neuter, object of
>   **allūdēbant** (67).
>   **quae:** the antecedents are **subtīlem ... mitram** (63), **levī ... amictū** (64),
>   and **teretī strophiō** (65).

dēlābor [dē-, *down* + **lābor, lābī, lāpsus sum,** *to slip, fall*], **dēlābī, dēlāpsus**
sum, *to drop; to slip down.*

passim, adv., *indiscriminately, in every direction, here and there.*

67   **ipsius:** note that the second *i* is short here; **ipse** and **ipsa** often mean *master*
and *mistress* (cf. 2.9 and 3.7); so here translate *of their mistress/owner.*

***flūctus, -ūs,** m., *wave.*

sāl, salis, m., *salt;* here, by synecdoche, *sea.*
>   **flūctūs salis:** subject of **allūdēbant.**

allūdō [ad-, *to, toward* + **lūdō, lūdere, lūsī, lūsus,** *to play*], **allūdere, allūsī,**
allūsus, *to play beside/around; to play/sport with.*
>   **allūdēbant:** spondaic fifth foot.

63   nōn flāvō retinēns subtīlem vertice mitram,
64   nōn contēcta levī vēlātum pectus amictū,
65   nōn teretī strophiō lactentīs vīncta papillās,
66   omnia quae tōtō dēlāpsa ē corpore passim
67   ipsius ante pedēs flūctūs salis allūdēbant.

continued

Initial Explorations

8.   Find an example of anaphora in lines 63–65. Explain how the physical description here of Ariadne on the seashore contributes to her psychological characterization.
9.   How do the waves of the sea (67) respond to the psychological state of Ariadne?

68   neque tum . . . neque tum: anaphora.
       fluitō, -āre, -āvī, -ātūrus, *to flow, float*; of clothes, *to hang loose.*
           mitrae . . . fluitantis amictūs: take each with vicem (69). For mitrae, see
               line 63, and for amictūs, see line 64.
               fluitantis: picking up flūctūs (67) and flūctuat (62).
69   vicis, gen. (no nom. sing.), f., accusative, vicem + gen., *plight* (of), *situation* (of),
           lot (of).
               neque (68) . . . / . . . vicem cūrāns: *caring neither for the lot (of).* . . .
       tōtō . . . pectore . . . / tōtō animō, tōtā . . . mente (70): translate *with* . . .
       ex tē: take with pendēbat (70).
       Thēseu: apostrophe.
70   *perditus, -a, -um, *ruined, lost; hopeless; in a state of desperation.*
71   *ā, interj., *alas.*
       *assiduus, -a, -um [ad-, *to, toward* + sedeō, sedēre, sēdī, sessūrus, *to sit*],
           incessant, constant.
       *lūctus, -ūs, m., *mourning, lamentation; sorrow, grief.*
       *ex(s)ternō [may be a Catullan coinage; ex-, *out* + sternō, sternere, strāvī,
           strātus, *to lay; to spread; to stretch; to strike down*], -āre, -āvī, -ātus, *to strike out of
           one's wits, put in a panic.*
72   spīnōsus, -a, -um, *thorny; prickly.*
       Erycīna, -ae, f., *Erycina, Venus* (so titled from her association with Mt. Eryx in
           Sicily and the temple of Venus on its summit).
       serō, serere, sēvī, satus, *to plant, sow.*
73   tempestās, tempestātis, f., *period of time; stormy weather; time.*
           illā tempestāte . . . quō ex tempore: *from that time when*, poetic periphrasis.
74   curvus, -a, -um, *curved.*
       Pīraeus, -ī, m., *Piraeus* (the port of Athens).
       lītoribus Pīraeī: spondaic fifth foot.
75   attingō [ad-, *to, toward* + tangō, tangere, tetigī, tactus, *to touch*], attingere,
           attigī, attactus, *to touch; to reach.*
       iniūstus, -a, -um, *unjust.*
           iniūstī: from the narrow point of view of the Athenians, inasmuch as he
               exacted a heavy penalty for the death of Androgeos (see below, line 77,
               and Myth on line 77); in mythology Minos was generally regarded as
               just, and he became the judge in the underworld.
       Gortȳnius, -a, -um, *Gortynian, of or pertaining to Gortyna* (a city in Crete);
           generally, *Cretan.*
       templum, -ī, n., *a piece of ground set aside for religious purposes; a temple; a region*
           (of the earth; if this is the meaning here, the reference would be to the land
           mass of Crete); here perhaps, *palace* (i.e., of Minos).

68 Sed neque tum mitrae neque tum fluitantis amictūs
69 illa vicem cūrāns tōtō ex tē pectore, Thēseu,
70 tōtō animō, tōtā pendēbat perdita mente.
71 Ā misera, assiduīs quam lūctibus externāvit
72 spīnōsās Erycīna serēns in pectore cūrās,
73 illā tempestāte, ferōx quō ex tempore Thēseus
74 ēgressus curvīs ē lītoribus Pīraeī
75 attigit iniūstī rēgis Gortȳnia templa.

continued

Text

73 illā tempestāte, ferōx quō ex tempore Thēseus

Thomson reads: **illā tempestāte, ferōx quā rōbure Thēseus**. The word **ex** does not appear in the manuscripts; Thomson quotes Kroll's argument against inserting **ex**: "It is a question of the *moment when* Venus sows her cares in the heart." With **quā** supply **tempestāte**; **rōbure** is ablative of respect with **ferōx**; Thomson's reading translates: *at that time, at which [time] Theseus fierce with physical strength.* . . .

  rōbur, rōburis, n., *oak-tree; physical strength.*

Comparison

Compare Ariadne in lines 60–69 as she watches the departing Theseus from a distance, who is likened to a bacchante, is tossed on great waves of anguished emotion, and shows no concern for the clothes that slip from her body, to Andromache as she learns of the death of her husband Hector in Homer, *Iliad* 22.460–70, given on page 316.

Initial Explorations

10. Find an example of a tricolon with anaphora and alliteration in lines 69–70. What do these rhetorical devices emphasize?
11   Find two examples of apostrophe in lines 69–71 and describe their rhetorical effect.
12. What shift in time frame follows the apostrophe **Ā misera** (71)?
13. What is being described in lines 71–72? Why is it Erycina/Venus who sows panic, grief, and anxiety in Ariadne's heart?
14. What ambiguities does the adjective **ferōx** (73) lend to the poet's depiction of Theseus?

76 *perhibeō [per-, intensive + habeō, -ēre, -uī, -itus, *to have*] -ēre, -uī, -itus, *to regard, hold; to say.*
    perhibent: introducing indirect statement, Cecropiam solitam esse . . . (79); with verbs such as perhibent here and in line 124 and ferunt in line 212, the poet appeals to the authority of legend for the story he is telling rather than taking responsibility for it himself.
  pestis, pestis, f., *pestilence, plague.*
  coāctam: perfect passive participle modifying Cecropiam (79) and taking the complementary infinitive exsolvere (77).
77 Androgeōnēus, -a, -um, *of Androgeos/Androgeon* (son of Minos and Pasiphaë).
  exsolvō [ex-, *thoroughly* + solvō, solvere, solvī, solūtus, *to loosen; to pay*], exsolvere, exsolvī, exsolūtus, *to pay.*
    poenās exsolvere, idiom + gen., *to pay the penalty* (for).
78 ēlēctus, -a, -um, *choice, select.*
  decus, decoris, n., *honor; glory; beauty, grace.*
  innūpta, -ae, f., *maiden.*
  ēlēctōs iuvenēs . . . et decus innūptārum: objects of dare (79).
    decus innūptārum: we might say *the flower of* . . .
      innūptārum / . . . Mīnōtaurō (79) / . . . vexārentur (80): three consecutive spondaic fifth feet.
79 *Cecropia, -ae, f., *Cecropia* (the city of Cecrops; Cecrops was the first king of the city that was later called Athens from its patron Athena).
  Cecropiam solitam esse: accusative + perfect infinitive in an indirect statement introduced by perhibent (76).
  daps, dapis, f., *religious feast, sacrificial meal.*
    dapem: [*as a*] *sacrificial meal*, in apposition to ēlēctōs iuvenēs . . . et decus innūptārum (78).
  dare: complementary infinitive with solitam esse.
  Mīnōtaurus, -ī, m., *Minotaur* (son of Minos and Pasiphaë).
80 Quīs: = Quibus, linking Quī, = Et eīs, with malīs.
  angustus, -a, -um, *narrow; closely surrounding.*
    angusta . . . moenia: i.e., of Cecropia/Athens, small at that time.
  cum: delayed temporal conjunction.
  moenia: metonymy for the city of Cecropia, = Athens.
81 ipse: = ultrō, adv., *voluntarily.*
  ipse suum Thēseus prō cārīs corpus Athēnīs: note the double interlocking word order: ABA . . . CBC.
  Athēnae, -ārum, f. pl., *Athens.*
82 prōiciō [pro-, *forward* + iaciō, iacere, iēcī, iactus, *to throw*], prōicere, prōiēcī, prōiectus, *to throw forth; to risk.*
  optō, -āre, -āvī, -ātus, *to wish; to choose.*
  potius quam: supply ut, *rather than* [*that*].
  *Crēta, -ae, f., *Crete* (island south of Greece, home of Minos).
  Crētam: accusative of end of motion without a preposition.
83 fūnus, fūneris, n., *funeral; corpse.*

76 Nam perhibent ōlim crūdēlī peste coāctam
77 Androgeōnēae poenās exsolvere caedis
78 ēlēctōs iuvenēs simul et decus innūptārum
79 Cecropiam solitam esse dapem dare Mīnōtaurō.
80 Quīs angusta malīs cum moenia vexārentur,
81 ipse suum Thēseus prō cārīs corpus Athēnīs
82 prōicere optāvit potius quam tālia Crētam
83 fūnera Cecropiae nec fūnera portārentur.

continued

Myth

77 **Androgeōnēae . . . caedis:** Androgeos, son of Minos and Pasiphae, conquered all his competitors at wrestling in Athens, and was, through jealousy, assassinated while on his way to the games at Thebes. According to another story, King Aegeus himself caused his death by sending him against the fire-breathing Marathonian bull. Minos thereupon besieged the Athenians, who were compelled to yield to him by a pestilence sent by the gods, and to accept his hard conditions of peace. —Merrill

Initial Explorations

15. How is Theseus portrayed in the narrative account of lines 73–83, especially in counterpoint to King Minos? What particular moral language is used in this narrative?
16. What is the meaning of the unusual expression in line 83, **fūnera . . . nec fūnera?**

84   *nītor, nītī, nixus sum + abl. object, *to lean on, rely on;* + abl. of means, *to press*
      forward (with).
      lēnis, -is, -e, *gentle.*
      *aura, -ae, f., *breeze.*
         Chiasmus: **nāve : levī :: lēnibus : aurīs** and alliteration: <u>n</u>āve <u>l</u>evī <u>n</u>ītēns
         ac <u>l</u>ēnibus aurīs.
85   magnanimus, -a, -um, *great-spirited.*
      Mīnōs, Mīnōis, acc., Mīnōa, m., *Minos* (king of Crete, husband of Pasiphaë).
      *sēdēs, sēdis, f., *seat; home.*
         sēdēs superbās: poetic plural.
         Chiasmus: **magnanimum : Mīnōa :: sēdēs : superbās.**
86   *cupidus, -a, -um, *longing, desirous.*
      *lūmen, lūminis, n., *light; lamp; eye.*
87   rēgius, -a, -um, *royal.*
         virgō (86) / rēgia: i.e., Ariadne.
      exspīrō [ex-, *out* + spīrō, -āre, -āvī, -ātus, *to breathe*], -āre, -āvī, -ātus, *to*
         breathe out, emit, give forth.
      odor, odōris, m., *odor, scent, fragrance.*
88   lectulus, -ī, m. [dim. of lectus, -ī, m., *couch, bed*], *little/dear couch/bed.*
         suāvīs exspīrāns castus odōrēs (87) / lectulus: Catullus may be thinking
         of Helen's bedchamber in *Odyssey* 4.121, described as *fragrant.*
89   quālēs: the antecedent is suāvīs . . . odōrēs (87): the similes in lines 89–90
         are a highly compressed version of the following: *such as [the sweet*
         fragrances that] the myrtles [that] border the Eurotas river [give forth] or [such as
         the sweet fragrances given forth by] the flowers of variegated colors [that] the
         springtime breeze brings forth.
      Eurōtas, -ae, m., *Eurotas River* (the chief river in Laconia, flowing through
         Sparta, where the palace of Menelaus and Helen was located).
      praecingō [prae-, *in front, ahead* + cingō, cingere, cīnxī, cīnctus, *to surround,*
         encircle], praecingere, praecīnxī, praecīnctus, *to gird; to surround, encircle;*
         to border.
      flūmen, flūminis, n., *stream, river;* pl., *the streams* (of a river).
      mȳrtūs: this noun, 2nd declension in the singular, has 4th declension forms
         in the nominative and accusative plural. Myrtle is commonly associated
         with Venus, the goddess of love.
90   distīnctus, -a, -um, *separate, different, variegated.*
      vernus, -a, -um, *of spring, vernal.*
      colōrēs: metonymy or synecdoche for flōrēs.
         aurave distīnctōs . . . verna colōrēs: interlocking word order or
         synchysis.
91   prius . . . / quam (92): = priusquam.
      flagrō, -āre, -āvī, *to be on fire; to blaze.*
      dēclīnō, -āre, -āvī, -ātus, *to turn away.*
         dēclīnāvit: spondaic fifth foot.

84   Atque ita nāve levī nītēns ac lēnibus aurīs

85   magnanimum ad Mīnōa venit sēdēsque superbās.

86   Hunc simul ac cupidō cōnspexit lūmine virgō

87   rēgia, quam suāvīs exspīrāns castus odōrēs

88   lectulus in mollī complexū mātris alēbat,

89   quālēs Eurōtae praecingunt flūmina mȳrtūs

90   aurave distīnctōs ēdūcit verna colōrēs,

91   nōn prius ex illō flagrantia dēclīnāvit

continued

Text

89   **praecingunt**

Thomson and Godwin read **prōgignunt**, as in manuscript θ, instead of Baehrens' reading **praecingunt**, which is in the Oxford Classical Text. The expanded translation would then be: *such as [the sweet fragrances that] the myrtles [that] the streams of the Eurotas produce [give forth].*

prōgignō [**pro-**, *forward* + **gignō, gignere, genuī, genitus,** *to bring to birth, create*], **prōgignere, prōgenuī, prōgenitus,** *to give birth to; to produce.*

Initial Explorations

17.   What is the effect of the alliteration and diction in lines 84–85?

18.   What would one expect the poet to describe after line 85, as Theseus, son of the king of Athens, arrives at the *proud home* of *great-spirited Minos*? What does the poet describe instead?

19.   What do lines 86–87a suggest is going to happen? What word suggests this? What is created by the interposition of the relative clause (87b–88) and the two similes (89–90) between the introductory subordinate clause in lines 86–87a and the main clause in lines 91–93?

20.   How are lines 87b–90 relevant to what the poet is describing in lines 86–87a and 91–93?

92   lūmina: picking up lūmine (86).

concipiō [con-, intensive + capiō, capere, cēpī, captus, *to take*], concipere,
concēpī, conceptus, *to take in; to catch; to conceive*.

cūnctō concēpit corpore: alliteration; also in flammam / funditus (93).

93   funditus, adv., *from the depths*.

īmus, -a, -um, *lowest, deepest*.

exārdēscō [ex-, intensive + ārdeō, ārdēre, ārsī, *to burn* + -scō, ingressive
suffix], exārdēscere, exārsī, *to catch fire, blaze up, burst into flames*.

tōta: translate as an adverb.

*medulla, -ae, f., *marrow of the bones* (cf. Catullus 35.15, ignēs interiōrem
edunt medullam, and Catullus 45.16, ignis mollibus ārdet in medullīs).

94   Heu: apostrophizing Cupid (sāncte puer, 95) and Venus (quae . . . regis, 96).

miserē, adv., *pitifully*.

exagitō [ex-, intensive + agō, agere, ēgī, āctus, *to do; to drive* + -itō, iterative or
intensive suffix], -āre, -āvī, -ātus, *to stir up*.

*immītis, -is, -e [in-, *not* + mītis, *gentle*], *pitiless; harsh; cruel*.

immītī corde: *with pitiless/cruel heart*, ablative of manner.

furōrēs: cf. furōrēs (54).

95   sāncte puer: i.e., Eros/Cupid; cf. Catullus 36.3, sānctae Venerī Cupīdinīque.

quī: delayed relative pronoun.

96   quaeque regis: *and [you] who rule. . . .* , i.e., Aphrodite/Venus.

quaeque . . . quaeque: both relative pronouns refer to Aphrodite/Venus;
repeat regis with the second relative pronoun.

Golgī, -ōrum, m. pl., *Golgi* (a town on Cyprus noted for the worship of
Aphrodite/Venus).

Īdalium, -ī, n., *Idalium* (a town on Cyprus sacred to Aphrodite/Venus).

quaeque regis Golgōs quaeque Īdalium: cf. Catullus 36.12–15.

frondōsus, -a, -um, *leafy*.

97   quālis, -is, -e, exclamatory here, *what sort of*.

iactāstis: syncopated, = iactāvistis.

mente: ablative of respect with incēnsam.

98   flūctibus: *waves* [of emotion/passion]; cf. flūctuat (62).

flāvō: cf. flāvō (63).

suspīrō [sub-, *under* + spīrō, -āre, -āvī, -ātus, *to breathe*], -āre, -āvī, -ātūrus, *to
sigh*.

suspīrantem: spondaic fifth foot.

99   Quantōs . . . timōrēs!: note the emphasis by positioning Quantōs at the
beginning and timōrēs at the end of the line.

langueō, languēre, languī, *to be weak, enfeebled, languid, faint*.

languentī: *swooning*.

100   Quantō: *By how much . . . !*, with magis.

fulgor, fulgōris, m., *brightness, luster*.

fulgōre: ablative of comparison.

fulgōre aurī: "Several editors point out that Mediterranean complexions
have a yellowish tinge when they 'pale'" (Thomson).

expallēscō [ex-, intensive + palleō, -ēre, *to be pale* + -scō, ingressive suffix],
expallēscere, expalluī, *to turn pale*.

92   lūmina, quam cūnctō concēpit corpore flammam
93   funditus atque īmīs exārsit tōta medullīs.
94   Heu miserē exagitāns immītī corde furōrēs
95   sāncte puer, cūrīs hominum quī gaudia miscēs,
96   quaeque regis Golgōs quaeque Īdalium frondōsum,
97   quālibus incēnsam iactāstis mente puellam
98   flūctibus, in flāvō saepe hospite suspīrantem!
99   Quantōs illa tulit languentī corde timōrēs!
100 Quantō saepe magis fulgōre expalluit aurī,

continued

Text

100   **Quantō**

Thomson reads **Quam tum**, the emendation of Faernus, with **Quam** going
with **saepe**, *How often.* **Quantō** is the reading of V and the Oxford Classical
Text.

Comparisons

With lines 86–100, compare the description in Apollonius, *Argonautica* 3.275–98, of
Medea falling in love with Jason at first sight, given on page 317.

95   sāncte puer, cūrīs hominum quī gaudia miscēs

For Eros/Cupid as a god who mixes *joys* (**gaudia**) with *cares/emotional distress*
(**cūrīs**), see the passages from Sappho and Theognis given on pages 317 and
318.

100 Quantō saepe magis fulgōre expalluit aurī

Compare the last two lines of the passage from Apollonius' *Argonautica*,
given on page 317.

Initial Explorations

21.   What imagery is used in lines 91–93 to describe what happens when
      Ariadne looks upon Theseus? What poetic device enhances the statement
      here?
22.   What is the effect of Catullus' use of apostrophe in lines 94–96?
23.   What metaphorical imagery is used in lines 97–98 to describe Ariadne's
      emotional turbulence? What is the effect of enjambement between these
      lines?

101 **cum**: introducing a **cum** circumstantial clause.

cupiēns: modifying the subject, **Thēseus** (102).

contendō [con-, intensive + **tendō, tendere, tetendī, tentus** or **tēnsus**, *to stretch*], **contendere, contendī, contentus**, *to compete, contend, fight*.

> **cum saevum cupiēns contrā contendere**: alliteration and repetition of cu- and con-.

102 **appetō** [ad-, *to, toward* + **petō, petere, petīvī, petītus**, *to look for, seek*], **appetere, appetīvī, appetītus**, *to try to reach; to seek to obtain; to strive after*.

***praemium, -ī**, n., *payment; prize, reward*.

***laus, laudis**, f., *praise; praiseworthy action*.

> **praemia laudis**: **praemia** is poetic plural; both meanings of **laus** are present in this phrase, *reward [consisting] of praise* and *reward for [his] praiseworthy action*.

103 **ingrātus, -a, -um**, *thankless, unwelcome*.

> **ingrāta**: modifying **mūnuscula**.

tamen: although terribly fearful for Theseus' safety (99–102), Ariadne *nevertheless* prayed to the gods and promised offerings (**vōta**, 104) if Theseus should be successful.

frūstrā, adv., *in vain, fruitlessly*.

> **frūstrā**: take with **ingrāta**, *fruitlessly unwelcome*. The little gifts that Ariadne promised to the gods were *not* (**nōn**) *fruitlessly unwelcome*, i.e., they were received by the gods with gratitude, and the desired outcomes occurred: Theseus slew the Minotaur and escaped from the labyrinth.

mūnusculum [dim. of **mūnus, mūneris**, n., *gift*], **-ī**, n., *little/dear gift*.

dīvus, -ī, m., *god*.

104 **tacitō**: "variously interpreted as 'silent (sc. in order to escape her parents' notice)' or 'hushed in adoration (of the beloved)'; the latter seems more probable" (Thomson).

succipiō [archaic for **suscipiō**; sub-, *under* + **capiō, capere, cēpī, captus**, *to take*], **succipere, succēpī, succeptus**, *to undertake/make* (a vow).

> **succēpit**: the subject (Ariadne) is resumed from line 100.

vōtum, -ī, n. (see Catullus 36.2), *vow* (a promise to dedicate or sacrifice something to a deity if the deity should grant a favor or answer a prayer).

labellum, -ī, n. [**labrum, -ī**, n., *lip* + -**lum**, dim. suffix] (see 8.18), *little/dear lip*.

105 **quatiō, quatere, _____, quassus**, *to shake*.

brac(c)hium, -ī, n., *arm*; rare, *branch* (of a tree).

Taurus [**taurus, -ī**, m., *bull*], **-ī**, m., *Taurus Mountains* (a range in southern Asia Minor).

> **Taurō**: the name of the mountain in the simile connects with the name of the monster that Theseus slays.

106 **quercus, -ūs**, f., *oak tree*.

cōniger, cōnigera, cōnigerum: hapax [**cōnus, -ī**, m., *cone* + **gerō, gerere, gessī, gestus**, *to bear*], *bearing pine cones, cone-bearing*.

sūdō, -āre, -āvī, -ātūrus, *to sweat*.

cortex, corticis, m., *bark*.

pīnus, -ūs, f., *pine tree*.

> **quercum aut . . . pīnum**: objects of **ēruit** (108).

101 cum saevum cupiēns contrā contendere mōnstrum

102 aut mortem appeteret Thēseus aut praemia laudis!

103 Nōn ingrāta tamen frūstrā mūnuscula dīvīs

104 prōmittēns tacitō succēpit vōta labellō.

105 Nam velut in summō quatientem brachia Taurō

106 quercum aut cōnigeram sūdantī cortice pīnum

continued

24. Is Theseus' success described in lines 105–111 to be thought of as the result of Ariadne's promise of gifts to the gods and of her prayers or vows (103–4), or is the reader to assume that Theseus would have successfully slain the Minotaur whether or not Ariadne had promised gifts and prayed to the gods?

25. What, according to the myth, did Ariadne do to assure Theseus' salvation that is not mentioned in lines 99–104?

26. How do lines 99–104 advance the author's intention to show us the progression and depth of Ariadne's love for Theseus?

107 *indomitus [in-, *not* + domō, domāre, domuī, domitus, *to tame, break in; to subdue*] -a, -um, *not broken in, untamed; unrestrained, violent.*

*turbō, turbinis, m., *whirlpool; whirlwind; tornado.*

contorqueō [con-, intensive + torqueō, torquēre, torsī, tortus, *to twist*], contorquēre, contorsī, contortus, *to twist; to rotate; to whirl; to wrench.*
    turbō con<u>torq</u>ēns: note the play on sounds.

flāmen, flāminis, n., *blast, gust* (of wind).

rōbur, rōboris, n., *oak tree; trunk* (of any tree).

108 ēruō [ē-, ex, *out* + ruō, ruere, ruī, *to rush; to overthrow*], ēruere, ēruī, ērutus, *to remove; to uproot.*

illa: i.e., the pīnus (106), feminine.

rādīcitus, adv., *from the roots.*

exturbō [ex-, *out* + turbō, -āre, -āvī, -ātus, *to shake, disturb*], -āre, -āvī, -ātus, *to drive out; to force out; to remove.*
    exturbāta: spondaic fifth foot; with the sound and meaning of the word, cf. turbō (107).

109 lātē, adv., *widely.*

quīvīscumque, quaevīscumque, quodvīscumque [also written as two words], *every conceivable.*

obvius, -a, -um, *in the path/way.*

110 domō, domāre, domuī, domitus, *to tame, break in; to subdue.*
    domitō: cf. indomitus (107).

saevum: substantive here, *the savage one,* i.e., the Minotaur.

prōsternō [prō-, *forward* + sternō, sternere, strāvī, strātus, *to lay; to spread; to stretch; to strike down*], prōsternere, prōstrāvī, prōstrātus, *to bring to the ground; to lay low.*
    prōstrāvit: cf. prōna cadit (109).

111 vānus, -a, -um, *empty.*

vānīs . . . ventīs: cf. indomitus turbō (107).

cornū, -ūs, n., *horn.*

iactantem cornua: cf. quatientem brachia (105).

112 *sōspes, sōspitis, *safe and sound, unscathed.*

laude: cf. laudis (102).

reflectō [re-, *back, again* + flectō, flectere, flexī, flexus, *to bend*], *to turn back.*

113 errābundus, -a, -um, *wandering.*

regēns: *guiding.*

tenuis, -is, -e, *thin.*

114 labyrinthēus, -a, -um [hapax], *labyrinthine.*

flexus, -ūs, m., *bending, turning.*

ēgredientem: i.e., Theseus, *[as he was] leaving.*

115 *tēctum, -ī, n., *roof; house; building.*

frūstror, -ārī, -ātus sum, *to deceive; to frustrate; to baffle.*

inobservābilis, -is, -e, *difficult to trace/observe, untraceable.*

error, errōris, m., *wandering; maze.*

107 indomitus turbō contorquēns flāmine rōbur
108 ēruit (illa procul rādīcitus exturbāta
109 prōna cadit, lātē quaevīs cumque obvia frangēns),
110 sīc domitō saevum prōstrāvit corpore Thēseus
111 nēquīquam vānīs iactantem cornua ventīs.
112 Inde pedem sōspes multā cum laude reflexit
113 errābunda regēns tenuī vēstīgia fīlō,
114 nē labyrinthēīs ē flexibus ēgredientem
115 tēctī frūstrārētur inobservābilis error.

continued

Comparisons

With the simile in lines 105–11, compare the similes in Homer, *Iliad* 13.389–93, Apollonius, *Argonautica* 4.1682–88, and Vergil, *Aeneid* 2.624–31, given on page 318.

Initial Explorations

27. What does the simile in lines 105–11 describe? How is it like the comparable similes in the *Iliad* and the *Argonautica*? What is the major difference, and how is it significant?

28. What does Catullus describe in lines 112–15? What words suggest the impossibility of the task? What and who are responsible for his success here? What credit is given to that person?

116　quid: interrogative, *why?*

dīgredior [dis-, dī-, *apart* + **gradior, gradī, gressus sum**, *to step, walk, go*], dīgredī, dīgressus sum, *to deviate, digress.*

carmen, carminis, n., *song.*

ā prīmō carmine: i.e., from the first part of this episode.

117　commemorō [con-, intensive + **memorō, -āre, -āvī, -ātus**, *to say; to relate, tell*], -āre, āvī, -ātus, *to recall; to mention, relate, recount.*

commemorem: deliberative subjunctive.

ut, conj., *how.*

ut . . . praeoptārit (120): indirect question.

genitor, genitōris, m., *father.*

vultum: here, *sight.*

118　ut [linquēns] cōnsanguineae complexum, ut [linquēns] dēnique mātris [complexum].

cōnsanguinea, -ae, f., *female blood relation; sister* (probably Phaedra, who later married Theseus and fell in love with his stepson, Hippolytus; Ariadne had two other sisters as well, Acale and Xenodice).

dēnique, adv., *at last, finally.*

ut dēnique mātris, / quae . . . (119): the third member of a tricolon.

119　gnāta, -ae, f., *daughter.*

dēperditus, -a, -um [from **dēperdō, dēperdere, dēperdidī, dēperditus**, *to lose; passive, to be utterly lost or ruined*], *utterly ruined, lost; desperate.*

dēperdita: cf. **perdita** (70).

*laetor, -ārī, -ātus sum, *to rejoice, be glad;* + in + abl., *to delight* (in).

dēperdita laetābātur: oxymoron; translate **dēperdita** as an adverb.

120　Thēseī: genitive, disyllabic.

Thēseī . . . amōrem: ambiguous: if the genitive is objective, the phrase would refer to Ariadne's love of Theseus; if it is subjective, it would refer to his love of her.

*dulcis, -is, -e, *sweet.*

praeoptō [prae-, *before* + **optō, -āre, -āvī, -ātus**, *to desire; to choose*], -āre, -āvī, -ātus, *to choose something* (acc.) *before something else* (dat.); *to prefer something* (acc.) *to something* (dat.)

praeoptārit, syncopated and scanned as three syllables by synizesis; = praeoptāverit; the subject is fīlia (117), i.e., Ariadne.

121　ut . . . / vēnerit, aut ut . . . (122) / līquerit (123): indirect questions.

vecta: modifying the subject of the verb, i.e., Ariadne.

ratis, ratis, f., *raft; boat, ship.*

ratī: ablative of means.

spūmōsus, -a, -um, *foamy.*

122　dēvinciō [dē-, *completely* + **vinciō, vincīre, vīnxī, vīnctus**, *to bind*], dēvincīre, dēvīnxī, dēvīnctus, *to tie/bind fast.*

dēvīnctam lūmina somnō: *having bound her eyes with sleep/her eyes bound with sleep;* see on **contēcta pectus**, line 64.

lūmina: cf. **lūmina** (92).

123　immemorī: cf. **immemor** (58).

coniūnx, *betrothed* or ironically, *husband.*

116 Sed quid ego ā prīmō dīgressus carmine plūra

117 commemorem, ut linquēns genitōris fīlia vultum,

118 ut cōnsanguineae complexum, ut dēnique mātris,

119 quae miserā in gnātā dēperdita laetābātur,

120 omnibus hīs Thēseī dulcem praeoptārit amōrem:

121 aut ut vecta ratī spūmōsa ad lītora Dīae

122 vēnerit, aut ut eam dēvīnctam lūmina somnō

123 līquerit immemorī discēdēns pectore coniūnx?

continued

Text

119   **laetābātur**

Connington suggested **lāmentāta est**, *she grieved*, which is printed by Godwin; the Oxford Classical Text and Thomson read **laetābātur**, of which the first four letters are preserved in the manuscripts and the last five are a supplement suggested by Lachmann and accepted by most editors. In choosing between the two readings one must decide whether Ariadne's mother is more likely to be described at this point as hopelessly grieving over her lovesick daughter or desperately fond of her. Thomson quotes Fordyce's comment that **lāmentāta est** is "palaeographically impossible," and he points out that in lines 117–19 there is a "gradual climax in expressions of affection (*vultum—complexum—deperdita laetabatur*)" and that "grief is not the theme of ll. 117–20."

Initial Explorations

29.   What is the function of this segment of the narrative?

30.   In lines 117–20 how does Catullus differentiate the familial relationships that Ariadne leaves behind when she departs, presumably secretly, with Theseus?

31.   What is the focus of the **ut** clause in lines 122–23, and how does the poet thematically connect this scene with the initial tableau of Ariadne abandoned in lines 52–70?

124 **Saepe. . . . :** this line picks up the theme from line 75.
illam . . . / . . . fūdisse (125): accusative + infinitive indirect statement.
perhibent: cf. **perhibent** (76).
ārdentī: cf. **exārsit** (93).
furō, furere, *to be mad; to be crazed* (with passionate desire).
   furentem: cf. **furōrēs** (54).
125 **clārisonus, -a, -um** [very rare word], *clear-sounding, shrill.*
   clārisonās īmō . . . pectore vōcēs: embedded word order.
īmus, -a, -um, *lowest; the bottom* (of).
fundō, fundere, fūdī, fūsus, *to pour forth.*
126 **praeruptus, -a, -um,** *broken off in front; precipitous, steep.*
trīstem: translate as an adverb.
cōnscendō [**con-,** intensive + **scandō, scandere,** *to climb*]*,* **cōnscendere,**
   cōnscendī, cōnscēnsus, *to climb up.*
      [**illam**] **trīstem cōnscendere:** accusative + infinitive indirect statement;
         translate as imperfect, *that [she] was sadly climbing up.*
127 **aciēs, aciēī,** f., *sharp edge; vision.*
   ***pelagus, -ī,** n., *sea.*
   ***vastus, -a, -um,** *desolate; vast.*
prōtendō [**prō-,** forward + **tendō, tendere, tetendī, tentus** or **tēnsus,** *to*
   stretch]*,* **prōtendere, prōtendī, prōtentus,** *to stretch forth.*
aestus, -ūs, m., *heat; ebb and flow; surge, swelling.*
128 **tremulus, -a, -um,** *trembling; quivering; rippling.*
sāl, salis, m., *salt;* by metonymy, *the sea.*
adversus, -a, -um, *turned toward; opposite; facing.*
prōcurrō [**prō-,** *forward* + **currō, currere, cucurrī, cursūrus,** *to run*],
   prōcurrere, prōcurrī, prōcursūrus, *to run forward.*
      prōcurrere: translate as imperfect.
129 **nūdō, -āre, -āvī, -ātus,** *to lay bare.*
   nūdātae: proleptic.
tegmen, tegminis, n., *covering.*
sūra, -ae, f., *calf* (of the leg).
   tegmina sūrae: for **tegmen sūrārum,** referring to her chiton as the covering
      of her calfs.
         mollia . . . sūrae: a golden line (see note to line 59); for the theme, cf.
            lines 63–67.
130 ***extrēmus, -a, -um,** *last; final.*
   [**illam**] **maestam dīxisse:** accusative + infinitive indirect statement.
      maestam: cf. **trīstem** (126) and **maestīs** (60).
   ***querella, -ae,** f., *complaint, protest, lament.*
      extrēmīs . . . querellīs: *in her. . . .*
131 **frīgidulus, -a, -um** [dim. of **frīgidus, -a, -um,** *chilly, cold*], *chilly, cold.*
ūdus, -a, -um, *wet.*
singultus, -ūs, m., *sob.*
cieō, ciēre, cīvī, citus, *to move; to raise, produce* (sounds).
   frīgidulōs ūdō singultūs ōre: interlocking word order or synchysis.

124 Saepe illam perhibent ārdentī corde furentem

125 clārisonās īmō fūdisse ē pectore vōcēs,

126 ac tum praeruptōs trīstem cōnscendere montēs,

127 unde aciem in pelagī vastōs prōtenderet aestūs,

128 tum tremulī salis adversās prōcurrere in undās

129 mollia nūdātae tollentem tegmina sūrae,

130 atque haec extrēmīs maestam dīxisse querellīs,

131 frīgidulōs ūdō singultūs ōre cientem:

continued

Initial Explorations

32. How does line 124 establish a thematic connection with the way Ariadne's passion has been previously described?

33. Lines 124–31 show us another tableau of Ariadne that matches the initial portrait in lines 52–70. What activities of Ariadne does the present segment show? In what essential way does this portrait differ from the earlier one?

34. The scene described in lines 124–31 is vividly pictorial. What phrases contribute most to the pictorial description?

35. What words and phrases in lines 124–31 contribute most to the portrayal of Ariadne's emotional state?

132 **Sīcine . . . / . . . / Sīcine** (134): anaphora.

patrius, -a, -um, *paternal; ancestral.*

    patriīs . . . ab ārīs: note the separation to enhance the meaning; the
    reference is to the sacred altars of her ancestral home.

āvehō [ā-, ab-, *from* + **vehō, vehere, vexī, vectus,** *to carry*], **āvehere, āvexī,**
    āvectus, *to carry off.*

***perfidus, -a, -um,** *treacherous, perfidious.*

    perfide . . . / perfide (133): note the repetition.

133 **līquistī . . . lītore**: alliteration.

134 ***nūmen, nūminis,** n., *nod (of the head); divine power.*

dīvum: = **dīvōrum** = **deōrum.**

    neglēctō nūmine dīvum: ablative absolute.

135 **immemor**: cf. **immemorī** (123) and **immemor** (58).

dēvōtus, -a, -um, *that have been cursed, accursed.*

***periūrium, -ī,** n., *false oath, perjury.*

    dēvōta domum periūria portās: alliteration.

136 **flectō, flectere, flexī, flexus,** *to bend; to turn; to change.*

137 **clēmentia, -ae,** f., *pity, mercy.*

praestō, adv., *ready, available.*

138 **immīte**: cf. **immītī** (94).

ut . . . vellet: result clause with delayed conjunction.

nostrī: genitive of **nōs**, poetic plural.

miserēscō, miserēscere + gen., *to pity.*

139 **quondam,** adv., *formerly, once.*

blandus, -a, -um, *charming; sweet; seductive.*

prōmissum, -ī, n., *promise.*

140 **mihī**: note the long *i* to fit the meter.

nōn haec: repeated from 139, but here **haec** is substantive, *these things.*

miserae: if correct, this is dative with **iubēbās**; supply **mihi**; see **Text.**

141 **sed [spērāre] cōnūbia laeta, sed [spērāre] optātōs hymenaeōs**: anaphora.

***cōnūbium, -ī,** n., *marriage.*

    cōnūbia: poetic plural.

hymenaeī, -ōrum, m. pl., *wedding.*

    cōnūbia laeta . . . optātōs hymenaeōs: chiasmus; Vergil took over these
    words of Ariadne in Dido's complaint to Aeneas (*Aeneid* 4.316), **per**
    cōnūbia nostra, per inceptōs hymenaeōs.

142 **quae cūncta**: the antecedents are **cōnūbia laeta** and **optātōs hymenaeōs**
    (141); translate *all which [things].*

āerius, -a, -um, *of the air, airy.*

discerpō [dis-, *apart* + **carpō, carpere, carpsī, carptus,** *to pluck; to seize*],
    discerpere, discerpsī, discerptus, *to tear to pieces.*

irrita: cf. **irrita** (59); here proleptic, *[and render them] vain/empty.*

    cūncta āeriī . . . irrita ventī: interlocking word order or synchysis.

        irrita ventī: cf. 59, **irrita ventōsae**; cf. also Catullus 70.3–4, **sed mulier**
        cupidō quod dīcit amantī, / in ventō et rapidā scrībere oportet
        aquā, and Catullus 30.10, **ventōs irrita.**

132 "Sīcine mē patriīs āvectam, perfide, ab ārīs,
133 perfide, dēsertō līquistī in lītore, Thēseu?
134 Sīcine discēdēns neglēctō nūmine dīvum,
135 immemor ā! dēvōta domum periūria portās?
136 Nūllane rēs potuit crūdēlis flectere mentis
137 cōnsilium? Tibi nūlla fuit clēmentia praestō,
138 immīte ut nostrī vellet miserēscere pectus?
139 At nōn haec quondam blandā prōmissa dedistī
140 vōce mihī, nōn haec miserae spērāre iubēbās,
141 sed cōnūbia laeta, sed optātōs hymenaeōs,
142 quae cūncta āeriī discerpunt irrita ventī.

continued

Text

140 **miserae**

Thomson reads **miseram**, as in a manuscript of 1482, with the usual accusative after **iubēbās**; supply **mē**. With regard to the reading **miserae** in the Oxford Classical Text, Thomson remarks, "There is no convincing parallel for *iubeo* + dative."

Comparisons

With Ariadne's lament (132–201), compare Catullus 30.

Compare also Medea's complaint to Jason in Apollonius' *Argonautica* 4.355–69 and 378–90, given on page 319, which served as a model for some of the themes in Ariadne's lament (64.132–201). Reread the passage from the *Argonautica* when you have finished reading Ariadne's lament.

Initial Explorations

36. What accusations does Ariadne make in the first four lines of her complaint (132–35)? What crucial adjectives does she use to describe Theseus that underscore that complaint?
37. What additional accusation does Ariadne go on to make in lines 136–38 that complements her initial complaint?
38. What specific accusation does Ariadne begin to develop in lines 139–42?
39. How is the unreliability of promises in the relationship of Theseus to Ariadne similar to the unreliability of words in the relationship of Lesbia to Catullus as seen in poem 70?

143 **Nunc iam**: cf. 8.9, **Nunc iam**.

    crēdat: jussive subjunctive.

      Nunc iam nūlla . . . fēmina crēdat: *Now at last let no woman trust. . . .* ; cf. Catullus 70.

        nūlla virō iūrantī fēmina: a particularly effective example of embedding and chiasmus.

144 **nūlla virī**: echoing **nūlla virō** (143).

    spēret: jussive subjunctive, echoing **spērāre** (140).

    sermōnēs esse fidēlēs: accusative + infinitive construction.

145 **quīs**: = **quibus**, dative of reference (translate as possessive with **animus**); its antecedent is **virī** (144), now generalized in the plural.

    cupiēns: emphatic redundancy with **praegestit**.

    praegestiō [rare; **prae-**, intensive + **gestiō, gestīre, gestīvī** or **gestiī**, *to desire eagerly*], **-īre** + infin., *to have an overpowering desire* (to), *to be especially eager* (to).

    apīscor [archaic; later usually **adipīscor; apiō, apere, aptus**, *to fasten, attach, bind* + **-scō**, ingressive suffix], **apīscī, aptus sum**, *to seize, grab; to obtain*.

146 **nīl . . . nihil**: anaphora.

    metuō, metuere, metuī, metūtus, *to fear; to be afraid* (to) + infinitive.

    parcō, parcere, pepercī, *to refrain* (from) + infinitive.

      Chiasmus: **metuunt : iūrāre :: prōmittere : parcunt**.

147 **cupidae**: echoing **cupiēns** (145).

    satiō, -āre, -āvī, -ātus, *to satisfy*.

      satiāta . . . est: neatly enclosing **libīdō**.

    libīdō, libīdinis, f., *desire, longing; wish; passion, lust*.

148 **nihil**: adverbial, *not at all*.

    metuēre: = **metuērunt**, if correct, a gnomic perfect; translate as present; see **Text**.

    periūria: cf. **periūria** (135).

143 "Nunc iam nūlla virō iūrantī fēmina crēdat,
144 nūlla virī spēret sermōnēs esse fidēlēs;
145 quīs dum aliquid cupiēns animus praegestit apīscī,
146 nīl metuunt iūrāre, nihil prōmittere parcunt:
147 sed simul ac cupidae mentis satiāta libīdō est,
148 dicta nihil metuēre, nihil periūria cūrant.

continued

Text

148 **metuēre**

Thomson reads **meminēre**, following Czwalina, instead of **metuēre**, as in V and the Oxford Classical Text; **meminēre** = **meminērunt**, perfect with present meaning.

Initial Explorations

40. How in lines 143–48 does Ariadne express her complaint that Theseus has led her on with false promises? What reason does she give to explain his behavior?

41. Even though Ariadne makes her statement about the unfaithfulness of men in a generalizing form, some of her language echoes specific points that she already made about herself and Theseus. Point out examples of such language.

42. What verbal repetition and parallelism does Ariadne use in lines 145–48 to emphasize her point?

149 **ego tē**: effective juxtaposition.
tē in mediō versantem turbine: interlocking word order or synchysis.
***versō, -āre, -āvī, -ātus**, *to turn; to writhe.*
turbine: cf. **turbō** (107).
lētum, -ī, n., *death.*
   in mediō versantem turbine lētī: referring to Theseus' heroic and life-
      theatening encounter with the Minotaur (105–11).
150 **ēripuī**: emphasized by enjambement.
potius, adv., *more, more than, rather.*
germānus, -ī, m., *brother.*
   germānum: i.e., the Minotaur (actually only Ariadne's half-brother); it may
      seem odd that Ariadne refers to the monstrous Minotaur as her *brother*;
      there may, however, be an allusion here to the parallel myth of Medea, in
      which she or Jason kills her brother Apsyrtus in order to make it possible
      for Jason to escape and sail home with the golden fleece.
āmittō [ā-, ab-, *from* + **mittō, mittere, mīsī, missus**, *to send*], **āmittere, āmīsī,
   āmissus**, *to give up, lose.*
cernō, cernere, crēvī, crētus, *to distinguish, separate; to decide.*
   crēvī: archaic; later usually **dēcrēvī** in this sense.
151 **quam**: with **potius** (150), *than*; supply **ut**, *than [that] I should. . . .*
fallācī: cf. **fallācī** (56).
suprēmus, -a, -um, *highest; final; critical.*
   suprēmō in tempore: *in a critical moment.*
dēsum [dē-, expressing removal + **sum, esse, fuī, futūrus**, *to be*], **dēesse,
   dēfuī**, *to be wanting/lacking*; + dat., *to fail to support* (someone).
   dēssem: = **dēessem**.
152 **prō**, prep. + abl., *for; as a reward or punishment for; in return for.*
dīlacerō [dī-, dis-, *apart* + **lacerō, -āre, -āvī, -ātus**, *to tear*], **-āre, -āvī, -ātus**, *to
   tear to pieces.*
fera, -ae, f., *wild beast.*
āles, ālitis, m./f., *large bird, bird of prey.*
   ferīs dabor ālitibusque: **dabor** is surrounded by **ferīs** and **ālitibus**,
      highlighting its meaning.
153 **praeda, -ae**, f., *prey.*
   praeda: emphasized by enjambement.
      Embedded word order: **dīlaceranda ferīs . . . ālitibusque** (152) **/ praeda**.
iniciō [in-, *in, on* + **iaciō, iacere, iēcī, iactus**, *to throw*], **inicere, iniēcī,
   iniectus**, here, **iniactus** (see **Text**), *to throw in/on.*
tumulō, -āre, -āvī, -ātus, *to bury.*
   iniactā . . . terrā: the souls of those left unburied were not allowed to enter
      the underworld (cf. Sophocles' *Antigone*).

149 "Certē ego tē in mediō versantem turbine lētī
150 ēripuī, et potius germānum āmittere crēvī,
151 quam tibi fallācī suprēmō in tempore dēssem.
152 Prō quō dīlaceranda ferīs dabor ālitibusque
153 praeda, neque iniactā tumulābor mortua terrā.

continued

Text

153 **iniactā**

Thomson reads **iniectā**, as in a manuscript of 1481, rather than leaving the unreduced vowel of **iniactā**.

Comparisons

With line 152, compare the opening of Homer's *Iliad*, given on page 320.

Initial Explorations

43. As Ariadne returns to the theme of Theseus' betrayal of herself, what particularly outrageous injustice does she complain of in lines 149–53?
44. Compare the way that lines 152–53 echo lines 4–5 of Homer's *Iliad*.
45. Identify ways in which word order in lines 152–153 emphasizes the way Ariadne sees herself victimized.

154 **quīnam, quaenam, quodnam,** interrogative adjective, *what, which.*

    Quaenam . . . leaena: note this interrogative adjective/noun pair and the other pairs that follow in lines 155–56.

    gignō, gignere, genuī, genitus, *to give birth to.*

    sōlā; cf. **sōlā** (57).

    rūpēs, rūpis, f., *crag, cliff.*

    leaena, -ae, f., *lioness.*

155 **concipiō** [**con-,** intensive + **capiō, capere, cēpī, captus,** *to take*], **concipere, concēpī, conceptus,** *to conceive.*

    conceptum: translate as a finite verb and supply **tē,** *conceived [you].*

    spūmō, -āre, -āvī, -ātūrus, *to froth, foam.*

    exspuō [**ex-,** *out* + **spuō, spuere, spuī, spūtus,** *to spit*], **exspuere, exspuī, exspūtus,** *to spit out.*

    spūmantibus exspuit: alliteration.

156 **quae Syrtis, quae Scylla rapāx, quae vasta Charybdis:** with each phrase supply **exspuit tē conceptum spūmantibus undīs** from line 155; note the ascending tricolon.

    Syrtis, Syrtis, f., *Syrtis* (shoals and sandbanks off the North African coast that were dreaded by mariners).

    Scylla, -ae, f., *Scylla* (a cliff-dwelling monster in the straits of Messina; it had six heads, each with a triple row of teeth, and would devour passing sailors).

    rapāx, rapācis, *predatory, rapacious.*

    vasta: see 127, **vastōs;** here *dreadful.*

    Charybdis, Charybdis, f., *Charybdis* (a whirlpool on the Sicilian side of the Strait of Messina, opposite Scylla).

157 **tālia quī:** delayed relative.

    tālia . . . dulcī praemia vītā: interlocking word order or synchysis.

158 **cordī esse alicuī,** idiom with double dative, *to be pleasing to someone's heart.*

    Sī tibi nōn cordī fuerant: "The pluperfect *fuerant* takes us back to a time before the coaxing promises of 139–40, suggesting that Theseus had rejected any thought of marriage from the outset (despite what he said to Ariadne) because of the supposed *praecepta* of his father" (Quinn).

        fuerant . . . / . . . (159) / . . . potuistī (160): pluperfect and perfect indicatives in a past contrary-to-fact condition instead of pluperfect subjunctives.

    cōnūbia: cf. **cōnūbia** (141).

    cōnūbia nostra: *my marriage, marriage to me;* **nostra:** poetic plural.

    nōn cordī . . . cōnūbia nostra: note the chiastic pattern of alliteration.

159 **quod:** here, *because;* delayed conjunction.

    horreō, horrēre, horruī, *to shudder at; to dread.*

    prīscus, -a, -um, *of olden times, ancient; old-fashioned; stern.*

    praeceptum, -ī, n., *precept.*

    parentis: this could refer to Minos, but more likely it refers to Aegeus (see note to line 158, **Sī tibi nōn cordī fuerant** above).

    prīscī praecepta parentis: alliteration.

154 "Quaenam tē genuit sōlā sub rūpe leaena,
155 quod mare conceptum spūmantibus exspuit undīs,
156 quae Syrtis, quae Scylla rapāx, quae vasta Charybdis,
157 tālia quī reddis prō dulcī praemia vītā?
158 Sī tibi nōn cordī fuerant cōnūbia nostra,
159 saeva quod horrēbās prīscī praecepta parentis,

continued

Comparisons

With lines 154–56, compare Catullus 60 and the passages from Homer and Euripides given for comparison with that poem on page 177.

Initial Explorations

46. What three themes does Ariadne develop rhetorically in lines 154–57 that have already been prominent in her complaint?
47. What excuse does Ariadne suggest that Theseus could offer for not wanting to marry her? (158–59) Would it exculpate him?

160   **attamen**, conj., *but yet*.
      vestrās . . . sēdēs: i.e., "the home of Theseus and his father" (Quinn).
      dūcere: supply **mē**.
161   **quae**: introducing a relative clause of purpose; translate *so that I* . . . ; the
          antecedent is **mē** (understood) from line 160.
      iūcundō: with **labōre**; ambiguous: pleasant to her or to Theseus or to both?
      famulor, -ārī, -ātus sum, *to be a servant;* + dat., *to serve*.
      serva, -ae, f., *female slave*.
          serva: *[as] a slave*.
162   **candida . . . liquidīs vēstīgia lymphīs**: interlocking word order or
          synchysis.
      permulceō [per-, intensive + **mulceō, mulcēre, mulsī**, *to touch lightly, stroke,*
          caress], **permulcēre, permulsī, permulsus**, *to stroke, caress*.
      liquidus, -a, -um, *fluid, liquid; clear*.
      vēstīgium, -ī, n., *footprint; underside of the foot, sole*.
      lympha, -ae, f., *spring water*.
          liquidīs . . . lymphīs: ablative of means.
163   **purpureus, -a, -um**, *dark-violet, purple*.
          purpureā . . . veste: ablative of means.
      cōnsternō [con-, intensive + **sternō, sternere, strāvī, strātus**, *to lay; to spread;*
          to stretch; to strike down], **cōnsternere, cōnstrāvī, cōnstrātus**, *to cover by*
          strewing; to spread.
      cubīle, cubīlis, n., *bed*.
          purpureāve tuum cōnsternēns veste cubīle: a golden line (see note to line
              59).
164   **Sed quid ego**: = 116.
      ignārus, -a, -um, *ignorant; unaware*.
      nēquīquam . . . aurīs: cf. **nēquīquam . . . ventīs** (111).
      conqueror [con-, intensive + **queror, querī, questus sum**, *to complain*],
          conquerī, conquestus sum, *to bewail;* + dat., *to cry out* (to).
          conquerar: deliberative subjunctive.
165   **externāta**: modifying the subject, **ego** (164); for the word, see line 71.
      quae: the antecedent is **aurīs** (164).
      sēnsus, -ūs, m., *feeling; sense*.
      augeō, augēre, auxī, auctus, *to increase, enrich*.
          auctae: + abl., *endowed* (with).
166   **missās**: *uttered*.
          missās audīre . . . reddere vōcēs: effective embedding of the paired
              infinitives.
      queō, quēre, quīvī, *to be able*.
167   **prope**: adverb, *nearly*.
      mediīs versātur in undīs: the word order complements the meaning.
      versātur: *he turns himself, he is*, passive in reflexive sense; cf. **versantem** (149).
168   **quisquam, quisquam, quicquam (quidquam)**, indefinite adjective, *any*.
      vacuus, -a, -um, *empty*.
      mortālis, mortālis, m., *human being, mortal*.
      algā: cf. **algā** (60).

160 "attamen in vestrās potuistī dūcere sēdēs,
161 quae tibi iūcundō famulārer serva labōre,
162 candida permulcēns liquidīs vēstīgia lymphīs,
163 purpureāve tuum cōnsternēns veste cubīle.
164 Sed quid ego ignārīs nēquīquam conquerar aurīs,
165 externāta malō, quae nūllīs sēnsibus auctae
166 nec missās audīre queunt nec reddere vōcēs?
167 Ille autem prope iam mediīs versātur in undīs,
168 nec quisquam appāret vacuā mortālis in algā.

continued

Initial Explorations

48. How are lines 160–63 appropriate as the climax of Ariadne's complaints against Theseus?
49. What word in line 164 indicates an abrupt shift in Ariadne's thinking? What reality does she now confront in lines 164–68?
50. What words and lines earlier in the poem are recalled in lines 164–68?

169 īnsultō [in-, *in, on* + saliō, salīre, salīvī or saliī, saltus, *to jump* + -tō, iterative
      or intensive suffix], -āre, -āvī, -ātus, *to leap upon; to mock.*
        īnsultāns: supply mē.
      extrēmō tempore: *at my last hour;* cf. suprēmō in tempore (151).
170 fors, fortis, f., *fortune.*
      etiam: adv., *even now,* modifying invīdit.
      nostrīs: poetic plural for meīs.
      invideō [in-, *in, on* + videō, vidēre, vīdī, vīsus, *to see*], invidēre, invīdī,
        invīsus, *to envy, be jealous of; to begrudge; to refuse to grant something* (acc.) *to
        someone* or *something* (dat.).
      questus, -ūs, m., *complaint, lament.*
      auris, auris, f., *ear.*
        aurīs: = aurēs, possibly with a pun on aurīs as dative plural of aura, -ae, f.,
          breeze.
171 omnipotēns, omnipotentis, *all-powerful.*
      utinam, adv. + pluperfect subjunctive for an unfulfilled wish with regard to
        past time, *would that . . . !, oh that . . . !, I wish that . . . !*
      tempore prīmō: we would say *in the first place.*
172 Gnōsius, -a, -um, *belonging to Cnossus* (in Crete); *Cretan.*
        Gnōsia Cecropiae: effective juxtaposition.
      tetigissent . . . / . . . / . . . religāsset . . . (174) / . . . / . . . requiēsset (176):
        pluperfect subjunctives of wish with utinam (171).
      puppis, puppis, f., *stern* (of a ship); by synecdoche, *ship.*
        Gnōsia . . . puppēs: a golden line (see note to line 59).
173 indomitō: cf. domitō (110) and indomitus (107).
      nec: delayed conjunction.
      dīrus, -a, -um, *horrible, dreadful.*
      ferēns: modifying the subject, nāvita (174).
      stīpendium, -ī, n., *tribute.*
      *taurus, -ī, m., *bull.*
        indomitō . . . dīra ferēns stīpendia taurō: embedded phrasing.
174 perfidus: cf. perfide (132, 133).
      religō [re-, *back* + ligō, -āre, -āvī, -ātus, *to fasten, bind*], -āre, -āvī, -ātus, *to tie
        up.*
        religāsset: = religāvisset.
      nāvita: archaic for nauta, -ae, m., *sailor.*
      fūnis, fūnis, m., *rope, cord; cable* (of a ship).
        nec (173) . . . / . . . in Crētā religāsset . . . fūnem: *had not tied up the cable [of
          his ship] in Crete;* see Text.
175 fōrma, -ae, f., *form; appearance.*
        dulcī crūdēlia fōrmā / cōnsilia: interlocking word order or synchysis.
176 requiēscō [re-, intensive + quiēscō, quiēscere, quiēvī, quiētūrus, *to rest*].
      requiēscere, requiēvī, requiētūrus, *to rest.*
        requiēsset: = requiēvisset.
      hospes: *stranger* or *guest.*
        malus . . . (175) / . . . hospes: echoing perfidus . . . nāvita (174).

169 "Sīc nimis īnsultāns extrēmō tempore saeva
170 fors etiam nostrīs invīdit questibus aurīs.
171 Iuppiter omnipotēns, utinam nē tempore prīmō
172 Gnōsia Cecropiae tetigissent lītora puppēs,
173 indomitō nec dīra ferēns stīpendia taurō
174 perfidus in Crētā religāsset nāvita fūnem,
175 nec malus hic cēlāns dulcī crūdēlia fōrmā
176 cōnsilia in nostrīs requiēsset sēdibus hospes!

continued

Text

173–74: nec . . . / . . . in Crētā religāsset . . . fūnem

This is the reading of Thomson and Godwin, following the reading of
manuscript O, *had not tied up the cable [of his ship] in Crete*. The Oxford
Classical text has **in Crētam**, *had not untied the cable [of his ship] for Crete*, i.e.,
had not set sail for Crete; Thomson regards this as "doubtful Latin." The verb
religāre usually means *to tie*, not *to untie*.

175 hic

Thomson reads **haec**, modifying **crūdēlia . . . / cōnsilia** (176).

Comparisons

With lines 171–72, compare the beginning of Euripides' *Medea* and the beginning
of Ennius' *Medea*, given on page 320.

Initial Explorations

51. How does the phrase **extrēmō tempore** (169) emphasize how *excessively
     mocking* (**nimis īnsultāns**) and *cruel* (**saeva**) fortune is to Ariadne?
52. Of what three sets of ears (**aurīs**, 170) have Ariadne's complaints been
     deprived?
53. Whom does Ariadne address in lines 171–76? With what three wishes?
54. How is Theseus described in these lines?
55. What is the significance of the allusions to Euripides and Ennius?
56. To what famous mythological figure might the word **hospes** (176), in the
     emphatic position at the end of the line and sentence, allude? How would
     this allusion reflect on the love affair of Theseus and Ariadne?

177   sē referre, idiom, *to take oneself back, to return.*
    mē referam: deliberative subjunctive.
    *spēs, speī, f., *hope.*
    perdita: cf. dēperdita (119) and perdita (70).
    nītor: cf. nītēns (84).
178   Īdaeus, -a, -um, *Idean, of Mt. Ida* (a mountain in Crete).
    petam: deliberative subjunctive.
    *gurges, gurgitis, m., *whirlpool; water* (of a river or sea).
    lātus, -a, -um, *wide, broad.*
179   discernō [dis-, *apart* + cernō, cernere, crēvī, crētus, *to distinguish, separate*],
      discernere, discrēvī, discrētus, *to divide, separate.*
    pontus, -ī, m., *sea.*
    truculentus, -a, -um, *ferocious.*
    dīvidit: pleonastic with discernēns; supply mē ab Īdaeīs montibus.
180   spērem: deliberative subjunctive.
    ipsa: here, *voluntarily, of my own free will.*
181   *respergō [re-, *back, again* + spargō, spargere, sparsī, sparsus, *to scatter; to
      sprinkle*], respergere, respersī, respersus, *to sprinkle.*
      respersum: modifying iuvenem.
    frāternā: cf. germānum (150).
    caede: here, *blood.*
    secūta: perfect participles of deponent verbs are often best translated as
      present tense.
182   Coniugis: see line 123.
    fīdus, -a, -um, *faithful.*
    cōnsōlor [con-, intensive + sōlor, -ārī, -ātus sum, *to comfort, console*], -ārī,
      -ātus sum, *to comfort, console.*
      cōnsōler: deliberative subjunctive.
    mēmet: an intensified mē.
183   lentus, -a, -um, *slow; flexible, pliant; bending under strain.*
    incurvō [in-, intensive + curvus, -a, -um, *curved, bent* + -ō], -āre, -āvī, -ātus, *to
      bend; to make X curve.*
      incurvāns: "a sign of urgent haste" (Thomson).
184   nūllō . . . tēctō: ablative with colitur and effectively surrounding the verb
      and subject.
    colō, colere, coluī, cultus, *to cultivate; to inhabit.*
    sōla: cf. sōlā (154).
185   pateō, -ēre, -uī, *to be open; to be available.*
    ēgressus, -ūs, m., *egress, escape.*
    cingō, cingere, cīnxī, cīnctus, *to surround, encircle.*
      pelagī cingentibus undīs: ablative absolute.
186   Nūlla . . . nūlla: anaphora, and picking up nūllō (184).
    fuga, -ae, f., *escape, flight.*
    ratiō, ratiōnis, f., *manner, method, means.*
187   omnia (186) . . . / omnia . . . omnia: anaphora and ascending tricolon.
    ostentō [ob-, *against* + tendō, tendere, tetendī, tentus or tēnsus, *to stretch*
      + -tō], -āre, -āvī, -ātus, *to exhibit, display; to hold out the prospect of* X (acc.).

177   "Nam quō mē referam? Quālī spē perdita nītor?

178   Īdaeōsne petam montēs? At gurgite lātō

179   discernēns pontī truculentum dīvidit aequor.

180   An patris auxilium spērem? Quemne ipsa relīquī

181   respersum iuvenem frāternā caede secūta?

182   Coniugis an fīdō cōnsōler mēmet amōre?

183   Quīne fugit lentōs incurvāns gurgite rēmōs?

184   Praetereā nūllō colitur sōla īnsula tēctō,

185   nec patet ēgressus pelagī cingentibus undīs.

186   Nūlla fugae ratiō, nūlla spēs: omnia mūta,

187   omnia sunt dēserta, ostentant omnia lētum.

continued

Comparisons

With lines 177–81, compare Euripides' *Medea* 502–5 and Ennius' *Medea*, fragment 284–85, given on page 321.

With line 181, compare Apollonius, *Argonautica* 4.464–74, where Jason, with Medea's help, slays Medea's brother, Apsyrtus, and she is sprinkled with her brother's blood; see page 321.

Initial Explorations

57.   Compare lines 177–81 with Euripides, *Medea* 502–5 and Ennius, *Medea*, fragment 284–85. What is the essential point that Ariadne makes in lines 177–81?

58.   Now that Ariadne realizes that she has no recourse to her father, to whom might she look for sympathy? (182) Why would this be to no avail? (183)

59.   To what thought about her predicament does Ariadne finally come in lines 184–87? How do these lines bring a conclusion to her complaint that began in line 164?

60.   Explain the effects of anaphora and the ascending tricolon in lines 186–87.

188 ante . . . / . . . prius . . . (189) / quam (190): = antequam/priusquam, *before*,
      with the subjunctives exposcam (190) and comprecer (191).
    mihī: dative of reference expressing possession, *my*.
    languēscō, languēscere, languī, *to grow weak, grow faint; to swoon*.
       languēscent: cf. languentī (99).
    lūmina: cf. lūmina (122).
    morte: ablative with languēscent.
189 fessus, -a, -um, *weary, tired*.
    sēcēdō [sē-, *apart* + cēdō, cēdere, cessī, cessūrus, *to go*], sēcēdere, sēcessī,
       sēcessūrus, *to go away, withdraw*.
    sēnsus, -ūs, m., *feeling, sense*.
       sēnsūs: note the location of this word beyond the word corpore,
          complementing the meaning of the clause.
190 iūstus, -a, -um, *just, rightful*.
    dīvus, -ī, m., *god*.
    *exposcō [ex-, intensive + poscō, poscere, poposcī, *to demand*], exposcere,
       expoposcī, *to demand*.
    prōdō [prō-, *forward* + dō, dare, dedī, datus, *to give*], prōdere, prōdidī,
       prōditus, *to betray*.
    multa, -ae, f., *fine; punishment*.
       iūstam ā dīvīs exposcam prōdita multam: cf. Medea's and Dido's
          determination to avenge themselves on the men who betray them.
191 *caelestis, caelestis, m./f., *heavenly one, god/goddess*; pl., *gods*.
    caelestum: = caelestium.
    postrēmus, -a, -um, *last, final*.
    comprecor [con-, intensive + precor, -ārī, -ātus sum, *to pray*], -ārī, -ātus
       sum, *to pray to, call upon*.
192 multō, -āre, -āvī, -ātus, *to punish*.
    multantēs: modifying the vocative Eumenidēs (193); cf. multam (190).
       multantēs vindice poenā: pleonastic for emphasis.
    vindex, vindicis, m./f., *vindicator, avenger*; here as adjective, *avenging*.
193 Eumenidēs, Eumenidum, f. pl., *Eumenides* ("the gracious ones," a
      euphemism for the avenging spirits, the Erinyes or Furies).
       Eumenidēs: vocative with the imperatives adventāte . . . audīte (195)
          and nōlīte (199); the Furies are described specifically as punishing
          perjurers in Homer, *Iliad* 19.259–60, and Hesiod, *Works and Days* 803–4.
    quibus: *whose*, dative of reference expressing possession.
    anguīnus: = anguīneus, -a, -um, *snaky*.
    redimītus, -a, -um, *bound, crowned*.
       anguīnō redimīta capillō / frōns (194): interlocking word order.
194 exspīrō [ex-, *out* + spīrō, -āre, -āvī, -ātus, *to breathe*], -āre, -āvī, -ātus, *to breathe
      forth*.
       exspīrantīs (acc. pl.) . . . pectoris īrās: *the wrath of* [your] *chest as it* [i.e.,
          your wrath] *breathes forth*. pectoris: seat of the lungs and of emotions.
    praeportō [prae-, *before* + portō, -āre, -āvī, -ātus, *to carry*], -āre, -āvī, -ātus, *to
       carry in front*; here, *to display*.
       exspīrantīs praeportat pectoris: alliteration.

188   "Nōn tamen ante mihī languēscent lūmina morte,
189   nec prius ā fessō sēcēdent corpore sēnsūs,
190   quam iūstam ā dīvīs exposcam prōdita multam
191   caelestumque fidem postrēmā comprecer hōrā.
192   Quārē facta virum multantēs vindice poenā
193   Eumenidēs, quibus anguīnō redimīta capillō
194   frōns exspīrantīs praeportat pectoris īrās,

continued

Initial Explorations

61.   What is Ariadne determined to do before she dies? What single word in line 190 expresses her justification for her determination to do this?
62.   Why does Ariadne appeal specifically to the *faithfulness of the gods* (caelestum . . . fidem, 191)?
63.   How does Ariadne's description of the Furies reflect her own emotional state?

195   **adventō** [**ad-**, *to, toward* + **veniō, venīre, vēnī, ventūrus**, *to come* + **-tō**,
        iterative or intensive suffix], **-āre, -āvī, -ātūrus**, *to approach, arrive at; to come.*
     querellās: cf. **querellīs** (130).

196   **vae**, interjection, expressing pain or anger, usually + dat., *alas!*
        vae misera: *alas, wretch [that I am]*; here **vae** + nom., but see **Text.**
        extrēmīs . . . medullīs: ablative of source without a preposition; for the
          phrase, cf. **īmō . . . ē pectore** (125) and **īmīs medullīs** (93).
        prōferō [**prō-**, *forward* + **ferō, ferre, tulī, lātus**, *to bring*], **prōferre, prōtulī,**
          prōlātus, *to bring forth.*

197   **inops, inopis**, *weak, helpless.*
     ārdēns: cf. **ārdentī** (124).
     āmēns, āmentis, *mindless; insane.*
     *caecus, -a, -um, *blind, blinded.*
     furōre: cf. **furentem** (124) and **furōrēs** (54).
        inops, ardēns, āmentī caeca furōre: asyndeton; ascending tricolon.

198   **Quae**: the antecedent is **querellās** (195).
     vērae: translate as an adverb, *truly, sincerely.*
     īmus, -a, -um, *lowest/deepest (part of).*
        pectore ab īmō: note the chiasmus created with **extrēmīs . . . medullīs** or
          īmīs . . . medullīs, see **Text** (196) and again cf. **īmō . . . ē pectore** (125).

199   **nōlīte patī**: *do not allow.*
     nostrum: poetic plural for **meum.**
     vānēscō, vānēscere, *to pass away, vanish.*
     lūctum: cf. **lūctibus** (71).

200   **quālī . . . mente**: *with the sort of mind with which*, ablative of manner. The
        quality of mind to which Ariadne is referring is, of course, Theseus'
        forgetfulness, which he has displayed in abandoning her; cf. **immemor**
        (135).
     sōlam Thēseus mē: note how the words **sōlam . . . mē** embrace **Thēseus.**

201   **tālī mente**: *with such a mind*, ablative of manner, answering **quālī . . . mente**
        (200).
     fūnestō, -āre, -āvī, -ātus, *to defile/pollute with murder/death.*
     fūnestet: optative subjunctive expressing a wish.
     -que . . . -que: *both . . . and*, polysyndeton.

195 "hūc hūc adventāte, meās audīte querellās,
196 quās ego, vae misera, extrēmīs prōferre medullīs
197 cōgor inops, ārdēns, āmentī caeca furōre.
198 Quae quoniam vērae nāscuntur pectore ab īmō,
199 vōs nōlīte patī nostrum vānēscere lūctum,
200 sed quālī sōlam Thēseus mē mente relīquit,
201 tālī mente, deae, fūnestet sēque suōsque."

continued

Text

196 **vae misera, extrēmīs**

Thomson reads **vae miserae, īmīs**. This provides a dative case with **vae**; the substitution of **īmīs** (cf. **īmīs . . . medullīs**, 93) for **extrēmīs** produces hiatus.

Initial Explorations

64. What descriptive language in lines 196–97 recalls ways in which Ariadne is portrayed in earlier portions of her complaint?

65. In line 190, Ariadne asserted that, *betrayed* (**prōdita**), she would demand *just punishment* (**iūstam . . . multam**) *from the gods* (**ā dīvīs**). As she addresses the Furies in lines 196–99, she no longer speaks in terms of justice. How does she instead appeal to the Furies' and the reader's pity?

66. The curse ends in lines 200–201 with what specific request? What principle of justice, which has been featured throughout Ariadne's complaint, does it exemplify?

202   **maestō**: cf. **maestam** (130); lines 130–31 and 202 frame Ariadne's lament.

       prōfundō [**prō-**, *forward* + **fundō, fundere, fūdī, fūsus**, *to pour*], **prōfundere, prōfūdī, prōfūsus**, *to pour forth.*

203   **supplicium, -ī**, n., *punishment.*

       ***ānxius, -a, -um**, *worried, disturbed, distressed.*

       ānxia: cf. **inops, ārdēns, āmentī caeca furōre** (197).

204   ***annuō** [**ad-**, *to, toward* + **nuō** (unattested), *to nod*], **annuere, annuī, annūtus**, *to nod assent.*

       invictus, -a, -um, *unconquered; invincible; firm, resolute.*

       nūmine: see 134, **nūmine.**

         annuit . . . nūmine: an etymological play on words since both words are derived from the unattested verb ***nuō.**

       invictō . . . nūmine: ablative of means, *with resolute nod.*

       rēctor, rēctōris, m., *ruler.*

205   **mōtus, -ūs**, m., *movement, motion.*

       tellūs, tellūris, f., *ground; the earth.*

       horridus, -a, -um, *rough.*

       contremēscō [**con-**, intensive + **tremō, tremere, tremuī**, *to tremble* + **-scō**, iterative or intensive suffix], **contremēscere, contremuī**, *to tremble violently.*

206   **concutiō** [**con-**, intensive + **quatiō, quatere, _____, quassus**, *to shake*], **concutere, concussī, concussus**, *to shake violently.*

         concussit: *caused to shiver* (Thomson).

       micō, micāre, micuī, *to quiver; to flash; to gleam; to flicker.*

       sīdus, sīderis, n., *heavenly body; planet, star.*

       mundus, -ī, m., *the heavens; the firmament.*

207   **caecus, -a, -um**, *blind; dark, black; blinding.*

       cālīgō, cālīginis, f., *darkness.*

         caecā . . . cālīgine: ablative with **cōnsitus** (208); with **caecā**, cf. **caeca** (197).

208   **cōnserō** [**con-**, intensive + **serō, serere, sēvī, satus**, *to sow, plant*], **cōnserere, cōnsēvī, cōnsitus**, *to sow.*

         caecā mentem cālīgine . . . (207) / cōnsitus: *having sown his mind with . . . .*; for this use of a perfect passive participle in a reflexive sense denoting an action that one performs upon oneself, see the note on **nōn contēcta pectus** (64). Cf. **spīnōsās Erycīna serēns in pecore cūrās** (72); while Venus sowed prickly emotional distress in Ariadne's heart, Theseus' mind was sown with the blinding darkness of forgetfulness. Cf. Ariadne's description of herself as **āmentī <u>caeca</u> furōre** (197).

       oblītus, -a, -um, *forgetful.*

       cūncta, / quae mandāta (209): = **cūncta mandāta, quae.**

209   ***cōnstāns, cōnstantis**, *firm, stable, steady.*

210   **nec**: *and not*; take the negative with both **sustollēns** and **ostendit** (211).

       maestō: cf. **maestō** (202).

       ***sustollō, sustollere** [**sub-**, *up from below* + **tollō, tollere**, *to lift, raise*], *to raise.*

211   **sōspitem**: cf. **sōspes** (112).

       Erechthēus, -a, -um, *of/associated with Erechtheus* (legendary king of Athens and great-grandfather of Aegeus); *Athenian.*

         210–11: note the alliteration of s's.

202 Hās postquam maestō prōfūdit pectore vōcēs,
203 supplicium saevīs exposcēns ānxia factīs,
204 annuit invictō caelestum nūmine rēctor;
205 quō mōtū tellūs atque horrida contremuērunt
206 aequora concussitque micantia sīdera mundus.
207 Ipse autem caecā mentem cālīgine Thēseus
208 cōnsitus oblītō dīmīsit pectore cūncta,
209 quae mandāta prius cōnstantī mente tenēbat,
210 dulcia nec maestō sustollēns signa parentī
211 sōspitem Erecthēum sē ostendit vīsere portum.

continued

Comparisons

With lines 204-6, compare Homer, *Iliad* 1.524–30, given on page 322.

Initial Explorations

67. What is the response in lines 202–6 to Ariadne's demand? What might this response suggest about her demand?
68. What is emphasized in the picture of Jupiter nodding assent? How does Catullus' description differ from that of Homer in *Iliad* 1.524–30?
69. What is the result in lines 207–11 of Jupiter's assent to Ariadne's curse?
70. Identify a word picture in lines 207–8 and a pattern of alliteration that highlights it.

212 **Namque ferunt ōlim**: cf. **Nam perhibent ōlim** (76).
     classī: = **classe**, again of a single ship; cf. **classe** (53, the usual ablative).
     cum: delayed conjunction.
     moenia: object of **linquentem** (213).
     dīva, -ae, f., *goddess*.
        dīvae: i.e., Athena.
213 *__gnātus, -ī__, m., *son*.
     concrēdō [**con-**, intensive + **crēdō, crēdere, crēdidī, crēditus**, *to trust; to
        believe*], **concrēdere, concrēdidī, concrēditus**, *to entrust*.
     Aegeus, -ī, m., *Aegeus* (father of Theseus).
        Aegeus: pronounced as two syllables.
214 **complector** [**con-**, intensive + **plectō, plectere, plexī, plexus**, *to twine*],
        complectī, complexus sum, *to embrace*.
           complexum: supply **eum**, i.e., Aegeus, as subject of the infinitive **dedisse**
              in the indirect statement dependent on **ferunt** (212), and supply
              gnātum as object of **complexum**.
     mandāta: cf. **mandāta** (209).
215 **Gnāte . . . / gnāte** (216): vocative; anaphora.
     ūnicus, -a, -um, *sole, one and only*.
        ūnice: take with **Gnāte**, *[My] one and only son*. The word **iucundior** is also
           vocative and is in apposition to the phrase **Gnāte. . . ūnice**.
216 **dubius, -a, -um**, *uncertain*.
     dīmittere: cf. **dīmīsit** (208).
     cāsus, -ūs, m., *fall; event; misfortune; circumstances*.
217 **reddite**: vocative, continuing the address to Theseus.
     extrēmus, -a, -um, *last, final, extreme*.
     fīne: feminine here.
     senecta, -ae, f., *old age*.
218 **quandoquidem fortūna . . . / ēripit . . . mihi tē** (219): cf. Catullus 101.5,
        quandoquidem fortūna mihī tētē abstulit ipsum.
     fervidus, -a, -um, *hot, burning; hot-blooded, ardent*.
     virtūs, virtūtis, f., *manliness; valor; worth; virtue*.
219 **invītō mihi**: dative of separation with **ēripit**.
     cui: *whose*, dative of reference; the antecedent is **mihi**, not **tē**.
     languidus, -a, -um, *ailing; enfeebled; faint, swooning*.
        languida: cf. **languēscent** (188).
220 **lūmina**: cf. **lūmina** (188) and earlier references to Ariadne's eyes.
     saturō, -āre, -āvī, -ātus, *to satisfy, satiate*.
221 **gaudēns laetantī pectore**: pleonastic for emphasis.
222 **secundus, -a, -um**, *second; favorable*.
223 **exprōmō** [**ex-**, *out* + **prōmō, prōmere, prōmpsī, prōmptus**, *to bring out/forth
        (from some storage place)*], **exprōmere, exprōmpsī, exprōmptus**, *to bring
        out/forth (from some storage place); to bring forth, give expression to*.
     querellās: cf. **querellās** (195).

212 Namque ferunt ōlim, classī cum moenia dīvae
213 linquentem gnātum ventīs concrēderet Aegeus,
214 tālia complexum iuvenī mandāta dedisse:
215 "Gnāte mihī longā iūcundior ūnice vītā,
216 gnāte, ego quem in dubiōs cōgor dīmittere cāsūs,
217 reddite in extrēmā nūper mihi fīne senectae,
218 quandoquidem fortūna mea ac tua fervida virtūs
219 ēripit invītō mihi tē, cui languida nōndum
220 lūmina sunt gnātī cārā saturāta figūrā,
221 nōn ego tē gaudēns laetantī pectore mittam,
222 nec tē ferre sinam fortūnae signa secundae,
223 sed prīmum multās exprōmam mente querellās,

continued

Text

215 **longā**

Thomson reads **longē**.

Myth

217 **reddite in extrēmā nūper mihi fīne senectae**: Theseus passed his early life with his mother Aethra in the home of her father Pittheus, king of Troezene, and when he finally came to Athens, found Aegeus already an old man. —Merrill

Initial Explorations

71. What is the significance of the fact that the words **Namque ferunt ōlim** (212) recall the words **Nam perhibent ōlim** (76)?
72. What do we learn about Aegeus and Theseus as the father addresses his son in lines 215–17? What is the tone of the father's address to his son?
73. Identify a chiasmus in line 218 and an effective juxtaposition of words in line 219.
74. What words used by Aegeus in lines 219b–220 recall words of Ariadne? To what effect?

224 **cānitiēs, -ēī**, f., *grayness* (of hair); concrete, *gray hair* (of old people).

īnfundō [**in-**, *in, on* + **fundō, fundere, fūdī, fūsus**, *to pour*], **īnfundere, īnfūdī, īnfūsus**, *to pour on.*

foedō, -āre, -āvī, -ātus, *to soil, defile.*

225 ***īnficiō** [**in-**, *in* + **faciō, facere, fēcī, factus**, *to make; to do*], **īnficere, īnfēcī, īnfectus**, *to dye; to darken with dye.*

vagus, -a, -um, *wandering; moving.*

***linteum, -ī**, n., *linen cloth; towel; sail.*

mālus, -ī, m., *pole; mast.*

226 **lūctūs**: cf. **lūctum** (199) and **lūctibus** (71) of Ariadne's grief.

incendia: *fires*, here, *emotional turmoil*; cf. **incēnsam . . . mente** (97) and lines 91–93.

227 **carbasus, -ī**, f., *canvas; sail.*

obscūrō, -āre, -āvī, -ātus, *to hide; to darken.*

dicō, -āre, -āvī, -ātus, *to indicate, show.*

   dicet: subjunctive; note that this is not from **dīcō, dīcere**; the compound verb **indicō, -āre**, would normally be used for the sense required here.

ferrūgō, ferrūginis, f., *iron-rust* (used as a dye, producing a color between dark purple and black).

Hibērus, -a, -um, *Iberian, Spanish.*

228 **Quod . . . sī**: *But if.*

concēdō [**con-**, intensive + **cēdō, cēdere, cessī, cessūrus**, *to go; to yield*], **concēdere, concessī, concessus**, *to go away; to yield; to grant.*

   concesserit: followed by **ut . . . respergās** (230).

Itōnus, -ī, m., *Itonus* (the name of Thessalian and Boeotian towns having cults of Athena).

   incola Itōnī: i.e., Athena.

229 **Erechtēus, -ī**, m., *Erechtheus* (legendary king of Athens).

   Erechthēī: pronounced as three syllables.

230 **annuit**: see line 204; here + infin., *has given her assent (to), has agreed (to).*

ut: introducing a clause dependent on **concesserit** (228).

respergās: cf. **respersum** (181).

231 **facitō**: solemn future imperative; **facitō ut**, *see to it that* (introducing two substantive clauses of result dependent on this verb of effort).

memorī: cf. **immemor** (135).

condō, condere, condidī, conditus, *to store up for future use, preserve.*

232 **vigeō, -ēre, -uī**, *to be active; to flourish, thrive; to live on* (in the memory).

mandāta: cf. **mandāta** (214).

ūlla: modifying **aetās**.

oblitterō [cf. **oblīvīscor, oblīvīscī, oblītus sum**, *to forget*], **-āre, -āvī, -ātus**, *to cause to be forgotten.*

   oblitteret: supply **haec mandāta** or **ea** as object.

***aetās, aetātis**, f., *age; passage of time.*

224 cānitiem terrā atque īnfūsō pulvere foedāns,
225 inde īnfecta vagō suspendam lintea mālō,
226 nostrōs ut lūctūs nostraeque incendia mentis
227 carbasus obscūrāta dicet ferrūgine Hibērā.
228 Quod tibi sī sānctī concesserit incola Itōnī,
229 quae nostrum genus ac sēdēs dēfendere Erechthēī
230 annuit, ut taurī respergās sanguine dextram,
231 tum vērō facitō ut memorī tibi condita corde
232 haec vigeant mandāta, nec ūlla oblitteret aetās;

continued

Comparisons

With line 224, compare Homer, *Iliad* 18.23–27, Achilles' grief at the death of Patroclus, and *Iliad* 24.163–65, Priam's grief at the death of Hector, given on page 322.

Initial Explorations

75. What words used by Aegeus in line 226 continue to recall Ariadne?
76. The gesture referred to in line 224 of pouring dust over one's head is modeled on two scenes in Homer, *Iliad* 18.23–27 and 24.163–65 (see **Comparisons** above). What is the significance of Catullus' allusion here?
77. What word used by Aegeus in line 231 recalls a word previously associated with Theseus? What is the effect of the recall?

233 **ut**: introducing two clauses of result with the verbs **dēpōnant** (234) and
       sustollant (235).
     invīsō [in-, *in, on* + **vīsō, vīsere, vīsī,** *to see*], **invīsere, invīsī, invīsus,** *to visit;
       to see.*
         invīsent: cf. **vīsere** (211).
     lūmina: cf. **lūmina** (220, of Aegeus' eyes, here of Theseus').
234 ***fūnestus, -a, -um,** *of or concerned with death or mourning, funereal.*
         fūnestam . . . vestem: *the garb of mourning* (Merrill), but the phrase is here
            used of the sails of Theseus' ship; cf. **fūnestet** (201).
     antenna, -ae, f., *yard* (of a sailing ship), *yardarm.*
235 **intortus, -a, -um,** *twisted.*
     sustollant: cf. **sustollēns** (210).
     ***vēlum, -ī,** n., *sail.*
     rudēns, rudentis, m., *rope.*
         candidaque . . . rudentēs: a golden line (see note to line 59).
236 **quam prīmum:** *as soon as.*
     cernō, cernere, crēvī, crētus, *to distinguish; to discern* (with the eyes); *to see.*
     ut: conjunction delayed from the beginning of the line.
     laetā gaudia: effective juxtaposition.
237 **redux, reducis,** *coming back, returning.*
     aetās: cf. **aetās** (232); here translate *day* (Thomson).
     prosperus, -a, -um, *successful.*
         aetās prospera: *the day of your success.*
     sistō, sistere, stetī or **stitī, status,** *to make* (someone) *stand; to present* (a
       person).
238 **Haec mandāta**: cf. **mandāta** (232); in line 238 the words **Haec mandāta** serve
       as the accusative direct object of **tenentem**; then they serve as the
       nominative subject of **līquēre** (240).
239 **ceu**, particle, *in the same way as, as.*
     pellō, pellere, pepulī, pulsus, *to strike; to drive.*
     flāmen, flāminis, n., *blast, gust* (of wind).
         flāmine: cf. **flāmine** (107), used there in a simile describing Theseus' victory
            over the Minotaur but used here in a simile describing Theseus' undoing
            when he forgets his father's orders.
240 **āereus, -a, -um** [four syllables; Greek loan word], *reaching high into the air,
       lofty.*
     niveus, -a, -um, *snowy.*
     līquēre: = **līquērunt**; the perfect tense verb here represents a simple past
       action when it serves as the verb with **Haec mandāta** (238) as its subject and
       Thēsea (239) as its object. Within the simile, with **nūbēs** (239) as its subject
       and **cacūmen** (240) as its object, it is a gnomic perfect, to be translated as a
       present tense.
     cacūmen, cacūminis, n., *top, peak.*

233 "ut simul ac nostrōs invīsent lūmina collīs,
234 fūnestam antennae dēpōnant undique vestem,
235 candidaque intortī sustollant vēla rudentēs,
236 quam prīmum cernēns ut laetā gaudia mente
237 agnōscam, cum tē reducem aetās prospera sistet."
238 Haec mandāta prius cōnstantī mente tenentem
239 Thēsea ceu pulsae ventōrum flāmine nūbēs
240 āereum niveī montis līquēre cacūmen.

continued

Initial Explorations

78. What is Aegeus' command in lines 233–35? Why does it make sense that he issue this command?
79. What is accomplished by having line 238, **Haec mandāta prius cōnstantī mente tententem**, recall line 209, **quae mandāta prius cōnstantī mente tenēbat**?
80. In lines 239–40 Catullus uses a simile that likens Theseus' forgetting of his father's commands to clouds driven by the winds and scattering from a high mountain summit. What specific aspect of Theseus' relationship to Ariadne does mention of the winds here recall? To what effect?

241 **ut**, conj. + indicative, *while*.
  prōspectus, -ūs, m., *viewpoint, prospect, view*.
    prōspectum: cf. **prōspectāns** (53, of Ariadne) and **prōspicit** (61, 62, of Ariadne), here of Aegeus.
242 **ānxia**: cf. **ānxia** (203).
  assiduōs: cf. **assiduīs** (71).
  absūmō [**ab-**, *completely, thoroughly* + **sūmō, sūmere, sūmpsī, sūmptus**, *to take up*], **absūmere, absūmpsī, absūmptus**, *to use up; to waste*.
    in assiduōs . . . flētūs: **in** + acc. of the thing on or with which one wastes one's resources.
  lūmina: cf. **lūmina** (233, of Theseus' eyes), here of Aegeus'.
243 **cum prīmum**: cf. **quam prīmum** (236).
  īnfectī: cf. **īnfecta** (225); but see **Text**.
244 **praeceps** [**prae-**, *in front, ahead* + **-ceps**, from **caput, capitis**, n., *head*], **praecipitis**, *headlong*.
  scopulus, ī, m., *rock* (projecting into the sea).
    scopulōrum ē vertice: cf. Ariadne in lines 126–27; cf. **ex arce** (241).
245 **āmittō** [**ā-, ab-**, *from, away* + **mittō, mittere, mīsī, missus**, *to send*], **āmittere, āmīsī, āmissus**, *to send away; to lose*.
    amissum: supply **esse**.
  crēdēns: cf. **crēdit** (55).
246 **fūnesta**: = **fūnestāta** (see line 201; cf. **fūnestam**, 234), modified by **paternā / morte** (247).
  domūs . . . tēcta: periphrasis for *house/home*.
  paternus, -a, -um, *paternal, a father's*.
247 **ferōx**: cf. **ferōx** (73).
  quālem . . . / . . . tālem (248): cf. **quālī . . . mente . . . / tālī mente** (200–201) in Ariadne's curse, which is fulfilled here.
  Mīnōidi: dative sing., here with short *i*, as in Greek; for the name, cf. **Mīnōis** (60).
  lūctum: cf. **lūctūs** (226) of Aegeus' grief and **lūctum** (199) and **lūctibus** (71) of Ariadne's grief.
248 **immemorī**: cf. **immemor** (135) and **immemorī** (58).
249 **Quae**: *And she*; the antecedent is **Mīnōidi** (247).
  prōspectāns: cf. **prōspectum** (241).
    prōspectāns cēdentem . . . carīnam: cf. **prōspicit** (61, 62) and **prōspectāns . . . / Thēsea cēdentem** (52–53).
  maesta: cf. **maestō** (210) and **maestīs** (60).
  carīna, -ae, f., *keel, hull; ship*.
250 **multiplex, multiplicis**, *having many twists or turns; multitudinous*.
  volvō, volvere, volvī, volūtus, *to roll; to turn over* (in the mind).
  saucius, -a, -um, *wounded; distressed*.
  cūrās: cf. **cūrās** (72) and **cūrārum** (62); with the entire line 250, cf. line 54.

241 At pater, ut summā prōspectum ex arce petēbat,
242 ānxia in assiduōs absūmēns lūmina flētūs,
243 cum prīmum īnfectī cōnspexit lintea vēlī,
244 praecipitem sēsē scopulōrum ē vertice iēcit,
245 āmissum crēdēns immītī Thēsea fātō.
246 Sīc fūnesta domūs ingressus tēcta paternā
247 morte ferōx Thēseus, quālem Mīnōidi lūctum
248 obtulerat mente immemorī, tālem ipse recēpit.
249 Quae tum prōspectāns cēdentem maesta carīnam
250 multiplicēs animō volvēbat saucia cūrās.

continued

Text

243 **īnfectī**

Thomson and Godwin keep the manuscript reading **īnflātī**, instead of changing it to **īnfectī** with Sabellicus, Guarinus, and the Oxford Classical Text.
> **īnflō** [**in-**, *in, on* + **flō, -āre, -āvī, -ātus,** *to blow*], **-āre, -āvī, -ātus,** *to fill with wind; to cause to swell.*

Myth

241 **summā . . . ex arce**: i.e., from the Acropolis, whence he would have an unimpeded view over the sea southward. . . . Another form [of the story] makes the promontory of Sunium the place whence Aegeus watched for the return of the ship, on descrying which he threw himself into the thence-named Aegean Sea. . . . —Merrill

Myth

Line 244, **praecipitem sēsē scopulōrum ē vertice iēcit,** may allude to the alternate story of Aegeus' death (see the **Myth** note on line 241).

Initial Explorations

81. Lines 241–42 present an image of Aegeus looking out across the sea from the top of the citadel in Athens and weeping. What earlier scenes does this recall? To what effect?
82. Compare line 245 with line 55. How is the echo of **crēdit** (55) in **crēdēns** (245) significant?
83. Identify the numerous verbal and thematic echoes in lines 246–50 of words and themes in the preceding body of the *ecphrasis*. What is the purpose and effect of these echoes?

251 **parte ex aliā**: i.e., of the coverlet that is being described in this entire passage.
flōrēns, flōrentis, *flowering; in the flower of one's youth.*
volitō [volō, -āre, -āvī, -ātūrus, *to fly* + **-tō,** iterative or intensive suffix], **-āre, -āvī, -ātūrus,** *to fly.*
Iacchus, -ī, m., *Iacchus* (another name for Dionysus or Bacchus).

252 **thiasus, -ī,** m. [Greek loan word], *band* (of people or Satyrs taking part in orgiastic dancing in honor of Dionysus).
Satyrus, -ī, m., *Satyr* (a type of young mythological woodland creature half human and half goat associated with Dionysus).
Nȳsigena, -ae, m., adj., *born on Mount Nysa* (in India or Arabia or Thrace, the birthplace of Dionysus).
Sīlēnus, -ī, m., *Silenus* (a type of elderly mythological woodland creature half human and half goat associated with Dionysus).
Sīlēnīs: spondaic fifth foot.

253 **Ariadna:** apostrophe.
īncēnsus: cf. **incēnsam** (97, of Ariadne), here, of Bacchus.

251　At parte ex aliā flōrēns volitābat Iacchus

252　cum thiasō Satyrōrum et Nȳsigenīs Sīlēnīs,

253　tē quaerēns, Ariadna, tuōque incēnsus amōre.

Initial Explorations

84.　What separate picture on the tapestry begins in lines 251–53?

85.　In what basic way does this picture counterbalance the long description of scenes centered around Ariadne that was previously narrated?

Discussion

1.　Discuss the literary structure of the *ecphrasis* in lines 50–253. How would you describe its segments? What purpose does such a structure serve? What are the proportions between visual representation, such as we would expect in an *ecphrasis*, and epic narrative?

2.　Discuss the value of heroism in the *ecphrasis*.

3.　Whose voice, or voices, do we hear in the *ecphrasis*? Who is the audience?

4.　Discuss Ariadne's relation to the tragic heroine Medea. What problems of chronology are involved in making Medea a model for Ariadne?

Meter: elegiac couplet

1   **etsī**, conj., *although.*
    assiduus, -a, -um, *incessant, constant.*
    cōnficiō [**con-**, intensive + **faciō, facere, fēcī, factus**, *to make; to do*], *to*
        accomplish, finish; to overwhelm.
    cūra: *distress.*
2   **sēvocō** [**sē-**, *away, apart* + **vocō, -āre, -āvī, -ātus**, *to call*], **-āre, -āvī, -ātus**, *to*
        call away.
    doctus, -a, -um, *learned.*
        doctīs . . . virginibus: i.e., the Muses.
    Ortalus, -ī, m., *Ortalus*, more commonly spelled Hortalus (Quintus
        Hortensius Hortalus, 114–50 B.C., an orator who was a rival of Cicero and a
        poet and historian).
3   **potis** or **pote**, indeclinable adjective + infin., *having the power* (to), *able* (to).
    dulcis, -is, -e, *sweet; fair; pleasant.*
    exprōmō [**ex-**, *out* + **prōmō, prōmere, prōmpsī, prōmptus**, *to bring out/forth*
        (from some storage place)], **exprōmere, exprōmpsī, exprōmptus**, *to bring*
        out/forth (from some storage place); *to give expression to.*
        exprōmere: cf. 64.223, **multās exprōmam mente querellās**.
    fētus, -ūs, m., *bearing, birth; fruit; offspring.*
4   **mēns animī**: *the mental power of my mind*, a periphrasis for "mind" found in
        Lucretius.
    flūctuō, -āre, -āvī, -ātūrus, *to rise in waves; to be agitated; to seethe.*
        flūctuat: cf. 64.62, **magnīs cūrārum flūctuat undīs**.
5   **namque**, conj., *for in fact, for.*
    nūper: modifying **mānāns alluit** (6).
    Lēthaeus, -a, -um, *of/belonging to Lethe* (the River of Forgetfulness in the
        underworld).
    gurges, gurgitis, m., *whirlpool; water* (of a river or sea).
        Lēthaeō gurgite: all shades of the dead pass through and drink from this
            river in the underworld; ablative of place where without a preposition
            (Thomson reads **Lēthaeō in gurgite**).
6   **pallidulus** [dim. of **pallidus, -a, -um**, *pale*], **-a, -um**, *pale.*
    pallidulum: the adjective **pallidus** is often used to describe the shades of
        the deceased.
    mānō, -āre, -āvī, *to flow.*
    alluō [**ad-**, *to, toward* + **luō, luere, luī**, *to wash*], **alluere, alluī**, of water, *to touch,*
        wet, lap.
    pedem: poetic singular for plural.

CATULLUS 65

A Brother's Lament

Catullus' grief over his brother's death has made it difficult for him to compose poetry.

1   Etsī mē assiduō cōnfectum cūra dolōre
2   sēvocat ā doctīs, Ortale, virginibus,
3   nec potis est dulcīs Mūsārum exprōmere fētūs
4   mēns animī, tantīs flūctuat ipsa malīs—
5   namque meī nūper Lēthaeō gurgite frātris
6   pallidulum mānāns alluit unda pedem,

continued

Explorations

1.   What basic context is established by the first four lines?
2.   The initial word **Etsī** indicates that these first four lines form what kind of clause? What complementary word should we expect to find at some point to introduce a clause that will complete the thought begun here? What at this point might you conjecture about the contents of this coming declarative statement?
3.   In the first two lines, identify interlocking word order, alliteration, and effective juxtaposition of words.
4.   Find a chiasmus in the arrangement of the first four lines.
5.   Explain the phrase **dulcīs Mūsārum . . . fētūs** (3) as a metaphor for poetry. What do the words **exprōmere** (3) and **mēns animī** (4) add to the description of how poetry is created?
6.   What prevents Catullus from fulfilling his function as a mouthpiece of the Muses? (4)
7.   What does the clause beginning with **namque** in line 5 explain? How does it logically follow from what precedes it? How does it fit within the development of thought in the poem?
8.   The description of the death of Catullus' brother (5–6) is couched in the mythology of the underworld. On what does the poet focus, and what is not mentioned that might have been expected in a mythological description of death?
9.   What pattern of word arrangement and what sound effects do you find in line 6?

7   **Troius, -a, -um,** *Trojan, of Troy.*
      Troia: the consonantal *i* stands for a double consonant, thus making the preceding syllable long or heavy. The *a* is metrically long or heavy by diastole.
      Rhoetēus, -a, -um, *of Rhoeteum* (a promontory and city in Troas on the Hellespont).
      subter, prep. + acc., *under;* + abl. (rare), *under.*
        subter: delayed preposition.
      tellūs, tellūris, f., *earth, ground.*

8   **nostrīs:** poetic plural.
      obterō [**ob-,** *against* + **terō, terere, trīvī, trītus,** *to rub; to wear down*], **obterere, obtrīvī, obtrītus,** *to trample on; to crush; to lie heavily upon.*

10   **amābilis, -is, -e,** *worthy to be loved.*

11   **aspiciō** [**ad-,** *to, toward* + **speciō, specere, spexī, spectus,** *to see*], **aspicere, aspexī, aspectus,** *to catch sight of, look upon.*
      posthāc, adv., *hereafter.*
      semper . . . / semper (12): note the repetition.

12   **maestus, -a, -um,** *sad, gloomy, mournful; saddened.*
      tuā . . . morte: with **maesta,** *saddened.*
      carmen, carminis, n., *song; poem.*

13   **quālis, -is -e,** *of what sort; of such a sort as.*
      dēnsus, -a, -um, *dense; thick.*

14   **Daulias, Dauliados,** f. adj., *Daulian, of/belonging to Daulis* (a town in Phocis, where Tereus ruled).
        Daulias: supply **avis,** = the nightingale (see **Myth,** page 253).
      absūmō [**ab-,** *from* + **sūmō, sūmere, sūmpsī, sūmptus,** *to take*], **absūmere, absūmpsī, absūmptus,** *to use up, consume, devour; to carry off, take away.*
      Itylus, -ī, m., *Itylus = Itys* (son of Tereus and Procne, killed by Procne).

15   **Sed tamen:** introducing the apodosis after **Etsī** (1).
      maeror, maerōris, m., *mourning, sadness.*

16   **expressus, -a, -um,** *translated.*
      carmina: not *poems* but *verses,* referring to poem 66 (not included in this book), a translation of a poem by Callimachus, the *Lock of Berenice,* a clever conceit in which Callimachus with mock solemnity gives voice to a lock of hair vowed by Queen Berenice for the safe return of her husband Ptolemy III from a campaign in Syria. The lock is carried into heaven and proclaims its devotion to the queen.
      Battiadēs, Battiadae, m., *Battiades* (a patronymic, equivalent to *Descendant of Battus.* Battus was the legendary founder of Cyrene, the birthplace of the Hellenistic poet Callimachus; Battiades was a pseudonym adopted by Callimachus; see Catullus 7.4–6).

17   **tua dicta:** i.e., Ortalus' request for some verses from Catullus.
      vagus, -a, -um, *wandering, roaming.*
        vāgīs nēquīquam crēdita ventīs: cf. Catullus 30.9–10 and 64.59 and 142.

18   **effluō** [**ex-,** *out* + **fluō, fluere, fluxī,** *to flow*], **effluere, effluxī,** *to flow out, slip away.*

7   Troia Rhoetēō quem subter lītore tellūs
8   ēreptum nostrīs obteret ex oculīs.
9   <Numquam ego tē poterō posthāc audīre loquentem,>
10   numquam ego tē, vītā frāter amābilior,
11   aspiciam posthāc? At certē semper amābō,
12   semper maesta tuā carmina morte canam,
13   quālia sub dēnsīs rāmōrum concinit umbrīs
14   Daulias, absūmptī fāta gemēns Itylī.—
15   Sed tamen in tantīs maerōribus, Ortale, mittō
16   haec expressa tibī carmina Battiadae,
17   nē tua dicta vagīs nēquīquam crēdita ventīs
18   effluxisse meō forte putēs animō,

continued

Explorations

10. If the focus is on forgetfulness in lines 5–6, on what is the focus in lines 7–8?
11. What rhetorical device is employed in lines 9–11a with the supplement for line 9 given above? How does the thought of these lines relate to the thought of lines 7–8?
12. What will the poet always do in the face of the loss of his brother to death? (11b–12)
13. What is striking about the arrangement and the sound of words in lines 9–12?
14. In lines 5–6 the death of Catullus' brother is presented in terms of the water of the River of Forgetfulness lapping at his pale foot. How is this theme of forgetfulness reversed in lines 11b–12?
15. To what does Catullus liken the songs that he will sing? (13–14) How is the comparison appropriate? What in the comparison is not applicable to Catullus' situation?
16. How are lines 12–14 at odds with the message of lines 1–4?
17. In what specific ways do lines 15–16 resume the thought of lines 1–4?
18. What reason do lines 17–18 offer as to why Catullus is sending his translation of Callimachus to Ortalus? What do the echoes of passages in poems 30 and 64 tell us about Catullus' concerns here?

19   fūrtīvus, -a, -um, *stolen; hidden; secret.*
        fūrtīvō mūnere: *as a secret gift* (from her betrothed, spōnsī), ablative of
            manner.
        mālum: apples were sent by lovers to their beloveds as gifts or pledges of
            their love.
20   prōcurrō [prō-, *forward* + currō, currere, cucurrī, cursūrus, *to run*],
            prōcurrere, prōcurrī, prōcursūrus, *to run forward; to fall forward.*
        castō: transferred epithet; effective juxtaposition with virginis; note the
            pleonasm.
        gremium, -ī, n., *lap, bosom.*
21   miserae: *of the lovesick girl.*
        oblīvīscor, oblīvīscī, oblītus sum, *to forget.*
            oblītae: with miserae, *of the lovesick girl who has forgotten [it];* the idea of
                forgetfulness establishes the relevance of the simile; Catullus promises
                not to forget Ortalus' request (17–18) the way the lovesick girl forgot the
                apple as she leaped up at the approach of her mother (22).
22   adventus, -ūs, m., *arrival; approach.*
        prōsiliō [prō-, *forward* + saliō, salīre, saluī, *to jump*], prōsilīre, prōsiluī, *to
            jump forward; to leap up.*
            prōsilit: the subject is the virgō.
        excutiō [ex-, *out* + quatiō, quatere, _____, quassus, *to shake*], excutere,
            excussī, excussus, *to shake out.*
                excutitur: the subject is quod (21, i.e., the mālum, 19).
                prōsilit, excutitur: effective juxtaposition.
23   atque: here, beginning a main clause, *and thereupon, and suddenly.*
        prōnus, -a, -um, *face down; moving downward.*
        praeceps [prae-, *in front, ahead* + -ceps, from caput, capitis, n., *head*],
            praecipitis, *headlong.*
                prōnō praeceps: alliteration and effective juxtaposition.
        agitur: the passive voice here gives the normally transitive verb an
            intransitive sense; translate freely with something such as *plummets.*
        dēcursus [dē-, *down* + cursus, -ūs, m., *course, run*], -ūs m., *a running down,
            downward course.*
                agitur dēcursū: spondaic fifth foot.
24   huic . . . trīstī: note that initially these two words may be taken together
            with trīstī being regarded as dative case, *for her . . . sad,* but that upon
            reading the second half of the line it becomes clear that trīstī is ablative
            with ōre; huic will then be taken as a dative of reference to be translated as
            a possessive with trīstī . . . ōre, ablative of place where without a
            preposition, thus, *over her sad face.*
        mānat: cf. mānāns (6).
        cōnscius, -a, -um, *conscious, knowing; guilty.*
            cōnscius: transferred epithet.
        rubor, rubōris, m., *redness; blush.*
            trīstī cōnscius ōre rubor: interlocking word order or synchysis.
                trīstī . . . ōre: the girl's sadness ironically echoes the poet's distress and
                    grief, assiduō . . . cūra dolōre (1).

19   ut missum spōnsī fūrtīvō mūnere mālum
20   prōcurrit castō virginis ē gremiō,
21   quod miserae oblītae mollī sub veste locātum,
22   dum adventū mātris prōsilit, excutitur,
23   atque illud prōnō praeceps agitur dēcursū,
24   huic mānat trīstī cōnscius ōre rubor.

Myth

Daulias (avis) (14)
The allusion is to the story of Procne and Tereus, which was treated differently by Homer (*Odyssey* 19.515–24) and the Hellenistic and Roman poets (see Ovid, *Metamorpohoses* 6.424–674). In the later version, which Catullus follows, the sisters Procne and Philomela, daughters of Pandion, king of Athens, avenge themselves on Tereus, Procne's husband, who had raped Philomela, by killing Tereus' and Procne's son Itys and serving his cooked flesh to Tereus to eat. Procne, the mother, is changed into a nightingale, Philomela, into a swallow, or vice versa. According to the myth, the nightingale sings most beautifully but in sorrow for the death of Itys.

The Homeric version of the story (*Odyssey* 19.515–24) is quite different. The woman who kills her child is identified as the daughter of Pandareus and is simply called the nightingale. She slew her son Itylus unwittingly. Catullus takes the name of the child from this Homeric passage instead of using the later name, Itys. He also imitates line 520 of the Homeric passage where the nightingale is described as singing "perched in the thick leaves of trees" (compare Catullus, line 13: **sub dēnsīs rāmōrum concinit umbrīs**). Catullus' reference to the woman as Daulias (14) connects with the later version of the myth, in which Procne is the wife of Tereus, king of Daulis.

Explorations

19.   The poem ends with a long and complex simile. What is being compared to what? Does it seem to be an appropriate comparison?
20.   How are lines 19–24 at odds with the message of lines 12–14?
21.   What images earlier in the poem are transformed in the final simile?
22.   In what way can the apple be thought of as a metaphor for the **carmina** (16) that Catullus is sending Ortalus?

Meter: elegiac couplet

Background

Catullus writes this epistle from Verona shortly after his brother's death in the
Troad. He is writing a reply to a friend probably named Manlius, who is
presumably in Rome. Manlius has apparently been deserted by his mistress and is
so distraught that he can neither sleep nor find pleasure or comfort in old
(presumably Greek) poets. He has written to Catullus asking that Catullus rescue
him, and he seeks from Catullus gifts of the Muses and of Venus. Catullus replies
that his own sorrow over the loss of his brother has destroyed his love life, that he
has not brought much poetry with him to Verona, and that he therefore cannot
provide what Manlius has requested.

1   **Quod . . . / . . . mittis** (2): *[The fact] that you send;* picked up by **id** (9).
     cāsus, -ūs, m., *fall; event; disaster.*
     acerbus, -a, -um, *bitter, harsh.*
        acerbō: modifying both **fortūnā** and **cāsū.**
2   **cōnscrībō** [**cōn-**, intensive + **scrībō, scrībere, scrīpsī, scrīptus**, *to write*],
        cōnscrībere, cōnscrīpsī, cōnscrīptus, *to write.*
        cōnscrīptum . . . lacrimīs: we might say "tear-stained" (Merrill).
     hoc: "implying 'which I have in front of me'" (Thomson).
     epistolium, -ī, n. [Greek loan word], *short letter, little letter.*
3   **naufragus, -a, -um** [**nāvis, nāvis**, f., *ship* + **frangō, frangere, frēgī, fractus**,
        to break], *shipwrecked;* as substantive, *a shipwrecked person.*
        naufragum . . . ēiectum: supply **tē**; **naufragum** is a metaphor for a lover
           who has been rejected and deserted by his beloved.
     ut: delayed conjunction introducing a purpose clause with its verbs placed at
        the beginning and end of the next line.
     ēiciō [**ē-, ex-**, *out* + **iaciō, iacere, iēcī, iactus**, *to throw*], **ēicere, ēiēcī, ēiectus**,
        to throw out; of the sea, *to drive/cast ashore.*
     spūmō, -āre, -āvī, -ātūrus, *to foam.*
4   **sublevō** [**sub-**, *under, from below* + **levō, -āre, -āvī, -ātus**, *to lift*], **-āre, -āvī,**
        -ātus, *to lift up.*
     restituō [**re-**, *back, again* + **statuō, statuere, statuī, statūtus**, *to make stand*],
        restituere, restituī, restitūtus, *to restore, renew; to revive.*
5   **quem**: the antecedent is the implied **tē** of [**tē**] **naufragum . . . ēiectum** (3).
     sāncta Venus: cf. **sāncte puer**, Catullus 64.95, and **sānctae Venerī**
        Cupīdinīque, Catullus 36.3, for Catullus' religious elevation of the deities
        of love.
     requiēscō [**re-**, *back, again* + **quiēscō, quiēscere, quiēvī, quiētūrus**, *to rest*],
        requiēscere, requiēvī, requiētūrus, *to rest.*

CATULLUS 68.1–40

You're not the only one who is unhappy.

Catullus explains why he cannot send his friend the gifts that he has requested.

1 Quod mihi fortūnā cāsūque oppressus acerbō
2   cōnscrīptum hoc lacrimīs mittis epistolium,
3 naufragum ut ēiectum spūmantibus aequoris undīs
4   sublevem et ā mortis līmine restituam,
5 quem neque sāncta Venus mollī requiēscere somnō
6   dēsertum in lectō caelibe perpetitur,

continued

---

6   **dēsertus, -a, -um,** *deserted.*
      dēsertum: cf. **dēsertam,** Catullus 64.57, of Ariadne deserted by Theseus; in
        Catullus 68 the addressee has been deserted by an unnamed beloved
        with an equally devastating effect.
      caelebs, caelibis, *without a spouse* (because unmarried, widowed, or
        divorced); *without a partner.*
        caelibe: a transferred epithet.
      perpetior [per-, intensive + **patior, patī, passus sum,** *to suffer; to allow*],
        perpetī, perpessus sum, *to endure;* + acc. and infin., *to permit.*
        quem . . . (5) / . . . perpetitur (6): "Catullus presumably implies that the
          would-be lover's non-existent sex life leaves him insomniac with
          frustration rather than asleep in exhausted bliss" (Godwin).

Explorations

1. How did Manlius apparently describe himself in the letter he wrote to Catullus? How does Catullus describe the letter? What word in line 2 suggests the feeling with which Catullus assumes that the letter was written? (1–2)
2. According to lines 3–4, why did Manlius send the letter to Catullus? How did Manlius describe himself? What does his description of himself imply about what actually happened to him? What goddess is called to mind by *the foaming waves of the sea*? What hyperbole did Manlius apparently employ in his letter?
3. Rather than as a person shipwrecked, how did Manlius continue to describe himself? (5–6) Instead of being at the threshold of death, how is Manlius now described? Who is responsible for his condition? How is **caelibe** a transferred epithet?

7   **dulcis, -is, -e**, *sweet.*
     scrīptor, scrīptōris, m., *writer.*
      scrīptōrum: modified by **veterum.**
     carmen, carminis, n., *song, poem, poetry.*
      dulcī . . . carmine: ablative of means or instrument.
      veterum dulcī scrīptōrum carmine: interlocking order or synchysis.
8   **oblectō** [**ob-**, *against* + **lactō, -āre, -āvī, -ātus**, *to entice*], **-āre, -āvī, -ātus**, *to attract; to delight.*
     cum: temporal, *when.*
     ānxius, -a, -um, *worried, anxious; troubled.*
     pervigilō [**per-**, *through* + **vigilō, -āre, -āvī, -ātūrus**, *to stay awake*], **-āre, -āvī, -ātūrus**, *to keep vigil, spend the night awake.*
      nec . . . (7) / . . . pervigilat (8): "The addressee is lying awake bereft of his lover and is too distraught even to find solace in the reading of old (i.e. presumably Greek) poets" (Godwin).
9   **mihi, mē**: effective juxtaposition; polyptoton.
     tibi: *your*, dative of reference, indicating possession.
10   **mūnera . . . et Mūsārum . . . et Veneris**: "The two complaints made by Manlius in 5–9 (he finds it hard to sleep alone, and older books give no solace in his wakefulness) are taken up in reverse order" (Thomson); Catullus then takes up the request for **mūnera Veneris** in lines 15–30 and the request for **mūnera Mūsārum** in lines 33–36, reversing the order again.
     hinc, adv., *from here.*
     hinc: i.e., *from me.*
11   **ignōtus, -a, -um** [**in-**, *not* + **nōtus, -a, -um**, *known*], *unknown.*
      nē . . . sint ignōta: litotes.
     incommodus, -a, -um [**in-**, *not* + **commodus, -a, -um**, *suitable; favorable; agreeable*], *troublesome; unfavorable; disagreeable.*
      incommoda: *misfortunes.*
     Manlius, -ī, m., *Manlius* (the Oxford Classical Text reads **Mānī** here).
12   **neu**: = **nē + ve**, *and lest.*
     ōdī, ōdisse, ōsus, perfect in form, present in meaning, *to hate; to have no use for; to reject, avoid.*
     hospitis officium: *the obligation of a guest;* Catullus has apparently incurred an obligation involving hospitality and would normally reciprocate the favor by acceding to Manlius' request for **mūnera et Mūsārum . . . et Veneris.**
13   **accipe**: here, *learn, hear*, followed by an indirect question.
     quīs: = **quibus**, *by what*, introducing an indirect question; take with **flūctibus.**
     mersō, -āre, -āvī, -ātus, *to dip, immerse; to submerge, drown; to overwhelm.*
      merser: subjunctive in an indirect question.
     flūctus, -ūs, m., *wave.*
      quīs merser fortūnae flūctibus ipse: cf. Catullus 65.4, **tantīs flūctuat ipsa malīs.**

7   nec veterum dulcī scrīptōrum carmine Mūsae
8   oblectant, cum mēns ānxia pervigilat:
9   id grātum est mihi, mē quoniam tibi dīcis amīcum,
10   mūneraque et Mūsārum hinc petis et Veneris.
11   Sed tibi nē mea sint ignōta incommoda, Manlī,
12   neu mē ōdisse putēs hospitis officium,
13   accipe, quīs merser fortūnae flūctibus ipse,
14   nē amplius ā miserō dōna beāta petās.

continued

---

14   **amplius**, adv., *any longer.*
     ā miserō: supply **mē**, *from unhappy [me], from [me] in my unhappiness.*
     beātus, -a, -um, *happy; blessed.*
       dōna beāta: *gifts that only the happy can give* (Fordyce).

Explorations

4. What fails to delight Manlius? When does this happen? (7–8)
5. To what does **id** (9) refer? What two reasons does Catullus give for why he is pleased? (9–10)
6. Do lines 11–12 suggest that Catullus will respond positively to Manlius' request? To what earlier in the poem do the words **mea . . . incommoda** (11) respond?
7. What reason does Catullus give for declining Manlius' request? (13) How does the way he expresses it echo words in lines 1–3? How does Catullus describe his situation as more desperate than that of Manlius?
8. What does Catullus want Manlius to stop asking for? (14) Why?

15   **Tempore quō**: *Since the time when* (Merrill).
  vestis . . . pūra: the all-white **toga virīlis**, which Roman boys put on at the
    age of fifteen or sixteen in exchange for the **toga praetexta**, the toga with a
    purple border of boyhood.

16   **aetās, aetātis**, f., *period/time of life; age.*
  flōridus, -a, -um, *flowery; blooming.*
  vēr, vēris, n., *spring.*
    vēr ageret: *was keeping its springtime* (Fordyce).
      iūcundum . . . aetās flōrida vēr: embedded word order.

17   **multa satis**: **multa**, *a lot*, internal accusative with **lūsī**; translate the phrase
    freely, *often enough.*
  lūsī: *I played the lover* (Thomson), as in 68.156, **in quā lūsimus**, *in which we
    played at love*; not *I composed poetry*, as in 50.2 and 5 (Thomson).
  dea: Venus.
  nescius -a, -um [**ne-**, *not* + **scius, -a, -um**, *knowing*] + gen., *unaware* (of).
    nōn . . . nescia: litotes.
  nostrī: genitive of **nōs**, poetic plural.

18   **cūrīs**: the emotional distress of passionate love; cf. Catullus 64.72, **spīnōsās**
    Erycīna serēns in pectore cūrās.
  amāritiēs, -ēī, f., *bitterness.*
    <u>dulcem</u> **cūrīs miscet** <u>amāritiem</u>: oxymoron; cf. Catullus 64.95, **sāncte**
    puer, cūrīs hominum quī gaudia miscēs, and the note on that line.

15   Tempore quō prīmum vestis mihi trādita pūra est,
16   iūcundum cum aetās flōrida vēr ageret,
17   multa satis lūsī: nōn est dea nescia nostrī,
18   quae dulcem cūrīs miscet amāritiem.

continued

Explorations

9.   What does Catullus provide in lines 15–18? How does it relate to anything
     earlier in the poem?

19 **studium, -ī**, n., *earnest application of one's attention or energies to some specified or implied object; zeal, ardor.*

    tōtum hoc studium: i.e., all the ardor that Catullus had directed toward love affairs.

lūctū: *because of grief*, ablative of instrument or cause.

frāterna . . . mors: **frāterna** = **frātris**; for the death of Catullus' brother, cf. Catullus 65.5–14 and Catullus 101.

    mors / abstulit (20): note the monosyllable at the end of the line, enjambement, and the completion of the sentence in the first foot of the next line, all emphasizing finality and paving the way for the emotional apostrophe that begins in line 20b.

20 **Ō miserō frāter adēmpte mihi**: cf. Catullus 101.6, **heu miser indignē frāter adēmpte mihi.**

    miserō: proleptic.

21 **commodus, -a, -um**, *suitable; favorable; agreeable.*

    mea . . . commoda: *my blesssings*, i.e., the good things in my life; the opposite of **incommoda**, *misfortunes* (11).

        frēgistī commoda: the taking away of Catullus' brother (**frāter adēmpte**, 20) has shattered all Catullus' blessings.

22 **est**: with **sepulta**.

    est nostra sepulta domus: the burial of Catullus' brother has resulted in a metaphorical burial of Catullus' whole household.

23 **omnia tēcum ūnā**: a variation on **tēcum ūnā tōta** (22).

gaudia: picking up **commoda** (21).

nostra: picking up **nostra** (22).

    omnia . . . periērunt gaudia nostra: the third item in the series, which moves from the generalized **mea . . . frēgistī commoda** (21) to the domestic **tōta est nostra sepulta domus** (22), to the intensely personal **omnia . . . periērunt gaudia nostra** (23).

24 **quae . . . amor**: Catullus traces all the joys of his life back to his brother's sweet love for him; this is the climax of Catullus' tribute to his brother in lines 20–24.

    tuus: picking up **tēcum** (23), **tēcum** (22), and **tū . . . tū** (21), emphasizing the emotional bond between Catullus and his brother.

25 **interitus, -ūs**, m., *ruin; death.*

    interitū: ablative of cause.

tōtā dē mente: *entirely from my mind* (Fordyce).

fugō, -āre -āvī, -ātus, *to put to flight; to drive away.*

26 **haec studia**: referring to **tōtum hoc studium** (19), a phrase that summarizes Catullus' youthful erotic frolicking (17–18).

    omnēs dēliciās animī: *all the delights of my emotional being*, referring to the love affairs (17–18) that he has now given up. For **dēliciās**, cf. Catullus 45.24. With **mente** (25) and **animī** (26) here, compare the phrase **mēns animī** in Catullus 65.4 and the note on the phrase there.

19   Sed tōtum hoc studium lūctū frāterna mihi mors

20   abstulit. Ō miserō frāter adēmpte mihi,

21   tū mea tū moriēns frēgistī commoda, frāter,

22   tēcum ūnā tōta est nostra sepulta domus,

23   omnia tēcum ūnā periērunt gaudia nostra,

24   quae tuus in vītā dulcis alēbat amor.

25   Cuius ego interitū tōtā dē mente fugāvī

26   haec studia atque omnēs dēliciās animī.

continued

Explorations

10.   What event changed Catullus' life? How did it change his life? (19–20a)
11.   What is the tone of Catullus' apostrophe of his dead brother? (20b–24) How do these lines differ from the description of Manlius at the beginning of the poem?
12.   How do lines 21–24 constitute an ascending tricolon?
13.   How do lines 19–20a and 25–26 form a frame around Catullus' emotional apostrophe of his brother in lines 20b–24?
14.   What patterns of alliteration are evident in lines 19–21? To what do they draw our attention?
15.   What other effective repetitions and what rhetorical devices can you find in lines 19–26?

27   **quārē**, adv., *why; for which reason.*

    quod scrībis: *[the fact] that you write;* cf. **quod** . . . (1) / . . . **mittis** (2); **quod scrībis** is picked up by **id** (30), just as **quod** . . . (1) / . . . **mittis** (2) was picked up by **id** (9).

    Vērōna, -ae, f., *Verona* (the northern Italian town where Catullus' family lived and where Catullus is now).

    turpis, -is, -e, *foul; disgraceful.*

    Catullō: *for Catullus,* dative of reference.

        Vērōnae turpe Catullō / esse (28): truncated indirect statement; supply another **esse**: *that it is* (**esse**) *shameful for Catullus to be staying* (**esse**) *at Verona;* see **Text**.

28   **quod**, conj., *because, inasmuch as.*

        quod . . . / . . . **tepefactet** (29): the subjunctive implies that this statement was made by the addressee in his letter to Catullus and that Catullus in reporting it does not vouch for its truth or falsity.

    hīc: i.e., at Verona.

    quisquis, quisquis, quidquid, *anyone who, everyone who, anything that, all that.*

    nota, -ae, f., *mark;* of wine, *quality, brand;* of persons, *quality, character, status.*

    quisquis dē meliōre notā: supply **est**, *everyone who is of* . . .

29   **dēsertō**: here not *deserted* as in line 6, but *empty;* cf. the phrase **in lectō caelibe** (6).

    tepefactō: hapax [**tepeō, -ēre**, *to be warm* + **faciō, facere, fēcī, factus**, *to do, make* + **-tō**, intensive or iterative suffix], **-āre**, *to (habitually) make warm, warm.*

        tepefactet: for the subjunctive, see the note on **quod** . . . / . . . **tepefactet** above.

    membrum, -ī, n., *limb* (of the body).

    cubīle, cubīlis, n., *bed.*

        quod . . . (28) / . . . **cubīlī**: Catullus' addressee in his letter to Catullus had commented that it was shameful for Catullus to be in Verona inasmuch as all the young men of the upper crust there warm their limbs in lonely beds without partners, whereas, by implication, in Rome young men of the upper crust sleep with mistresses (except for the addressee who has been deserted by his).

        frīgida . . . **cubīlī**: a golden line (see note on Catullus 64.59).

30   **nōn est turpe**: Catullus rejects his addressee's characterization of his situation.

    magis: *[but] rather.*

    miserum: here, *pitiful, pitiable,* "a misfortune to be endured" (Quinn).

27   Quārē, quod scrībis Vērōnae turpe Catullō
28   esse, quod hīc quisquis dē meliōre notā
29   frīgida dēsertō tepefactet membra cubīlī,
30   id, Manlī, nōn est turpe, magis miserum est.

continued

Text

27   Quārē, quod scrībis Vērōnae turpe Catullō
28   esse,

Most editors print the text as given in the Oxford Classical Text and printed here. Manuscript V, however, reads **Catulle**, and some editors accept this reading and print as if Catullus were quoting directly from his addressee's letter. Quinn thus prints as follows:

27   Quārē, quod scrībis, "Vērōnae turpe, Catulle,
28   esse, quod hīc quisquis dē meliōre notā
29   frīgida dēsertō tepefactat membra cubīlī,"

Godwin regards fewer words as part of the direct quotation:

27   Quārē, quod scrībis, "Vērōnae turpe, Catulle,
28   esse," quod hīc quisquis dē meliōre notā
29   frīgida dēsertō tepefactet membra cubīlī,

Quinn interprets **hīc** as referring to Rome, and he sees in lines 28 and 29 a reference to all the upper crust young men warming their limbs in Clodia/Lesbia's bed, which is now deserted both by the death of her husband and by Catullus' being away in Verona. Godwin objects to this view: "One wonders at this point just how blunt and rude Catullus' friend could be about the behaviour of Catullus' beloved [Clodia/Lesbia] and still expect to stay his friend and receive poems to order." Godwin keeps the vocative but shortens the direct quotation; in his reading, given above, **hīc** refers to Verona, not Rome, just as it does in the Oxford Classical Text, and there is no allusion to Clodia/Lesbia: "the reference *hic* is then a gentle jibe at the expense of the sexual desert which is Verona rather than a direct stab at Catullus' beloved [Clodia/Lesbia], of whose behaviour he would not wish to be reminded."

Explorations

16.   Why would it be disgraceful for Catullus to be in Verona? Why is it not disgraceful but rather pitiable?
17.   What purpose might Manlius have had in chiding Catullus by saying that it was disgraceful for him to be in Verona?

31   **ignōscō** [**in-**, *not* + **nōscō, nōscere, nōvī, nōtus,** *to know*], **ignōscere,**
        ignōvī, ignōtus + dat., *to pardon, forgive; to excuse.*
          Ignōscēs: supply **mihi.**
        quae: the antecedent is **mūnera** (32).
        lūctus: picking up **lūctū** (19).

32   **tribuō, tribuere, tribuī, tribūtus,** *to bestow, give.*
        haec . . . mūnera: picking up **mūnera . . . Veneris** (10).
        cum: *[at a time] when.*
        nequeō [**ne-**, *not* + **queō, quīre, quīvī,** *to be able*], **nequīre, nequīvī,** *to be*
          unable.

33   **Nam:** *Now/Moreover,* here marking a transition to a new subject.
        quod: *[the fact] that.*
        scrīptōrum: the genitive of either **scrīptōrēs** (*writers*) or of **scrīpta** (*writings*);
          in line 7 the word means *writers,* but here it may mean *writers, writings,* or
          books. If it means *writings,* there is no way to tell whether Catullus is
          referring to his own writings or those of others.
        cōpia, -ae, f., *abundance; supply.*

34   **hoc fit:** *this happens,* or read **hōc fit,** *(it) happens for this reason.*
        quod: here, *because.*
        vīvimus: poetic plural.
        domus: cf. **domus** (22); here in line 34 the word means *home,* not *household.*
          illa domus: supply **est mea.**

35   **sēdēs, sēdis,** f., *seat; home; residence.*
        illīc, adv., *at that place; there.*
        carpō, carpere, carpsī, carptus, *to pluck; to seize; to wear away, reduce.*
        aetās: cf. **aetās** (16); here simply *life.*
          mea carpitur aetās: *my life is spent.*
            illa domus, (34) / **illa mihī sēdēs, illīc mea carpitur aetās:** anaphora
              and ascending tricolon.

36   **capsula, -ae,** f. [dim. of **capsa, -ae,** f., *a cylindrical case* (for holding papyrus
        rolls)], *a small cylindrical case* (for holding papyrus rolls).

31   Ignōscēs igitur sī, quae mihi lūctus adēmit,
32   haec tibi nōn tribuō mūnera, cum nequeō.
33   Nam, quod scrīptōrum nōn magna est cōpia apud mē,
34   hoc fit, quod Rōmae vīvimus: illa domus,
35   illa mihī sēdēs, illīc mea carpitur aetās;
36   hūc ūna ex multīs capsula mē sequitur.

continued

Explorations

18. How do lines 31–32 summarize what Catullus has been saying in lines 11–30?
19. What is Catullus explaining to Manlius in lines 33–36?
20. Why can Catullus not comply with Manlius' request? (33–36)
21. What words in lines 34–35 recall words earlier in the poem? What contrast is being made between what is described in lines 34–35 and the earlier section of the poem in which these words occur?

37   **Quod**: connecting relative; translate *this*.
       cum: delayed causal conjunction.
       nōlim: potential subjunctive, *I would not wish*.
       statuō, statuere, statuī, statūtus, *to make stand; to establish; to determine; to
          judge*.
              statuās: supply **ut**, *that you judge*.
       nōs: poetic plural.
       malignus, -a, -um, *ungenerous, unkind, grudging*.
38   **id facere**: **id** is explained by the **quod** clause in line 39.
       ingenuus, -a, -um, *typical of a free-born person; liberal, honorable, gentlemanly*.
39   **quod**: picking up **id** (38), *[namely] that*.
       nōn: take with **posta est**.
       cōpia, -ae, f., *abundance, supply*.
          utriusque . . . cōpia: *a supply of each [thing]*, i.e., gifts of both the Muses and
              of Venus, **mūnera et Mūsārum . . . et Veneris** (10).
       posta est: syncopated, = **posita est**, from **pōnō, pōnere, posuī, positus**,
          here with the sense *to set before, provide*.
40   **ultrō**, adv., *voluntarily, without being asked*.
       dēferō [**dē-**, *down* + **ferō, ferre, tulī, lātus**, *to carry; to bear*], **dēferre, dētulī,
          dēlātus**, *to bring down; to offer*.
              dēferrem . . . sī . . . foret: present contrary-to-fact condition.
       sīqua: = **sī** + **aliqua**.
       foret: = **esset**, from **fore**, the alternative future infinitive of **sum, esse, fuī,
          futūrus**, *to be*.
              cōpia sīqua foret: supply **mihi**, dative of the possessor.

37 Quod cum ita sit, nōlim statuās nōs mente malignā
38   id facere aut animō nōn satis ingenuō,
39 quod tibi nōn utriusque petentī cōpia posta est:
40   ultrō ego dēferrem, cōpia sīqua foret.

Explorations

22. What two things does Catullus want to be sure that Manlius understands? (37–40)
23. How do lines 37–38 help round out the structure of the poem by recalling an earlier line?
24. What words in lines 39–40 help round out the structure of the poem by recalling earlier words or phrases?

Meter: elegiac couplet

1 **quārē**, adv., *for which reason, why.*
  tibi: dative with **supposuisse** (2).

2 **Rūfus, -ī**, m., *Rufus* (perhaps M. Caelius Rufus, the lover of Clodia defended
  by Cicero).
  tener, tenera, tenerum, *soft, tender, delicate.*
  suppōnō [sub-, *under* + **pōnō, pōnere, posuī, positus**, *to put, place*],
   suppōnere, supposuī, suppositus + dat., *to put under, to place next to.*
    supposuisse: archaic use of perfect for present, = **suppōnere.**
  femur, femoris, n., *thigh.*
   femur: a verbal play with **fēmina** in line 1.

3 **nōn sī**: *not [even] if.*
  rārus, -a, -um, *loosely woven; rare; exquisite.*
   rārae . . . vestis: clothing made of very fine, transparent Coan silk.
  labefactō [**labō, -āre, -āvī,** *to stand unsteadily; to totter* + **faciō, facere, fēcī,**
   factus, *to make; to do* + **-tō**, iterative or intensive suffix], **-āre, -āvī, -ātus,** *to*
   loosen; to weaken; to shake/cause to waver (in resolve); *to seduce.*
    velit . . . (2) / **. . . labefactēs (3)**: subjunctives in an indirect question;
     translate as indicatives.

4 **perlūcidulus, -a, -um**: hapax [dim. of **perlūcidus, -a, -um,** *transparent,*
   translucent], *transparent, translucent.*
  dēliciīs: cf. 2.1, **dēliciae.**

5 **fābula**: *rumor.*
  tibi: dative of reference; translate as possessive with **ālārum** (6).
  fertur: *is said.*

6 **vallēs, vallis,** f., *valley.*
   valle: diction appropriate to the world of the **caper.**
  āla, -ae, f., *wing; armpit.*
  trux, trucis, *savage, fierce.*
  caper, caprī, m., *goat.*

7 **metuō, metuere, metuī, metūtus,** *to fear.*

8 **quīcum**: = **cum quā**; the antecedent is **bēstia.**
  bellus, -a, -um, *pretty.*
  cubō, cubāre, cubuī, cubitus, *to lie down, to lie in bed.*
   cubet: subjunctive in a relative clause of characteristic.

9 **interficiō** [inter-, intensive + **faciō, facere, fēcī, factus,** *to make, do*],
   interficere, interfēcī, interfectus, *to kill; to destroy.*
  pestis, pestis, f., *destruction; plague; destructive creature; pest.*

10 **fugiunt**: the indicative instead of the subjunctive is found in indirect
  questions in archaic and colloquial Latin; the subject is **omnēs** (7).

CATULLUS 69

Rufus reeks!

Catullus thinks he knows why the girls reject Rufus.

1 Nōlī admīrārī, quārē tibi fēmina nūlla,
2   Rūfe, velit tenerum supposuisse femur,
3 nōn sī illam rārae labefactēs mūnere vestis
4   aut perlūcidulī dēliciīs lapidis.
5 Laedit tē quaedam mala fābula, quā tibi fertur
6   valle sub ālārum trux habitāre caper.
7 Hunc metuunt omnēs, neque mīrum: nam mala valdē est
8   bēstia, nec quīcum bella puella cubet.
9 Quārē aut crūdēlem nāsōrum interfice pestem,
10   aut admīrārī dēsine cūr fugiunt.

Explorations

1. At what should Rufus not be surprised?
2. How do lines 3–4 reinforce the point made in lines 1–2?
3. With what repetitions of sounds does Catullus play in line 2? With what repetitions of sounds does he play in line 4?
4. Why do women refuse to sleep with Rufus? (5–6)
5. **Caper** (6) as used here is an example of what figure of speech?
6. Trace the development of the **mala fābula** (5) and the image of the **caper** (6) in the poem.
7. Locate a double chiasmus created by words in lines 1 and 9–10.

Meter: elegiac couplet

1   **Nūllī**: substantive = **Nēminī**, *No one*, dative with **nūbere**.
    dīcit mulier mea: the verb of the main clause of the sentence (**dīcit**) and its
       subject (**mulier mea**) are embedded in the indirect statement, **Nūllī sē** . . .
       nūbere mālle.
          sē . . . **mālle**: *that she would prefer*, the main clause (apodosis) of a future-
             less-vivid condition in indirect statement.
2   **nōn sī**: *not [even] if*.
    Iuppiter, Iovis, m., *Jupiter, Jove* (king of the gods).
    petat: subjunctive in the if-clause (protasis) of a future-less-vivid condition.
3   **mulier** . . . **quod dīcit**: delayed relative without an antecedent, *[that] which* =
       what a woman says. . . . This clause is the object of **scrībere** in line 4.
    cupidus, -a, -um [**cupiō, cupere, cupīvī, cupītus**, *to desire, want* + **-idus, -a,**
       -um, adjectival suffix], *passionately longing, desirous*.
    amāns, amantis, m., *lover*.
4   **rapidus, -a, -um** [**rapiō, rapere, rapuī, raptus**, *to snatch, seize* + **-idus, -a,**
       -um, adjectival suffix], *flowing so violently as to carry anything along in its*
       path, swiftly flowing.
    scrībere oportet: the infinitive with its object clause is the grammatical sub-
       ject of the impersonal verb, *to write what a woman says . . . is fitting = one ought*
       to write what a woman says or *what a woman says ought to be written*. The
       language is proverbial; the Greek tragedian Sophocles (ca. 496–406 B.C.)
       wrote: "I write the oath of a woman onto water." Other examples of the
       proverb speak of writing on water (as here) and of letting winds *carry*
       words away (cf. Catullus 30.9–10, 64.59 and 142, and 65.17) rather than of
       writing on the wind (as here).

Explorations

1. Which lines of Callimachus' poem has Catullus used?
2. What are the similarities between Catullus' epigram and the first two cou-
    plets of Callimachus'?
3. Of what significance are the following differences between Catullus' epi-
    gram and the first two couplets of Callimachus'?
    a. Callimachus is writing about fictional characters, while Catullus is writ-
        ing about himself and his **mulier**.
    b. In Callimachus' epigram, it is a man who swears the oath, while in
        Catullus it is a woman who makes the statement.
    c. Catullus has introduced the idea of marriage and the possibility of mar-
        riage with Jupiter.
4. Why do you suppose Catullus did not use Callimachus' third couplet?

CATULLUS 70

Words, Words, Words!

This is one of several poems in which Catullus tries to analyze the failure of his love affair with Lesbia. Here he adapts an epigram from the Greek poet Callimachus.

1 Nūllī sē dīcit mulier mea nūbere mālle
2   quam mihi, nōn sī sē Iuppiter ipse petat.
3 Dīcit: sed mulier cupidō quod dīcit amantī,
4   in ventō et rapidā scrībere oportet aquā.

Comparison

Catullus adapted this epigram from an epigram of the Greek poet Callimachus (ca. 305–ca. 240 B.C.) preserved in the *Palatine Anthology* (5.6):

1 ὤμοσε Καλλίγνωτος Ἰωνίδι, μήποτε κείνης
2   ἕξειν μήτε φίλον κρέσσονα μήτε φίλην.
3 ὤμοσεν· ἀλλὰ λέγουσιν ἀληθέα, τοὺς ἐν ἔρωτι
4   ὅρκους μὴ δύνειν οὔατ' ἐς ἀθανάτων.
5 νῦν δ' ὁ μὲν ἀρσενικῷ θέρεται πυρί· τῆς δὲ ταλαίνης
6   νύμφης, ὡς Μεγαρέων, οὐ λόγος οὐδ' ἀριθμός.

1 Callignotus swore to Ionis that he would have
2   neither male beloved nor female beloved in preference to her.
3 He swore: they speak the truth, that lovers' oaths
4   do not enter into the ears of the immortals.
5 Now he burns with a flame for a male, but of the poor girl,
6   as of the Megarians, there is no word nor accounting.

The names Callignotus and Ionis are fictional, the former meaning "Known as Handsome" and the latter suggesting a girl (perhaps a freed slave girl) from Ionia. The Megarians were proverbial for being of no historical or cultural account whatsoever.

Meter: elegiac couplet

1   **quondam**, adv., *formerly.*
    sōlum: modifying **Catullum.**
    nōscō, nōscere, nōvī, nōtus, inceptive, *to get to know, learn;* perfect, *to know*
        (a person or thing; here the verb is used of carnal knowledge).
        nōsse: syncope for **nōvisse.**
            sōlum tē nōsse Catullum: ambiguous, *that you knew only Catullus*
                (with **tē** as subject of the infinitive) or *that only Catullus knew you*
                (with **tē** as object of the infinitive).
2   **prae**, prep. + abl., *before, instead of.*
    Iuppiter, Iovis, m., *Jupiter, Jove* (king of the gods).
        nec prae mē velle tenēre Iovem: supply **tē** from line 1 as the subject of
            velle; now the ambiguity of line 1 is eliminated and **tē** must be taken as
            the subject of the infinitive there.
3   **nōn tantum**: *not only*, picked up in the next line by **sed**; the usual idiom
        would have **sed etiam**, *but also.*
    vulgus, -ī, n., *the common people, general public;* abstract for concrete, *a*
    commoner.
        ut vulgus amicam: supply **dīligit**; **amīcam** here = *courtesan, prostitute.*
4   **gnātus** (= **nātus**), **-ī**, m., *son.*
    gener, generī, m., *son-in-law.*
5   **cognōscō** [**con-**, intensive prefix + **nōscō**, see above], **cognōscere,**
        cognōvī, cognitus, inceptive, *to get to know, learn, become acquainted with;*
        perfect, *to know* (a person or thing; here the verb is used of intellectual
        knowledge).
    etsī, conj., *even if, although.*
    impēnsē, adv. [perhaps from perfect passive participle of **impendō,**
        impendere, impendī, impēnsus, *to pay out, disburse, spend; to spend to no*
        purpose, waste], *to an immoderate degree, lavishly;* comparative, *to a more*
        immoderate degree, more earnestly; at greater expense, more heavily.
    ūrō, ūrere, ūssī, ūstus, *to destroy by fire; to inflame with desire;* passive,
        intransitive, *to burn.*
6   **vīlis, -is, -e**, *costing little, worthless; contemptible; cheap.*
    levis, -is, -e, *of little worth; inconstant, fickle; light.*
7   **quī**, adv. [old ablative form], *how.*
    potis or **pote**, indeclinable adjective + infinitive (see Catullus 45.5), *having the*
        power (to), *able* (to).
        potis est: = **potest**; supply **fierī.**
    amāns, amantis, m., *lover.*
    iniūria, -ae, f., *unlawful conduct; an injustice, a wrong* (here specifically of un-
        faithfulness, which a husband would punish in a wife by divorcing her, but
        which a lover must put up with).
8   **bene velle**, idiom, *to wish* (a person) *well* (used of normal friendly feelings be-
        tween two people), *to have affection.*

CATULLUS 72

Now I know you!

In this poem Catullus probes deeper into his complex feelings for Lesbia.

1   Dīcēbās quondam sōlum tē nōsse Catullum,
2   Lesbia, nec prae mē velle tenēre Iovem.
3   Dīlēxī tum tē nōn tantum ut vulgus amīcam,
4   sed pater ut gnātōs dīligit et generōs.
5   Nunc tē cognōvī: quārē, etsī impēnsius ūror,
6   multō mī tamen es vīlior et levior.
7   Quī potis est, inquis? Quod amantem iniūria tālis
8   cōgit amāre magis, sed bene velle minus.

Explorations

1. Compare this poem with Catullus 70. What are the similarities and differences?
2. What has Catullus borrowed in this poem from Callimachus' epigram (see Catullus 70) that he did not borrow in poem 70?
3. How is what Lesbia is reported to have said in lines 1 and 2 of poem 72 different from what the **mulier** is reported to say in the first two lines of poem 70?
4. How does Catullus define his love for Lesbia in lines 3–4?
5. What has Catullus come to know (5) and what effect has that knowledge had on him (5–6)?
6. What is accomplished by the addition of the final couplet, introduced by Lesbia's reported question?
7. Examine the relationship between the sentences and clauses in this epigram and the metrical structures of the hexameter and the pentameter lines. How do the grammatical and metrical structures enhance the meaning expressed in each of the couplets?
8. Locate significant placement of words, significant repetition of words, metrical patterns, and sounds, and other verbal echoes in the epigram.

Meter: elegiac couplet

1   **quisquam, quisquam, quicquam,** indefinite pronoun, *anyone, anything.*
      velle . . . / . . . putāre (2): complementary infinitives dependent on **dēsine.**
      mereor, -ērī, -itus sum, *to deserve.*
         bene merērī + dē + abl., *to deserve well* (of anyone), *to deserve thanks* (from
           anyone).
               quicquam bene . . . merērī: *to deserve any thanks.*
2   **pius, -a, -um,** *faithful to one's moral, religious, or social obligations; dutiful.*
3   **ingrātus, -a, -um,** *ungrateful; unappreciated.*
         omnia . . . ingrāta: omnia could mean *the whole world,* in which case **in-**
           grāta would have the first of its meanings given above, or it could mean
           all the things one does, in which case **ingrāta** would have the second of its
           meanings given above.
      nihil: adverbial with **prōdest** (4).
      fēcisse: *to have acted.*
      benignē, adv., *with friendliness, kindly, generously.*
4   **prōsum, prōdesse, prōfuī,** *to be of use; to help; to be beneficial.*
         prōdest: the infinitive phrase **fēcisse benignē** (3) is the subject. See below
           for a different version of lines 3–4.
      immō, particle serving to correct a previous statement, *rather.*
      obsum, obesse, obfuī, *to get in the way, be harmful.*
         taedet obestque: the infinitive phrase **fēcisse benignē** is still the subject.
      magis, adv., *more; rather, instead.*
5   **ut mihi:** supply **est.**
      quem nēmō . . . / quam . . . quī (6): *whom no one . . . / than . . . [he] who. . . .*
      acerbus, -a, -um, *bitter; cruel.*
      urgeō, urgēre, ursī, *to press, weigh down, oppress.*
6   **modo,** adv., *just now, recently.*
      ūnicus, -a, -um, *only.*
      habeō, habēre, habuī, habitus, *to have, hold; to consider;* here with double
      predicate, *to regard/treat X as Y.*

Text

3–4   The word **prōdest** at the beginning of line 4 is not in the manuscripts but has
        been supplied by modern editors to fill out the metrical pattern of the line.
        Thomson proposes a different reading for lines 3 and 4 as follows, supply-
        ing the words in brackets:
            3   Omnia sunt ingrāta, nihil fēcisse benignē \<est\>;
            4   immō etiam taedet, \<taedet\> obestque magis;
        The verb **est** and the second **taedet** have been supplied; **nihil . . . est**
        means *is no good,* and the subject of **est** is **fēcisse benignē,** which is also the
        subject of **taedet, \<taedet\> obestque.**

Catullus 73

Ingratitude Everywhere

The poet complains that no good deed is rewarded.

1	Dēsine dē quōquam quicquam bene velle merērī
2	aut aliquem fierī posse putāre pium.
3	Omnia sunt ingrāta, nihil fēcisse benignē
4	<prōdest,> immō etiam taedet obestque magis;
5	ut mihi, quem nēmō gravius nec acerbius urget
6	quam modo quī mē ūnum atque ūnicum amīcum habuit.

Explorations

1. How does the large number of infinitives (five of them) in lines 1–2 affect your ability to comprehend what is being expressed in these lines? Does the similarity of sound of the words **quōquam, quicquam,** and **aliquem** help or hinder your understanding of the meaning of the lines? What poetic device links the words together? What is the tone of the lines?
2. Which version of lines 3–4 is more effective?
3. What is the logical relationship of the second couplet to the first?
4. The words **merērī** (1), **pium** (2), **ingrāta** (3), **benignē** (3), and **prōdest** (4) refer to traditional values in Roman society. These values put great store in a network of mutual loyalties, favors, and gratitude between individuals, between individuals and the state, and between individuals and the gods. What view does Catullus urge that the reader take of these mutual interrelationships in the first two couplets of this poem?
5. What is the effect of the elisions in the last line of the poem?
6. What imagery (use of descriptive language to represent people or objects, often appealing to our senses) does Catullus use in this poem, if any? From what does this poem draw its power?
7. Some scholars believe that Catullus arranged his poems in essentially the order in which they are preserved in the manuscripts; others believe that the arrangement is due to an editor who collected Catullus' poems after his death. Why would either Catullus or an editor put poem 73 after poem 72?

Meter: elegiac couplet

1   **dēdūcō** [**dē-**, *down, from, away* + **dūcō, dūcere, dūxī, ductus**, *to lead, take, bring*], **dēdūcere, dēdūxī, dēductus**, *to lead down; to lead off/along* (to a certain destination); *to bring down, reduce* (to a certain state or condition).
      culpa, -ae, f., *fault, blame; wrongdoing;* (of sexual misconduct) *infidelity.*
         culpā: ablative of cause; see Catullus 11.22.

2   **officium, -ī**, n., *a helpful/beneficial act* (done to someone to whom one owes an obligation); *duty, obligation, commitment, devotion* (to a person, to the state); *function, job* (i.e., what one does to fulfill one's role).
         officiō . . . suō: *by [performing] its own function/job; by its own commitment/devotion.*
      ipsa: i.e., **mēns**.

3   **ut**: introducing a result clause.
      bene velle: see Catullus 72.8.
      queō, quīre, quīvī or **quiī**, *to be able.*
      tibi: dative with **bene velle**.

4   **dēsistō** [**dē-**, *down, from, away* + **sistō, sistere, stetī, status**, *to cause* (a person or thing) *to stand*], **dēsistere, dēstitī**, *to cease.*
         nec dēsistere amāre: supply **queat** from line 3.
      omnia: *[anything and] everything* = the worst things possible.

Text

1   **mea**: Thomson takes this as modifying **Lesbia** instead of **mēns** and places the comma after **tuā**, thus:
        1   Hūc est mēns dēducta tuā, mea Lesbia, culpā

Catullus 75

The Love-Hate Deepens.

Catullus admits in this short poem that personal reflection and analysis have worsened his condition.

1   Hūc est mēns dēducta tuā mea, Lesbia, culpā
2   atque ita sē officiō perdidit ipsa suō,
3   ut iam nec bene velle queat tibi, sī optima fīās,
4   nec dēsistere amāre, omnia sī faciās.

Explorations

1. Catullus has put strong emphasis on the opening word **Hūc**. To what state of mind does **Hūc** refer? How does the compound verb **est . . . dēducta** color the assertion?
2. In lines 1–2, what is Catullus claiming he did and that Lesbia did not do? Consider the words **culpā** (1) and **officiō** (2) in your answer. What is the consequence of Catullus' actions according to line 2?
3. In your own words state what the last two lines say. The phrase **bene velle** (3) clearly relates this poem to Catullus 72, where the same phrase is used in the final line. What are the similarities and the differences between the two poems?
4. Specific words in Catullus 73 highlight traditional Roman values based on mutual loyalties, favors, and gratitude between individuals. What words in Catullus 75 highlight these values? Are any words of this sort found in Catullus 72?
5. Read the poem in meter. Where do you feel that the first comma should go in line 1? Find chiastic arrangements of words in lines 1 and 2. Analyze the parallel structure of lines 3 and 4. How many elisions do you find? Why are the ones in line 4 so effective?

Meter: elegiac couplet

1   **quī, qua, quod**, indefinite adjective after **sī**, *any*.
      qua: sometimes written together with the **sī** as one word, **sīqua**; the indefinite adjective modifies **voluptās**.
      recordor [**re-**, *back, again* + **cor, cordis**, n., *heart, mind*], **-ārī, -ātus sum**, *to call to mind, recollect*.
      recordantī . . . / . . . hominī (2): dative of the possessor.
      benefactum, -ī, n., *kindness, good deed*.
      benefacta: cf. Catullus 73.3, **fēcisse benignē**.
2   **cōgitat**: here, *recollects, bears in mind*.
      esse: not simply *is*, but *has been and still is*.
      pium: *dutiful*; see Catullus 73.2.
3   **nec . . . nec**: *and not . . . and not*.
      violō, -āre, -āvī, -ātus, *to violate*.
      violāsse: syncope for **violāvisse**.
      nec . . . nūllō: double negative, *and not in any*. Thomson prints **in ūllō**, eliminating the double negative.
      foedus, foederis, n., *formal agreement, treaty; contract, compact*.
      fidēs . . . foedere: note the alliteration of **fid- . . . foed-** in these key words.
4   **dīvus, -ī**, m., *god*.
      dīvum: syncope for **dīvōrum**; take with **nūmine**.
      fallō, fallere, fefellī, falsus, *to deceive*.
      ad fallendōs . . . hominēs: gerundive with **ad** to express purpose.
      nūmen, nūminis, n., *divinity, power*.
      abūtor [**ab-**, *completely, thoroughly* + **ūtor, ūtī, ūsus sum**, *to use*], **abūtī, abūsus sum** + abl., *to misuse, abuse*.
         abūsum: supply **esse**.
5   **multa**: with **gaudia** (6).
      parō, -āre, -āvī, -ātus, *to prepare, get ready; to produce, bring about; to win, earn*.
      parāta: with **ex hōc ingrātō . . . amōre** (6).
      aetās, aetātis, f., *age* (the years of one's life).
      in longā aetāte: *in the long years ahead, for the remainder of your life, over a long life*.
6   **ingrātō**: see the meanings given at Catullus 73.3; here, *unappreciated, received with no gratitude*.
7   **quīcumque, quaecumque, quodcumque**, indefinite relative pronoun, *whoever, whatever*.
      bene: take with **dīcere** and **facere** (8).
      quisquam, quisquam, quicquam, indefinite pronoun, *anyone, anything*.
8   **dīcere . . . (7) / . . . facere . . . dicta . . . facta**: note the parallelism.
      dictaque factaque: polysyndeton.

CATULLUS 76

An Urgent Plea for a "Quid pro Quo"

Catullus appeals to the gods for salvation.

1   Sī qua recordantī benefacta priōra voluptās
2   est hominī, cum sē cōgitat esse pium,
3   nec sānctam violāsse fidem, nec foedere nūllō
4   dīvum ad fallendōs nūmine abūsum hominēs,
5   multa parāta manent in longā aetāte, Catulle,
6   ex hōc ingrātō gaudia amōre tibi.
7   Nam quaecumque hominēs bene cuiquam aut dīcere possunt
8   aut facere, haec ā tē dictaque factaque sunt,

continued

Explorations

1.   When doing what might a person experience pleasure (**voluptās**)? (1–4)
2.   What lies in store for Catullus? (5–6) Why is this so? (7–8)
3.   A syllogism consists of a major and a minor premise and a conclusion. Identify the elements of a syllogism in the thoughts contained in lines 1–8 (the elements of the syllogism are there, but not in the usual order).
4.   It was a philosophical commonplace in antiquity "that the recollection of past good deeds is a source of pleasure" (J. G. F. Powell, "Two Notes on Catullus," *The Classical Quarterly* 40, 1990, 199). Powell continues: "One of the chief problems in ancient moral philosophy was the need to show that virtue is profitable to those who practise it. One of the arguments employed to this end was that virtuous deeds are a source of pleasurable memories and that the enjoyment of a good conscience has a greater value than more mundane pleasures" (Powell, 199). Powell quotes the following example of this thinking from Cicero's *De senectute* (9): **cōnscientia bene āctae vītae multōrumque benefactōrum recordātiō iūcundissima est**, *knowledge of a life well lived and memory of many good deeds is most pleasant.* Compare Cicero's statement with lines 1–5 of Catullus 76.
5.   Is there anything in lines 1–5 that would lead you to expect that this poem will deal with a love affair?
6.   Are lines 5–6 straightforward? That is, is Catullus flooded with **voluptās** and **gaudia** at the thought of his good deeds and clean conscience? If not, why not? What words in line 6 undercut the optimism of lines 1–5?
7.   The truth or falsity of the conclusion of a syllogism depends on the truth or falsity of each of its premises. Which premise (1–4, 7–8) when applied to Catullus' situation may be false here?

9   **omnia quae:** delayed relative. Other editors make line 9 an independent
sentence with **quae** a connecting relative introducing a main clause.

    ingrātae: here, *ungrateful, thankless;* cf. **ingrātō** (6).

    crēdō, crēdere, crēdidī, crēditus + dat., *to trust; to believe; to commit, entrust.*

10   **tētē:** emphatic **tē.**

    amplius, comparative adv., *more, further.*

    excruciō [ex-, *thoroughly* + **cruciō, -āre, -āvī, -ātus,** *to crucify; to torture;* from
crux, crucis, f., *cross* (on which slaves could be punished by being impaled
and allowed to die)], **-āre, -āvī, -ātus,** *to crucify; to torture, torment.*

        excruciēs: deliberative subjunctive.

            Quārē . . . excruciēs: this is Thomson's reading; other texts give
Quārē iam tē cūr amplius excruciēs?

11   **quīn,** interrogative adv., *why . . . not?*

    animō: = **in animō.**

    offirmō [ob-, *against* + **firmō, -āre, -āvī, -ātus,** *to make strong*] **-āre, -āvī,
-ātus,** *to make firm;* intransitive, *to be determined; to become strong.*

    istinc, adv., *from there; from the state you are in.*

    tē ipse: this is Thomson's reading; other texts have **tēque,** with an unneeded
connective.

12   **dīs:** = **deīs.**

    dīs invītīs: *because/since the gods are unwilling* (i.e., to help or to guarantee
that she love you in return).

    dēsinis esse miser: compare Catullus 8.1.

13   **longum subitō:** note the effective juxtaposition of words.

14   **vērum,** conj., *but.*

    quā lubet = quā libet [quā, *in any way* + **libet,** impersonal, *(it) pleases*], *in any
way it pleases, no matter how, somehow or other.*

    efficiō [ex-, *thoroughly* + **faciō, facere, fēcī, factus,** *to make, do*], **efficere, ef-
fēcī, effectus,** *to accomplish, carry out, bring about.*

        efficiās: jussive subjunctive, *you must. . . .* ; cf. Catullus 8.1, **dēsinās.**

15   **salūs, salūtis,** f., *safety; health; salvation.*

    haec: feminine singular in place of the neuter **hoc,** by attraction to the gen-
der of **salūs.**

    hoc: scanned as a long or heavy syllable (originally spelled **hocc**). The four
demonstratives in lines 14–16 (**hoc, haec, hoc,** and **hoc;** note the anaphora)
refer to **longum subitō dēpōnere amōrem** (13).

    pervincō [per-, *thoroughly* + **vincō, vincere, vīcī, victus,** *to conquer, win*],
pervincere, pervīcī, pervictus, *to win a complete victory over; to overcome.*

        est . . . pervincendum: note the effect of the spondaic fifth foot.

16   **sīve . . . sīve,** conj., *whether . . . or.*

    potis or **pote,** indeclinable adjective + infinitive (see Catullus 45.5 and 72.7),
having the power (to), *able* (to).

        pote: supply **est,** = **potest,** and supply **fierī,** *to become, to be done.*

9   omnia quae ingrātae periērunt crēdita mentī.
10   Quārē cūr tētē iam amplius excruciēs?
11   Quīn tū animō offirmās atque istinc tē ipse redūcis,
12   et dīs invītīs dēsinis esse miser?
13   Difficile est longum subitō dēpōnere amōrem.
14   Difficile est, vērum hoc quā lubet efficiās:
15   ūna salūs haec est, hoc est tibi pervincendum,
16   hoc faciās, sīve id nōn pote sīve pote.

continued

Explorations

8. Explain the commercial connotations of the words **periērunt** and **crēdita** (9).
9. Compare the idea expressed in lines 8–9 with Catullus 73. What specific example of ingratitude does the poet give in poem 76?
10. What is the relationship between the question in line 10 and what has preceded it in the poem?
11. What answer does Catullus give in lines 11–12 to the question he asks of himself in line 10?
12. Lines 13–14 stand in the exact middle of the poem. Explain them as an internal dialogue.
13. What devices of rhetoric, grammar, and meter does Catullus use in lines 15–16 to emphasize the necessity of accomplishing the task? Does he think he can accomplish it?

17   **dī**: = **deī**.

      vestrum: genitive of **vōs**.

        vestrum est + infinitive, *is characteristic of you, is within you.*

      misereor, -ērī, -itus sum, *to have pity; to feel compassion.*

        miserērī: the infinitive serves as the subject of **vestrum est**.

      quis, qua/quae, quid, indefinite pronoun after **sī**, *anyone, anything.*

18   **extrēmus, -a, -um**, *last, final, last-minute.*

      ops, opis, f., *power; aid, help.*

19   **aspiciō** [**ad-**, *to, toward* + **speciō, specere, spexī, spectus**, *to see, observe*],

        aspicere, aspexī, aspectus, *to look at.*

      pūriter [**pūrus, -a, -um**, *clean* + **-ter**], adv. [a formal, archaic formation for the

        later and more usual **pūrē**], *in a clean manner; without moral blemish.*

20   **pestis, pestis**, f., *disease, plague.*

      perniciēs, -ēī, f., *destruction, ruin.*

        pestem perniciemque: alliteration and hendiadys, = *destructive disease* or

          ruinous plague.

      mihi: dative of separation.

21   **mihi**: dative of reference, indicating possession, with **īmōs . . . in artūs**.

      subrēpō [**sub-**, *under* + **rēpō, rēpere, rēpsī**, *to crawl, creep*], **subrēpere, sub-**

        rēpsī, subrēptūrus, *to creep under/into.*

      īmus, -a, -um, *deepest, innermost.*

      torpor, torpōris, m., *numbness, paralysis.*

      artus, -ūs, m., *joint; limb.*

22   **laetitia, -ae**, f., *gladness, joy.*

23   **illud . . . ut . . . illa**: *the following . . . that she.*

      contrā, adv., *in return.*

        contrā: take with **dīligat**.

          contrā ut mē, this is Thomson's reading, replacing **contrā mē ut** of other

            editions; it avoids delaying the conjunction and obviates the tempta-

            tion to take **contrā** as a preposition governing **mē**.

24   **quod**: *[something] that.*

      quod nōn potis est: supply **fierī**, *[something] that is not possible [to happen].*

      pudīcus, -a, -um, *virtuous, honorable, chaste.*

        esse pudīca velit: supply **ut** from line 23.

25   **ipse**: over against **illa** (23).

      taeter, taetra, taetrum, *offensive, revolting, foul.*

26   **prō**, prep. + abl., *for, in return for.*

      pietās, pietātis, f., *dutifulness.*

        pietāte: cf. **pium** (2).

17   Ō dī, sī vestrum est miserērī, aut sī quibus umquam
18   extrēmam iam ipsā in morte tulistis opem,
19   mē miserum aspicite et, sī vītam pūriter ēgī,
20   ēripite hanc pestem perniciemque mihi,
21   quae mihi subrēpēns īmōs ut torpor in artūs
22   expulit ex omnī pectore laetitiās.
23   Nōn iam illud quaerō, contrā ut mē dīligat illa,
24   aut, quod nōn potis est, esse pudīca velit:
25   ipse valēre optō et taetrum hunc dēpōnere morbum.
26   Ō dī, reddite mī hoc prō pietāte meā.

Explorations

14. To whom does Catullus turn in his helplessness?
15. Catullus incorporates standard elements of ancient prayers to the gods, such
     as the if-clauses in lines 17–18, but how are these two clauses particularly rel-
     evant to Catullus' condition?
16. What lines at the beginning of the poem do the words **sī vītam pūriter ēgī**
     (19) recall?
17. For what does Catullus pray? (20–22)
18. With what kind of imagery does the poet now describe his love? (20) What
     words in the remaining lines of the poem develop this imagery?
19. What words in lines 19–21 recall words in Catullus 51?
20. What two words in the first part of the poem are recalled by the word **laeti-
     tiās** (22)?
21. What does Catullus no longer seek, and why? (23–24)
22. What line earlier in the poem is echoed by line 25 and to what effect?
23. How does the last line of the poem round out the prayer to the gods and the
     poem as a whole?

Comparisons

How does Catullus 76 compare with Catullus 8 in theme and in tone?

Compare the following translations by William Walsh and Horace Gregory both with each other and with Catullus 76.

William Walsh (1663–1708)

Is there a pious pleasure that proceeds
From contemplation of our virtuous deeds?
That all mean sordid action we despise,
And scorn to gain a throne by cheats and lies?
Thyrsis, thou hast sure blessings laid in store
From thy just dealing in this curst amour.
What honour can in words or deeds be shown
Which to the fair thou hast not said and done?
On her false heart they all are thrown away:
She only swears more easily to betray.
Ye powers that know the many vows she broke,
Free my just soul from this unequal yoke.
My love boils up, and like a raging flood
Runs through my veins and taints my vital blood.
I do not vainly beg she may grow chaste,
Or with an equal passion burn at last—
The one she cannot practise, though she would,
And I contemn the other, though she should—:
Nor ask I vengeance on the perjured jilt;
'Tis punishment enough to have her guilt.
I beg but balsam for my bleeding breast,
Cure for my wounds and from my labours rest.

Horace Gregory (1898–1982)

If man can find rich consolation, remembering his good deeds
    and all he has done,
if he remembers his loyalty to others, nor abuses his religion
    by heartless betrayal
of friends to the anger of powerful gods,
then, my Catullus, the long years before you shall not sink
    in darkness with all hope gone,
wandering, dismayed, through the ruins of love.
All the devotion that man gives to man, you have given,
    Catullus,

your heart and your brain flowed into a love that was desolate, wasted, nor can it return.
But why, why do you crucify love and yourself through the
   years?
Take what the gods have to offer and standing serene, rise
   forth as a rock against darkening skies;
and yet you do nothing but grieve, sunken deep in your
   sorrow, Catullus,
for it is hard, hard to throw aside years lived in poisonous
   love that has tainted your brain
and must end.
If this seems impossible now, you must rise
to salvation. O gods of pity and mercy, descend and witness
   my sorrow, if ever
you have looked upon man in his hour of death, see me now
   in despair.
Tear this loathsome disease from my brain. Look, a subtle
   corruption has entered my bones,
no longer shall happiness flow through my veins like a river.
   No longer I pray
that she love me again, that her body be chaste, mine forever.
Cleanse my soul of this sickness of love, give me power to
      rise, resurrected, to thrust love aside,
I have given my heart to the gods, O hear me, omnipotent
   heaven
and ease me of love and its pain.

Meter: Elegiac couplet

1   **Rūfus, -ī**, m., *Rufus* (perhaps M. Caelius Rufus, the lover of Clodia defended
       by Cicero).
       mihi: take with **amīce**, *my friend*, or with **crēdite**, *believed by me*, or with both.
       frūstrā ac nēquīquam: near synonyms, meaning *in vain*, the former empha-
         sizing disappointment, the latter failure (Fordyce).
2   **immō**, particle serving to correct a previous statement, *rather*.
       malum, -ī, n., *trouble; distress, pain; damage*.
3   **sīcine**: = **sīc + -ne**.
       subrēpō [sub-, *under* + **rēpō, rēpere, rēpsī**, *to crawl, creep*], **subrēpere, sub-**
         rēpsī, subrēptūrus + dat. (see Catullus 76.21), *to creep under; to steal upon*.
            subrēpstī: syncope for **subrēpsistī**.
       intestīna, -ōrum, n. pl., *intestines*.
       perūrō [per-, *thoroughly* + **ūrō, ūrere, ūssī, ūstus**, *to burn*], **perūrere,**
         perūssī, perūstus, *to consume, burn*.
4   **ei**, interj., *alas!*
       miserō: supply **mihi**, dative of separation with **ēripuistī; miserō** is proleptic,
         [and made me] wretched.
       bona: neuter plural, but translate with a singular abstract noun such as *hap-*
         piness.
5   **heu heu**: Thomson prints **ēheu** instead of **heu heu** here and in line 6.
       venēnum, -ī, n., *poison*.
         venēnum: vocative.
6   **pestis, pestis**, f. (see Catullus 76.20), *disease, plague* (often applied to a person
         as an agent responsible for destroying something).
            pestis: vocative.
       amīcitia, -ae, f., *friendship*.
         nostrae . . . amīcitiae: *of our friendship*; i.e., of Catullus' friendship with
            Rufus, cf. **amīce** (1).

Catullus 77

Friend?

No, betrayal!

1   Rūfe mihi frūstrā ac nēquīquam crēdite amīce
2   (frūstrā? immō magnō cum pretiō atque malō),
3   sīcine subrēpstī mī, atque intestīna perūrēns
4   ei miserō ēripuistī omnia nostra bona?
5   Ēripuistī, heu heu nostrae crūdēle venēnum
6   vītae, heu heu nostrae pestis amīcitiae.

Explorations

1. Compare the theme of this poem with that of Catullus 73. What are the similarities? What are the differences?
2. Poems 73 and 77 both find echoes in poem 76. What lines in poems 73 and 76 express the futility of behaving toward anyone with the kindness and generosity that would engender friendship? What lines in poem 76 are recalled by words, phrases, and clauses in poem 77?
3. Locate four nouns in the vocative case.
4. In lines 1–2 locate an ascending triad of two adverbs and a prepositional phrase.
5. In lines 3–4 locate the members of an ascending tricolon.
6. Study the pattern of *m*-, *s*-, and *ō*-sounds in the poem. How do they enhance its effectiveness?
7. Locate all repeated words. How does repetition emphasize the forward movement of the rhetorical structures in the poem?
8. The Rufus of this poem is sometimes identified with M. Caelius Rufus, a lover of Clodia Metelli, the woman who is often identified as Catullus' Lesbia. If these two identifications were to be made, how would this affect your interpretation of this poem? How would your interpretation of the poem be different if these two identifications were not made?

Meter: elegiac couplet

1   **praesēns, praesentis,** *being in the same place, present.*
       praesente virō: if we identify Lesbia as Clodia Metelli, then this will refer
         to Clodia's husband Quintus Metellus Celer, who died in 59 B.C.
       mala . . . dīcit: tmesis for **maledīcit**, from **maledīcō** [**male,** *badly* + **dīcō,**
         dīcere, dīxī, dictus, *to say*], **maledīcere, maledīxī, maledictus** + dat., *to*
         curse, heap abuse (upon).

2   **haec**: i.e., the verbal abuse mentioned in line 1; for the feminine singular
         form, see the use of **haec** in line 15 of Catullus 76.
       fatuus, -a, -um, *mentally lacking, foolish.*
         illī fatuō: i.e., Lesbia's husband.
       laetitia, -ae, f., *happiness, joy.*
         laetitia: predicate nominative.

3   **mūlus, -ī,** m., *mule.*
       nostrī: genitive of **nōs,** perhaps in the sense of *the relationship between us;* or
         plural for singular, = **meī.**
       oblītus, -a, -um + gen., *forgetful* (of).
       tacēret: the subject is Lesbia.

4   **sānus, -a, -um,** *sane, rational, in one's right mind, emotionally sound* (i.e., free of
         passionate involvement).
       quod: here, *in as much as.*
       ganniō, gannīre, (often of dogs) *to growl, snarl.*
       obloquor [**ob-,** *against* + **loquor, loquī, locūtus sum,** *to speak*], **obloquī,**
         oblocūtus sum, *to break in* (on a speaker or a conversation), *interrupt.*
       gannit et obloquitur: hysteron proteron.

5   **meminit**: supply **nostrī** from line 3.
       quae . . . rēs: the antecedent **rēs** is included in the relative clause, translate,
         a matter that. . . .
       ācer, ācris, ācre, *keen, sharp; serious.*

6   **Hoc est**: *That is [to say].*
       Hoc: scanned here as long or heavy
       ūrō, ūrere, ūssī, ūstus, *to burn;* passive (cf. Catullus 72.5), *to be inflamed* (with
         desire or passion).

CATULLUS 83

Lesbia's stinging words are not what they seem. Or are they?

What does Lesbia's behavior mean?

1   Lesbia mī praesente virō mala plūrima dīcit:
2   haec illī fatuō maxima laetitia est.
3   Mūle, nihil sentīs? Sī nostrī oblīta tacēret,
4   sāna esset: nunc quod gannit et obloquitur,
5   nōn sōlum meminit, sed, quae multō ācrior est rēs,
6   īrāta est. Hoc est, ūritur et loquitur.

Explorations

1. What is the situation described in this poem? Some commentators identify Lesbia with Clodia Metelli and believe that the reader is to imagine Catullus as being with Lesbia/Clodia and her husband, Q. Metellus Celer. Others, noting the words **nostrī oblīta** (3) and **meminit** (5), maintain that Catullus cannot be imagined as being present.
2. Why does Catullus call the husband a mule in the second couplet?
3. Explain **gannit et obloquitur** as an example of hysteron proteron.
4. How does the poet in lines 5–6 interpret Lesbia's state of mind and actions as reported in lines 1–4?
5. How do the words **ūritur et loquitur** (6) correspond to **gannit et obloquitur** (4)?
6. Propertius, a love poet of the Augustan age, had Catullus 83 in mind when he wrote a poem on "the theme that an angry tongue is a proof of love" (Quinn, 418). The following lines are extracts from Propertius' poem (3.8.3–4, 9–12, 28):
   > When maddened with wine you push over the dining table and fling full cups at me with frenzied hand . . . there's no doubt that you are giving me signs of truly passionate love: for no woman is so upset unless overwhelmed with love. The woman who hurls insults with frenzied tongue grovels at the feet of great Venus. . . . I would always wish to be the pale lover of an angry woman (**Semper in īrātā pallidus esse velim**).

   How does Propertius' poem help you understand the argument that Catullus is making?
7. Some see in lines 3–6 "a deliberate evasion of the unpleasant conclusions that might be drawn from the situation described in lines 1–2" (Holoka, 119). Is this view defensible?

Meter: elegiac couplet

1   **chommoda:** = **commoda**, n. pl., *advantages*. This is the first of three words in
     the poem that Arrius mispronounces by aspirating the initial letter, i.e., by
     adding a rough breathing sound equivalent to the letter *h*, so that here *c*
     becomes *ch*. *Ch, ph,* and *th* sounds were not native to Latin, but they were
     frequent in Greek and in the parent language from which both Greek and
     Latin evolved. When Latin began borrowing words from Greek that con-
     tained aspirated consonants, it did not borrow the aspiration, so that Greek
     theatron, "theater," originally became Latin **teātrum**. By Catullus' time,
     however, Latin had begun to incorporate the aspirated consonants in
     Greek loan words, thus giving **theātrum**, and there was a tendency to
     overdo this Greek influence by incorporating aspiration into Latin words
     where it did not belong, hence **pulcher** instead of **pulcer** and **phius** instead
     of **pius**. This practice bothered Cicero (*Orator* 160), and it was a source of
     amusement for Catullus, as this poem shows. (See Fordyce, 373–74.)
     sī quandō, here with the imperfect subjunctive instead of the usual pluper-
          fect indicative, *if ever, whenever*.
2   **īnsidiae, -ārum**, f. pl., *ambush*.
     īnsidiās Arrius hīnsidiās: ellipsis, implying repetition of the earlier
          clauses, only in reverse order, i.e., **sī quandō Arrius vellet īnsidiās**
          dīcere, hīnsidiās dīcēbat. Aspiration (an *h* sound) before an initial
          vowel was native to Latin, but in popular speech it tended to disappear,
          thus **arēna** instead of **harēna**, *sand; arena*, and **ortus** instead of **hortus**,
          garden. Conversely, it was sometimes added where it did not belong,
          giving **hūmidus** instead of **ūmidus**, *wet, moist*, and **have** instead of **ave**,
          greetings! Arrius makes the latter mistake. (See Fordyce, 374.)
     Arrius, -ī, m., *Arrius* (possibly Quintus Arrius, an orator of whom Cicero
          thought very little, describing him as a man of low birth who though lack-
          ing education and native talent managed to gain political office, wealth,
          and the favor of powerful patrons, including Marcus Crassus; see Cicero,
          Brutus 242).
3   **mīrificē** [**mīrus, -a, -um**, *extraordinary, remarkable* + **-ficus**, adjectival suffix,
          making, causing + **-ē**, adverbial ending] (see Catullus 53.2), *in an amazing*
          manner, remarkably well.
     mīrificē: take with **esse locūtum**.
     spērō, -āre, -āvī, -ātus, *to look forward to, hope for; to hope; to flatter oneself* (that +
          acc. and infin.).
          spērābat . . . / cum . . . dīxerat (4): past general, with imperfect
               indicative in the main clause and pluperfect indicative in the temporal
               clause; translate the temporal clause *whenever he said. . . .*
4   **quantum poterat:** *with as much force as possible*.
5   **līber, lībera, līberum**, *free*.
6   **māternus, -a, -um**, *maternal*.
     avus, -ī, m., *grandfather*.
     avia, -ae f., *grandmother*.

CATULLUS 84

Aspirations reveal aspirations.

The affected pronunciation of a social climber doesn't impress Catullus.

1	Chommoda dīcēbat, sī quandō commoda vellet
2	dīcere, et īnsidiās Arrius hīnsidiās,
3	et tum mīrificē spērābat sē esse locūtum,
4	cum quantum poterat dīxerat hīnsidiās.
5	Crēdō, sīc māter, sīc līber avunculus eius,
6	sīc māternus avus dīxerat atque avia.

continued

Text

5   **līber**: it is difficult to explain why Catullus would describe the uncle as **līber**, and R. G. M. Nisbet has suggested that **semper** is what Catullus wrote here.

Explorations

1. How does Catullus use word placement and chiasmus to highlight Arrius' humorous mispronunciations? (1–2)
2. What do we learn about Arrius in lines 3–4? Compare this behavior to that of Suffenus described in lines 15–17 of Catullus 22. What is the similarity? What is the poet's attitude toward this behavior?
3. Arrius' mispronunciations are often explained as misguided attempts on the part of someone of lower class to imitate the speech of the upper classes. Explain this in the light of the information on aspiration supplied in the notes on lines 1 and 2 and in the light of what Cicero says about Quintus Arrius (see note on line 2), assuming that he is the Arrius of this poem.
4. Why does Catullus mention Arrius' family in lines 5–6? Is **līber** to be taken literally or sarcastically? What is implied about the social status of Arrius' maternal relatives?

7   **Hōc**: i.e., Arrius. If Arrius is the Quintus Arrius described by Cicero in his *Brutus*, he may have been sent to Syria by Crassus on a diplomatic mission in conjunction with Crassus' military expedition to Parthia in 55 B.C.

      requiēscō [re-, intensive + **quiēscō, quiēscere, quiēvī, quiētūrus,** inceptive, *to fall asleep; to take rest*], **requiēscere, requiēvī, requiētūrus,** inceptive, *to rest; to find relief.*

         requiērant: syncope for **requiēverant.**

      omnibus: dative of reference, *for all concerned, everyone's.*

      auris, auris, f., *ear.*

8   **audībant**: syncope for **audiēbant.**

      eadem haec: supply **verba** (i.e., the words **commoda** and **īnsidiae**) and **dicta**, *pronounced.*

      lēniter, adv., *gently; with a smooth breathing* (i.e., without the rough breathing or aspiration, the *h*-sound of Greek aspirated vowels and consonants), *without aspiration, smoothly.*

      leviter, adv., *lightly, gently, softly.*

9   **sibi**: dative of reference, *for themselves.*

      postillā, adv., *afterwards, after that time.*

      metuō, metuere, metuī, metūtus, *to fear, be afraid of.*

10   **affertur**: historical present.

      nūntius: sometimes an indirect statement is introduced through a reference to speech, as here; i.e., *a message is brought, that.* . . .

      horribilis, -is, -e, *inspiring fear/horror; dreadful, horrible.*

11   **Īonius, -a, -um,** *Ionian* (referring to the Ionian Sea off the west coast of Greece).

      flūctus, -ūs, m., *wave.*

      īsset: relative and temporal clauses inside indirect statements take the subjunctive.

Comparison

Here is an Anglicized version of Arrius. What is the particularly British mistake in pronunciation that Sir 'Arry makes? Which of the two poems do you prefer? Why?

Sir 'Arry, though lately created a knight,
Is unable to order his h's aright.
He expounds the wise views of a man of haffairs
Or explains 'ow 'e 'ates haristocracy's hairs.
(To his mother, nee 'Awkins, he owes, I expect,
This unpleasant, invincible vocal defect.)
His victims had looked for a respite at least
While Sir 'Arry is occupied doin' the Heast.
But alas for our hopes! You've not heard the news? What?
Sir 'Arry finds Hindia 'ellishly 'ot.

                                               Anonymous

7   Hōc missō in Syriam requiērant omnibus aurēs:
8   audībant eadem haec lēniter et leviter,
9   nec sibi postillā metuēbant tālia verba,
10   cum subitō affertur nūntius horribilis,
11 Īoniōs flūctūs, postquam illūc Arrius īsset,
12   iam nōn Īoniōs esse sed Hīoniōs.

Explorations

5. What do the words **Hōc missō in Syriam** (7) and **requiērant omnibus au-rēs** (7) imply about the social status of Arrius at this time?
6. How do the words **lēniter** and **leviter** (8) correspond to descriptions of Ar-rius' speech in lines 1–4?
7. Explain the point of the final couplet.

Meter: elegiac couplet

1   **ōdī, ōdisse**, perfect in form, present in meaning, *to hate*.
     quārē, interrogative adv., *for what reason, why*.
       Quārē id faciam: indirect question dependent on **requīris**.
     requīrō [re-, intensive + **quaerō, quaerere, quaesīvī, quaesītus**, *to ask*],
       requīrere, requīsīvī, requīsītus, *to ask*.
2   **Nescio**: see note on Catullus 2.6.
     fierī: infinitive in an indirect statement dependent on **sentiō**; supply **id** as
       subject of the infinitive and **mihi** as dative of reference, *that [it] is being
       done/is happening [to me]*.
     excruciō [ex-, *thoroughly* + **cruciō, -āre, -āvī, -ātus**, *to crucify; to torture*; from
       crux, crucis, f., *cross* (on which slaves could be punished by being impaled
       and allowed to die)] (see Catullus 76.10), **-āre, -āvī, -ātus**, *to crucify; to tor-
       ture, torment*.

Comparisons

Grade these versions for their faithfulness to the original, their success in convey-
ing its tone and sentiment, and their simplicity of expression.

I hate, and yet I love thee too;
How can that be? I know not how;
Only that so it is I know;
And feel with torment that 'tis so.

—Abraham Cowley, 1667

I hate and love. Why? You may ask but
It beats me. I feel it done to me, and ache.

—Ezra Pound, 1885–1972

I hate and I love. And if you ask me how,
I do not know: I only feel it, and I'm torn in two.

—Peter Whigham, 1966

I HATE and love.
And if you ask me why,
I have no answer, but I discern,
can feel, my senses rooted in eternal torture.

—Horace Gregory, 1898–1982

Of course I hate what I love, and can't explain, for how is one to syllogize
    his pain?

—Gary Wills, 1966

CATULLUS 85

I Hate and I Love.

How does Catullus' analysis of his predicament differ now from what it was in poems 72 and 75?

1 Ōdī et amō. Quārē id faciam, fortasse requīris.
2 Nescio, sed fierī sentiō et excrucior.

Explorations

1. How many verbs are there in this couplet? How many nouns and adjectives can you find? On what does the poet focus in poem 85?
2. Read the poem aloud and in meter. How many elisions can you find and what is the effect of the first and of the last elision?
3. Identify the members of an ascending tricolon in the poem. What word does the ascending tricolon highlight?
4. Locate two caesuras in the first line and two diaereses in the second line.
5. Divide the poem into segments based on the pauses (caesuras, diaereses, and sentence-ends).
6. Using these divisions of the poem into segments, label each of the segments as members of a ring composition or chiasmus consisting of ABCCBA.
7. Label the members of the ring composition or chiasmus as (A) feelings felt by an active agent, (B) action performed by an active agent, (C) inquiry by an active agent, (C) response by an active agent, (B) suffering experienced by a passive victim, and (A) feelings felt by a passive victim. What pattern do you detect?
8. How does the final word of the poem relate to the first three words?
9. How do the words that immediately precede the second pause in each line (labeled B in the ring composition or chiasmus) relate to one another?
10. What are the main oppositions or antitheses in the poem?
11. Who is the *you* of **requīris**?
12. Compare this poem with Catullus 72 and 75. How does it carry to its logical conclusion and crystallize the basic antithesis expressed in those poems?
13. Catullus 72 contains elements of a dialogue. How does the implied dialogue in Catullus 85 lead the poet to a different conclusion and to a different state of mind?
14. In poem 72 the clause **Nunc tē cognōvī** (5) shows the poet fully in command of his rational faculties, and with these rational faculties he clearly describes his emotional situation twice over, first in the second half of line 5 and line 6 and then in answer to Lesbia's reported question, in the second half of line 7 and line 8. What word in Catullus 85 reverses this sense of intellectual knowledge expressed in Catullus 72?

Meter: elegiac couplet

1   **Quīntia, -ae** f., *Quintia* (a woman whom Catullus is comparing to Lesbia).
     fōrmōsus, -a, -um, *beautiful.*
       fōrmōsa: the word occurs in Catullus only in this poem.
     multīs: *in the eyes of many,* dative of reference or dative of the person judging.
     candidus, -a, -um (see Catullus 13.4), *white, fair-skinned, pretty.*
     longus, -a, -um, *long, tall.*
2   **rēctus, -a, -um** (see Catullus 10.20), *tall, straight.*
     haec: substantive, *these [characteristics].*
     singulī, -ae, -a, *taken separately, individual.*
     cōnfiteor [con-, intensive + **fateor, fatērī, fassus sum,** *to accept as true, ad-
       mit*], **cōnfitērī, cōnfessus sum,** *to admit* (a fact).
3   **Tōtum illud "fōrmōsa" negō:** the phrase **Tōtum illud "fōrmōsa"** as a
     whole is the object of **negō,** *I deny.* The word **fōrmōsa** is quoted from line 1
     and remains in the nominative case instead of becoming accusative to
     match the words with which it is in apposition (**tōtum illud**); translate, *that
     [expression/description] fōrmōsa as a whole I deny.*
     venustās, venustātis (see Catullus 3.2, 10.4, 12.5, 13.6, 22.2, 31.12, 35.17, 36.17),
       f., *charm, attractiveness.*
4   **in tam magnō . . . corpore:** a complimentary phrase in itself; the ancients
     admired stature in both men and women.
     mīca, -ae f., *particle, grain.*
     sal, salis, m., *salt;* by metonymy, *wit, "spice."*
       salis: compare Catullus 13.5, **sale,** 10.33, **īnsulsa male,** and 12.4, **salsum;**
       here in 86.4 the word refers less to verbal wit or intellectual sophistica-
       tion than to sexual charm and appeal.
5   **cum . . . / tum (6),** *both . . . and, not only . . . but also.*
     pulcerrima: = **pulcherrima.**
6   **omnibus:** *from all women.*
     omnīs: = **omnēs.**
     surripiō [sub-, *from below* + **rapiō, rapere, rapuī, raptus,** *to snatch, seize*], **sur-
     ripere, surripuī, surreptus,** *to steal.*
     Venerēs: for the plural, see Catullus 3.1; some editors print the word with a
     small *v* here; in either case it refers to the qualities of a woman that excite
     sexual desire in men, *charms, graces,* the sources of a woman's sex appeal.

CATULLUS 86

A Beauty Contest

Catullus displays his high standards and flatters Lesbia in the process.

1   Quīntia fōrmōsa est multīs. Mihi candida, longa,
2   rēcta est: haec ego sīc singula cōnfiteor.
3   Tōtum illud "fōrmōsa" negō: nam nūlla venustās,
4   nūlla in tam magnō est corpore mīca salis.
5   Lesbia fōrmōsa est, quae cum pulcerrima tōta est,
6   tum omnibus ūna omnīs surripuit Venerēs.

Explorations

1. Where in the first line does Catullus deliberately place words next to each other in order to set himself and his values against society and its values?
2. Examine the placement of the word **fōrmōsa** in each of the three couplets. What do you discover?
3. What qualities does Catullus admit that Quintia has? (1–2)
4. Why does Catullus refuse to admit that Quintia measures up to the full definition of the word **fōrmōsa**? (3–4)
5. What does Lesbia have that Quintia does not? (5–6)
6. What does Catullus mean by the phrase **omnīs . . . Venerēs** (6)?

Meter: elegiac couplet

1   **Nūlla . . . mulier . . . sē dīcere. . . .** : reminiscent of Catullus 70.1, **Nūllī sē
      dīcit mulier. . . .** , and inviting comparison of the two poems.
      tantum . . . / quantum (2), *as much . . . as.*
      amātam: supply **esse**.
2   **vērē**: modifying **dīcere** (1).
3   **foedus, foederis**, n., *formal agreement, treaty; contract, compact.*
      ūllō . . . foedere: = **in ūllō foedere**.
         fidēs . . . foedere: note the alliteration of **fid- . . . foed-** in these key
            words here as in Catullus 76.3, reinforced here by **fuit**. For **foedus**, see
            also Catullus 109.6.
      tanta, / quanta (4): *as great . . . as.*
4   **in amōre tuō**: conceivably either *in your love [for me]* or *in [my] love for you.*
      reperiō [re-, *back* + **pariō, parere, peperī, partus**, *to give birth to, produce; to
         get*], **reperīre, repperī, repertus**, *to find.*
         reperta . . . est: the subject is **fidēs**.

Text

2   **est**: Thomson prints **es**, removing the awkward shift from third person in the
         first couplet to second person in the next; the words **Lesbia . . . mea** then
         become vocative, and the line could be punctuated as follows:
            vērē, quantum ā mē, Lesbia, amāta, mea, es.

3   **ūllō . . . foedere**: Thomson prints **ūllō . . . in foedere**, thus:
            Nūlla fidēs ūllō fuit umquam in foedere tanta,

CATULLUS 87

A Love Unparalleled but Flawed

Find the sting in the final words of this epigram.

1   Nūlla potest mulier tantum sē dīcere amātam
2   vērē, quantum ā mē Lesbia amāta mea est.
3   Nūlla fidēs ūllō fuit umquam foedere tanta,
4   quanta in amōre tuō ex parte reperta meā est.

Explorations

1.   What words establish a parallelism between the two couplets of this poem?
2.   What is gained and what is lost by reading **es** instead of **est** in line 2?
3.   How does alliteration enhance the diction in line 3?
4.   Thomson remarks, "The sting of this epigram lies, of course, in *ex parte mea*." Explain how this could be true. What is the flaw in this unparalleled love?
5.   Compare the reciprocity of love and faithfulness expressed in the dialogue between Septimius and Acme in Catullus 45 with the one-sided declaration of love and faithfulness in Catullus 87.

Comparison

With what other poem(s) of Catullus has Walter Savage Landor (1775–1864) joined poem 87 in the following translation? Why did Landor join the poems together?

Love's Madness

None could ever say that she,
Lesbia! was so loved by me;
Never, all the world around,
Faith so true as mine was found.
If no longer it endures,
(Would it did!) the fault is yours.
I can never think again
Well of you: I try in vain.
But, be false, do what you will,
Lesbia! I must love you still.

Meter: elegiac couplet

1　**dīcit . . . male**: see Catullus 83.1.
2　**Lesbia mē . . . nisi amat**: = nisi Lesbia mē amat.
　dispereō [dis- *apart* or with intensive force + **pereō, perīre, periī, peritūrus**, *to perish, die*], **disperīre, disperiī**, *to be ruined; to perish, die.*
　　dispeream: optative subjunctive expressing a wish, *may I perish.*
3　**Quo signo?**: *By what sign [do I know that she loves me]?*
　quia, conj., *because.*
　totidem [**tot**, indeclinable adjective, *as many* + **īdem, eadem, idem**, *the same*], indeclinable adjective, *as many.*
　sunt totidem mea: colloquial, *my [things] are as many*, = *the same things/symptoms are mine*, = *it's the same with me.*
　dēprecor [**dē-**, *down, away* + **precor, -ārī, -ātus sum**, *to pray*], **-ārī, -ātus sum**, *to try to avert by prayer; to beg relief from, pray to be rid of.*
　　dēprecor illam / assiduē (4): Thomson: *I am forever running her down.*
4　**assiduē** [**ad-**, *to, near* + **sedeō, sedēre, sēdī, sessūrus**, *to sit*], adv., *continually, all the time.*
　vērum, conj., *but.*

CATULLUS 92

How do I know she loves me?

In this poem, as in poem 83, Catullus manages to read Lesbia's behavior in a para-doxical or contradictory way. Is he deceiving himself again?

1   Lesbia mī dīcit semper male nec tacet umquam
2   dē mē: Lesbia mē dispeream nisi amat.
3   Quō signō? Quia sunt totidem mea: dēprecor illam
4   assiduē, vērum dispeream nisi amō.

Explorations

1. What examples of parallel wording do you find in this poem?
2. What is unusual about the word order of the two clauses contained in the words **Lesbia mē dispeream nisi amat** (2)?
3. What is the structural and logical point of the phrase **Quō signō** (3)?
4. Compare the theme of this poem with that of Catullus 83.
5. Compare poem 104, given below in Latin and in a very literal English translation. Does Catullus' denial there that he was ever able to heap abuse upon Lesbia suggest a flaw in the argument of poem 92?

Comparison

Catullus 104

Crēdis mē potuisse meae maledīcere vītae,
    ambōbus mihi quae cārior est oculīs?
nōn potuī, nec, sī possem, tam perditē amārem:
    sed tū cum Tappōne omnia mōnstra facis.

> **Tappō, Tappōnis,** m., *Tappo* (unknown; perhaps "a stock character in farcical plays," Thomson).

Do you believe that I was capable of heaping abuse upon the light of my
    life,
who is more dear to me than my two eyes?
I was not capable [of this], and, if I were, I would not be loving [her] as
    desperately [as I do]:
but you and that clownish friend of yours exaggerate everything.

Meter: elegiac couplet

1   **Zmyrna, -ae,** f. [Greek word], *Zmyrna* or *Smyrna* (the name of a short epic
     poem, a so-called epyllion, written by C. Helvius Cinna, see Catullus 10.30,
     about the unnatural passion of a young woman, Zmyrna/Smyrna,
     sometimes called Myrrha, for her father, her transformation into a tree, and
     the birth of her son, the ill-fated Adonis, from the trunk of the tree; see
     Ovid, *Metamorphoses* 10.298–528).
          Zmyrna: the noun **Zmyrna,** the subject of the sentence, is modified by
          ēdita (2) and is repeated at the beginning of line 5 after the interrup-
          tion of the subordinate clause in lines 3–4 and then finds its main verb
          mittētur (5). Or, less likely, supply **est** with **ēdita** to constitute the
          main verb; line 5 will then be a new main clause.
     nōnam post . . . messem / . . . nōnamque . . . post hiemem: prepositional
          phrases modifying **ēdita** (2), *published after the ninth . . . / . . . and after the
          ninth . . .*
     dēnique, adv., *finally, at last.*
     messis, messis, f., *harvest.*
2   **coepī, coepisse, coeptus,** perfect stem only, *to begin.*
          post . . . (1) / quam coepta est: *after it was begun:* **post** (1 and repeated in
          2) serves as both a preposition with the accusatives and as part of the con-
          junction **postquam.**
     ēdō [ex-, *out* + **dō, dare, dedī, datus,** *to give*], **ēdere, ēdidī, ēditus,** *to give out;
          to give forth* (offspring), *give birth to; to publish.*
3   **cum,** conj. + indicative, *when, while.*
     intereā, adv., *meanwhile, in the meantime;* with adversative force, *nevertheless,
          however, anyhow, at any rate.*
          intereā: Thomson translates *for his part.*
     Hatriēnsis, -is, -e, *of/belonging to Hatria;* here, *the [man] of Hatria, Volusius*
          (Hatria, a town in northern Italy on the Adriatic coast, the modern Adria, is
          presumably the birthplace of Volusius, the author of the *Annals* scathingly
          criticized by Catullus in poem 36. The word **Hatriēnsis** is A. E. Housman's
          conjectural correction of the manuscript reading, **Hortēnsius,** which most
          commentators find problematic because of poem 65, in which Catullus ded-
          icates a translation he has made of a poem of Callimachus to Hortensius,
          who had requested it; the two men seem to have very similar literary
          tastes. Here in poem 95 the person described in lines 3–4 is the diametric
          opposite of what Catullus admires in a poet and can scarcely be Horten-
          sius).
4   Line 4 has been lost from the manuscripts and what is printed here is a con-
          jecture; other conjectures have been suggested, including **versiculōrum
          annō quōlibet ēdiderit [quōlibet** = *any*].
     versiculī, -ōrum, m. pl., *light verse, verse.*
     pūtidus, -a, -um, *rotten, foul.*
          pūtidus: translate as an adverb.
     ēvomō [ex-, *out* + **vomō, vomere, vomuī, vomitus,** *to vomit*], **ēvomere,
          ēvomuī, ēvomitus,** *to vomit.*

CATULLUS 95

Cinna's *Zmyrna* is born.

Catullus stakes out his poetics with reference to such Latin and Greek poets as Cinna, Volusius, Philetas, and Antimachus.

1 Zmyrna meī Cinnae nōnam post dēnique messem
2   quam coepta est nōnamque ēdita post hiemem,
3 mīlia cum intereā quīngenta Hatriēnsis in ūnō
4   <versiculōrum annō pūtidus ēvomuit,>

continued

Explorations

1. What contrast is being made between Cinna's production of poetry as described in the first couplet and Volusius' production of poetry as described in the second couplet?
2. What words in the first couplet mirror the time frame of a human pregnancy?
3. What word in the second couplet suggests that Volusius' production of poetry can best be described with vocabulary describing a bodily function? How does it contrast with the vocabulary of the first couplet?
4. What words are highlighted by their placement in line 3?
5. In what other poem does Catullus castigate a poet for writing too many verses?

5   **cavus, -a, -um**, *hollow, deep-channeled*.
       cavās: transferred epithet.
    Satrachus, -ī, m., *Satrachus* (a river in Cyprus, related to the myth of Adonis, the son of Zmyrna).
    penitus, adv., *to a remote distance, far off*.

6   **cānus, -a, -um**, *gray*.
    saeculum, -ī, n. (see Catullus 1.10), *age; lifetime; generation*.
       cāna . . . saecula: *gray-haired generations [of men]*, subject of **pervoluent**.
    pervolvō [per-, *through, continuously* + **volvō, volvere, volvī, volūtus**, *to roll*], **pervolvere**, *to go on unrolling* (a papyrus roll for reading).
       pervoluent: scanned as four syllables = **pervolvent**.

7   **Volusī annālēs**: see Catullus 36.1.
    Padua, -ae, f., *Padua* (one of the mouths of the Po river in northern Italy).
       Paduam . . . ad ipsam: delayed preposition; **ad** = *at/by* here.

8   **laxus, -a, -um**, *loose*.
    scomber, scombrī, m., *scomber* (a fish, possibly mackerel).
    tunica, -ae, f., *tunic; covering, wrapping*.
       laxās scombrīs saepe dabunt tunicās: some think Catullus means that the papyrus sheets on which Volusius' *Annals* are written will be used to wrap fish at the fish-market; Thomson argues persuasively that they will be used as wrappers within which the fish will be cooked. In either case there will be plenty of papyrus from Volusius' *Annals* to use often (**saepe**) for either purpose, with no need to wrap the fish tightly (cf. **laxās**), in spite of the fact that papyrus was very expensive.

9   **Parva . . . / . . . Antimachō** (10): it is uncertain whether lines 9 and 10 belong to poem 95 or not; some editors make them a separate poem labeled 95b.
    meī: the genitive of a noun or proper name is missing from the manuscripts at the end of the line; editors have supplied various possibilities, such as **sodālis**, *buddy*, and **poētae**, *poet*. In any case, the reference should be to Cinna, e.g., **meī . . . poētae**, *of my poet* would mean *of the poet I have been speaking of*, namely Cinna. Solodow's conjecture, **Philītae** (for which, see below), is printed in the text here.
    mihi sint cordī: optative subjunctive in idiom with double dative, *may . . . be to/for the heart to me, may . . . be dear/pleasing to me*.
    monimentum, -ī, n., *monument*; pl., *literary works, writings*.
    Philītās (Philētās), -ae, m., *Philetas* (of Cos in the Eastern Mediterranean; a Greek poet of the early third century B.C., the founder of the Alexandrian school of scholar-poets, the most famous of whom was Callimachus).
       Philītae: by metonymy for **Cinnae**, as **Antimachō** (10) is for **Volusiō**.

10   **tumidus, -a, -um**, *swollen, bloated*; of literary works, *inflated, pretentious*.
    gaudeat: jussive subjunctive + abl.
    Antimachus, -ī, m., *Antimachus* (of Colophon; a Greek scholar and poet of the late fifth/early fourth centuries B.C., author of a famous epic poem, the *Thebais*, dealing with the first expedition against Thebes, and an elegiac poem titled *Lyde*, perhaps written after the death of his wife or mistress of the same name; Callimachus condemned him for his verbosity).

5   Zmyrna cavās Satrachī penitus mittētur ad undās,
6   Zmyrnam cāna diū saecula pervoluent.
7   At Volusī annālēs Paduam morientur ad ipsam
8   et laxās scombrīs saepe dabunt tunicās.
9   Parva meī mihi sint cordī monimenta <Philītae>,
10   at populus tumidō gaudeat Antimachō.

Explorations

6.   What rhetorical device is used in lines 5 and 6?
7.   How do lines 5 and 7 contrast the fate of Cinna's poem with the fate of Volusius' verses?
8.   How do lines 6 and 8 contrast the fate of Cinna's poetry with the fate of Volusius' verses in a different way from that seen in lines 5 and 7?
9.   The production and publication of Cinna's *Zmyrna* were described in the first couplet in language suggesting childbearing. How do lines 6 and 7 continue the metaphor of poetry as a living creature?
10. What is the poet's wish for himself in line 9? What does he order the vulgar crowd to do in line 10? What contrasts are established?
11. What is accomplished by Catullus' referring to Cinna with the phrase **meī . . . Philītae** and by his referring to Volusius as Antimachus?
12. How is this poem structured?
13. What is Catullus saying in this poem about good poetry and bad poetry, and how does what he says compare with what Callimachus says about poetry in the passage for comparison?

Comparison

Callimachus in his *Hymn to Apollo*, 108–12, has Apollo, the god of poetry, express his poetic preferences through metaphors of the Assyrian river (the Euphrates) and a trickling spring:

The stream of the Assyrian river is great, but it carries
much filth of the earth and refuse on its waters.
The Bees do not carry water to Demeter from every source
but whatever springs up pure and undefiled,
a trickling spring from a holy fountain, the choicest, the flower of its kind.

Meter: elegiac couplet

1   **quisquam, quisquam, quicquam**, indefinite pronoun, *anyone, anything*.
    mūtus, -a, -um, *mute, silent*.
       mūtīs . . . sepulcrīs: dative with **grātum** and **acceptum**. The adjective is
          described as a transferred epithet by Thomson since it is really the silent
          ashes of the dead that are on the speaker's mind.
    grātus, -a, -um, *grateful, appreciative; received with gratitude or appreciation;* +
       dat., *welcome, pleasing*.
    acceptus, -a, -um + dat., *acceptable, pleasing, welcome*.
    -ve, enclitic conj., *or*.

2   **accidō [ad-**, *to* + **cadō, cadere, cecidī, cāsūrus**, *to fall*], **accidere, accidī**, *to
       fall down, descend; to occur, happen*.
    Calvus, -ī, m., *Calvus* (a close friend of Catullus—see Catullus 14a, 50, and
       53—whose wife or mistress, Quintilia, has died).
    dolor, dolōris, m. (see Catullus 2.7 and 50.17), *pain, smart, love-ache; grief*.

3   **dēsīderium, -ī**, n. (see Catullus 2.5), *something longed for, object of desire; sweet-
       heart; desire, longing* (for a lost person or thing).
       quō dēsīderiō: the antecedent of **quō** is **dolōre** (2), and that antecedent
          is picked up and repeated in the more specific word **dēsīderiō** in the
          relative clause itself; in line 3 translate **quō dēsīderiō** as ablative of in-
          strument or means, *by means of which desire/longing*; repeat the phrase
          at the beginning of line 4 but now translate it as ablative of cause, *be-
          cause of which desire/longing*.

4   **ōlim**, adv., *once, of old*.
       ōlim missās: *long sent away/rejected/abandoned*, or (Davis) *long since bidden
          farewell, long departed*.
    amīcitia, -ae, f., *friendship*.

5   **nōn tantō . . . dolōrī est / Quīntiliae** (6): double dative, *is not [a matter] for
       such great grief to Quintilia*.
    mors: i.e., Quintilia's.
    immātūrus, -a, -um, *premature, untimely*.

6   **quantum**, relative adv., *to the extent to which, as much as, as*.
       quantum: correlating with **tantō** (5).

CATULLUS 96

To Calvus, on the Sad Occasion of His Wife's or Mistress's Death

Catullus tries to console Calvus with the thought that death may not be a final break between the living and the dead, and he redefines Calvus' grief as an expression of his continuing love for and friendship with the departed.

1 Sī quicquam mūtīs grātum acceptumve sepulcrīs
2   accidere ā nostrō, Calve, dolōre potest,
3 quō dēsīderiō veterēs renovāmus amōrēs
4   atque ōlim missās flēmus amīcitiās,
5 certē nōn tantō mors immātūra dolōrī est
6   Quīntiliae, quantum gaudet amōre tuō.

Explorations

1. What is the grammatical structure of the single sentence of which this poem is composed?
2. What proposition does the poet put forth in the first and the third couplets?
3. What words in the third couplet recall a specific word and a specific phrase in the first couplet? What central thematic contrast in the poem do these words and this phrase define?
4. How does the relative clause that makes up the second couplet define its antecedent, **dolōre** (2)?
5. What are the similarities and what are the differences between the two clauses in lines 3 and 4?
6. What words suggest that Catullus is generalizing about the human condition in lines 1–5?
7. How do lines 3 and 4 lead to the conclusion expressed in the final couplet?

Comparison

Sulpicius, a friend of Cicero's, wrote to him, reproving his excessive grieving over the death of his beloved daughter, Tullia, as follows (*Epistulae ad familiares*, 4.5.6):

There is no grief that the passage of time does not lessen and soothe. For you to await this time rather than to use your wisdom to take care of the grief is shameful of you. But if any consciousness belongs to the inhabitants of the underworld, such was your daughter's love for you and devotion to her family that certainly this is not what she wants you to do.

Meter: elegiac couplet

1   **vectus**, *having been carried, having traveled.*
2   **frāter**: the word occurs in the vocative three times in the poem, here and in
       lines 6 and 10, always at the same metrical position. It was a customary
       part of funeral rites to call upon the deceased three times.
    ad, prep. + acc., *to; at;* here, *for the purpose of.*
    īnferiae, -ārum, f. pl. [**in-**, *in, into* + **ferō**, *I carry;* but thought by the ancients to
       be related to **īnferī, -ōrum**, m. pl., *the inhabitants of the underworld*], *offerings
       for the dead* (such as milk, honey, wine, and flowers).
          miserās . . . īnferiās: the rites are so described because they evoke sad-
             ness in those who perform them.
3   **dōnō, -āre, -āvī, -ātus**, *to give; to present* (somebody, acc., with something,
       abl.).
          dōnārem: an imperfect subjunctive is used here and in line 4 in spite of
             the fact that the main verb of the sentence, **adveniō** (2) is present tense.
             Some explain the secondary sequence as dependent on the perfect
             passive participle, **vectus** (1).
    mūnus, mūneris, n., *task; duty; gift, offering* (given as a duty).
       mūnere mortis: the noun in the genitive is adjectival in sense, *with a
          duty/offering associated with death,* = *with a funereal gift.*
4   **mūtus, -a, -um**, *mute, silent.*
    nēquīquam, adv., *in vain.*
    alloquor [**ad-**, *to* + **loquor, loquī, locūtus sum**, *to speak*], **alloquī, allocūtus
       sum**, *to address, speak to.*
          alloquerer: imperfect subjunctive; see note on line 3 above.
    cinis, cineris, m., here f., *ash.*
5   **quandoquidem**, conj., *since.*
    fortūna, -ae, f., *fortune.*
    mihī: dative of separation here and in line 6.
    tētē: emphatic **tē**.
6   **indignē**, adv., *undeservedly; outrageously;* here more specifically, *prematurely.*
       indignē: translate with **adēmpte**.
          heu miser indignē frāter adēmpte mihi: apostrophe; compare Catullus
             68.20, **Ō miserō frāter adēmpte mihi**. Here in poem 101, Thomson
             (followed in this edition) punctuates with a period after this line
             instead of the comma in most editions and with a comma instead of the
             period in most editions at the end of line 4, making line 6 a "climactic
             outburst" that concludes the first six lines of the poem.

Comparison (continued on next page)

With the opening line of poem 101, compare the opening lines of Homer's *Odyssey*:

Tell me, O Muse, the tale of the man much-traveled, who wandered
<u>many</u> ways, when he had sacked the holy city of Troy;

CATULLUS 101

Here rests his head upon the lap of Earth
A youth to Fortune and to Fame unknown.

(Thomas Gray, 1716–71)

Catullus' brother has died in Asia Minor near Troy. How does Catullus stress the
distance he has traveled to the site of the grave? What must he do there?

1　Multās per gentēs et multa per aequora vectus
2　　adveniō hās miserās, frāter, ad īnferiās,
3　ut tē postrēmō dōnārem mūnere mortis
4　　et mūtam nēquīquam alloquerer cinerem,
5　quandoquidem fortūna mihī tētē abstulit ipsum,
6　　heu miser indignē frāter adēmpte mihi.

continued

Comparison (continued from previous page)

and he saw the cities of <u>many men</u> and came to know their mind,

yes, and he suffered in his spirit <u>many</u> woes on the <u>sea,</u>

trying to win his life and the homecoming of his companions.

Explorations

1.　What letters and sounds predominate in lines 1–4?
2.　Read lines 1–4 aloud. How does Catullus use dactyls and spondees effectively here?
3.　How does Catullus effectively position words in lines 3 and 4 to highlight the verbs?
4.　How does the poet evoke sympathy for his task in the first four lines?
5.　Observe the placement of the words in line 4: **et mūtam nēquīquam alloquerer cinerem**. What would be expressed by taking **nēquīquam** as modifying **mūtam**?
6　a.　What feelings are expressed in lines 5–6? Look closely at the individual words in this couplet.
　　b.　What words are emphatically juxtaposed in line 5?
　　c.　What is the point of using **tētē** and **ipsum** in combination?
　　d.　What is the force of the words **abstulit** and **adēmpte**?
　　e.　How do the three words **heu miser indignē** build on each other?
　　f.　Why is **mihi** repeated?

7   **intereā**, adv., *meanwhile, in the meantime;* with adversative force, *nevertheless, however, anyhow, at any rate.*

      haec: i.e., the traditional offerings for the dead. **Haec** is the antecedent of **quae** and the object of **accipe** in line 9.

      prīscus, -a, -um, *ancient.*

      quae . . . trādita sunt . . . ad īnferiās: *which have been handed over/given [by me] for. . . .* Others take **trādita sunt** to mean *have been handed down.*

      mōre: *in the manner of . . .*

      parentum: = **maiōrum,** *ancestors.*

8   **trīstī mūnere:** ablative of manner, *as a sad duty/offering.*

9   **frāternus, -a, -um,** *of/belonging to a brother, a brother's.*

      multum, adv., *much, abundantly.*

      mānō, -āre, -āvī, -ātūrus, *to flow;* + abl., *to be wet (with), drip (with).*

      flētus, -ūs, m., *crying, tears.*

10   **perpetuus, -a, -um,** *everlasting, continuous, uninterrupted.*

      in perpetuum: *forever.*

      avē: *hail!*

7   Nunc tamen intereā haec, prīscō quae mōre parentum

8   trādita sunt trīstī mūnere ad īnferiās,

9   accipe frāternō multum mānantia flētū,

10   atque in perpetuum, frāter, avē atque valē.

Explorations

7.   What is the structure of the poem?

8.   What is the effect of the threefold repetition of **frāter** in the poem?

9.   Comment on alliteration and assonance in the last four lines.

10. This poem speaks of last rites performed by the poet for his brother. How does the poem itself enact and become part of the ritual?

Comparison

Compare the following epigram by the Hellenistic Greek poet Meleager, who was writing about 100 B.C. What similarities do you find between Meleager's epigram and Catullus 101, Catullus 96, and Catullus 3?

Tears I bestow upon you, Heliodora, even down
    through the earth to Hades, the last gift of my love,
tears sorely wept; and on your tomb, much wept over, I pour them
    as an offering, a memorial of longing, a memorial of affection.
For piteously, piteously do I Meleager mourn for you
    even among the dead, a useless favor to Acheron.
Alas, where is the lovely blossom I desire? Hades has snatched
    her away, snatched her away; the dust has desecrated the flower in
       bloom.
But I implore you, Earth nurturer of all, enfold gently in your bosom,
    mother, the girl who is mourned by all.

                               —*Palatine Anthology* 7.476

Meter: elegiac couplet

1   **Sī quicquam . . . optigit . . . / . . . hoc est grātum** (2): perfect indicative in
       the if-clause and present indicative in the main clause constituting a
       present-general condition, *If anything [ever] happens . . . / . . . this is [always]*
       pleasing. . . .
       quisquam, quisquam, quicquam, indefinite pronoun, *anyone, anything.*
       cupidus, -a, -um [**cupiō, cupere, cupīvī, cupītus**, *to desire, want* + **-idus, -a,**
         -um, adjectival suffix], *passionately longing, desirous, eager.*
           cupidō optantīque: supply the pronoun **cuiquam**, *to anyone*, for these
              two adjectives to modify. Hiatus occurs between the two adjectives; do
              not elide.
       optingō [**ob-**, *against* + **tangō, tangere, tetigī, tāctus**, *to touch*] **optingere,**
         optigī + dat., *to fall* (to as one's lot), *to happen* (to someone to his/her advan-
         tage or disadvantage).
2   **īnspērāns, īnspērantis**, *not hoping/expecting.*
         īnspērantī: predicative to **(cuiquam) cupidō optantīque** in line 1, translate
          when not hoping [for it]/expecting [it].
       hoc: scanned here and in line 3 as a long or heavy syllable (originally
         spelled **hocc**), referring to **quicquam** (1).
       grātus, -a, -um (see Catullus 96.1), *grateful, appreciative; received with gratitude*
         or appreciation; + dat., *welcome, pleasing.*
       propriē, adv., *on one's own account; properly, strictly speaking, rightly.*
         propriē: *in the true sense of the word*, take with **grātum** (in the third sense
          above).
3   **hoc**: referring to the good news expressed in the relative clause, **quod. . . .**
         (4), *[the fact] that. . . .*
       nōbīs: here and in line 6 = **mihi**.
       cārus, -a, -um, *dear, precious.*
         et cārius aurō: this is Heyworth's emendation.
4   **restituō** [**re-**, *back, again* + **statuō, statuere, statuī, statūtus**, *to set; to stand up;*
         to place], **restituere, restituī, restitūtus**, *to set up again; to restore; to bring back;*
         + dat., *to bring X* (acc.) *back into favor with Y* (dat.).
5   **restituis**: supply **tē mihi**.
       ipsa: *yourself* or *of your own accord.*
6   **lūx, lūcis**, f., *light; day.*
       candidus, -a, -um, *white, bright, dazzling; cheerful, favorable, happy.*
       nota, -ae, f., *mark* (here, to indicate a lucky day on a calendar).
         candidiōre notā: ablative of description; for the idea, compare Catullus 8.3
          candidī sōlēs.
7   **mē ūnō**: *than I alone, than I myself.*
       vīvit: = **est** (cf 8.10 and 10.33).
       aut magis umquam / optandam vītam dūcere quis poterit: this is Lyne's
         emendation.
         magis: take with **optandam** (8).
8   **quis**: note the postponement of the interrogative pronoun.

CATULLUS 107

Lesbia returns!

Catullus expresses his ecstatic joy when the unexpected happens.

1 Sī quicquam cupidō optantīque optigit umquam
2   īnspērantī, hoc est grātum animō propriē.
3 Quārē hoc est grātum nōbīs, et cārius aurō,
4   quod tē restituis, Lesbia, mī cupidō,
5 restituis cupidō atque īnspērantī, ipsa refers tē
6   nōbīs. Ō lūcem candidiōre notā!
7 Quis mē ūnō vīvit fēlīcior, aut magis umquam
8   optandam vītam dūcere quis poterit?

Text

The Oxford Classical Text prints lines 3 and 7–8 as follows:

3 quārē hōc est grātum †nōbīs quoque† cārius aurō

7 Quis mē ūnō vīvit fēlīcior, aut magis †hāc est
8   †optandus vītā dīcere quis poterit?

The daggers indicate textual corruptions. Compare the lines carefully with the text given above, which contains emendations suggested by Heyworth and Lyne.

Explorations

1. What is the logical structure of thought in this poem?
2. Catullus has created an extraordinarily elaborate verbal mosaic in this poem. What words are repeated from the first couplet in the last couplet?
3. What words are repeated from the first couplet in the central second and third couplets?
4. What words are repeated within the central two couplets?
5. Are any words repeated in the final couplet from the central second and third couplets?
6. Analyze the example of repetition that is at the exact center of the poem.
7. Identify the members of a tricolon in the central second and third couplets.
8. Comment on the placement of the name Lesbia in line 4.
9. What words in lines 3 and 6 express how welcome what has happened is?
10. What is unusual about this poem when you compare it with the rest of the short elegiac poems you have read?

Meter: elegiac couplet

1   **Iūcundum:** *a pleasant thing,* direct object of **prōpōnis.**
    mea vīta: cf. 45.13.
    prōpōnō [**pro-,** *forward* + **pōnō, pōnere, posuī, positus,** *to put, place*],
      prōpōnere, prōposuī, prōpositus, *to set forth, state, declare; to propose.*
    amōrem: modified by **hunc nostrum** (2), introducing indirect statement.
2   **perpetuus, -a, -um,** *continuous, uninterrupted, everlasting.*
    usque, adv., *continuously, to the end.*
    fore: = **futūrum esse,** future infinitive in indirect statement. The text of
      lines 1–2 as given here is that of Thomson. The text as given in the Oxford
      Classical Text edition and by Quinn and Fordyce is printed below, with
      notes on attempts to make sense of it.
3   **Dī magnī:** cf. Catullus 14a.12 and 53.5.
    facite ut + subjunctive, *bring it about that.* The verb **facere** may be used to
      introduce a subjunctive clause of result, particularly in situations that
      imply effort.
4   **sincērē,** adv., *faithfully, truly, sincerely.*
5   **ut liceat . . . :** a result clause.
    tōtā . . . vītā: ablative instead of accusative of extent of time (here for the first
      time in extant Latin literature).
    perdūcō [**per-,** *through* + **dūcō, dūcere, dūxī, ductus,** *to lead, take, bring*],
      perdūcere, perdūxī, perductus, *to protract, prolong, carry through, extend.*
6   **aeternus, -a, -um,** *eternal, everlasting;* in a weakened sense, *enduring, life-*
      long.
    sānctae: cf. Catullus 76.3.
    foedus, foederis, n., *formal agreement, treaty; contract, compact.*
    foedus: cf. Catullus 76.3 and 87.3.
    amīcitia, -ae, f., *friendship.*

Text

The text of lines 1–2 is given as follows in the Oxford Classical Text:
   1   Iūcundum, mea vīta, mihi prōpōnis amōrem
   2   hunc nostrum inter nōs perpetuumque fore.
fore: = **futūrum esse,** future infinitive in indirect statement introduced by
prōpōnis (1), with **amōrem / hunc nostrum inter nōs** as the subject of the indirect statement and **Iūcundum . . . perpetuumque** as predicate adjectives.
Alternatively, Quinn suggests taking **Iūcundum . . . amōrem** as a simple direct object of **prōpōnis,** *you propose a pleasant love,* with **hunc nostrum inter nōs**
in apposition to **Iūcundum . . . amōrem** and **perpetuum . . . fore** as a further
expansion, *[and] that it will last forever.*

CATULLUS 109

More Promises

What does Lesbia promise Catullus in the opening lines of this poem? What is Catullus' response?

1 Iūcundum, mea vīta, mihi prōpōnis: amōrem
2   hunc nostrum inter nōs perpetuum usque fore.
3 Dī magnī, facite ut vērē prōmittere possit,
4   atque id sincērē dīcat et ex animō,
5 ut liceat nōbīs tōtā perdūcere vītā
6   aeternum hoc sānctae foedus amīcitiae.

Explorations

1. Compare Thomson's version of the first couplet printed in the text above with the traditional version printed below the notes on the opposite page. Do you find any problems with the traditional version? Is Thomson's version an improvement?
2. What is the relationship between the first couplet and the remainder of the poem? Compare the structures of Catullus 70 and 72.
3. In poem 70 Catullus is skeptical of Lesbia's protestations, and in poem 72 he has caught her lying. Through his prayer to the gods in lines 3–4 of poem 109, what attitude does Catullus reveal toward Lesbia's proposal in lines 1–2?
4. What result does Catullus envision in the third couplet as coming from the gods' enabling Lesbia to promise *truly, sincerely,* and *from the heart*?
5. The two major themes of this poem are (1) life-long continuance of love/friendship and (2) sincerity. How are the themes allocated to couplets?
6. Consider the final line of the poem. Locate its interlocking word order. Are there examples of transferred epithets here? If so, what are their implications? What kind of relationship is described in these words?
7. What is the relationship between **amōrem** (end of line 1) and **amīcitiae** (end of line 6)? With the concepts and words here, compare Catullus 72.3–4 and Catullus 96.3–4.

Passages for Comparison

Catullus 64.60–69

60   Quem procul ex algā maestīs Mīnōis ocellīs,
61   saxea ut effigiēs bacchantis, prōspicit, ēheu,
62   prōspicit et magnīs cūrārum flūctuat undīs,
63   nōn flāvō retinēns subtīlem vertice mitram,
64   nōn contēcta levī vēlātum pectus amictū,
66   omnia quae tōtō dēlapsa ē corpore passim
67   ipsius ante pedēs flūctūs salis allūdēbant.
68   Sed neque tum mitrae neque tum fluitantis amictūs
69   illa vicem cūrāns. . . .

Compare Ariadne in lines 60–69 as she watches the departing Theseus from a distance, who is likened to a bacchante, is tossed on great waves of anguished emotion, and shows no concern for the clothes that slip from her body, to Andromache as she learns of the death of her husband Hector in Homer, *Iliad* 22.460–70:

> Speaking thus, she rushed through the hall like a Maenad,
> with throbbing heart; and with her went her serving-women.
> But when she reached the tower and the crowd of men,
> she stood on the wall looking about, and she perceived
> him being dragged before the city; swift horses
> were dragging him pitilessly to the hollow ships of the Achaeans.
> But black night veiled her eyes,
> she fell backwards and lost consciousness.
> She dropped far from her head her shining head-band,
> her diadem, her hair net, its woven band,
> and her veil. . . .

Catullus 64.86–100

86   Hunc simul ac cupidō cōnspexit lūmine virgō
87   rēgia, quam suāvīs exspīrāns castus odōrēs
88   lectulus in mollī complexū mātris alēbat,
89   quālēs Eurōtae praecingunt flūmina mȳrtūs
90   aurave distīnctōs ēdūcit verna colōrēs,
91   nōn prius ex illō flagrantia dēclīnāvit
92   lūmina, quam cūnctō concēpit corpore flammam
93   funditus atque īmīs exarsit tōta medullīs.
94   Heu miserē exagitāns immītī corde furōrēs
95   sāncte puer, cūrīs hominum quī gaudia miscēs,
96   quaeque regis Golgōs quaeque Īdalium frondōsum,

97   quālibus incēnsam iactāstis mente puellam
98   flūctibus, in flāvō saepe hospite suspīrantem!
99   Quantōs illa tulit languentī corde timōrēs!
100   Quantō saepe magis fulgōre expalluit aurī. . . .

Compare the description in Apollonius, *Argonautica* 3.275–98, of Medea falling in love with Jason at first sight:

> Meanwhile Eros arrived through the bright air unseen,
> bringing trouble, just as a horsefly attacks heifers
> who are grazing, which herdsmen call the gadfly.
> And in the porch under the lintel, having quickly strung his bow,
> he selected from his quiver a grievous arrow that had not yet been used.
> And on swift feet he passed through the entrance without being noticed,
> giving a quick glance around. Rolling into a crouching position near Jason
> himself, he put the notched end of the arrow in the middle of his bowstring,
> and then immediately he drew apart both hands and
> shot at Medea; speechlessness seized her.
> He himself darted out of the high-roofed hall
> rejoicing; but the arrow burned deep
> in the young woman's heart, like a flame. She was constantly
> casting glances back at Jason, and whatever sensible thoughts she had
> fluttered from her mind in her lovesickness, nor did she have memory
> of anything else, but her heart overflowed with sweet pain.
> As a poor woman spreads wood chips on a smoldering stick,
> as she busies herself with spinning wool,
> so that she might have light in the house at night,
> sitting very close to the hearth; an enormous fire from the small
> stick is aroused and annihilates all the wood chips together.
> Such was the baleful love that, rolled tightly under her heart,
> was blazing secretly; her soft cheeks turned
> pale, then red, due to the anguish of her mind.

Catullus 64.95

95   sāncte puer, cūrīs hominum quī gaudia miscēs

For Eros/Cupid as a god who mixes *joys* (**gaudia**), *with cares/emotional distress* (**cūrīs**), see the following quotations from Sappho (Greek poet, 7th century B.C., from Lesbos) and Theognis (Greek poet, 6th century B.C., from Megara), who describe Eros as "bitter-sweet":

Sappho 130:

> Again Love, the bitter-sweet (γλυκύπικρον), irresistible creature

that loosens the limbs, shakes me.
Theognis 1353–56:

> Cyrnus, love is bitter (πικρός) and sweet (γλυκύς), alluring and harsh
>   for the young, until it is fulfilled.
> For if it is fulfilled, it becomes sweet, but if pursuing it
>   one does not fulfill it, of all things it is the most painful.

Catullus 64.105–11

105   Nam velut in summō quatientem brachia Taurō
106   quercum aut conigeram sūdantī cortice pīnum
107   indomitus turbō contorquēns flāmine rōbur,
108   ēruit (illa procul rādīcitus exturbāta
109   prōna cadit, lātē quaevīs cumque obvia frangēns),
110   sīc domitō saevum prōstrāvit corpore Thēseus
111   nēquīquam vānīs iactantem cornua ventīs.

With the simile in lines 105–9, compare the following similes in Homer, Apollonius, and Vergil:

Homer, *Iliad* 13.389–93 (a warrior named Asius is slain by Idomeneus):

> And he fell just as when an oak falls or a white poplar,
> or tall pine, which carpenters in the mountains
> have cut down with freshly sharpened axes to be used for building a ship;
> so he lay stretched out in front of his horses and chariot,
> moaning and grasping the bloody dust.

Apollonius, *Argonautica* 4.1682–88 (Medea's magic powers overcome the giant Talos, who falls to his death):

> But just as some huge pine tree high on the mountains,
> which the woodcutters left only half-felled by their sharp axes
> when they returned down from the forest; in the night
> it is shaken at first by gusts of wind, but then later
> utterly torn away it falls down; so Talos swayed
> for a while, standing on untiring feet,
> but then later, drained of his strength, he fell with an enormous thud.

Vergil, *Aeneid* 2.624–31 (Aeneas describes a moment in the fall of Ilium/Troy):

> "Then indeed all of Ilium seemed to me to collapse
> in the fires and Neptune's Troy to be overturned from its foundation;
> and just as on the tops of mountains when farmers vie with one another
> to hew with iron an ancient ash tree and press to fell it

with numerous ax blows, it continuously threatens to fall
and shivering sways its leaves with shaking top,
until gradually overcome by its wounds it gives a final
groan and torn up from the ridge crashes in collapse."

Catullus 64.132–201

Compare Medea's complaint to Jason in Apollonius' *Argonautica* 4.355–69 and 378–90, which served as a model for some of the themes in Ariadne's lament (64.132–201). At this moment in the story of Jason and Medea's return to Greece after Medea helped Jason steal the golden fleece, Medea is terribly afraid that Jason is about to desert her:

"Jason, what plot did you Argonauts eagerly agree to accomplish
with regard to me? Has your triumph utterly infused you with
forgetfulness, and don't you care at all for all that you were saying
when you were caught in need? Where have those oaths of yours gone,
made in the name of Zeus, god of suppliants, and your honey-sweet promises?
For which I, improperly and with shameless will,
abandoned my country, the fame of my house, and my parents
themselves, all of which were of supreme importance to me; but far away
and alone I am borne along on the sea with the baleful kingfishers,
because of your troubles, so that you might be preserved for me
while you fulfilled the trials with the oxen and the earthborn men.
Last of all, moreover, the fleece also, for which you made this voyage,
you won by my folly; and I have poured destructive shame
on the female race. Wherefore I say that I follow you
to the land of Greece as your child, bride, and sister. . . .
How shall I come before my father's eyes?
With a great reputation? What vengeance or grievous
destruction shall I not painfully suffer for the terrible things
I have done? And will you win the return that your heart desires?
May the royal wife of Zeus, in whom you boast, not bring
that to pass. May you remember me even at a time
when you are worn out with troubles; and may the fleece depart like a dream
to the darkness of the underworld, making your efforts all in vain.
May my Furies drive you at once from your country—exactly what even I
myself have suffered by your cruelty. It is not right for these curses to fall
on the earth unfulfilled. For certainly you have violated a great oath,
pitiless man. Surely not for long hereafter will you and your companions be
carefree and eye me with mockery, escaping through the plot you have
    agreed upon."

Catullus 64.152

152   Prō quō dīlaceranda ferīs dabor ālitibusque

Compare the opening of Homer's *Iliad*:

> Sing, goddess, of the cursed wrath of Achilles,
> the son Peleus, which brought countless woes on the Achaeans,
> and hurled many brave souls of warriors
> to Hades, and made their bodies a prey for dogs
> and all the birds, and the will of Zeus was accomplished.

Catullus 64.171–72

171   Iuppiter omnipotēns, utinam nē tempore prīmō
172   Gnōsia Cecropiae tetigissent lītora puppēs,

Compare Euripides, *Medea* 1–8:

> Would that the ship Argo had not sped on wings
> through the dark blue Symplegades to the land of Colchis,
> nor that the pine in the glens of Mount Peleus had ever
> been cut and felled and supplied with oars the hands
> of those noblest men who went after
> the golden fleece for Peleus. For then my mistress
> Medea would not have sailed to the towers of Iolcus
> smitten in heart with love for Jason. . . .

Compare Ennius, *Medea* 1–9 (= tragedies, fragment 253–61):

> Would that the fir trees in the Pelian grove had not been cut
> and fallen to the earth to make a ship's timbers,
> nor that from there the first stage of work
> had begun on the ship, which is now called
> Argo, because in it chosen Argive heroes
> were carried to seek from the Colchians the golden ram's fleece
> because of the treacherous order of King Pelias;
> for thus never would my mistress Medea in delusion have set foot
> outside her house wounded by cruel love and with a sick heart.

Catullus 64.177–81

177   Nam quō mē referam? Quālī spē perdita nītor?

178 Īdaeōsne petam montēs? At gurgite lātō
179 discernēns pontī truculentum dīvidit aequor.
180 An patris auxilium spērem? Quemne ipsa relīquī
181 respersum iuvenem frāternā caede secūta?

Compare Euripides, *Medea* 502–5:

> Now where am I to turn? To my father's house,
> which I betrayed for you along with my country too and came here?
> Or to the wretched daughters of Pelias? They, whose
> father I murdered, would receive me well in their house!

Compare Ennius, *Medea* (tragedies, fragment 284–85):

> Where now am I to turn? What road am I to begin to walk on?
> To my father's house or to the daughters of Pelias?

Catullus 64.181

181 respersum iuvenem frāternā caede secūta?

Godwin (p. 155) remarks: "One wonders how much affection her father bore for the monster born of his wife's bestiality, whom he locked in the labyrinth." The image of Theseus sprinkled with the blood of Ariadne's brother calls to mind the parallel myth of Jason and Medea. In Apollonius, *Argonautica* 4.464–74, Jason in desperation and with Medea's help, slays Medea's brother, Apsyrtus, and she is sprinkled with her brother's blood:

> Immediately Jason leapt out from his hidden ambush,
> holding up in his hand a bare sword. Medea quickly
> turned her eyes back, covering them with her veil,
> that she might not look upon the murder of her brother when he was struck.
> But Jason struck him, as a butcher strikes a large, strong-horned bull,
> keeping his eye on him near the temple that the
> Brygians, who are neighbors on the opposite side, once built for Artemis.
> In its entrance hall Apsyrtus fell on bended knee, and at last the hero,
> breathing out his life, caught with both hands the dark blood
> from the wound and stained the silver-white veil
> and robe of his sister red as she tried to evade him.

Catullus 64.204–6

204 annuit invictō caelestum nūmine rēctor;
205 quō mōtū tellūs atque horrida contremuērunt
206 aequora concussitque micantia sīdera mundus.

Compare Homer, *Iliad* 1.524–30, where Zeus gives his nod of assent to Thetis' request that Zeus honor her son, Achilles. Zeus is speaking:

"Come! I will give a nod of assent with my head for you that you may trust me;
for among the immortals this is the greatest pledge
on my part; for no pledge of mine is taken back or is proved deceitful
or goes unfulfilled, whatever I assent to with a nod of my head."
Zeus spoke and gave a nod with his dark-blue eyebrows;
so then the ambrosial locks flowed waving from the king's
immortal head; and he set great Olympus quaking.

Catullus 64.224

224 cānitiem terrā atque īnfūsō pulvere foedāns,

Compare Homer, *Iliad* 18.23–27, Achilles' grief at the death of Patroclus:

Taking the grimy dust with both hands
he poured it over his head and disfigured his lovely face;
and the black ashes settled upon his fragrant tunic.
But he himself great in his greatness lay fully extended
in the dust, and he disfigured his hair, tearing it with his own hands.

Compare Homer, *Iliad* 24.163–65, Priam's grief at the death of Hector:

There was much
dung on the head and neck of the old man,
which he had heaped on himself with his hands as he rolled about.

Vocabulary

A

ā, interj., *alas*

ab or **ā**, prep. + abl., *from, by*

abeō [ab-, *from, away* + eō, īre, iī/īvī, itūrus, *to go*], **abīre, abiī** or **abīvī, abitūrus**, *to go away*

ac, conj., *and*

accipiō [ad-, *to* + capiō, capere, cēpī, captus, *to take*], **accipere, accēpī, acceptus**, *to accept, get, receive, welcome*

ad, prep. + acc., *to, toward;* expressing purpose, *for*

adēmpte: from **adēmptus**, see **adimō**

adeō [ad-, *to* + eō, īre, iī/īvī, itūrus, *to go*], **adīre, adiī, aditus**, *to come to, approach*

adimō [ad-, *to* + emō, emere, ēmī, ēmptus, *to take*], **adimere, adēmī, adēmptus** + dat., *to take away* (from)

admīror [ad-, *to* + mīror, -ārī, -ātus sum, *to be surprised*] **-ārī, -ātus sum**, *to wonder (at); to be surprised*

adsum [ad-, *to* + sum, esse, fuī futūrus, *to be*], **adesse, adfuī, adfutūrus**, *to be present, be near*

adveniō [ad-, *to* + veniō, venīre, vēnī, ventūrus, *to come*], **advenīre, advēnī, adventūrus**, *to reach, arrive*

aequor, aequoris, n. (see 11.8), *sea*

afferō [ad-, *to* + ferō, ferre, tulī, lātus, *to carry*], **afferre, attulī, allātus**, *to bring*

ager, agrī, m., *field, territory, land*

agnōscō [ad-, intensive + nōscō, nōscere, nōvī, nōtus, *to get to know*], **agnōscere, agnōvī, agnitus**, *to recognize*

agō, agere, ēgī, āctus, *to do, drive*

agricola, -ae, m., *farmer*

aliquī, -ae, -a, indefinite adjective, *some*

aliquis, aliquis, aliquid, indefinite pronoun, *someone, anyone, something, anything*

alius, alia, aliud, *another, other*

alō, alere, aluī, altus, *to feed, nourish, rear*

Alpēs, Alpium, f. pl., *the Alps*

alter, altera, alterum, *another*

altus, -a, -um, *tall, high*

ambō, ambae, ambō, *both*

amīca, -ae, f., *friend*

amictus, -ūs, m., *clothing*

amīcus, -ī, m., *friend*

amō, -āre, -āvī, -ātus, *to like, love*

amor, amōris, m. (see 6.16, 7.8, 13.9), *love*

an, conj., *or*

anima, -ae, f., *soul, "heart"*

animus, -ī, m. (see 45.20), *mind*

annuō [ad-, *to, toward* + nuō (unattested), *to nod*], **annuere, annuī, annūtus**, *to nod assent.*

annus, -ī, m., *year*

ante, adv., *previously, before*

ante, prep. + acc., *before, in front of*

anteā, adv., *previously, before*

ānxius, -a, -um, *worried, disturbed, distressed*

appāreō [ad-, *to, toward* + pāreō, -ēre, -uī, -itūrus, *to obey; to be visible*], **-ēre, -uī, -itūrus**, *to appear*

apud, prep. + acc., *with, at the house of*

aqua, -ae, f., *water*

āra, -ae, f., *altar*

ārdeō, ārdēre, ārsī, ārsūrus, *to burn, blaze*

Ariadna, -ae, f., *Ariadne* (daughter of Minos)

ars, artis, f., *skill*

arx, arcis, f., *citadel*

assiduus, -a, -um [ad-, *to, toward* + sedeō, sedēre, sēdī, sessūrus, *to sit*], *incessant, constant*

at, conj., *but*

atque, conj., *and also; and what is more, and in fact, and indeed*

attineō [ad-, *to, toward* + teneō, tenēre, tenuī, tentus, *to hold*], **attinēre, attinuī, attentus**, *to hold back;* + ad + acc., *to be of concern* (to) audeō, audēre, ausus sum + infin., *to dare* (to)

audiō, -īre, -īvī, -ītus, *to hear, listen to*

auferō [ab-, *from* + ferō, ferre, tulī, lātus, *to carry*], auferre, abstulī, ablātus, *to carry away, take away*

augeō, augēre, auxī, auctus, *to increase*

aura, -ae, f., *breeze*

aurum, -ī, n., *gold*

aut, conj., *or*

aut . . . aut, conj., *either . . . or*

autem, conj., *however, but, moreover*

auxilium, -ī, n., *help*

avunculus, -ī, m., *maternal uncle*

B

bene, adv., *well*

bēstia, -ae, f., *beast*

bonus, -a, -um, *good*

brevis, -is, -e, *short*

Britannī, -ōrum, m. pl., *inhabitants of Britain, Britons*

C

cadō, cadere, cecidī, cāsūrus, *to fall*

caecus, -a, -um, *blind*

caedēs, caedis, f., *slaughter, killing*

caelestis, caelestis, m./f., *god/goddess;* pl., *heavenly ones, gods*

caelum, -ī, n., *sky, heaven*

campus, -ī, m., *plain, field*

candidus, -a, -um, *white, fair-skinned, beautiful*

canō, canere, cecinī, cantus (see 34.4), *to sing*

capillus, -ī, m., *hair*

capiō, capere, cēpī, captus, *to take, catch, capture, seize*

caput, capitis, n., *head*

cārus, -a, -um, *dear, beloved*

castus, -a, -um, *virtuous, chaste*

caveō, cavēre, cāvī, cautus, *to be careful, watch out for, beware*

Cecropia, -ae, f., *Cecropia* (the city of Cecrops; Cecrops was the first king of the city that was later called Athens from its patron Athena)

cēdō, cēdere, cessī, cessūrus, *to go; to go away; to depart; to recede*

celer, celeris, celere, *swift*

cēlō, -āre, -āvī, -ātus, *to hide, conceal*

cēna, -ae, f., *dinner*

cēnō, -āre, -āvī, -ātus, *to dine, eat dinner*

centum, indeclinable adjective, *a hundred*

certē, adv., *certainly*

cibus, -ī, m., *food*

clāmō, -āre, -āvī, -ātūrus, *to shout*

classis, classis, f., *fleet*

cliēns, clientis, m., *client, dependent*

cōgitō, -āre, -āvī, -ātus, *to think*

cōgō [con-, intensive + agō, agere, ēgī, āctus, *to do, drive*], cōgere, cōēgī, cōāctus, *to compel, force*

collis, collis, m., *hill*

colō, colere, coluī, cultus (see 36.14), *to cultivate*

color, colōris, m., *color*

comes, comitis, m./f., *companion , comrade*

commemorō [con-, intensive + memorō, -āre, -āvī, -ātus, *to speak of, mention*], -āre, -āvī, -ātus, *to mention, recount*

comparō [con-, intensive + parō, -āre, -āvī, -ātus, *to prepare, get ready*], -āre, -āvī, -ātus, *to buy, obtain,*

complexus, -ūs, m., *embrace*

concinō [con-, *together* + canō, canere, cecinī, *to sing*], concinere, concinuī, *to sing together, sing*

cōnficiō [con-, intensive + faciō, facere, fēcī, factus, *to make, do*], cōnficere, cōnfēcī, cōnfectus, *to accomplish, finish*

coniungō [con-, *with, together* + iungō, iungere, iūnxī, iūnctus, *to join*], coniungere, coniūnxī, coniūnctus, *to join*

coniūnx, coniugis, m./f., *husband; wife; spouse*

cōnor, -ārī, -ātus sum, *to try*

cōnsilium, -ī, n., *plan*

cōnspiciō [con-, intensive + speciō, specere, spexī, spectus, *to see*], cōnspicere, cōnspexī, cōnspectus, *to catch sight of*

cōnstāns, cōnstantis, *firm, stable, steady*

contrā, prep. + acc., *against*

cōnūbium, -ī, n., *marriage*

convīva, -ae, m., *guest (at a banquet)*

cor, cordis, n., *heart*

corpus, corporis, n., *body*

crēdō, crēdere, crēdidī, crēditus + *dat.*, *to trust; to believe*

creō, -āre, -āvī, -ātus, *to create*

Crēta, -ae, f., *Crete* (island south of Greece, home of Minos)

crūdēlis, -is, -e, *cruel*

culpa, -ae, f. (see 11.22, 73.1), *fault, blame*

cum, conj., *when, whenever; since; although*

    cum prīmum, *as soon as*

cum, prep. + abl., *with*

cūnctus, -a, -um, *all, the whole*

Cupīdō, Cupīdinis, m. (see 3.1), *Cupid* (son of Venus and god of love)

cupidus, -a, -um, *longing, desirous*

cupiō, cupere, cupīvī, cupītus, *to desire, want*

cūr, adv., *why*

cūr, *why*

cūra, -ae, f. (see 2.10), *care; emotional distress; anguished emotion; feeling*

cūrō, -āre, -āvī, -ātus, *to care; to take care of; to look after*

currō, currere, cucurrī, cursūrus, *to run*

D

dē, prep. + abl., *down from, concerning, about*

dea, -ae, f., *goddess*

decem, indeclinable adjective, *ten*

decet, decēre, decuit, impersonal, *(it) is becoming, fitting; should*

dēdicō [dē-, thoroughly, completely + dicō, -āre, -āvī, -ātus, *to indicate; to dedicate*], -āre, -āvī, -ātus, *to dedicate*

dēfendō, dēfendere, dēfendī, dēfēnsus, *to defend*

dēferō [dē-, *down* + ferō, ferre, tulī, lātus, *to carry*], dēferre, dētulī, dēlātus, *to carry down*

dēfessus, -a, -um, *tired*

deinde, adv., *then, next*

dēliciae, -ārum, f. pl., *delight*

dēpōnō [dē-, *down* + pōnō, pōnere, posuī, positus, *to put*], dēpōnere, dēposuī, dēpositus, *to lay down, put aside, set down*

dēsertus, -a, -um, *deserted, lonely*

dēsīderō, -āre, -āvī, -ātus, *to long for, desire, miss*

dēsinō [dē-, thoroughly, completely + sinō, sinere, sīvī, situs, *to leave alone, let be*], dēsinere, dēsiī, dēsitus + infin., *to cease (from), stop (doing)*

dēspondeō [dē-, thoroughly, completely + spondeō, spondēre, spopondī, spōnsus, *to pledge; to contract*], dēspondēre, dēspondī, dēspōnsus, *to pledge, promise; to betroth, promise in marriage*

deus, -ī, nom. pl., dī, dat., abl. pl., dīs, m., *god*

dēvorō [dē-, *down* + vorō, -āre, -āvī, -ātus, *to swallow*], -āre, -āvī, -ātus, *to devour*

dexter, dext(e)ra, dext(e)rum, *right*

    dextra, -ae, f., *right hand*

dī: nom. pl. of deus

Dīa, -ae, f., *Dia* (an island five and a half miles from Heracleon, Crete; confused in the myth with Naxos)

dīcō, dīcere, dīxī, dictus (see 34.14), *to say, tell*

dicta, -ōrum, n. pl., *words*

diēs, diēī, m., *day*

difficilis, -is, -e, *difficult*

digitus, -ī, m., *finger*

dīligō [dis-, dī-, *apart* + legō, legere, lēgī, lēctus, *to choose, select, pick*], dīligere, dīlēxī, dīlēctus, *to esteem, cherish, love* dīmittō [dis-, dī-, *apart* + mittō, mittere, mīsī, missus, *to send*], dīmittere, dīmīsī, dīmissus, *to send away, dismiss*

discēdō [dis-, dī-, *apart* + cēdō, cēdere, cessī cessūrus, *to go*], discēdere, discessī, discessūrus, *to go away, depart*

diū, adv., *for a long time*

dīversus, -a, -um, *different*

dīvidō, dīvidere, dīvīsī, dīvīsus, *to divide*

dō, dare, dedī, datus, *to give*

doleō, -ēre, -uī, -itūrus, *to be sorry, be in pain*

dolor, dolōris, m., *grief*

domina, -ae, f. (see 3.10), *mistress, lady of the house*

domus, -ūs, f., *house*
    domī, *at home*
    domum, *homeward, home*

dōnō, -āre, -āvī, -ātus, *to give.*

dōnum, -ī, n., *gift*

dormiō, -īre, -īvī, -ītūrus, *to sleep*

dūcō, dūcere, dūxī, ductus (see 8.2), *to lead, take, bring; to consider*

dulcis, -is, -e, *sweet*

dum, conj., *while, as long as*

duō, duae, duō, *two*

E

ē or ex, prep. + abl., *from, out of*

ēbrius, -a, -um, *drunk*

edō, ēsse, ēdī, ēsus, *to eat*

ēdūcō [ex-, ē-, *from, out of* + dūcō, dūcere, dūxī, ductus, *to lead*], ēdūcere, ēdūxī, ēductus, *to lead out, bring forth*

efferō [ex-, *from, out of* + ferō, ferre, tulī, lātus, *to carry, bring*], efferre, extulī, ēlātus, *to carry out, bring out*

egō, pronoun, *I*

ēgredior [ex-, ē-, *from, out of* + gradior, gradī, gressus sum, *to step, walk*], ēgredī, ēgressus sum, *to go out, leave, disembark*

ēheu, interj., *alas*

ēiciō [ex-, ē-, *from, out of* + iaciō, iacere, iēcī, iactus, *to throw*], ēicere, ēiēcī, ēiectus, *to throw out*

ēlegāns, ēlegantis, *elegant, tasteful*

enim, conj., *for*

eō, īre, iī/īvī, itūrus, *to go*

ēripiō [ex-, *out* + rapiō, rapere, rapuī, raptus, *to snatch, seize*], ēripere, ēripuī, ēreptus, *to snatch from; to rescue*

et, conj., *and, also*
    et . . . et, conj., *both . . . and*

etiam, adv., *also, even*

ex or ē, prep. + abl., *from, out of*

excitō [ex-, *from, out of* + citō, citāre, citāvī, citātus, *to rouse*], -āre, -āvī, -ātus, *to rouse, wake up*

expellō [ex-, *out* + pellō, pellere, pepulī, pulsus, *to drive*], expellere, expulī, expulsus, *to drive out, expel*

exposcō [ex-, intensive + poscō, poscere, poposcī, *to ask for, demand*], exposcere, expoposcī, *to demand*

exprimō [ex-, intensive + premō, premere, pressī pressus, *to press*], exprimere, expressī, expressus, *to press out, express*

exspectō [ex-, *out* + spectō, -āre, -āvī, -ātus, *to look at, watch*], -āre, -āvī, -ātus, *to look out for, wait for*

ex(s)ternō [may be a Catullan coinage; ex-, *out* + sternō, sternere, strāvī, strātus, *to lay; to spread; to stretch; to strike down*; but by folk etymology the verb ex(s)ternāre may have been thought of as related to externus, -a, -um, *on the outside, external*], -āre, -āvī, -ātus, *to strike out of one's wits, put in a panic.*

extrēmus, -a, -um, *last; final*

F

fābula, -ae, f., *story*

facilis, -is, -e, *easy*

faciō, facere, fēcī, factus, *to make, do; to consider, regard*

factum, -ī, n., *deed*

fallāx, fallācis, *deceitful, deceptive;
  traitorous*
fātum, -ī, n., *fate*
faveō, favēre, fāvī, fautūrus + dat., *to
  give favor* (to), *favor*
fēlīx, fēlīcis, *lucky, happy, fortunate*
fēmina, -ae, f., *woman*
ferō, ferre, tulī, lātus, *to bring, carry,
  bear, say*
ferōx, ferōcis, *fierce; high-spirited*
fidēlis, -is, -e, *faithful, devoted, reliable*
fidēs, fideī, f., *good faith, reliability, trust*
figūra, -ae, f., *figure*
fīlia, -ae, f., *daughter*
fīlum, -ī, n., *thread*
fīnis, fīnis, m., *end*
fīō, fierī, factus sum, *to become; to be
  made; to be done; to happen*
flamma, -ae, f., *flame*
flāvus, -a, -um, *blond(e)*
fleō, flēre, flēvī, flētus, *to weep, cry; to
  weep for, lament*
flētus, -ūs, m., *weeping, tears*
flōs, flōris, m., *flower*
flūctus, -ūs, m., *wave, billow; waters of
  the sea*
fōrma, -ae, f., *form, shape*
fōrtasse, adv., *perhaps*
forte, adv., *by chance*
fortūna, -ae, f., *fortune* (good or bad);
  luck (good or bad)
frangō, frangere, frēgī, frāctus, *to
  break, shatter*
frāter, frātris, m., *brother*
frāternus, -a, -um, *brotherly*
frīgidus, -a, -um, *cool, cold*
frōns, frontis, f., *forehead*
frūstrā, adv., *in vain*
fugiō, fugere, fūgī, fugitūrus, *to flee; to
  escape*
fuī: see **sum**
fundus, -ī, m., *farm*
fūnestus, -a, -um, *of or concerned with
  death or mourning; funereal*
fūnus, fūneris, n., *funeral*
fūr, fūris, m., *thief*

furor, furōris, m., *frenzy; fury; rage;
  anger; passionate desire*

G

gaudeō, gaudēre, gavīsus sum, *to be
  glad, rejoice;* + abl., *to find delight* (in),
  take pleasure (in)
gaudium, -ī, n., *joy, pleasure*
geminus, -a, -um, *twin, double*
gemō, gemere, gemuī, gemitus, *to
  groan; to lament*
gēns, gentis, f., *family, clan; nation, people;* pl., *peoples*
genus, generis, n., *race, stock, nation*
gerō, gerere, gessī, gestus, *to wear; to
  bear, carry*
gnātus, -ī, m., *son*
grātia, -ae, f., *gratitude, thanks*
  grātiās/grātēs agere + dat., *to thank*
grātus, -a, -um + dat., *pleasing* (to)
gravis, -is, -e, *heavy, oppressive, severe*
gurges, gurgitis, m., *whirlpool; water* (of
  a river or sea)

H

habeō, -ēre, -uī, -itus, *to have, hold*
habitō, -āre, -āvī, -ātus, *to live, dwell*
harēna, -ae, f., *sand*
heu, interj., *alas*
hic, haec, hoc, *this*
hīc, adv., *here*
hiems, hiemis, f., *winter*
homō, hominis, m., *man*
hōra, -ae, f., *hour*
horreō, -ēre, -uī, *to shudder; to be
  unwilling*
hospes, hospitis, m., *guest, host, friend;
  stranger*
hostis, hostis, m., *enemy*
  hostēs, hostium, m. pl., *the enemy*
hūc, adv., *here, to here, to this place*

I

iaceō, -ēre, -uī, -itūrus, *to lie, be lying
  down*
iaciō, iacere, iēcī, iactus, *to throw*
iactō, -āre, -āvī, -ātus, *to toss about,*

drive to and fro
iam, adv., *now, already*
ibi, adv., *there*
īdem, eadem, idem, *the same*
identidem, adv., *again and again, repeatedly*
igitur, conj., *therefore*
ignis, ignis, m., *fire*
ille, illa, illud, *that; he, she, it; the former; that famous*
illīc, adv., *there, in that place*
illūc, adv., *there, to that place*
imber, imbris, m., *rain*
immemor, immemoris + gen., *forgetful*
immītis, -is, -e [in-, *not* + **mītis**, *gentle*], *pitiless; harsh; cruel*
in, prep. + abl., *in, on*
in, prep. + acc., *into, onto, against*
incendium, -ī, n., *fire*
incendō, incendere, incendī, incēnsus, *to burn, set on fire, inflame*
incidō [in-, *into/onto* + **cadō, cadere, cecidī, casūrus**, *to fall*], **incidere, incidī, incāsūrus** (see 10.5), *to fall into/onto*
incipiō [in-, *in/on* + **capiō, capere, cēpī, captus**, *to take*], **incipere, incēpī, inceptus**, *to begin*
incola, -ae, m./f., *inhabitant*
incolumis, -is, -e, *unhurt, safe and sound*
inde, adv., *from there; then*
indomitus, -a, -um, *not broken in, untamed; unrestrained, violent, savage*
īnficiō [in-, *in* + **faciō, facere, fēcī, factus**, *to make; to do*], **īnficere, īnfēcī, īnfectus**, *to dye; to darken with dye*
ingredior [in-, *in, into* + **gradior, gradī, gressus sum**, *to step, walk*], **ingredī, ingressus sum**, *to go in, enter*
iniciō [in-, *on* + **iaciō, iacere, iēcī, iactus**, *to throw*], **inicere, iniēcī, iniectus** + dat., *to throw/fling* (on)
inquam, inquis, inquit, perf., **inquiī**, *to say*
īnsula, -ae, f., *island*

inter, prep. + acc., *between, among*
intereā, adv. (see 36.18, 95.3, 101.7), *meanwhile*
invideō [in-, *in, on* + **videō, vidēre, vīdī, vīsus**, *to see, look*], **invidēre, invīdī, invīsus** + dat., *to envy, be jealous of*
invītus, -a, -um, *unwilling*
iocus, -ī, m., *joke, joking, jest*
ipse, ipsa, ipsum, *himself, herself, itself, themselves; very*
īra, -ae, f., *anger*
īrātus, -a, -um, *angry*
irritus, -a, -um, *vain; empty; invalid*
is, ea, id, *he, she, it; this, that*
iste, ista, istud, often contemptuous or derogatory, *that (of yours)*
ita, adv., *thus, so*
Italī, -ōrum, m. pl., *the Italians*
iter, itineris, n., *journey, route, road*
iubeō, iubēre, iussī, iussus, *to order, bid*
iūcundus, -a, -um, *pleasant, delightful*
iungō, iungere, iūnxī, iūnctus, *to join*
Iuppiter, Iovis, m., *Jupiter* (king of the gods)
iūrō, -āre, -āvī, -ātus, *to swear* (as in an oath)
iuvenis, iuvenis, m., *young man*

L

labor, labōris, m., *work, toil*
lacrima, -ae, f., *tear*
laedō, laedere, laesī, laesus, *to harm, hurt*
laetor, -ārī, -ātus sum, *to rejoice, be glad; + in + abl., to delight* (in), *be fond* (of)
laetus, -a, -um, *happy, glad*
lapis, lapidis, m., *stone*
lateō, -ēre, -uī, *to lie in hiding, hide*
lātrō, -āre, -āvī, -ātūrus, *to bark*
laus, laudis, f., *praise; praiseworthy action*
lectīca, -ae, f., *litter*
lectus, -ī, m., *bed, couch*
legō, legere, lēgī, lēctus, *to read*

lentus, -a, -um, *slow*

lepidus, -a, -um, *charming*

levis, -is, -e, *light*

libenter, adv., *gladly*

licet, licēre, licuit, impersonal + dat., (*it*) *is allowed*

ligō, -āre, -āvī, -ātus, *to bind up*

līmen, līminis, n., *threshold*

lingua, -ae, f., *tongue*

linquō, linquere, līquī, *to leave*

linteum, -ī, n., *linen cloth; towel; sail*

lītus, lītoris, n., *shore*

locō, -āre, -āvī, -ātus, *to place*

locus, -ī, m.; m. or n. in pl., *place*

longus, -a, -um, *long, tall*
  longē, adv., *far*

loquor, loquī, locūtus sum, *to speak, talk, say*

lūceō, lūcēre, lūxī, *to shine*
  lūcet, lūcēre, lūxit, *it is light, it is day;* (*it*) *shines*

lūctus, -ūs, m., *grief, mourning*

lūdō, lūdere, lūsī, lūsūrus, *to play*

lūmen, lūminis, n., *light; lamp; eye*

lūx, lūcis, f., *light*

M

maestus, -a, -um, *sorrowful, gloomy; grieving; sad*

magis, adv., *more; rather, instead*

magister, magistrī, m., *master*

magistra, -ae, f., *mistress*

magnus, -a, -um, *big, great, large*

maior, maior, maius, gen., maiōris, *bigger*

mālō, mālle, māluī, *to prefer*

mālum, -ī, n., *apple*

malus, -a, -um, *bad, evil*
  male, adv. (see 3.13, 16, 10.33, 83.1, 92.1), *badly*

mandātum, -ī, n., *order, instruction*

maneō, manēre, mānsī, mānsūrus (see 8.15), *to remain, endure, last*

mānō, -āre, -āvī, *to flow*

manus, -ūs, f., *hand*

mare, maris, n., *sea*

marītus, -ī, m., *husband*

māter, mātris, f., *mother*

maximus, -a, -um, *biggest, greatest*

medius, -a, -um, *mid-, middle of*

medulla, -ae, f., *marrow of the bones*

melior, melior, melius, gen., meliōris, *better*

meminī, meminisse, *to remember*

memor, memoris, *remembering, mindful, unforgetting*

mēns, mentis, f., *mind.*

mēnsa, -ae, f., *table*

meus, -a, -um, *my, mine*

mī = mihi or vocative of meus

migrō, -āre, -āvī, -ātūrus, *to change one's residence; to go away*

mīlia, mīlium, n. pl., *thousands*

mīlle, indeclinable adjective, *a thousand*

minimus, -a, -um, *very small, smallest*

Mīnōis, Mīnōidis, f., *daughter of Minos* (Ariadne)

minus, adv., *less*

mīror, -ārī, -ātus sum, *to admire, wonder at*

mīrus, -a, -um, *wonderful, marvelous, strange*

misceō, miscēre, miscuī, mixtus, *to mix*

miser, misera, miserum, *unhappy, miserable, wretched;* as a term describing lovers, *obsessed with erotic passion, lovesick*

mitra, -ae, f., *headdress* (a cloth or cap worn by Greek girls at night)

mittō, mittere, mīsī, missus (see 96.4), *to send, let go*

modus, -ī, m., *way*

moenia, moenium, n. pl., *walls* (of a town or city)

molestus, -a, -um, *troublesome, annoying*

mollis, -is, -e, *soft*

mōns, montis, m., *mountain, hill*

mōnstrum, -ī, n., *monster*

morbus, -ī, m., *illness, sickness*

morior, morī, mortuus sum, *to die*

moror, -ārī, -ātus sum, *to delay, remain,*

stay

mors, mortis, f., *death*

mortālis, -is, -e, *mortal*

mortuus, -a, -um, *dead*

mōs, mōris, m., *custom*

moveō, movēre, mōvī, mōtus, *to move*

mulier, mulieris, f., *woman*

multus, -a, -um, *much*

 multī, -ae, -a, *many*

 multum, adv., *greatly, much, abundantly*

mūnus, mūneris, n., *gift, service*

Mūsa, -ae, f., *Muse (goddess of song and poetry)*

mūtus, -a, -um, *silent*

mūtuus, -a, -um, *mutual, shared*

mȳrtus, -ī, f., *myrtle-tree*

N

nam, conj., *for*

namque, conj., *for; well then, now*

nārrō, -āre, -āvī, -ātus, *to tell* (a story); *to say*

nāscor, nāscī, nātus sum, inceptive, *to be born*

nāsus, -ī, m., *nose*

nāvis, nāvis, f., *ship*

-ne: indicates a question

nē, conj. + subjunctive, *not, not to, so that . . . not*

nec, conj., *and . . . not*

 nec . . . nec . . . , conj., *neither . . . nor*

necesse, adv. or indeclinable adjective, *necessary*

neglegēns, neglegentis, *negligent, careless, inattentive*

neglegō, neglegere, neglēxī, neglēctus, *to neglect, ignore*

negō, -āre, -āvī, -ātus, *to deny*

nēmō, nēminis, m./f., *no one*

neque, conj., *and . . . not*

 neque . . . neque/nec, conj., *neither . . . nor*

nēquīquam, adv., *in vain, to no purpose*

nesciō, -īre, -īvī, -ītus, *to be ignorant, not to know*

niger, nigra, nigrum, *black*

nihil, indeclinable noun, *nothing*

nīl, indeclinable noun, *nothing*

nimis, adv., *too, too much*

nisi, conj., *if . . . not, unless*

nītor, nītī, nixus sum + abl. object, *to lean on, rely on;* + abl. of means, *to press forward* (with)

nocte, *at night*

nōlō, nōlle, nōluī, *to be unwilling, not to wish, refuse*

nōmen, nōminis, n., *name*

nōn, adv., *not*

 nōn mīrum, *no wonder, it is not surprising*

nōndum, adv., *not yet*

nōnus, -a, -um, *ninth*

nōs, pronoun, *we, us*

noster, nostra, nostrum, *our*

nōtus, -a, -um, *known*

novus, -a, -um, *new*

nōx, noctis, f., *night*

 nocte, *at night*

nūbēs, nūbis, f., *cloud*

nūbō, nūbere, nūpsī, nūptūrus + dat., *to marry*

nūllus, -a, -um, *no, none*

num, adv., *surely . . . not* (introduces a question that expects the answer "no")

nūmen, nūminis, n., *nod (of the head); divine power*

numerus, -ī, m. (see 50.5), *number*

numquam, adv., *never*

nunc, adv., *now*

nūntius, -ī, m., *messenger, message*

nūper, adv., *recently*

O

ō, interj., used with vocative and in exclamations

octō, indeclinable adjective, *eight*

oculus, -ī, m., *eye*

offerō [ob-, *against* + **ferō, ferre, tulī, lātus,** *to bring*], **offerre, obtulī, oblātus,** *to provide*

officium, -ī, n., *duty*

ōlim, adv., *once (upon a time)*

ōlīva, -ae, f., *olive, olive tree*

omnis, -is, -e, *all, the whole, every*

onus, oneris, n., *load, burden*

oportet, oportēre, oportuit, impersonal, *(it) is fitting; one ought*

opprimō [ob-, *against* + premō,
premere, pressī, pressus, *to press*],
opprimere, oppressī, oppressus, *to
overwhelm*

optimus, -a, -um, *best*

optō, -āre, -āvī, -ātus, *to wish for, desire*

ōrātiō, ōrātiōnis, f., *oration, speech*

ōrō, -āre, -āvī, -ātus, *to beg*

ōs, ōris, n., *mouth; face; expression*

ostendō [ob-, *against* + tendō, tendere,
tetendī, tentus, *to stretch/hold out, offer*], ostendere, ostendī, ostentus, *to
show, point out*

P

paene, adv., *almost*

parātus, -a, -um, *ready, prepared*

parcō, parcere, pepercī + dat., *to spare*

parēns, parentis, m./f., *parent*

pāreō, -ēre, -uī, -itūrus + dat., *to obey*

parō, -āre, -āvī, -ātus, *to prepare, get
ready; to purchase, buy*

    parātus, -a, -um, *ready, prepared*

pars, partis, f., *part, direction, region*

parvus, -a, -um, *small*

pateō, patēre, patuī, *to extend*

pater, patris, m., *father*

patior, patī, passus sum, *to suffer,
endure*

patria, -ae, f., *nation, native land*

patrōnus, -ī, m., *patron*

paucī, -ae, -a, *few*

paulum, adv., *a little, for a little while*

pectus, pectoris, n., *chest, breast*

pecus, pecoris, n., *livestock, sheep and
cattle*

pelagus, -ī, n., *sea*

pendeō, pendēre, pependī, *to be
suspended, hang*

per, prep. + acc., *through; along; on account of*

perditus, -a, -um, *ruined, lost; hopeless;
in a state of desperation*

perdō [per-, here of upset or perversity
+ dō, dare, dedī, datus, *to give*],
perdere, perdidī, perditus, *to destroy;
to lose.*

    perditus, -a, -um, *ruined, lost;
hopeless; in a state of desperation*

pereō [per-, here of upset or perversity
+ eō, īre, iī/īvī, itūrus, *to go*], perīre,
periī, peritūrus (see 8.2, 45.5, 76.9), *to
die, perish; to come to an end; to perish
(with love), be madly in love.*

perfidus, -a, -um, *treacherous,
perfidious*

perhibeō [per-, intensive + habeō,
-ēre, -uī, -itus, *to have*] -ēre, -uī, -itus,
to regard, hold; to say, assert

periūrium, -ī, n., *false oath, perjury*

perveniō [per-, completion + veniō,
venīre, vēnī, ventūrus, *to come*],
pervenīre, pervēnī, perventūrus +
ad + acc., *to arrive (at), reach*

pēs, pedis, m. (see 4.21), *foot*

pessimus, -a, -um, *worst*

    pessimē, adv., *worst*

petō, petere, petīvī, petītus, *to seek*

placeō, -ēre, -uī + dat., *to please*

plēnus, -a, -um + gen., *full (of)*

plūrēs, plūrēs, plūra, gen., plūrium,
more

plūrimī, -ae, -a, *most, very many*

plūrimum, adv., *very much, especially,
most*

plūs, adv., *more*

poena, -ae, f., *punishment, penalty*

poēta, -ae, m., *poet*

populus, -ī, m., *people*

portō, -āre, -āvī, -ātus, *to carry*

portus, -ūs, m., *port, harbor.*

possum, posse, potuī, *to be able; I can*

post, adv., *after(ward), later, hereafter*

post, prep. + acc., *after*

postquam, conj., *after*

postrēmus, -a, -um, *final, last*

    postrēmō, adv., *finally*

potius, adv., *rather*
  potius quam, *rather than*
praemium, -ī, n., *payment; reward, prize*
praentereā, adv., *besides, too, moreover*
praetereō [praeter-, *past, by* + **eō, īre, iī/īvī, itūrus**, *to go*], **praeterīre praeteriī** or **praeterīvī, praeteritus**, *to go past, pass by; to surpass*
pretium, -ī, n., *price*
prīmus, -a, -um, *first; first part of*
  prīmum, adv., *first, at first*
prior, prior, prius, gen., **priōris**, *previous*
  prius, adv., *earlier, before, previously*
priusquam, conj., *before*
prīscus, -a, -um, *of olden times, ancient*
prō, prep. + abl., *for, on behalf of*
procul, adv., *in the distance, far off, far*
prōferō [pro-, *forward* + **ferō, ferre, tulī, lātus**, *to carry*], **prōferre, prōtulī, prōlātus**, *to carry forward, continue*
proficīscor [pro-, *forward* + **faciō, facere, fēcī, factus**, *to make, do* + **-scō**, inceptive suffix], **proficīscī, profectus sum**, inceptive, *to set out, leave*
prōmittō [pro-, *forward* + **mittō, mittere, mīsī, missus**, *to send*], **prōmittere, prōmīsī, prōmissus**, *to promise*
prōnus, -a, -um, *face down*
prope, adv., *near, nearly*
prope, prep. + acc., *near*
prōspectō [prō-, *forward* + **speciō, specere, spexī, specus**, *to see; to watch* + **-tō**, intensive or iterative suffix], **-āre, -āvī, -ātus**, *to look out at, watch*
prōvincia, -ae, f., *province*
puella, -ae, f., *girl, girlfriend, swetheart*
puer, puerī, m., *boy*
pugnō, -āre, -āvī, -ātūrus, *to fight;* + dat., *to fight with*
pulcher, pulchra, pulchrum, *beautiful, pretty, handsome*
  pulcherrimus, -a, -um, *most/very beautiful*

pulvis, pulveris, m., *dust*
pūrus, -a, -um, *spotless, clean, plain white*
putō, -āre, -āvī, -ātus, *to think, consider*

Q

quaerō, quaerere, quaesīvī, quaesītus, *to seek, look for, ask (for)*
quālis, -is, -e, *what sort of; such as, as, like*
quam, adv., *how; what a; than; as*
  quam prīmum, *as soon as*
quandō, adv., *when*
quandōquidem or **quandoquidem**, adv., *since*
quantus, -a, -um, *how big, how much, as*
  quantum, adv., *as much as*
quārē, adv., *for which reason, therefore*
quasi, adv., *as if*
-que, enclitic conj., *and*
querella, -ae, f., *complaint, protest, lament*
quī, quae, quod, interrog. adj., *what, which*
quī, quae, quod, relative pronoun, *who, which, that*
quīdam, quaedam, quoddam, indefinite adjective, *a certain*
quiēs, quiētis, f. (see 4.26), *rest, repose*
quīngentī, -ae, -a, *five hundred*
quis, qua/quae, quid, indefinite pronoun after **nē, nī, seu, sī**, *anyone, anybody, somebody, anything, something*
quis, quis, quid, interrogative pronoun, *who, what*
quō, adv., *where, to where, where to*
quod, conj., *because*
quod: see **quī, quae, quod**
quoniam, conj., *since*
quoque, adv., *also*
quot, interrogative adv., *how many*

R

rāmus, -ī, m., *branch*
recipiō [re- *back* + **capiō, capere, cēpī, captus**, *to take*], **recipere, recēpī, receptus**, *to receive*

reddō [re-/red-, *back* + dō, dare, dedī, datus, *to give*], reddere, reddidī, redditus, *to give back, return; to restore*

redeō [re-, *back* + eō, īre, iī/īvī, itūrus, *to go*], redīre, rediī or redīvī, reditūrus, *to return*

redūcō [re-, *back* + dūcō, dūcere, dūxī, ductus, *to lead*], redūcere, redūxī, reductus, *to lead back, take back*

referō [re-, *back* + ferō, ferre, tulī, lātus, *to take, bring*], referre, rettulī, relātus, *to take/bring back; to report; to write down*

reficiō [re-, *back* + faciō, facere, fēcī, factus, *to make*], reficere, refēcī, refectus, *to remake, redo, restore* (to health)

regō, regere, rēxī, rēctus, *to rule*

relinquō [re-, *back* + linquō, linquere, līquī, lictus, *to leave*], relinquere, relīquī, relictus, *to leave behind*

remittō [re-, *back* + mittō, mittere, mīsī, missus, *to send*], remittere, remīsī, remissus, *to send back*

rēmus, -ī, m., *oar*

renovō [re-, *back, again* + novō, -āre, -āvī, -ātus, *to make something new*], -āre, -āvī, -ātus, *to renew, revive*

reportō [re-, *back* + portō, -āre, -āvī, -ātus, *to carry*], -āre, -āvī, -ātus, *to bring back*

requīrō [re-, *repeated action* + quaerō, quaerere, quaesīvī, quaesītus, *to seek, look for; to ask for*], requīrere, requīsīvī, requīsītus, *to ask, inquire, search*

rēs, reī, f., *thing, matter, affair*

respergō [re-, *back, again* + spargō, spargere, sparsī, sparsus, *to scatter; to sprinkle*], respergere, respersī, respersus, *to sprinkle*

respondeō [re-, *back* + spondeō, spondēre, spopondī, spōnsus, *to give a pledge*], respondēre, respondī, respōnsūrus, *to reply*

retineō [re-, *back* + teneō, tenēre, tenuī, tentus, *to hold*], retinēre,

retinuī, retentus, *to hold back, keep*

revocō [re-, *back* + vocō, -āre, -āvī, -ātus, *to call*], -āre, -āvī, -ātus, *to recall, call back*

rēx, rēgis, m., *king*

rīdeō, rīdēre, rīsī, rīsus, *to laugh (at), smile*

rixa, -ae, f., *quarrel*

rogō, -āre, -āvī, -ātus, *to ask*

Rōma, -ae, f., *Rome*
   Rōmae, *in Rome*

rumpō, rumpere, rūpī, ruptus, *to burst, rupture*

rūs, rūris, n., *country, countryside, farmlands*

S

sacculus, -ī, m. [dim. of saccus, -ī, m., *sack, bag*], *small sack, bag, purse, pouch*

saeculum, -ī, n., *age, era*

saepe, adv., *often*

saevus, -a, -um, *fierce, savage*

Salvē!/Salvēte! *Greetings! Hello!*

sānctus, -a, -um, *holy, sacred; sanctified, hallowed*

sanguis, sanguinis, m., *blood*

satis, indeclinable substantive, adv., *enough*

sciō, -īre, -īvī, -ītus, *to know*

sē, *himself, herself, oneself, itself, themselves*

secundus, -a, -um (see 4.21), *second*

sed, conj., *but*

sedeō, sedēre, sēdī, sessūrus, *to sit*

sēdēs, sēdis, f., *seat; home; dwelling*

semper, adv., *always*

senex, senis, m., *old man*

sentiō, sentīre, sēnsī, sēnsus, *to feel, notice, realize*

sepeliō, sepelīre, sepelīvī, sepultus, *to bury*

sepulcrum, -ī, n., *tomb*

sequor, sequī, secūtus sum, *to follow*

sermō, sermōnis, m., *conversation, talk*

serviō, -īre, -īvī, -ītūrus + dat., *to serve*

sī, conj., *if*

sīc, adv., *thus, so, in this way*

signum, -ī, n., *signal, sign*

silva, -ae, f., *woods, forest*

simul, adv. (see 11.14, 18), *together, at the same time*

> simul ac, conj. (see 22.15, 51.6), *as soon as*

sine, prep. + abl., *without*

sinister, sinistra, sinistrum, *left*

sinō, sinere, sīvī, situs, *to allow*

sīve . . . sīve, conj., *whether . . . or if or or whether*

sōl, sōlis, m., *sun*

soleō, solēre, solitus sum + infin., *to be accustomed (to), be in the habit (of)*

sōlus, -a, -um, *alone; deserted*

solvō, solvere, solvī, solūtus (see 36.2), *to loosen, untie; to relax, relieve*

somnus, -ī, m., *sleep*

sonitus, -ūs, m., *sound, noise*

sōspes, sōspitis, *safe and sound, unscathed*

spectō, -āre, -āvī, -ātus, *to watch, look at*

spērō, -āre, -āvī, -ātus, *to hope*

spēs, speī, f., *hope*

spōnsus, -ī, m., *betrothed man, bridegroom*

stō, stāre, stetī, statūrus, *to stand*

studium, -ī, n., *eagerness, enthusiasm; study*

suāvis, -is, -e, *sweet, delightful*

sub, prep. + abl., *under, beneath*

sub, prep. + acc., *under*

subitō, adv., *suddenly*

sum, esse, fuī, futūrus, *to be*

summus, -a, -um, *greatest, very great; highest, topmost; the top of . . .*

sūmō, sūmere, sūmpsī, sūmptus, *to take, take up*

super, indeclinable substantive, adv., *over, above, more than enough*

superbus, -a, -um, *proud, arrogant, haughty*

surgō, surgere, surrēxī, surrēctūrus, *to get up, rise*

suspendō [sub-, *under* + pendō, pendere, pependī, pēnsus, *to place in the scales, weigh*], suspendere,

suspendī, suspēnsus, *to suspend, hang*

sustollō [sub-, *under* + tollo, tollere, *to lift, raise*], sustollere, *to raise, haul up*

suus, -a, -um, *his, her, one's, its, their (own)*

T

tabellārius, -ī, m., *courier*

taceō, -ēre, -uī, -itus (see 6.3), *to be quiet/silent*

tacitus, -a, -um, *silent*

taedet, taedēre, taesum est, impersonal, *(it) bores, makes one tired/sick*

tālis, -is, -e, *such, like this, of this kind*

tam, adv., *so, as, such*

tamen, adv., *however, nevertheless*

tandem, adv., *at last, at length*

tangō, tangere, tetigī, tāctus, *to touch*

tantus, -a, -um, *so great, as great, such a big, so much*

> tantum, adv., *only; so much; so*

taurus, -ī, m., *bull*

tēctum, -ī, n., *roof; house; building*

tegō, tegere, tēxī, tēctus, *to cover*

temptō, -āre, -āvī, -ātus, *to try*

tempus, temporis, n., *time*

teneō, tenēre, tenuī, tentus, *to hold*

tergum, -ī, n., *back*

terra, -ae, f., *earth*

tertius, -a, -um, *third*

Thēseus, Thēseī, m., acc., Thēsea, voc., Thēseu (all except the accusative pronounced as two syllables), *Theseus (Greek hero, son of Aegeus)*

timor, timōris, m., *fear*

tollō, tollere, sustulī, sublātus, *to lift, raise; to take away; to steal*

tot, indeclinable adjective, *so many*

tōtus, -a, -um, *all, the whole*

trādō [trāns-, *across* + dō, dare, dedī, datus, *to give*], trādere, trādidī, trāditus, *to hand over*

trāns, prep. + acc., *across*

trēs, trēs, tria, *three*

trīstis, -is, -e, *sad*

tū, pronoun, *you (sing.)*

tulī, see ferō

tum, adv., *at that moment, then*

turbō, turbinis, m., *whirlpool; whirlwind; tornado*

tuus, -a, -um, *your* (sing.)

U

ubi, adv., conj., *where*

ūllus, -a, -um, *any*

umbra, -ae, f., *shade*

umquam, adv., *ever*

ūnā, adv., *together*

unda, -ae, f., *wave*

unde, adv., *from where*

undique, adv., *on all sides, from all sides*

ūnus, -a, -um, *one, one alone*

ūnā, adv., *together*

urbs, urbis, f., *city*

ut, conj. + indicative, *as, when*

ut, conj. + subjunctive, *so that, that*

uterque, utraque, utrumque, *each* (of two), *both*

ūtor, ūtī, ūsus sum + abl., *to use*

utrum . . . an . . . , conj. (see 10.31), *whether . . . or . . .*

ūva, -ae, f., *grape, bunch of grapes*

V

valdē, adv., *very, very much, exceedingly*

valeō, -ēre, -uī, -ītūrus (see 6.12, 11.17), *to be strong, be well*

valē/valēte, *goodbye*

varius, -a, -um, *different, various, varied*

vastus, -a, -um, *desolate; vast*

-ve, enclitic conj., *or*

vehō, vehere, vexī, vectus, *to carry;* pass., *to be carried; to travel*

vectus, -a, -um, *having been carried, having traveled*

velle: see volō

vēlum, -ī, n., *sail*

velut, adv., *just as*

veniō, venīre, vēnī, ventūrus, *to come*

ventus, -ī, m., *wind*

Venus, Veneris, f. (see 3.1, 45.26), *Venus* (the goddess of love)

versō, -āre, -āvī, -ātus, *to turn; to writhe;* pass. in reflexive sense, *to pass one's time; to be*

versus, -ūs, m., *verse*

vertex, verticis, m., *whirlpool; top; top of the head; head*

vērus, -a, -um, *true*

vērē, adv., *truly*

vērō, adv., *truly, really, indeed*

vester, vestra, vestrum, *your* (pl.)

vēstīgium, -ī, n., *track, footprint, trace*

vestis, vestis, f., *clothing; cloth; coverlet*

vetus, veteris, *old, ancient*

vexō, -āre, -āvī, -ātus, *to annoy, trouble*

via, -ae, f., *road*

victōria, -ae, f., *victory*

videō, vidēre, vīdī, vīsus, *to see*

videor, vidērī, vīsus sum, *to seem, be seen*

vigilō, -āre, -āvī, -ātūrus, *to stay awake*

vīlla, -ae, f., *country house, villa*

vincō, vincere, vīcī, victus, *to conquer; to win*

vīnum, -ī, n., *wine*

vir, virī, m., *man; husband*

virgō, virginis, f., *maiden*

vīsō, vīsere, vīsī, *to see*

vīta, -ae, f., *life*

vīvō, vīvere, vīxī, vīctūrus (see 5.1, 8.10, 10.33, 107.7), *to live*

vix, adv., *scarcely, with difficulty, hardly, barely*

vocō, -āre, -āvī, -ātus, *to call; to invite*

volō, velle, voluī, *to wish, want, be willing*

voluptās, voluptātis, f., *pleasure, delight*

vōs, pronoun, *you* (pl.)

vōx, vōcis, f., *voice*

vultus, -ūs, m., *face*